Research Methods in Applied Behavior Analysis

Issues and Advances

Edited by

Alan Poling

and

R. Wayne Fuqua

Western Michigan University
Kalamazoo, Michigan

Plenum Press • New York and London

Library of Congress Cataloging in Publication Data

Research methods in applied behavior analysis.

(Applied clinical psychology)
Includes bibliographies and index.
1. Behavior modification. 2. Psychology, Applied—Methodology. I. Poling, Alan D.
II. Fuqua, R. Wayne. III. Series. [DNLM: 1. Behavior. 2. Research—methods. BF 76.5
R432]
BF637.B4R47   1986   616.89′142   86-4894
ISBN 0-306-42127-5

d 651 10·86

© 1986 Plenum Press, New York
A Division of Plenum Publishing Corporation
233 Spring Street, New York, N.Y. 10013

Printed in the United States of America

Contributors

Jan Bachman • Department of Psychology, Western Michigan University, Kalamazoo, Michigan

Donald M. Baer • Department of Human Development, University of Kansas, Lawrence, Kansas

Elbert Blakely • Department of Psychology, Western Michigan University, Kalamazoo, Michigan

Robert G. Brown, Jr. • Department of Psychology, Western Michigan University, Kalamazoo, Michigan

James Cleary • Department of Psychology, University of Minnesota, Minneapolis, Minnesota

Jeffrey Cross • Department of Psychology, Allegheny College, Meadville, Pennsylvania

Robert Epstein • Cambridge Center for Behavior Studies, 11 Ware Street, Cambridge, Massachusetts, Department of Psychology, University of Massachusetts, Amherst, Massachusetts

R. Wayne Fuqua • Department of Psychology, Western Michigan University, Kalamazoo, Michigan

Deborah Grossett • Richmond State School, 2100 Preston Avenue, Richmond, Texas

Bradley E. Huitema • Department of Psychology, Western Michigan University, Kalamazoo, Michigan

Brian A. Iwata • Division of Behavioral Psychology, The John F. Kennedy Institute, Johns Hopkins University School of Medicine, Baltimore, Maryland

James M. Johnston • Department of Psychology, Auburn University, Auburn, Alabama

Richard W. Malott • Department of Psychology, Western Michigan University, Kalamazoo, Michigan

Nancy A. Neef • Department of Special Education, University of Maryland, College Park, Maryland

Terry J. Page • Division of Behavioral Psychology, The John F. Kennedy Institute, Johns Hopkins University School of Medicine, Baltimore, Maryland

Barry S. Parsonson • Department of Psychology, University of Waikato, Hamilton, New Zealand

H. S. Pennypacker • Department of Psychology, University of Florida, Gainesville, Florida

Alan Poling • Department of Psychology, Western Michigan University, Kalamazoo, Michigan

John Schwade • Murdoch Center, Butner, North Carolina

Preface

The branch of clinical psychology known as behavior modification or, synonymously, *applied behavior analysis*, has grown substantially from humble beginnings in the 1960s. Many colleges and universities now offer courses in applied behavior analysis, and more than a few grant degrees in the area. Although they remain controversial, behavior modification procedures have been used to good advantage in dealing with a range of problem behaviors and are now rather widely employed in schools, residential institutions, and other therapeutic facilities.

The two hallmarks of applied behavior analysis are utilization of the principles of operant conditioning to improve human behavior and utilization of scientific research methodology to assess the effectiveness of treatments.

The present text provides an overview of several issues peculiar to applied behavior analysis research methodology. Six general areas of concern are (a) trends in applied behavior analysis research, (b) assessment and measurement issues, (c) experimental designs and strategies, (d) interpretation of findings, (e) ethical issues in applied behavior analysis, and (f) the societal impact of studies in the area. As evidenced by a sizable number of recently published articles, these topics are of considerable interest to behavior analysts. They also are relevant for students of scientific epistemology and general psychological research methods.

In selecting chapters for inclusion in *Research Methods in Applied Behavior Analysis*, the editors attempted to provide a balanced coverage of controversial topics. Thus, some authors argue for the use of inferential statistics in applied behavior analysis, whereas others criticize the practice. No attempt is made to present as resolved issues that currently are being debated, nor to imply a consensus of expert opinion where none exists. Established behavior analysts speak for themselves in the selected articles, and they do not inevitably speak with one voice. Most, however, do appear to agree that applied behavior analysis will remain viable only so long as its practitioners wisely employ the methods of science to explore and beneficially alter human behavior.

The primary purpose of this text is to summarize scientific research methods and their applications in applied behavior analysis. If this objective is met, primary credit is due the individual contributors. We editors are deeply indebted to each of them. We also are grateful to the many other individuals who in one way or another contributed to the project in particular, Alan Bellack, Michel Hersen, Eliot Werner, Leonard Guida and Peter Strupp deserve special thanks.

ALAN POLING
R. WAYNE FUQUA

Contents

CHAPTER 8.   THE GRAPHIC ANALYSIS OF DATA

Barry S. Parsonson and Donald M. Baer

CHAPTER 9.   AUTOCORRELATION IN BEHAVIORAL RESEARCH:
             WHEREFORE ART THOU?

Bradley E. Huitema

CHAPTER 10. STATISTICAL ANALYSIS AND SINGLE-SUBJECT DESIGNS:
             SOME MISUNDERSTANDINGS

Bradley E. Huitema

Experimentation in Behavioral Psychology

The Flight to the Laboratory

RICHARD W. MALOTT

INTRODUCTION

The surest path to ultimate reality is through the experimental sciences. Only by experimentation can we establish functional relations (causal relations). Only by manipulating an independent variable can we prove that it affects a dependent variable. Otherwise we are restricted to mere speculation.

We may have a statistically reliable correlation between two variables, but we do not know for sure that one of those variables affects the other. We may know that having been a Boy Scout is correlated with later success in life, but we do not know that the early scouting caused the beneficial effect. Instead both variables might be caused by a third variable like parental income. The only way we can know for sure is to randomly assign some kids to the Scouts while preventing others from joining, and then checking them out a few years later.

But in the world of affairs, we do not even have a reliable correlation. Instead, we know one successful guy who had been a Boy Scout and one loser who had not. And from that we infer a correlation; and from the correlation we infer a causal relation.

Often we do not even have our rudimentary facts straight. For instance, we think the JC's man of the year had been in the Scouts,

RICHARD W. MALOTT • Department of Psychology, Western Michigan University, Kalamazoo, MI 49008.

though we are not sure. But surely he must have been, and we extrapolate from there.

The surest path to higher truth is through experimental research, not correlational field studies, and not speculations based on a few historical facts. Now, this is all fairly common knowledge in the philosophy of science, through I have jazzed it up a bit with a few pop words like *reality, cause, truth,* and *prove.* And I agree with this common knowledge, although it would exclude one of humanity's most important scientific discoveries—Darwin's notion of biological evolution as caused by the survival of the species, his theory of evolution.

DARWIN

Darwin had no experimentally verified functional relationships. And I doubt if he ever calculated that first correlation coefficient. At best, he had a few observations here and there. And a lesser, more conservative scholar would have been content with cataloguing and reporting of those observations, refraining from unsubstantiated speculations about the relationships among the observations. But fortunately Darwin was not so timid. He went way beyond his data base to suggest causal relations. He developed a framework, a theory that allowed him and us to make a little more sense of the world; it became one of the great intellectual accomplishments of all time. It was a scientific accomplishment, but not an experimental one. Of course, if he had been able to conduct a few experiments, we might not be replaying the Scopes Monkey Trial every few years. And that may point out one of the greatest difficulties in using a speculative framework, such as Darwin's theory of evolution. It is not so much that we cannot arrive at the truth through speculation; it is that we can never be sure when we have gotten there and when we are on the wrong path instead. It is hard to evaluate a theory or framework of this sort. Of course you can see if it fits what facts we know, but you can never perform a test of statistical significance that will allow you to rule it out, or fail to rule it out. What it really boils down to is that this framework or theory makes sense or it does not make sense. And if you do not want to believe it, you will always be able to find reasons to support your disbelief.

SKINNER

I think Skinner is even further away from the textbook model of the scientist than Darwin. But we can cloak him in the guise of the experimentalist, because early in his career he did stick a few rats and pigeons into experimental test chambers. And some of those early experiments may have indeed shaped his theorizing, but I think it is his theorizing or systematizing that is his major, revolutionary contribution to knowledge; and I suspect his theorizing could stand relatively independent of his experimental work, though often his experiments served as nice demonstrations of some of the basic concepts of behavior analysis.

But my guess is that Skinner could have, and perhaps did, derive most of the basic concepts of behavior analysis (e.g., reinforcement, extinction, generalization, and chaining) from already existing data, casual everyday observations, and common sense. Then he simply illustrated them with his experiments.

To me, his contributions were the systematizing of the principles and concepts of behavior and his bold extrapolation from a few simple rat studies to the most complex instances of human behavior. He was so far from his data base that it was out of sight. He outdid Darwin in his boldness. And best of all, he did it without reference to mentalistic concepts.

Interestingly, many methodological behaviorists are so enamored with the rhetoric of experimental science that they think Skinner's last significant contribution was *Behavior of Organisms* (1938) or maybe *Schedules of Reinforcement* (Ferster & Skinner, 1957). But I think he was just starting to hit his stride with his brilliant, speculative, systematizing, theoretical work *Contingencies of Reinforcement* (1969). However, the methodological behaviorists and experimental rhetoriticians often put down the contemporary Skinner as having sold out to arm-chair philosophizing.

So even Skinner's followers fail to agree about the value of his various contributions. And maybe the methodological folks are right, in the sense that after his teaching machine demonstrations in the fifties, most of the work Skinner has done may have had little impact on the field of behavior analysis. He got the ball rolling and now its own inertia keeps it going with little other than inspirational input from him.

But I think that may speak poorly of our field rather than of Skinner's more recent efforts. I think our field has simply failed to keep up with him. And I think the main reason is because of the blinders our experimental rhetoric has put on us. We are not able to grasp Skinner's scope of vision. I will admit the difficulty and abstractness of the topics and the difficulty of reading Skinner's writing may also be factors.

But in any case, it is going to be hard to evaluate Skinner as a theorist because his theories violate one of the oldest cannons of the experimental mentality—that they be testable, that they be capable of disproof. For instance, how are you going to do that crucial experiment to demonstrate that human behavior is or is not determined or lawful?

No one is ever going to prove or disprove Skinner's notions about a utopian experimental culture, problem solving, phylogeny and ontogeny of behavior, thinking, ethics, education, language, the shortcomings of mentalism, etc.

It may be that his notions will survive in a world of intellectual Darwinism because they are a little closer to the truth than are others, and because the followers of Skinner's notions are therefore able to deal more effectively with the world. But that survival will be no ultimate proof because the critics can point out that a lot of nonsense survives for the wrong reasons. Ironically, I can imagine critics of the future criticizing Skinnerian theory as being completely off base, while they enjoy the benefits of a world made a little more intelligible by Skinnerian theory and a little more habitable and humane by Skinnerian technology.) On the other hand, the failure of Skinnerian theory to survive would also be no ultimate proof of its falseness. Truth, beauty, and justice do not always win out over prejudice, ignorance, and political and economic expedience. Still, being right must surely increase the survival value of a theory, at least a little bit.

Skinner's theory, even more than Darwin's, is too big to be tested, in the tradition sense. His theory is a world of view. It does not involve a set of axioms from which we derive some specific, testable hypotheses. It talks more in general than in particular. Another theory or world view of perhaps a somewhat smaller scope would be Marxism. And a world view of comparable scope would be Christianity.

Now the Skinnerian world view differs from these others, including Darwin's, in that the basic principles or processes have been verified in the experimental laboratory. And many of the specific extrapolations to applied human concerns have also been experimentally verified. We know we are dealing with true causal relations. Still Skinner's speculations go way beyond this experimental data base. But it is nice to know that at least we're starting off with some verified concepts.

FEAR OF FIELD STUDIES

I find myself learning much more about human nature from a reading of Dale Carnegie's schmaltzy *How to Win Friends and Influence People* (1964) than I do from a whole volume of any of our leading behavior analysis journals. And yet Carnegie never set foot in a laboratory, so far as I know. He just looked around, listened to people's stories, and read about people's lives. And from that, he induced a few profound functional relations. People will be more likely to try to make you happy, if you make them happy. People will be less likely to try to make you happy, if you make them unhappy. And you can make them happy by knowing their name, spelling it correctly, smiling at them, listening to them, agreeing with them, and admiring them. Nothing new there, of course. Yes, there is. What is new is that this is almost a miniature world view. Everyone knows it is true. But no one knows how universally and powerfully and mountain-movingly true it is, except Carnegie and his followers. To write off these concepts as trivial is like writing off the principle of reinforcement as trivial. But Carnegie arrived at the notion of their power, without the benefit of an experimental analysis. And if you read his book, you will probably agree that he also makes a pretty good case for their power, without the benefit of experimental data. Now he may be a little light on the theoretical analysis of why his causal relations hold, but they do hold tenaciously nonetheless.

I think we would do well to train our scientists to spend more time speculating about the relevance of everyday life to their fields of study, in the manner of Darwin, Skinner, Marx, the Christians, and Carnegie—not in lieu of experimental analyses, but in addition to them. As it is, we are training most of our experimental scientists to have a very strong aversion to knowledge that comes from any source other than a laboratory; and we seem proud of it. True, that conservatism may prevent us from making fools of ourselves; but it may also condemn us to an ever tightening spiral of triviality.

FEAR OF UTILITY

We professors train our experimental scientists to believe that the only way they will be of professional worth is to do experimental research and publish in scholarly journals. Anything else is a lesser achievement. They should not be teachers, they should not be administrators, they should not be practitioners. But only a small percentage of them then get jobs as experimentalists, and the majority gets jobs as teachers, administrators, and practitioners. And that majority then attempts to distort those jobs into research positions, though that is not what they are paid for. And they evaluate their jobs in terms of how many research opportunities there are. And they hang their heads in shame when they are not able to publish as much as their colleagues in the big-time universities. So by such overemphasis on the experimental-scientist model, we are condemning the majority of our graduates to lives as unhappy misfits in jobs they will eventually find themselves in. Yet, the rhetoric of the experimental-scientist model is so strong and so deeply inculcated that to suggest another model is to blaspheme.

I believe it is time for the members of the experimental sciences to rethink this issue. We need to acknowledge the ability of speculative science to make worthwhile contributions, in the manner of Darwin and Skinner. We need to acknowledge casual field-study observations as valuable sources of data, in the manner of Carnegie. And we need to acknowledge the worth of other sorts of contributions to our field, in the areas of teaching, administration, and applications. Incidently, if we stop insisting on rigorous experimental analyses in support of all of our knowledge, then teachers, administrators, and practitioners can more readily make valuable contributions to that body of knowledge.

CONCLUSIONS

Psychologists dealing with learning, in general, and behavior analysis, in particular, tend to equate their areas of study with experimental methodology. Even in applied behavior analysis, they emphasize the application of experimental methodology. We give little support to engineering applications of our knowledge, for example, behavioral systems analysis; and we give even less support to the theoretical analyses of behavior.

In reviewing the literature, we seem to find it more rewarding to discard a study because it was not 100% methodologically clean than we do to praise a study because it gives us some new insight into human nature. But instead, I suggest we place less emphasis on our methodology and more on our subject matter. We should not decrease our rigorous experimental studies. But we should increase our creative, informal observation, including behavioral introspection; and we should increase the systematization of our field.

REFERENCES

Carnegie, D. (1964). *How to win friends and influence people*. New York: Pocket Books.
Ferster, C. B., & Skinner, B. F. (1957). *Schedules of reinforcement*. New York: Appleton-Century-Crofts.
Skinner, B. F. (1938). *The behavior of organisms*. New York: Appleton-Century-Crofts.
Skinner, B. F. (1969). *Contingencies of reinforcement*. New York: Appleton-Century-Crofts.

2

Basic Research Designs in Applied Behavior Analysis

ALAN POLING AND DEBORAH GROSSETT

INTRODUCTION

Applied behavior analysis relies on experimentation to assess the efficacy of interventions. Experimentation involves the measurement of one physical event, the dependent variable, under conditions where the value of a second physical event, the independent variable, is manipulated systematically. If the value of the dependent variable covaries lawfully with the value of the independent variable, a functional relation is evident. Functional relations are the basis of scientific laws; such relations allow for the prediction and control, hence the understanding, of phenomena studied as dependent variables. The logical configuring of conditions that allows changes in a dependent variable to be attributed to the actions of an independent variable is termed the experimental design. Although many specific experimental designs are capable of demonstrating functional relations, a limited number of designs are favored by applied behavior analysts. The purpose of this chapter is to describe these designs.

BETWEEN-SUBJECTS AND WITHIN-SUBJECT DESIGNS

Two general experimental strategies can be adopted in treatment evaluation. The first involves *between-subjects*, or group, comparisons. In such experiments, individuals in one group are treated differently from

ALAN POLING • Department of Psychology, Western Michigan University, Kalamazoo, MI 49008. **DEBORAH GROSSETT** • Richmond State School, 2100 Preston Avenue, Richmond, TX 77469. Manuscript preparation was partially supported by National Institutes of Health Research Grant R01 NS20216–01.

those in another group (or groups), and obtained differences in the performance of the groups are attributed to their differential treatment. In most between-subjects designs, the various groups are assumed to be equivalent at the onset of experimentation (this assumption typically is supported through random assignment of subjects to groups, or matching of groups on important dimensions) and inferential statistics are commonly used to evaluate obtained differences in performance.

Between-subjects designs have a long and illustrious history in science, but their widespread use in behavior analysis has been criticized on several grounds (see Hersen & Barlow, 1976; Kazdin, 1982; Sidman, 1960). These include (a) the need for many subjects, which are rarely available in clinical settings; (b) the possibility of obscuring individual responses to treatment through the grouping of data commonly associated with inferential statistics; and (c) the ethical problem of withholding treatment from a (control) group of subjects, which is an integral part of many between-subjects designs. In view of these shortcomings, it appears that the use of between-subjects designs in applied behavior analysis should be restricted to situations in which the experimental question necessitates their use (cf. Poling & Cleary, in press).

Experimental designs that involve the intensive study of individuals, each of whose behavior under one condition is compared to that same person's behavior under one or more other conditions, are termed *within-subject* designs. They also are sometimes designated *single-subject* or *single-case* designs.

In contrast to most between-subjects designs, where the behavior of interest is measured once or at most a few times in each of a large number of individuals, *within-subject* designs typically involve repeated measures of the behavior of a relatively small number of subjects. Also in contrast to most between-subjects designs, where individuals in a particular group are exposed to only one value of the independent variable, typical within-subject designs expose every individual to all values of the independent variable.

Hersen and Barlow (1976) examine the historical antecedents of within-subject designs in clinical investigations. It is sufficient for our purposes to mention only that within-subject designs have long been accepted in the natural sciences, including medicine. Claude Bernard, for example, in his *An Introduction to the Study of Experimental Medicine* (1865) opted for an approach to research very much like that currently favored by behavior analysts (see Thompson, 1984). A common but unappealing form of within-subject design is the case study method, an enduring favorite in clinical psychology and in certain areas of medicine.

Case Study Designs

The *case study*, or B (treatment only), design is the simplest type of within-subject design. In this experimental configuration, treatment is introduced prior to or in conjunction with observation of the target behavior. Because this design does not involve the collection of data in the absence of treatment, no conclusions can be drawn regarding the functional relation between treatment and the dependent variable. Although clients in clinical settings may require immediate treatment, which precludes the collection of baseline (treatment absent) data, authoritative sources (e.g., Boring, 1954; Campbell & Stanley, 1966) have deemed designs similar to the case study to be devoid of scientific worth. While B designs that incorporate careful measures of behavior may generate hypotheses worthy of rigorous test (cf. Hersen & Barlow, 1976), this seems to be their only role in a science of behavior.

A/B Designs

By convention, the letter *A* is used to designate a baseline (no treatment) condition, the letter *B* to designate treatment (different parametric values of treatment can be designated by subscripting). The *A/B* design involves a baseline phase followed by the introduction of treatment; the target behavior (i.e., the response that intervention is intended to change) is monitored repeatedly during both phases. A treatment effect is demonstrated by showing that performance differs from one phase to the next. Figure 1 (top frame) presents the results from a hypothetical experiment in which an A/B design was employed.

The A/B design is logically superior to the B design, but neither supports firm conclusions, and both suffer from what Campbell and Stanley (1966) termed "threats to their internal validity." These uncontrolled threats, which limit the confidence with which changes in a dependent variable can be attributed to an independent variable, include changes in the target behavior due to maturation of the subject, history effects, and unknown extraneous variables that impose on the client coincident with treatment. (Extraneous variables are objects and events other than the treatment of interest that affect a dependent variable.)

Consider, for example, a situation in which a researcher posits that providing verbal instructions will increase the on-task behavior of a hyperactive child. On-task behavior is appropriately defined and measured during an initial baseline (A) phase, followed (after behavior in the A phase stabilized) by the intervention (B). After a few days of

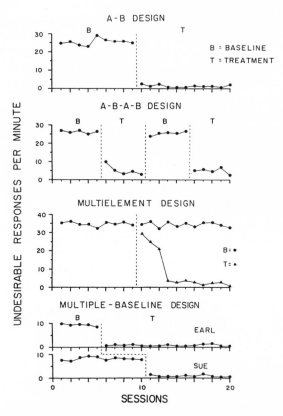

FIGURE 1. Hypothetical data from experiments utilizing A/B, A/B/A/B, multiple-baseline, and multielement baseline (or alternating-treatments) designs. Each set of data suggests that the treatment was effective in reducing undesirable behavior.

exposure to treatment, levels of on-task behavior clearly increase, and remain stable for several days. This suggests that the intervention was in fact effective. It is possible, however, that some extraneous variable became operative coincident with imposition of treatment, and was actually responsible for the observed, and quite real, improvement. Perhaps at the onset of the B phase a favored playmate of the child (and a potent disrupter of on-task activity) became ill and left school. The playmate's absence, not verbal prompting, actually accounted for the observed increase in on-task behavior. If the researcher failed to detect the confounding effects of the playmate's absence, which is likely, the researcher would attribute the increased on-task behavior to treatment, and err in so doing. This error of inference probably would have been avoided had a posttreatment baseline phase been added to the experiment, in which case a rudimentary withdrawal design (to be discussed) would have been employed.

Exposing other, independent (e.g., spatially separated) subjects to the intervention also would decrease the likelihood that the effects of verbal prompts would be confused with those of a friend's absence, for the effects of such an extraneous variable would be limited in space and time. Though a friend's absence might confound the effects of treatment for Kimberly, tested in Kalamazoo, that same absence could not similarly affect Kathy, exposed to treatment in Kathmandu 2 weeks later. Independent A/B designs, when arranged in a special configuration involving the temporally staggered introduction of treatment, constitute a multiple-baseline design, described later.

Withdrawal Designs

Withdrawal designs are widely used in basic behavioral research and, in the inaugural issue of the *Journal of Applied Behavior Analysis* (JABA), Baer, Wolf, and Risley (1968) noted that such designs are of great value in applied behavior analysis. Surely they are widely employed in the area; from 1968 to 1976, withdrawal designs were used in the majority of studies published in JABA (Kelly, 1977).

The logic of all withdrawal[1] designs is straightforward and compelling: If the dependent measure changes appreciably from the baseline level when treatment is implemented, and returns to at or near the initial baseline level when treatment is terminated, there is good reason to believe that the observed changes in the target behavior reflect the action of treatment.[2] It is, of course, possible that some extraneous variable begins to impose on the client when treatment is introduced, remains operative throughout the course of treatment, and ceases when treatment ends. Unless the extraneous variable is actually associated with treatment, the likelihood of this happening is small (but never nonexistent), and grows smaller with each additional implementation and termination of treatment. Repeatedly exposing a client to treatment and evaluating performance during treatment relative to pre- and posttreatment baselines can be conceptualized as replicating an experiment.

---

[1]Withdrawal designs are also commonly termed *reversal designs,* although the latter designation may be misleading as Hersen and Barlow (1976) explained.

[2]Multiple dependent measures (target behaviors) frequently are monitored in applied behavior analysis, regardless of the experimental design employed. To facilitate exposition, our discussion of designs will assume that, unless the design dictates otherwise (as does the multiple-baseline), only one target behavior is measured.

Sidman (1960) used the term *direct replication* to refer to the "replication of a given experiment by the same investigator" (p. 73), and noted that replicating an experiment with the same subject increases confidence in the reliability of findings, although it does not preclude the possibility that this subject is more or less sensitive to treatment than are other individuals. Direct replication of an experiment with additional subjects also increases confidence in the reliability of findings, and begins to address the issue of generalizability of findings, a topic to which we will return shortly.

It is important to recognize that in direct replication, either within or between subjects, conditions must be kept relatively constant. That is, treatment parameters and outcome measures must be consistent and, in replications across subjects, all individuals must be relatively homogeneous with respect to the behavior of interest and characteristics likely to affect its modifiability (e.g., age, presence of mental retardation). If this is done,

> interpretation of mixed results, where some clients benefit from the procedure and some do not, can be attributed to as few differences as possible, thereby providing a clearer direction for further experimentation. (Hersen & Barlow, 1976, p. 318)

Although there is no standard for the number of direct replications across individuals required for findings to be generally accepted by the scientific community, Hersen and Barlow (1976) suggested that one successful experiment and three successful replications across subjects provide sufficient support for the efficacy of treatment to merit tests by other researchers, in other settings, and with other kinds of subjects (i.e., systematic replications).

Data from a hypothetical study employing an A/B/A/B design are presented in the second frame of Figure 1. The actual use of such a design in applied behavior analysis is exampled by a recent study conducted by Murphy, Hutchinson, and Bailey (1983), who demonstrated that arranging organized games decreased the number of aggressive acts emitted by children during recess. Over 300 kindergarten, first-grade, and second-grade children served as subjects in this investigation, and the inappropriate behaviors (aggression, property abuse, and rule violations) of these individuals were recorded by trained undergraduates during daily 20-minute playground periods. Results of the study are shown in Figure 2.

Prior to the introduction of organized games, the average number of aggressive incidents observed during daily recording periods was over

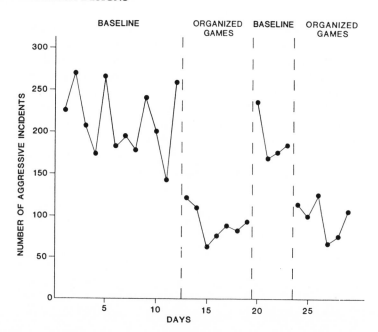

FIGURE 2. Frequency of undesirable incidents recorded during daily 20-min observational periods on the playground. An A/B/A/B design was employed in this study; A and B conditions are described in text. *Note.* From "Behavioral school psychology goes outdoors: The effect of organized games on playground aggression" by H. A. Murphy, J. M. Hutchinson, and J. S. Bailey, *Journal of Applied Behavior Analysis*, 1983, *16, 29–35.* Reprinted with permission of The Society for the Experimental Analysis of Behavior.

200. When games such as foot races and rope jumping were first introduced, the mean number of aggressive acts decreased by roughly 50%. Inappropriate behavior returned to initial baseline levels when treatment was terminated, and again declined with the reintroduction of games. In view of these findings, the researchers appear safe in concluding that the introduction of organized games appreciably reduced the overall frequency of young childrens' inappropriate playground activities.

Though this study involved a within-subject design, only data summarized across participants (i.e., group means with no measure of variability) were presented. This does not preclude meaningful conclusions of a general sort, but does leave unanswered the question of whether games similarly affected all children. Within-subject designs allow for a detailed description of treatment effects only when data for individual subjects are carefully analyzed; grouped data obscure idiosyncratic responses to treatment regardless of the design employed.

When used appropriately, various forms of withdrawal designs are adequate for comparing the effects of different treatments, and for determining the interactive effects of two or more treatments, as well as simply evaluating a single intervention. Two basic rules pertain to the use of all withdrawal designs. First, conditions should not be changed until behavior is relatively stable over time. In general, a behavior is stable if (a) variability over time is minimal, and (b) there is no upward or downward trend in performance over time. Stable data are important in that they facilitate analysis of the effects of an intervention, and also provide a measure of its full (i.e., steady-state) effects. Methods for assessing the stability of data and for analyzing data that evidence trends or appreciable variability are discussed by Parsonson and Baer in their chapter in this text, and experimental techniques for reducing the variability of data are reviewed by Sidman (1960).

Second, to provide for a true analysis of an intervention's effects, only one variable should be altered at a time. This typically becomes an issue only when two or more treatments are being compared. Consider a situation in which a researcher is interested in the combined effects of two treatments, B and C. This could be assessed appropriately via an A/B/A/B/BC/B/BC design (BC indicates both treatments are in effect). Although this design does not provide for an analysis of the C treatment alone, it does allow the combined effects of the two treatments to be examined by comparing performance between the adjacent B and BC phases, which differ with respect to a single variable (C) only. An A/B/ A/BC/A/A/BC design would not be adequate for evaluating the combined effects of the treatments, because the B and BC phases are not adjacent. Hersen and Barlow (1976) provided a detailed analysis of why it is important to alter only one variable from phase to phase in a study, and also introduce many variants of the basic withdrawal design (e.g., A/B/A/B/ A/B/A/B/A/C/A/C). These variants differ in complexity and the range of experimental questions they are suited to answer, but their logic is precisely that of the A/B/A design, and they share its general strengths and weaknesses.

The primary disadvantages of all withdrawal designs are two. One is that such designs cannot be used to evaluate treatments that produce irreversible effects. A second is that withdrawing an apparently effective treatment, and thereby inducing countertherapeutic behavior change, may be ethically unacceptable in applied settings. A third shortcoming of withdrawal designs, though perhaps less significant than the former two, is that many sessions (observation periods) are required to complete a typical experiment in which such a design is employed. Extended periods of evaluation may not be possible or desirable in certain settings or with certain populations (e.g., acutely depressed, hospitalized patients).

Multiple-Baseline Designs

The *multiple-baseline design* involves a sequence of A/B manipulations staggered in time. In this design, a number of target behaviors, typically three or four (Kazdin & Kopel, 1975), are recorded. These can be different behaviors of a single individual, the same or different behaviors of two or more individuals, or the same behavior of a single individual in different situations. Each target behavior must require change in like direction, and all dependent measures should be independent (i.e., changing one ought not affect the others).

The multiple-baseline design typically begins with all target behaviors being assessed during baseline conditions.[3] Once performance is stable, treatment is introduced for one target behavior. For example, if the aggressive responses of three different children constitute the target behaviors, one child's aggressive responding would be treated, whereas the other dependent measures (i.e., the aggressive behavior of the other two children) would continue to be recorded under baseline conditions. When the behavior first treated stabilizes in the presence of the intervention, treatment would begin for a second behavior, and continued for the first. Treatment for the third target behavior would begin only when the second had stabilized. Data showing the results of a hypothetical experiment in which a multiple-baseline-across-subjects design was employed are presented in the third frame of Figure 1.

With a multiple-baseline design, a treatment's efficacy is evident if each dependent measure changes when and only when treatment is initiated for that behavior. If two or more behaviors are apparently affected when treatment is implemented for one of them, the design's logic dictates that this effect cannot confidently be attributed to treatment. This is because such data might reflect a nonindependence of the target behaviors, but could also involve the action of some extraneous variable coincidentally activated at the onset of treatment. These two possibilities can be evaluated by terminating treatment and determining whether both behaviors return to pretreatment levels. If so, it is reasonable to

[3]The multiple-baseline design can also begin with all target behaviors being treated, after which treatment is withdrawn in a sequence that is temporally staggered across treatments. An example of this arrangement, which, of course, is useful for examining the effects of withdrawing treatment, is provided by Davis, Poling, Wysocki, and Breuning (1981).

conclude that treatment is effective and the two behaviors nonindependent. If not, the action of an extraneous variable cannot be ruled out, and the intervention's efficacy remains moot.

Poche, Brouwer, and Swearingen (1981) provided an example of the use of a multiple-baseline-across-subjects design in a study intended to evaluate a procedure for developing self-protective behavior in young children. Results of the investigation are shown in Figure 3.

Prior to training, which involved modeling, behavior rehearsal, and social reinforcement, all three subjects were susceptible to adult lures in that they remained in close proximity to, and agreed to go with, the adult. Following training, each subject responded appropriately to lures (e.g., moved away and said no when asked to accompany the adult). Follow-up data collected 4 months after treatment had ended indicated that treatment gains were well maintained over time.

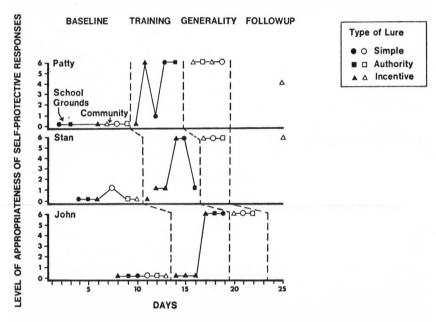

FIGURE 3. The level of appropriateness of self-protectiveness during baseline, training, and generality probes in both school and community settings. Closed symbols represent data gathered near the school (where children were trained); open circles in a location away from the school. A multiple-baseline design (with follow-up) was used in this study and conditions are described in text. *Note.* From "Teaching self-protection to young children" by C. Poche, R. Brouwer, and M. Swearingen, *Journal of Applied Behavior Analysis*, 1981, *14*, 169–176. Reproduced with permission of The Society for the Experimental Analysis of Behavior.

The multiple-baseline design is not limited by the two major short-comings of withdrawal designs. It is appropriate for evaluating treatments that produce irreversible effects (so long as the dependent measures are independent) and does not require countertherapeutic behavior change to demonstrate the efficacy of treatment. For these reasons, the design is quite popular in applied behavior analysis (Kelly, 1977).

Despite its popularity in applied research and the fact that many behavior analysts (e.g., Baer *et al.*, 1968) contend that the multiple-baseline design is capable of demonstrating a functional relation between independent and dependent variables, the design is essentially an A/B configuration with replications staggered in time. Hence, the multiple-baseline provides a less convincing demonstration of treatment effects than withdrawal designs (and perhaps for that reason is rarely used in basic behavioral research as published in the *Journal of the Experimental Analysis of Behavior*). Moreover, there are three potentially significant problems with the multiple-baseline design. First, withholding treatment during an extended baseline period may be ethically or practically undesirable. Second, the design is appropriate only when the behaviors of concern are independent and, as Kazdin and Kopel (1971) noted, independence of target behaviors is sometimes difficult to determine prior to the initiation of treatment. Third, it may be difficult to interpret the efficacy of an intervention when it produces the desired change in some target behaviors, but not in others.

Multiple-Probe Designs

The *multiple-probe design* (Horner & Baer, 1978) combines the logic of the multiple-baseline design with probe procedures to evaluate the effects of interventions designed to teach a sequence (chain) of responses. With this design, initial baseline data are collected on each of the steps (behaviors) in the training sequence. After initial baseline data are collected, treatment is introduced for the first behavior in the chain. Only when that response is acquired to criterion level are additional probe data collected for other behaviors in the sequence. These probe data represent a "true baseline" for the second response in the sequence, which is now treated. At the end of treatment for this second behavior, probe data are collected for all other responses; these data constitute follow-up data for the behavior initially treated and true baseline data for the third behavior in the sequence. The logic of the multiple-probe design and its relation to the multiple-baseline are evident in Figure 4,

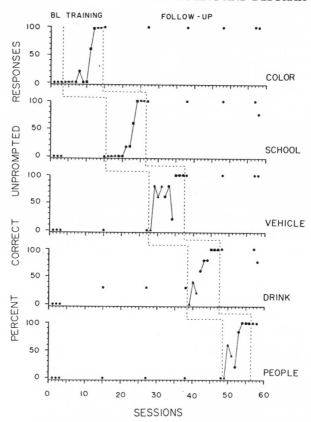

FIGURE 4. Percent correct unprompted intraverbal responses by a mentally retarded individual. A multiple-probe design was used in this study. Training began with immediate prompts (triangles), followed sequentially by sessions in which prompts were delayed by 1 sec (circles) and by 2 sec (squares). BL represents baseline. *Note.* From "Development of intraverbal behavior in mentally retarded individuals through transfer of stimulus control procedures: Classification of verbal responses" by S. J. Braam and A. Poling, *Applied Research in Mental Retardation*, 1983, 4, 279–302. Reproduced with permission of Pergamon Press.

which shows data collected by Braam and Poling (1983) in a study examining the use of transfer of stimulus control procedures to teach intraverbal responses to mentally retarded participants.

Data presented in Figure 4 indicate that prior to training (during the baseline, or BL, phase) the subject did not emit appropriate intraverbal responses (i.e., spoken words representing specific examples) in response to the generic nouns *color, school, vehicle, drink,* and *people*. Appropriate intraverbal responding to each of these nouns developed rapidly with exposure to a transfer of stimulus control procedure (during the training phase), and probe data collected after training ended indicated that treatment gains were well maintained over time.

As does the unelaborated multiple-baseline design, the multiple-probe design demonstrates the efficacy of treatment by showing that a particular behavior changes when and only when treatment is instituted for that behavior. General strengths and weaknesses of the two designs are precisely the same. However, because the multiple-probe procedure does not require extended baseline observations throughout the course of a study, it is of real value when "continuous measurement during extended multiple baselines proves impractical, unnecessary, or reactive" (Horner & Baer, 1978, p. 196).

Changing-Criterion Designs

Although sometimes described as a variant of the multiple-baseline design (e.g., Hartman & Hall, 1976), the *changing-criterion design* is perhaps better envisioned as an A/B design with the treatment phase divided into subphases, each of which involves a different criterion for reinforcement. As Hartmann and Hall (1976) noted:

> Each treatment phase is associated with a stepwise change in criterion rate for the target behavior. Thus, each phase of the design provides a baseline for the following phase. When the rate of the target behavior changes with each stepwise change in the criterion, therapeutic change is replicated and experimental control is demonstrated. (p. 527)

Figure 5 shows for one subject the results of a study by Foxx and Rubinoff (1979) in which a changing-criterion design was used to evaluate the efficacy of a procedure designed to reduce the caffeine intake of habitual coffee drinkers. Prior to treatment, which involved self-monitoring and contingency contracting, this individual consumed over 1000 mg of caffeine per day. Each of four successive treatment phases reduced the amount of caffeine allowed by 102 mg relative to the previous phase. Results indicate that the subject met the criterion at each phase of treatment, and that the reduced caffeine intake associated with treatment was retained over a prolonged follow-up period.

The changing-criterion design has three major strengths. First, treatment does not have to be withdrawn, thus ethical and practical problems related to countertherapeutic behavior change are obviated. Second, all subjects receive treatment after only a brief baseline period. Third, when performance closely matches specified criteria, the design allows for an unambiguous demonstration of a treatment's efficacy. However, problems of interpretation arise when behavior does not closely parallel criterion levels, which is one of the design's shortcomings.

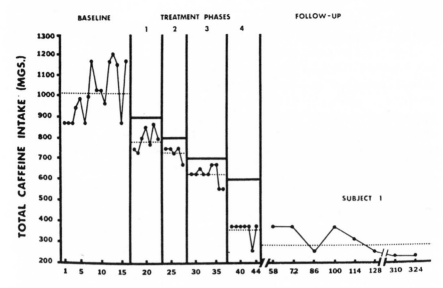

FIGURE 5. One subject's daily caffeine intake (mg) during baseline, treatment, and follow-up phases. A changing-criterion design was used in this study, and treatment involved self-monitoring and contingency contracting. *Note.* From "Behavioral treatment of caffeinism: Reducing excessive coffee drinking" by R. M. Foxx and A. Rubinoff, *Journal of Applied Behavior Analysis*, 1979, *12*, 335–344. Reproduced with permission of The Society for the Experimental Analysis of Behavior.

Another is that the design does not allow for the evaluation of treatments that do not specify stepwise changes in performance. This includes the majority of procedures employed by behavior analysts.

Alternating-Treatments Designs

The *alternating-treatments design* (Barlow & Hayes, 1978) involves repeated measurement of behavior while conditions rapidly alternate, typically between baseline and a single intervention phase, or between two separate intervention phases. Conditions may alternate either within a measurement session or from one session to the next, and the sequencing of conditions may be either regular or unpredictable. In many cases, a unique extereoceptive stimulus is paired with each condition, in which case the design resembles a multiple schedule and has been termed a multielement baseline design by Ulman and Sulzer-Azaroff (1975).

An experimental configuration similar to the alternating-treatments design also has been referred to as a simultaneous-treatment design (Kazdin & Hartmann, 1978). This designation appears to be misleading insofar as the treatments of concern are never in effect at the same time, that is, simultaneously.

The logic of the alternating-treatments design is evident in Figure 6, which presents data collected by Mosk and Bucher (1984). Those authors demonstrated via an alternating-treatments design that shaping plus prompting was more effective than prompting alone in teaching visual-motor (i.e., pegboard) skills to moderately and severely mentally retarded children.

One alleged advantage of the alternating-treatments design is in the analysis of highly variable behaviors. In clinical settings, levels of a target behavior often fluctuate widely across time; behavior may also consistently improve or worsen in the absence of treatment. In such cases, a phase change is not appropriate when multiple-baseline or withdrawal designs are employed. With the alternating-treatments design, conditions change regardless of the subject's behavior, and a comparison can legitimately be made between performance in two conditions (e.g., treatment and baseline) even though the target behavior improves or worsens during each. So long as behavior is consistently and appreciably better (or worse) during treatment than during baseline, variability across time does not preclude making a gross statement about the clinical value of treatment. However, when behavior does not inevitably differ greatly across conditions, the appropriate interpretation is unclear; the alternating-treatments design deals effectively with variability only when interventions produce such large effects as to overshadow other sources of variability. The effects of such interventions typically are evident regardless of experimental design. The alternating treatments design differs from other within-subject designs primarily in allowing phase changes while behavior is fluctuating; it cannot impose order on chaotic data. Moreover, one anticipates that a truly useful treatment will not only produce an overall improvement in behavior, but also will be associated with relatively stable performance over time.

A second advantage for the alternating treatments design involves its relative efficiency. Unlike withdrawal or multiple-baseline designs, the alternating treatments design allows for early initiation of treatment (although an initial pretreatment baseline phase is common when two interventions are to be compared), rapid exposure to all conditions of concern, and a quick evaluation of the success of treatment. Meaningful data (i.e., those that allow for a comparison of behavior under all of the conditions of interest) are generated early in the experiment and all is not lost if the project terminates prematurely. In addition, the design allows diverse treatments to be compared within a reasonable amount of time.

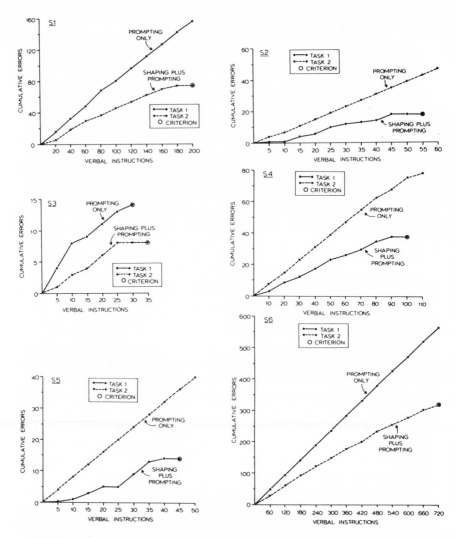

FIGURE 6. Cumulative errors in a pegboard-insertion task for subjects C1-C6. Cumulative errors are graphed as a function of the number of instructions, and the larger circle shows where criterion was reached. An alternating-treatments design was used in this study to compare a prompting procedure to a procedure in which promoting was combined with shaping. *Note.* From "Prompting and stimulus shaping procedures for teaching visual-motor skills to retarded children" by M. D. Mosk and B. Bucher, *Journal of Applied Behavior Analysis,* 1984, *17,* 23–34. Reproduced with the permission of The Society for Experimental Analysis of Behavior.

Because the design involves the rapid alternation of conditions, it has two major shortcomings. The first is that brief exposure to a treatment may be insufficient for its true actions to be observed. The second is that the design is inappropriate for evaluating treatments with long-lasting effects, because their actions will persist into, and confound, subsequent conditions.

Other Designs

Textbooks devoted to research methodology in applied behavior analysis (e.g., Hersen & Barlow, 1976; Kazdin, 1982) describe a number of experimental designs in addition to those previously described. Though other designs might be required for answering specific research questions (e.g., a concurrent schedule design would provide a useful means of determining which of two teaching techniques children prefer), the designs described in this chapter, used alone or in combination, are employed in the vast majority of published studies in applied behavior analysis, and fully illustrate the logic of within-subject research. Hence, no additional configurations will be described here.

EXTERNAL VALIDITY AND WITHIN-SUBJECT RESEARCH

The purpose of experimentation is to detect functional relations. When a study is designed so that changes in a dependent variable can be attributed with little or no ambiguity to the effects of an independent variable, it is said to be *internally valid*. The internal validity of a study is of obvious concern, but it is also important to consider the external validity of a study (Campbell & Stanley, 1968), that is, the extent to which functional relations observed therein can be reproduced under other circumstances.

> In applied research, considerations of external validity are especially critical because the purpose of undertaking the intervention may be to produce changes that are not restricted to conditions peculiar to the experiment. (Kazdin, 1982, p. 101)

As discussed elsewhere (Bracht & Glass, 1968; Kazdin, 1982), a wide range of factors can compromise the external validity of a study, regardless of the experimental design employed.

Some critics (e.g., Kiesler, 1971) have argued that all within-subject designs tell only how efficacious a treatment is in dealing with the problem behaviors of the tested subjects, and provide little or no information concerning the treatment's probable effects in other individuals. There appears to be no justification for such a contention; surely most of the interventions devised by applied behavior analysts (and demonstrated effective via within-subject designs) have proven widely effective. Nonetheless, the external validity of any one study is never fully apparent until the limits of reproducibility of functional relations reported therein are determined through systematic replication.

Systematic replication (Sidman, 1960) is the term used to describe attempts to assess the range of conditions under which a treatment is effective.

> We can define systematic replication in applied research as any attempt to replicate findings from a direct replication series, varying settings, behavior change agents, behavior disorders, or any combination thereof. It would appear that any successful systematic replication series in which one or more of the above-mentioned factors is varied also provides further information on generality of findings across clients since new clients are usually included in such efforts. (Hersen & Barlow, 1976, p. 339)

In principle, systematic replications ought to be begun under circumstances much like those in which treatment efficacy was first documented. That is, the behavior to be changed would not differ greatly, nor would other client characteristics, or the parameters of treatment. If treatment efficacy is evident under these circumstances, subsequent systematic replications would alter one variable, perhaps the kind of behavior targeted for change, until a point is reached at which the treatment is of no demonstrable value. Such a progression of systematic replications delineates the range of conditions under which a treatment is beneficial and, with respect to an individual study in the series, determines the external validity of its findings.

Though applied behavior analysts typically study potent interventions of broad efficacy, assessing the generality of a particular set of findings through logical inference, not systematic replication, is most difficult. As Sidman (1960) sagely noted, evaluating the probable external validity of a study is a behavioral process, one which in his words requires "maturity of judgement." An established scientist considering an intervention reported effective in a particular situation probably will consider several factors in determining the range of conditions under which similar effects should obtain. Among them are the experimental design employed, the kind and number of subjects studied, the ubiquity and magnitude of the treatment's effects, and whether other investigators have reported similar results. No formal rules will be employed in evaluating these factors, for none exist. Rather, the scientist will respond to them in light of a personal reinforcement history.

Sidman (1960) put it well when he wrote, "The experience and judgment of the individual scientist are always involved in the evaluation of data" (p. 71). Regardless of whether data are being evaluated as to reliability, generalizability, or scientific significance,

> mistakes are possible, but there are means for detecting and correcting them. The objectivity of science consists not so much in set rules of procedure as in the self-corrective nature of the scientific process. (Sidman, 1960, p. 43)

In this, perhaps, lies its primary virtue.

SELECTING AN EXPERIMENTAL DESIGN

Despite the potential complexities of experimental research and the many writings devoted to it, the essential features of a sound treatment evaluation are three, and can be simply stated: (a) the behavior to be changed (dependent variable) must be adequately defined and measured; (b) the treatment (independent variable) must be consistently administered according to the selected protocol; and (c) the sequencing of conditions (experimental design) and method of data analysis must allow observed changed in the dependent variable to be attributed with confidence to the intervention. If these three conditions are met, the evaluation is in principle sound.

There is no one design that is best, no panacean experimental configuration that succeeds where others fail. The experimental design that a researcher selects for a particular application will depend on several factors, perhaps the most important being the individual's training and theoretical persuasion. By virtue of their history, some investigators will favor between-subjects designs, others particular within-subject configurations. In addition to historical variables, current circumstances act to determine the design an investigator chooses to employ. To be fully satisfactory, an experiment must be designed so as to (a) fit the research question, (b) provide information that is useful to the intended research consumer, (c) be compatible with the available subject population, (d) effectively utilize available temporal and financial resources, and (e) be ethically acceptable.

Selection of an appropriate experimental design may seem difficult to the neophyte researcher, but the task is straightforward if one is aware of the logic, the strengths, and the weaknesses of common configurations. The present chapter is intended to provide this information, though in no great detail, for the designs typically employed by applied behavior analysts. More comprehensive coverages of within-subject experimental designs are provided by many authors (e.g., Hersen & Barlow, 1976; Johnston & Pennypacker, 1981; Kazdin, 1982; Sidman, 1960) to whose works the reader desiring further information is directed.

REFERENCES

Baer, D. M., Wolf, M. M., & Risley, T. R. (1968). Some current dimensions of applied behavior analysis. *Journal of Applied Behavior Analysis, 1,* 91–97.

Barlow, D. H., & Hayes, S. C. (1979). Alternating-treatments design: One strategy for comparing the effects of two treatments in a single subject. *Journal of Applied Behavior Analysis, 12,* 199–210.

Boring, E. G. (1954). The nature and history of experimental control. *American Journal of Psychology, 67,* 573–589.

Bracht, G. H., & Glass, G. V. (1968). The external validity of experiments. *American Educational Research Journal, 5,* 437–474.

Braam, S., & Poling, A. (1983). Development of intraverbal behavior in mentally retarded individuals through transfer of stimulus control procedures. *Applied Research in Mental Retardation, 4,* 279–302.

Campbell, D. T., & Stanley, J. C. (1966). *Experimental and quasi-experimental designs for research.* Chicago, IL: Rand McNally.

Davis, V. J., Poling, A., Wysocki, T., & Breuning, S. E. (1981). Effects of phenytoin withdrawal on matching to sample and workshop performance of mentally retarded persons. *The Journal of Nervous and Mental Disease, 169,* 718–725.

Foxx, R. M., & Rubinoff, A. (1979). Behavioral treatment of caffeinism: Reducing excessive coffee drinking. *Journal of Applied Behavior Analysis, 12,* 335–344.

Hartmann, D. P., & Hall, R. V. (1976). The changing-criterion design. *Journal of Applied Behavior Analysis, 9,* 527–532.

Hersen, M., & Barlow, D. H. (1976). *Single case experimental designs: Strategies for studying behavior change.* New York: Pergamon Press.

Horner, R. D., & Baer, D. M. (1978). Multiple-probe technique: A variation of the multiple baseline. *Journal of Applied Behavior Analysis, 11,* 189–196.

Johnston, J. M., & Pennypacker, H. S. (1981). *Strategies and tactics of human behavioral research.* New York: Erlbaum.

Kazdin, A. E. (1982). *Single-case research designs: Methods for clinical and applied settings.* New York: Oxford University Press.

Kazdin, A. E., & Hartmann, D. P. (1978). The simultaneous-treatment design. *Behavior Therapy, 9,* 912–922.

Kazdin, A. E., & Kopel, S. A. (1975). On resolving ambiguities of the multiple-baseline design: Problems and recommendations. *Behavior Therapy, 6,* 601–608.

Kelly, M. B. (1977). A review of the observational data-collection and reliability procedures reported in the *Journal of Applied Behavior Analysis. Journal of Applied Behavior Analysis, 10,* 97–101.

Kiesler, D. J. (1971). Experimental designs in psychotherapy research. In A. E. Bergin & S. L. Garfield (Eds.), *Handbook of psychotherapy and behavior change* (pp. 36–74). New York: Wiley.

Mosk, M. D., & Bucher, B. (1984). Prompting and stimulus shaping procedures for teaching visual-motor skills to retarded children. *Journal of Applied Behavior Analysis, 17,* 23–34.

Murphy, H. A., Hutchinson, J. M., & Bailey, J. S. (1983). Behavioral school psychology goes outdoors: The effect of organized games on playground aggression. *Journal of Applied Behavior Analysis, 16,* 29–36.

Poche, C., Brouwer, R., & Swearingen, M. (1981). Teaching self-protection to young children. *Journal of Applied Behavior Analysis, 14,* 169–176.

Poling, A., & Cleary, J. (in press). Within-subject designs. In K. D. Gadow & A. Poling (Eds.), *Advances in learning and behavioral disabilities (Supp. 1): Methodological issues in human psychopharmacology.* Greenwich, CT: JAI Press.

Sidman, M. (1960). *Tactics of scientific research.* New York: Basic Books.

Thompson, T. (1984). The examining magistrate for nature: A retrospective review of Claude Bernard's *An Introduction to the Study of Experimental Medicine. Journal of the Experimental Analysis of Behavior, 41,* 211–216.

Ulman, J. D., & Sulzer-Azaroff, B. (1975). Multielement baseline design in educational research. In E. Ramp & G. Semb (Eds.), *Behavior analysis: Areas of research and application* (pp. 359–376). Englewood Cliffs, NJ: Prentice-Hall.

3

Pure versus Quasi-Behavioral Research

JAMES M. JOHNSTON AND H. S. PENNYPACKER

BEHAVIOR AS A SCIENTIFIC SUBJECT MATTER

Introduction

Among the many struggles that, throughout its history, constitute psychology's attempts to study human activity, the conception of exactly what it is about human beings that should be the object of our investigations has been, and continues to be, a mighty one. This struggle is certainly appropriate; there can be no more central and pervasive an issue in psychological research than the definition of the phenomenon to be addressed by experimental methods. One of the reasons why an unambiguous definition of the subject matter is critical is so that the details of research method can be properly suited to the task of preserving the subject matter in the process ranging from definition, through measurement, design, and analysis to experimental inference in undiluted and uncontaminated form. Failures to maintain such purity depreciate to some degree (perhaps beyond any scientific value) the legitimacy of experimental conclusions, such bastardy taking the form of inferior reliability and generality. Eventually, these limitations on experimental data come to characterize entire literatures, thereby retarding the development of a human science and stunting its technological progeny.

Although it is by no means universally agreed upon, many in psychology and the social sciences describe behavior as the focus of their scientific efforts. Of this population, some refine their mission even further to the study of behavior as a natural phenomenon in its own right, rather than as an epiphenomenal means of investigating putative events inside the organism. However, even within this hearty minority,

JAMES M. JOHNSTON • Department of Psychology, Auburn University, Auburn, AL 36849.   H.S PENNYPACKER • Department of Psychology, University of Florida, Gainesville, FL 32611.

there is often considerable discrepancy between the intended subject matter and the subject matter that survives experimental methods. That is, the conception of behavior that guides the investigator's creation of the experiment and eventual inferences is often far from congruent with the subject matter that is defined by research methods and represented by the data. (Of course, nature speaks only through experimental procedures and without regard for the intentions of the investigator). This kind of slippage seems to issue partly from an inadequate understanding of what the biological phenomenon of behavior is, thereby ensuring insensitivity to the consequences of its characteristics for the selection of methods for studying it.

A Definition and Some Methodological Consequences

The following is a biologically and empirically functional definition of behavior:

> The behavior of an organism is that portion of the organism's interaction with its environment which is characterized by detectable displacement in space through time of some part of the organism and which results in a measurable change in at least one aspect of the environment. (Johnston & Pennypacker, 1980, p. 48)

Certain facets of this definition carry a major responsibility in guiding experimental investigation of the subsumed subject matter. Certainly, most fundamental is the stipulation that behavior is characteristic only of individual organisms. It is an intraorganism phenomenon, a result that can exist only when an interactive condition prevails between a single creature and some part of its environment. That environment may sometimes include other organisms, but it is still each individual that is behaving, not collections of individuals. In other words, there is no such phenomenon as group behavior, just as there is no such biological organism as a group; it is only our linguistic traditions and statistical machinations that create such illusions. Although this argument could be pursued at far greater length, it should already be clear that one of its methodological consequences is that the fundamental features of behavior can be clearly detected only at the level that they exist. A scientific effort to understand organism–environment interactions (behavior) must examine the effects of independent variables on those interactions. Given the uniqueness of individual organisms and their past and present environmental interactions, any attempt to abbreviate the search for empirical generalities by collating the effects of the independent variable on the behavior of different subjects can only obfuscate rather than extend the relations of interest.

Another methodological implication of this definition emerges from the reference to "the organism's interaction with its environment" and to "detectable displacement in space." The first phrase denotes behavior as the *interface* between the organism and the environment, not a property or attribute of the organism. Behavior is not possessed by the organism and is not something that the organism does: it is the result of a relational condition between the separate entities of organism and environment. The requirement for an interaction means that real or hypothetical states of the subject (being hungry or anxious) do not constitute behavioral events and that neither do independent conditions or changes in the environment (if you walk in the rain you will get wet, but *getting wet* is not behavior). The reference to "detectable displacement in space" removes any confusion by requiring movement, however gross or minute.[1] Furthermore, the last phrase of the definition—"which results in a measurable change in some aspect of the environment"—dictates that the movement of interest be detected and measured by its effects on the environment. This is not an unreasonable requirement; because behavior refers to organism–environment relations, there will unavoidably be relevant environmental changes to serve this definitional and measurement function. It is also a useful restriction because it tends to insure that the phenomenon being measured is indeed behavior.

A further methodological consequence of this definition stems from the requirement of organism–environment interaction and the reference to this process taking place through time. These elements define behavior as a dynamic, continuous, interactive process occurring through time, not as a discrete, static event or state. It follows that attempts to study such a phenomenon must strive to capture these qualities through the tactics of measurement and design that are selected.

In summary, behavior is first a phenomenon that exists only between individual organisms and their environments. Second, behavior involves some movement which is an interaction between the behavior organism and its environment. Third, such movements constitute a dynamic and continuous process through time. Whatever else may be true about behavior, it would seem difficult to deny the validity of these fundamental qualities.[2]

---

[1]That this definition was crafted primarily for methodological utility is clear by its requirement for detectable movement. This should not be taken to mean that events whose reality and nature are uncertain and that cannot now be directly measured may not satisfy the remainder of the definition and otherwise qualify. Consistent with the tenets of radical behaviorism, it does mean that the experimental study of such supposed events is relatively difficult and risky and that we must question very carefully the nature of the data and our interpretations.

[2]There are many other implications of this definition of behavior that are not narrowly relevant to this particular argument, although they are quite important in other contexts. A full discussion may be found in Johnston and Pennypacker (1980).

It may be important to remind ourselves here that although we may debate the details of a definition of behavior, the process itself is a real, natural, biological phenomenon whose existence and features will be no more affected by our convictions than lead was turned into gold by alchemists. To the extent that our conception of behavior and the ways in which we go about studying it are not concordant with its actual features, our experimental data and subsequent conclusions will suffer from insufficient reliability and inadequate generality.

PURE BEHAVIORAL RESEARCH METHODS

Introduction

Experiments embodying methodological practices that preserve the fundamental qualities of this subject matter in undisturbed and uncontaminated form constitute *pure behavioral research.* What is pure is the representation of the complete array of fundamental qualities of behavior in the experimental data. Pure behavioral research is created by measurement, design, and inferential procedures that respect these qualities by doing nothing to abridge, dilute, or distort their manifestation in the data. Although this hardly guarantees correct inferences, it at least affords them a proper basis in fact.

The standards for pure behavioral research are as uncompromising as the behavioral nature that dictates them. As with the phenomenon itself, we have no say in their specifications. Their violation may not doom an experiment to utter worthlessness, but it must suffer in direct proportion to the trespass. Of course, the limitations exist whether or not they are recognized, and therein lies nature's contingency for the scientist. What, then, are these requirements?

Unit of Analysis

Although important strategically, the formal definition of behavior only describes the general phenomenon of interest. The experimenter must select and define a particular piece of behavior for study, instances of which can then be repeatedly and accurately measured. In other words, out of this continuous stream of behaviors the experimenter must define the limits of a single class of behavioral instances that are homogeneous along certain dimensions. Because each unique instance of behavior is a relation between some part of the organism and some part of its environment, it should not be surprising that a class of responses must be defined in terms of the classes of surrounding environmental events (stimuli) to which its members are functionally related. Defining a response class with reference to antecedent and consequent environmental stimulus classes insures a class of responses that are homogeneous in the functional relations that each has with its controlling influences in the environment. This functional homogeneity avoids using topographical similarity or idiosyncratic verbal history as a basis for defining a class that would then include responses having different sources of environmental influences and that might therefore be differently affected by the independent variable. Functional response class definitions thereby facilitate realizing experimental inferences about treatment effects that can be reproduced by others and that may hold for additional response classes as well.

Dimensional Quantities and Units of Measurement

Another aspect of experimental method that is central to preserving the characteristics of behavior as a subject matter concerns the dimensions of responding that are quantified through observation and the ways in which the amounts of those dimensions are described. The fundamental properties of behavior dictate a number of those dimensional quantities. Duration, latency, and frequency are probably most commonly used, although there are many others, including those characteristic of a body in motion (velocity, acceleration, etc.). Selecting for measurement dimensions of responding that are real, quantifiable, and likely to show variability that is of experimental interest is required if the data are to reflect orderly and useful relations between responding and experimental conditions.

The proper use of dimensional quantities depends on the units of measurement that are used to describe the amount of the dimension being measured. These units must be absolute or unvarying in their meaning and that meaning must be standard for all users. Temporal dimensions are readily quantified with the units of time (seconds, minutes, etc.) whose meanings have long been absolute and standard. In the case of frequency, the compound unit, cycles/unit time, reflects the reference that the compound dimension of frequency makes to two different properties of behavior. The importance of absolute and standard units of measurement stems from the encouragement they lend to measuring real qualities of behavior, the facilitation of measurement accuracy that they provide, and the resulting clarity that is attached to the data from observation through design, analysis, and interpretation. The natural sciences have long enjoyed these benefits.

Observing and Recording

The observational practices that are necessary to preserve the characteristics of behavior are probably more obvious than dimensional issues. Certainly, observation must be of the defined responding of a single subject. If multiple subjects are used, each must be observed independently and their data maintained separately in recording and analytical processes. Because behavior is the interaction between the individual and the environment, attempting to analyze the influence of some independent variable on that interaction would be fatally complicated by mixing that result with the different effects from other subjects.

The dynamic and continuous nature of behavior must be acknowledged by scheduling periods of observation that are as long as possible and that occur as frequently as possible. Furthermore, it is even more important that the target response class be measured continuously while observational sessions are in progress, not only because this is required by the nature of the subject matter, but because discontinuous transduction of facts into data assures some degree of inaccuracy. Of course, these decisions depend on a great many factors that are sometimes difficult or impossible to turn to the service of experimentation. Nevertheless, the reasons for the importance of these tactics will remain influences in the data, whether or not they are accommodated.

Finally, the quality of the data yielded by the measurement process must be regularly assessed. The standard here is not validity or interobserver agreement, but accuracy, and the researcher's task is not to evaluate it passively but to guarantee it. Pure behavioral research requires that the data approximate the true state of nature, a condition that can be determined and certified only by examining the correspondence between obtained and true values and adjusting the transducer as necessary. This process is called calibration, and it is required whether the transducer is machine or human.

Experimental Design

Although there are many details that must be carefully considered in arranging an experimental design, there are a few elements that are mandatory if the characteristics of behavior as a subject matter are to be preserved. One of these characteristics—the dynamic nature of organism–environment interactions through time—dictates that measurement must be scheduled to occur repeatedly over some period of time under each different set of experimental conditions. The purpose of these repeated observations of responding is to allow the complete and stable effects of each condition on the measured dimensions of the target response class to be clearly seen. This is called the *steady state* strategy and it has a number of invaluable benefits, but clarifying the nature of responding under each condition is certainly the most important because these data will be the foundation on which experimental inferences are constructed.

However, a prerequisite to this benefit is that the data accumulated through repeated observations under each condition separately represent the responding of individual subjects. Any attempt to address prematurely the issue of intersubject generality by creating some amalgam of the behavior of different subjects under the same conditions only insures that the purity of the subject matter will be destroyed by mixing treatment-induced variability with intersubject variability, an extraneous artifact that has nothing to do with the description of and cannot ever be used to explain the behavior of a single organism.

Quantification and Display

The data that guide experimental inferences have usually been subjected to various quantifying operations and displayed in accordance with different graphic formats, and these manipulations can substantially influence the reliability and generality of interpretations. In order for this influence to be favorable, any treatments of the data must scrupulously conform to strategies dictated by the nature of the phenomenon. That is, the data representing the behavior of a single subject must not be tainted with that from other subjects, and their temporal continuity must be respected. Although these strategies leave a useful variety of quantification and display options, they foreclose many popular traditions.

Experimental Inference

Experimental inference refers to the translation the scientist makes from the language of nature to the language of the culture. Nature speaks through variations in behavior that are correlated with variations in experimental procedures. As interpreters, our scientific verbal behavior functions to direct others not having these experiences to act successfully. The reliability and generality of our inferences depends on their being properly tempered by the details of experimental method and the characteristics of variation in the subject's behavior as represented by the data. However, if the data do not properly represent the phenomenon that is the focus of our inferences, the reliability and the generality of those inferences must unavoidably suffer. In turn, the progress of the science will suffer.

Such progress can come only in the form of veridical descriptions of the relations between behavior and those variables that influence it, these relations being repeatedly verifiable (reliable) and having some meaning or effectiveness beyond the circumstances of their origin (generality). These characteristics will be attained only if our interpretive verbal behavior is adequately controlled by the details of both experimental procedure as well as the resulting data. This challenge can be met only if the foregoing strategies have been followed so that the basic characteristics of behavior have survived the vicissitudes of experimentation intact and untainted.

Uses and Limitations

It should be clear that pure behavioral research methods are required whenever it is necessary to make inferences about behavior in its phenomenal sense. In other words, if the overall research goal is to identify behavioral facts that will eventually accumulate into well understood behavioral laws of broad generality, then experimental inferences must be based on data that fully represent the qualities of the phenomenon and nothing else.

Another way of saying this is that these methods are required whenever the researcher's immediate inferences are to the level of the individual rather than the population; however, the phrase "the level of the individual" may need some definition. An obvious referent is to the individual subject; these methods are mandatory if there is to be discussion about the effects of experimental procedures on each separate subject. This interpretive preference does not mean that the researcher has no interest in the population of individuals from which the subject is drawn; indeed, one of the subject's functions may be to represent that population. But if the researcher's goal is to learn something about the subject's behavior whose generality to other individuals in the population can then be experimentally pursued, then pure behavioral research methods are obligatory. In other words, the researcher's desire to identify behavioral relations that hold for certain populations does not mean that the immediate experimental inferences should be to the population level. In fact, generality across individuals cannot be established or even reasonably guessed at on the basis of the data from a few or even a large number of subjects in a single study. This and the other dimensions of generality can be established only through many experiments that identify and explain the variables that influence the relation of interest.

In spite of this argument, some might still be tempted to insist that they do not want to discuss the effects of the independent variable on each subject, that they want to make probabilistic speculations about the effects that would be detected in the population *if each individual were actually tested*. This last phrase gives away the true interest, however; it is intended that the results will hold for individuals. Indeed, such population inferences are usually in the context of a research program designed to learn about behavioral laws that will apply to individuals.

Still another way to assess the need for using pure behavioral research methods is to ask if there is a desire to understand why different subjects reacted differently to the same treatment procedure. The honest answer is usually affirmative, and the requisite methods are those just described.

Now that we have established the fundamental use of pure behavioral research methods, it may be illuminating to consider the kinds of studies that require this function. Certainly that which is traditionally described as basic behavioral research qualifies. Here the interest is in discovering and explaining fundamental behavior–environment relations at the level of the individual that may eventually prove to be broadly general. However, there is nothing about this strategy that specifies nonhuman species, laboratory settings, and conditioning processes. This style of basic research can also use human subjects behaving in controlled nonlaboratory settings and can focus on the effects of variables whose mechanism does not depend on conditioning processes.

When the research goal is to develop a reliably effective technological procedure, pure behavioral research methods are usually no less appropriate. Even though this kind of research may seem quite distinct from basic research because of species and setting differences, from an inferential point of view these are superficial and irrelevant variations. To understand this argument, it is important to distinguish between technological research and technological application. The latter may require sound behavioral measurement, but formal cause–effect inferences are inappropriate (no matter how tempting) in the absence of the complete experimental regalia. And if the technology being applied has been properly (experimentally) developed, further experimentation in the difficult context of routine practice will infrequently be necessary.

Such procedures will come only from technological research that includes developing, analyzing, and evaluating practical procedures that can then be used to control behavior. Furthermore, this research will only attain the level of effectiveness and reliability that is common in other natural-science-based technologies if it uses pure behavioral research methods in most of its experiments. This standard is required not because technological procedures must be based on and understood in terms of the basic laws of behavior that they embody (which is true), but because adequate effectiveness and reliability can only be attained by establishing the exact behavioral (individual) effects of procedural variables. The development of a procedure is not completed until it is understood why it works and what the variables are that influence its effectiveness, and these research goals are unambiguously and thoroughly behavioral in nature, requiring experimental methods that respect the integrity of that subject matter.

The possible exception to this requirement concerns that portion of technological research that evaluates a procedure's effectiveness and reliability under realistic field conditions. In some of these studies it may be sufficient to merely describe the resulting behavioral effects, given that their relation to the procedures has long since been experimentally established. In fact, some of the effects of interest may be only indirectly behavioral, such as logistical and economic results. Although certain features of pure behavioral research are always advisable (standard and absolute units of measurement, for instance), other elements may here be unnecessary or even inappropriate, especially if any inferences are to the level of the population rather than the individual.

QUASI-BEHAVIORAL RESEARCH METHODS

Introduction

Experiments whose data originated with observations of behavior but whose methods prevent the data from representing its fundamental qualities fully and without distortion or contamination may be termed *quasi-behavioral research*. The prefix denotes the potential problem: such research seems to be behavioral although it is not by the standards of the phenomenon itself. Even though the data in quasi-behavioral research may indeed be based on behavior, at least one or, more commonly, many features of its method have in some way limited the representation in the data of the fundamental qualities of behavior that must be present if the research is to serve successfully as a basis for inferences about behavior. The problem is not that the methodological practices that create quasi-behavioral research are inherently improper; they can be quite appropriate in the service of many kinds of experimental questions. The problem lies in the risk of deception, of assuming that procedures and data allow inferences about behavior when they do not. Understanding those methodological practices that make research quasi-behavioral will diminish this risk.

Unit of Analysis

Beginning an experiment with a good understanding of behavior's properties is not sufficient to guarantee an adequate basis for eventual inferences about behavior. Each individual's behavior is made up of a myriad of different and continuously changing classes of responses, each class being determined by the surrounding environmental events that simultaneously define its existence. Not acknowledging these natural influences in defining the unit of analysis means that the designated class will actually be made up of multiple classes, each having differing environmental determinants and, possibly, differing susceptibility to the independent variable in the study. Thus, the changes observed in the designated class will be some mixture of the treatment variable's effects on the various natural or functional classes. This will not be detectable in any obvious way in the data (although they will probably be more variable than would otherwise be the case), but inferences drawn about the relation between the independent variable and the designated response class will have poorer reliability and generality than a properly defined response class would have afforded. A powerful treatment variable may minimize the damage, but this is hardly an auspicious way to begin an experiment.

There are a great many ways to avoid proper functional-response class definitions. One of the most common is to define responses into a class on the basis of their topography or form in three-dimensional space. Sometimes topographical features are not substantially divergent from functional considerations, but often such designated classes are aggregates of functional classes whose responses have very different environmental determinants. The popularity of this kind of criteria may be because form is easier to see and describe than function and (perhaps as a result) because common descriptors tend to be based on form. We often decide how to isolate some part of a subject's behavior on the basis of our verbal history. This history is manifest in coding systems which parcel pieces of behavior into large multiclass categories. One such system breaks all human behavior into 29 classes, but the most absurd version of this practice has only two categories: positive or appropriate behavior and negative or inappropriate behavior. Sometimes interest in the popular artifact called "group behavior" is expressed early in the experimental process by defining the response class in such a way that the behavior of different individuals must be collectively observed in order to meet definitional requirements.

All of these and the many other ways of defining responses into classes for the purpose of measurement that ignore the natural classes defined by environmental relations must pay some penalty, whether large or small, in the reliability and generality of any behavioral inferences. This is because the functional response class is the unit of analysis, the level at which individual behavioral effects occur and at which order is most clearly seen. Definitional procedures that violate this fact make the data and thus the research quasi-behavioral.

Dimensional Quantities and Units of Measurement

Another means of constraining the basis on which inferences about behavior are made concerns the dimensions of behavior that are observed and the ways in which those dimensions are quantified. Often there is no behavioral dimension that is clearly referred to by the measurement process. The ubiquitous questionnaire in psychological research is plagued with this problem. Even when there is a clear behavioral dimension, two like dimensional quantities are frequently put in ratio in order to form a relative quantity that may be expressed as a percentage. One difficulty with this practice is that the dimensional referents cancel with division. Another is that variation in the percentages across sessions may be the result of changes in the numerator, the denominator, or both, but the quotients hide the exact nature of behavioral variability.

The justification of inferences about behavior is further weakened when units are used whose definitions are vaganotic—based on variation in a set of underlying observations of behavior (see Chap. 4 of Johnston & Pennypacker, 1980). Thus, as in the case of Fechner's JND, the meaning of the unit varies from application to application both within and across experiments. Most standardized tests involve such variable units, although the units (like the IQ point) are not usually given a formal name. Often the underlying variability is only assumed and does not actually enter into the calculation of scale values or unit definition; rating scales typify this practice. Whatever the details, not quantifying the amount of the observed dimension of behavior with units of measurement whose meaning is absolute and standard insures that the representation of behavioral qualities in the data is not what it seems.

Observing and Recording

The most obvious threat to a sound basis for inferences about behavior that emerges from observing and recording practices involves mixing in some fashion the observations of the responding of different subjects. This may occur through actually observing a number of different subjects simultaneously and treating the data as if they were from a single subject, or the collating may occur at the recording stage when separate observations of different subjects are transcribed into some aggregate form, such as a mean or a median. The effect in either case is the same: The orderly relations that might exist in the individual data are hidden when contaminated with intersubject variability, and the experimenter and anyone else is prevented from seeing behavioral effects in pure form. Basing primary experimental inferences on grouped data from different subjects automatically defines the research as quasi-behavioral.

Another barrier to sound behavioral inference may come from inadequacies in the amount and distribution of periods of observation. If observational periods are very brief, occur intermittently or infrequently, or are few in number under each condition, or if observation is not continuous during each session, the data base for eventual interpretation will be insufficient, regardless of the propriety of other methodological decisions. These are routine sampling issues, but when the subject matter is behavior with its dynamic and continuous character, they take on primary significance. Without a complete representation of the ebb and flow of responding as the experiment proceeds through one phase to another, the risk that inferences will not be congruent with what really happened becomes unacceptably high.

Experimental Design

One of the reasons for the repeated observations already discussed has as much to do with the determinants of the inferential behavior of the experimenter as it does with the nature of behavior as a subject matter. The steady state strategy referred to earlier draws its justification in part from the effort to study individual subjects intensively over time. This necessitates making experimental comparisons using the data from two different conditions to which a single subject was sequentially exposed, rather than using the data from two different subjects, each exposed to only one of the conditions. In order to accomplish this within-subject comparison, it is important to be certain that the data taken as representative of the effects of each of the two conditions are fully characteristic of the subject's responding under each condition. If for whatever reason the data do not fully represent the actual relations between experimental variables and behavior, then inferences regarding those effects cannot be complete and accurate.

Certainly, the most common design practice that successfully misrepresents and contaminates the fundamental qualities of behavior is making inferences about the effects of an independent variable on behavior on the basis of data that represent the aggregate of its separate effects on the behavior of each of a number of different subjects, with any one subject having been exposed to only one of the two conditions being compared. This example of groups-comparison-design inferences is useful because it highlights the fatal flaw that makes it a quasi-behavioral research practice—the use of grouped data across subjects but within conditions or, conversely, the absence of inference based on the data of individual subjects obtained under repeated exposure to both conditions.

Quantification and Display

One of the unfortunate side effects of groups-comparison designs is their inextricable relation to inferential statistics, whose rules completely determine quantification and display practices. The consequences of inferential statistics for experimental method are sufficiently substantial and pervasive that they will be treated in a separate section. However, it should be clear that they require that the data from many different subjects be thoroughly homogenized and processed in a way that greatly limits access to pure behavioral data at the individual level, if they even exist. The rules for quantifying operations are extensive and rigid, and graphic displays are often preempted, in spite of their ability to highlight detailed relations between two variables. Because of their dominant influence on inferential behavior, quantifying and display practices alone can make research quasi-behavioral, even if all of the preceding elements of method supply pure behavioral data.

Experimental Inference

As suggested by its definition, quasi-behavioral research is created by any methodological practices that result in experimental inferences that are not under the control of all of the fundamental qualities of the phenomenon of behavior. Aside from their other methodological consequences, the interpretive process required by all inferential statistical models guarantees this final limitation, and the following section will detail the reasons for this and the many other effects of statistical practices on the subject matter.

In summary, then, quasi-behavioral research methods can be said to create a qualitatively different subject matter from that of pure behavioral research. It is composed of both pure behavioral qualities and artifactual qualities created by elements of research method, the exact proportions of each varying from one study to another depending on particular methodological practices. However, the scientist's mission is not to create subject matters but to understand natural phenomena. In order to accomplish this mission, experimental methods must do no more and no less than represent the natural phenomenon fully and without distortion or contamination. They must not create any discrepancies between the raw phenomenon and the experimental subject matter. When this occurs, the research may appear to be about something that it not quite is, and inferences about the phenomenon innocently based on a subject matter that is slightly or substantially different must suffer slightly or substantially weakened reliability and generality, whether or not we like it or even know it.

TRADITIONS AND PRACTICES OF INFERENTIAL STATISTICS

History of Application in Psychology

Psychology and the social sciences have a kind of familial relationship with statistics; to a great extent they grew up together, something like cousins. Their lineage actually goes back to biblical times when the first efforts at social enumeration were made, and by the 17th and 18th centuries formal censuses were conducted with the support of simple descriptive statistics. The utility of this technology to the business and financial world was obvious, and the need for economic quantification spurred statistical applications. The need to make predictions based on economic and other data was served by developments in the mathematics of probability, and by the turn of the 19th century it was possible to estimate with serviceable accuracy the likelihood of occurrence of particular instances.

It is not clear just when the notion emerged of using mathematical statistics and the new developments in probability theory to assist in making intergroup experimental comparisons. Augustus DeMorgan (1806–1871) may be able to lay claim to that accomplishment, but it was clearly Adolphe Quetelet (1796–1874) who became the dominant figure in this history. This Belgian statistician and astronomer is widely regarded as the founder of the social sciences (Woolf, 1963). His wide-ranging intellect saw the possibility of applying the calculus of probability to detailed demographic data cataloging all aspects of human affairs so as to estimate the ideals of human qualities. Like others of his time, he viewed the normal law of error as evidence of some supraordinate regularity, and his concept of the average man as a natural ideal was a major influence on 19th century concepts of behavior. It was Quetelet who suggested and popularized the practice of drawing inferences about dynamic individual phenomena on the basis of statistical comparisons between large groups of individuals (Walker, 1929).

Francis Galton (1822–1911) greatly assisted this practice by applying it to the task of mental measurement and the field of education. His development of the mathematical expression of correlation was an important advance that attracted the attention of Karl Pearson (1857–1936). Pearson not only developed fully the mathematics of correlation but also the idea of moments of any distribution, the term *standard deviation*, and the general mathematics of sampling distributions.

However, the modern concepts of experimental design were constructed by Ronald Fisher and his students. Like Pearson, he was interested in biological issues, and he turned his attention to the new field of agricultural research. Out of this work came the concept of experimental design in the sense of creating experimental conditions that allow statistical reasoning from large sets of data collected so as to permit comparisons between groups.

Meanwhile, the emerging disciplines of the social sciences needed an experimental method, and the new inferential statistical practices and reasoning were not only historically familiar, they brought with them a needed aura of scientific respectability. The ensuing decades have seen the practice of designing experiments in accordance with the requirements of tests of statistical significance ossify into the methodological backbone of the social sciences. This tradition has grown so secure that any other experimental procedures are called quasi-experimental (Campbell & Stanley, 1966).

Consequences for the Study of Behavior

Experimental Question. The effects of this tradition never were narrowly limited to experimental interpretation, and over the years they have pervaded all aspects of scientific method. Some of these methodological consequences are rigidly dictated by the mathematical model, but in turn they often strongly encourage still other practices until the invasion is complete.

These effects begin at the beginning with the experimental question. Its form is thoroughly subservient to the logic of inferential statistics, which is required by the underlying mathematical procedures. The technique requires calculating the probability of obtaining the observed difference between two sample group means given the assumption that there is no difference in the populations. Aside from the sham of the null hypothesis (which is a bit of logical sleight-of-hand necessary to give the reasoning the appearance of deductive validity), the real experimental question only asks, Is there a difference (between the measures of central tendency for the different groups being compared)?

This is a frustratingly crude question. It turns science into an inefficient game of 20 questions, in which questions must be phrased so that they can be answered only by yes or no. The chafing of this restriction is easily seen in discussion sections, where the experimenters routinely exceed their inferential limits by waxing poetic about the *nature* of the difference—the true theme of interest.

However, the effects of inferential statistical traditions on question asking are even more serious than the formalities of interrogatory form. They go to the very depths of our wonderings about behavior. They encourage a curiosity about differences, about whether "this" makes a difference or whether "this" is different from "that." Of course, it is not that observed differences are uninformative, but they are inevitably easy to find. Their availability may be experimentally gratifying, but their accumulation in the literature may improperly comfort us about our progress. For science advances by purusing similarities, and similarities are discovered by asking about the detailed nature of the relations between independent and dependent variables.

Measurement. The impact of inferential statistics on measurement is relatively indirect, though still powerful. For example, there is nothing about inferential statistics that specifies the means by which response classes are defined. However, the mathematical requirement for adequate sample size has the indirect effect of encouraging response class definitional practices that are compatible with a large number of subjects. This is especially true when their performances are measured simultaneously, but even when they are observed one at a time, definitional niceties are de-emphasized by observational logistics. As a result, the strenuous rigors of functional definitional strategies tend to be avoided in favor of simplicity, which usually means broad categorical labeling guided by cultural linguistic history and its topographical foundation.

Observational procedures become similarly subservient to large-N logistics. The perceived need to sample from a large number of individuals in a population indirectly though strongly encourages observational procedures that sample only a small portion of the occurrences in the response class's population. In other words, the tendency is to observe the behavior of each subject relatively few times, usually only once. The obvious consequence is data that depict an incomplete and misrepresentative picture of the true effects of experimental conditions. The dynamic character of behavior is lost to a static illusion that is comforting only if variability is viewed as an inconvenience useful for no more than algebraic manipulation in the service of the statistical model.

Experimental Design. This style of observational sampling creates part of experimental design as well. In its narrowest sense, experimental design refers to the arrangement of the independent variable (and, by implication, the scheduling of dependent variable measurement) throughout the entire course of the experiment. When large-N logistics encourage relatively few measurements, there is further encouragement for relatively limited exposure of each subject to experimental conditions. Of course, the number and duration of exposures to the independent variable varies greatly depending on its nature, but the contrast to repeated-measures designs with their repeated contacts with the treatment condition is easily drawn. Furthermore, whereas to the statistician the difference is simply a matter of the number of contacts, to the behaviorist one exposure each with many subjects is very different from many exposures with one subject. Only the later suits the nature of the phenomenon.

A more subtle effect of statistical traditions on experimental design is to make it a static and rigidly rulebound set of practices whose requirements in any one application are set down by an underlying mathematical model that has nothing to do with the nature of the phenomenon and the needs of the independent variable. The experiment then becomes a somewhat secondary process of filling cells with empirically derived numbers, and once begun, it must be completed regardless of how clearly the numbers suggest a better design or the futility of the effort, because the results cannot be "clearly" known until the statistic is fully computed. This static perspective thus forces the investigator to guess the results in advance in order to predict all of their experimental needs. In effect, it attempts to coerce nature to adapt to the design rather than the other way around.

Interpretation. Not surprisingly, the consequences of inferential statistics for experimental interpretation are direct, clear, and encompassing. They begin with detailed rules for quantifying the results of observation, and the most unfortunate one is the common requirement for aggregating data across subjects into various representations of the groups. However, the quantitative digestion of the data by statistical formulas continues by specifying the entire quantitative basis for experimental comparisons, regardless of the nature of the data. Along the way, intersubject variability and treatment-induced variability are thoroughly homogenized, and any chance of describing pure behavioral effects is completely lost.

Although they are not specifically precluded, any meaningful graphic traditions have been preempted by these quantitative traditions. In fact, descriptions of statistical outcomes do not tend to be regularly accompanied by graphic displays that relate even group "responding" to treatment conditions over time, and the displays that are used are usually highly summarized with few data points.

The results of all of this quantification is a rigid inferential process that is narrowly aimed at a probability-bound decision about the existence of a difference between groups. It is not a searching and inquisitive process, looking anywhere in the data where nature may have left a message. It is more like a blindered old workhorse following the same route each time.

The destination is equally predictable. As already discussed, the "official" inferential statement allows only acceptance or rejection of the null hypothesis. In the latter case, this then allows arguments about why an alternative hypothesis (the real one) might be responsible for the obtained difference. However, because data analysis procedures have usually focused solely on the mere existence of a difference, there is little if any formal basis for discussing the degree of the difference or its nature. This must make one wonder at the source of control over the inevitable inferential discussions that exceed these bounds.

Unfortunately, the legitimacy of their statements further depends on the correctness of a number of assumptions. This requirement is unfortunate because the assumptions are rarely viable on their face in the case of a behavioral subject matter. For example, these assumptions usually derive from the normal law of error, which asserts that as a result of random determination errors will be distributed evenly around a central value and tend to cancel. Furthermore, it is also often required that multiple distributions of such errors be roughly equivalent so that they can be pooled.

The problem is that these assumptions are rarely fit by behavioral data. The effects of uncontrolled variables on behavior cannot be assumed to resemble independent, random occurrences because behavior is a continuous process. The effects of any variable (extraneous or independent) are most likely to exhibit serial dependence. It is simply the nature of the phenomenon that every moment of our experience may influence subsequent actions. These assumptions are easily made and verified if ears of corn are the subject matter, but when it is behavior, they are only easily made.

Many of these and other shortcomings of inferential statistics are no longer novel, and a battery of further quantitative operations are often called on for resuscitation of the data. Such efforts suggest notions of statistical control that diverge sharply from the contrary tradition of experimental control. Experimental control refers to actual manipulation of real events in order to modulate their influence on the dependent variable. However, quantitative operations manipulate only numbers and have no impact on what they actually represent. In other words, statistics control no more than the verbal behavior of the investigator.

Generality. The great paradox of inferential statistics is that their use kills almost all hope of achieving one of their primary goals. Probably the most frequently articulated need motivating their use is to establish the generality of the results across subjects. To understand why this is ultimately impossible with these methods, it is important to understand that cross-subject generality (there are other flavors) first depends on the existence of a reliable behavioral relation or effect whose generality can then be queried. Knowledge about how well that effect holds for different members of some population comes from understanding how certain variables influence it. This understanding can be obtained only through experimental analysis of the relation and its controlling variables, and the experimental methods must accommodate their behavioral nature.

The statistical tradition misunderstands the task by attempting to make it an inferential process instead. Whereas inferences from the sample to the population are indeed proper statistically, they are not meaningful behaviorally because of the nature of the phenomenon. The grouped data supporting inferences to the population cannot properly describe the heterogeneity of actual individual effects. In other words, the group "effect" whose generality is being argued is not a behavioral phenomenon but a mathematical artifact. In fact, there are usually many different behavioral effects among the sampled subjects, and such variety suggests a fair amount of proper experimental spade work before enough will be known to produce a reliable (individual) effect whose generality can then be pursued. Of course, that accomplishment will inevitably identify a number of controlling variables that influence cross-subject generality.

Summary. Some have countered these limitations of inferential statistics by proposing nonparametric alternatives (e.g., Kazdin, 1976; Levin, Masascuilo, & Hubert, 1978). Although the substitution may be well-intentioned, it should be clear that nonparametric statistics suffer a sufficient number of the same problems to guarantee their quasi-behavioral status. They may avoid the plague of intersubject variability and assumptions about the nature of the hypothesized parent population, but they require or encourage many practices that compromise pure behavioral qualities. For example, their inferential focus on a single significance statement instead of detailed descriptions of responding under repeated exposures to experimental phases that are themselves repeated still discourages proper attention to measurement practices and the steady state strategy. Furthermore, even though they avoid intersubject variability, their quantification rules can easily obscure pure behavioral effects as successfully as their large-N relatives.

For that matter, descriptive statistical procedures must be applied with care lest they too befoul behavioral data. However, when descriptive quantitative methods are properly used to supplement graphic displays by adding a degree of descriptive precision about aspects of pure behavioral relations, they can be quite valuable. In fact, we have introduced a descriptive statistic (Kappa) designed to serve as a measure of variability in the responding of a single subject (Johnston & Pennypacker, 1980).

In other words, the concerns expressed here about various statistical traditions and practices should not be misconstrued as a condemnation of the quantitative operations themselves. Statistics, inferential and descriptive, are perfectly valid and very valuable methods for particular tasks, but methods and tasks must be properly matched. Given their tradition and sophistication, it is indeed unfortunate that inferential statistics and the study of behavior are such a poor match.

The social scientist's attempts to force the fit by adapting the subject matter to the method has furthered naive, culturally based conceptions of behavior instead of loosening these bonds. Inferential statistical traditions have encouraged the view that behavior is an intrinsically variable and autonomously inspired phenomenon that is complex beyond the capabilities of science. It has done this not only by obfuscating the orderliness of behavioral relations but by requiring, generating, and using behavioral variability instead of explaining it. Variability is thus viewed as inevitable and beyond reasonable, if not ultimate, explanation. Not surprisingly, this perspective provides limited experimental motivation to control variables and explain their influence, and the relative paucity of such evidence is only taken to affirm the consequence. It is a tragic circle.

LIMITATIONS AND USES OF QUASI-BEHAVIORAL RESEARCH METHODS

Where does this assessment of quasi-behavioral research methods leave us? It should be clear that they are poorly suited to the task of learning things about behavior. When our experimental questions require inferences about behavior (as a phenomenon, not in the general and vague cultural sense), we must use methods that generate data that retain all of the qualities of behavior intact and undiluted so that our inferences will be successfully reliable and general. Quasi-behavioral research methods fail to meet this requirement and, therefore, should not be used to support inferences about behavior or to the individual. It has already been pointed out that this is the type of inference required by all basic research and most technological research, and quasi-behavioral research methods are thus inappropriate in these areas of investigation.

Lest this seem too extreme an indictment, it should be acknowledged that it is not that quasi-behavioral research methods can tell us nothing at all about behavior. If a treatment effect is unusually powerful, it may survive such methodological mishandling with useful reliability and generality. The ancients learned much about the world without the niceties of scientific method, but they were often wrong, and what little they did learn pales into insignificance compared to the fruits of even a few years of modern science. At the most generous, quasi-behavioral research methods are a highly inefficient way to go about discovering the laws of behavioral nature, and the costs to our field and our culture are certainly more than we can afford.

These constraints may be difficult to accept in those cases where we can plainly see that quasi-behavioral research data originated from the subject's behavior. It looks like the data represent behavior—in the vague lay sense of behavior, they do—but we do not see or appreciate the gravity of their shortcomings. The problem lies in the strength of our culturally based linguistic practices about behavior and the relative weakness of our professional vocabulary, which should be under the control of the experimental facts about the phenomenon and their methodological implications. It may help to remember that the cost comes when we succumb to improper inferential temptations that are then published and become literature. Then, their value to others who wish to act successfully based on our findings is limited (if not worthless or possibly harmful), and they discover that they cannot do so. This is the real meaning of poor reliability and inadequate generality. When entire areas of behavioral literature are constituted predominantly of quasi-behavioral research, we are likely to find little progress in our understanding of behavior in such areas and meager technological benefits to society.

If analytical behavioral research (experimental or applied) is an improper use for quasi-behavioral research methods, then are there any experimental functions that they can successfully serve? The answer is certainly affirmative and does not conflict with all of the foregoing criticisms. The propriety of these procedures is not at issue in the abstract; they can only be evaluated in particular applications. Generically speaking, we can say that the appropriate behavioral applications are those in which the experimental question does not require inferences about behavior, even though the data may be behavioral. There are many occasions for such questions, although they collectively constitute a relatively small portion of our field's technological research efforts.

Some of these questions may indeed require a behavioral data base but only to support inferences to the population level. Much evaluation research is of this sort. When the problem clearly calls for comparing the aggregate performances of groups of individuals and drawing conclusions about the populations that the sampled individuals represent, then inferential statistical procedures are appropriate. For example, when the experimental question demands a comparison between the behavioral effects of two different procedures, a groups-comparison design accompanied by statistical analysis is proper.

However, this type of question is far less often appropriate than its prevalence in the literature might suggest. It should only follow a program of research in which each of the two procedures has been experimentally developed, analyzed, and refined so that exactly how and why each works is fully understood. Furthermore, the two procedures must be exactly equivalent in their goals and functions, as well as in the characteristics of their target populations. In other words, they must be fully and meaningfully comparable, and it takes a fairly extensive program of research to reach this point. Absent this comparability, such comparisons serve political rather than technological interests.

Other questions may require that experimental comparisons be within-group rather than between groups. Here inferential statistics might be inappropriate, but collating data across individuals would be necessary to describe and draw conclusions about collective effects. Such studies are only needed when there is no interest or value in understanding the nature and mechanism of behavioral effects for the individual. Many technological efforts designed to manage the behavior of large numbers of people with procedures that are not designed, selected, or managed for individuals may fall into this category. For instance, efforts to control the use of natural resources or to manage behavior in public settings often takes this form (e.g., Geller, Winett, and Everett, 1982). In these instances, the goal is to influence the behavior of individuals but only as members of a large population. However, the fact that the procedure's effects occur for each individual means that these technologies must first be developed with research conducted at the individual level. Nevertheless, the research program will eventually require group data, though the comparisons may be within rather than between groups.

Still other questions may examine logistical aspects of technological procedures. Here, behavioral data may be used to answer financial, personnel, and administrative questions in which inferences need not be made about the individual effects of behavior change procedures. These types of investigations also come only at the later stages of a technological research program, after the proper development and analysis using pure behavioral research methods. In these kinds of studies, the behavior of the procedure's target individuals is of interest only insofar as it provides aggregate data that can be used for calculating administrative needs or consequences. For example, such studies may use behavioral data from target individuals to determine the amount and distribution of staff time that must be provided. Of course, this answer would only be useful if the form of the procedures being used were already known to be maximally effective.

These examples of different types of questions that properly call for quasi-behavioral research methods should suggest that they cannot be so easily treated as a single method or even a related set of methodological procedures as the previous discussion may have implied. For instance, of two studies calling for grouped data, one may require between-groups comparisons whereas another may necessitate within-group comparisons, thus leading to very different quantitative and inferential procedures.

Furthermore, many of these studies may require pure behavioral measurement procedures, regardless of the nature of their design or interpretation. Indeed, pure behavioral measurement methods are probably rarely inappropriate, even though they may not be required. There are no inferential disadvantages to proper response class definition, standard and absolute units of measurement, and continuous and complete observation, for example. The only constraints that may preclude these procedures are logistical, and even then they may be avoided only if the inferences allow it.

METHODOLOGICAL CONTINGENCIES

In addition to the phenomenon, the nature of the experimental question and the inferences necessary to answer it thus emerge as the criteria for all of these methodological decisions. Properly read, they specify even the most detailed methodological features necessary for attaining experimental goals. Of course, the risk is that their dictates may be improperly interpreted. Investigators may be tempted to presume that their experiments do not require inferences about behavior or to the individual when in fact they do.

The quality of our research method (and thus our research) therefore seems to rest in part on how well we understand the nature of our subject matter, our questions, and our inferential verbal behavior. Somewhat more behaviorally, the critical issue is how well we can identify the natural contingencies between our experimental behavior and our subject's behavior. Those contingencies are the essence of scientific method. They are the means by which we come under control of the laws of nature, not only as individual scientists but as a culture.

Recognizing the behavioral relations that constitute research methods is important because it helps us realize that they are irrevocable. We learn about nature (behavioral or otherwise) by arranging conditions so that our behavior (nonverbal and verbal) is effectively controlled by some aspect of our natural subject matter. If our arrangements are improper, then our resulting behavior will not be effectively controlled by the facts of our subject matter, and other influences (theory, culturally based preconceptions, extraexperimental contingencies, etc.) are likely to be dominant. In other words, there is no short cut, no alternative way of discovering the facts and laws of nature. If the conditions we arrange do not exactly suit our subject matter and the particular facets of it that are of interest, then our subsequent behavior will not be exactly under its control. In other words, although we may have some choice about our experimental methods, we have no choice about their effects.

This assessment should suggest that our intentions and excuses have no bearing on what we learn. Whether or not we view a particular methodological procedure as troublesome, logistically inconvenient, practically impossible, or unnecessary is completely irrelevant. We will learn what our methods allow us to learn and no more. If we use measurement procedures that have been described here as quasi-behavioral, then we will see an incomplete and distorted picture of the dependent variable that will limit the reliability and generality of our (and everybody else's) inferences. This will be the case whether we are aware of the shortcomings of the measurement procedures or even whether they were the best procedures that were possible under the circumstances.

In conclusion, it would seem beneficial to approach our research in a thoroughly behavioral manner. Our own behavior thus becomes fully as much the target of analysis as that of our subjects, and the goal is to insure that our behavior is effectively under the control of our subject's behavior.

REFERENCES

Campbell, D. T., & Stanley, J. C. (1966). *Experimental and quasi-experimental designs for research*. Chicago, IL: Rand McNally.

Geller, E. S., Winett, R. A., & Everett, B. (1982). *Preserving the environment: New strategies for behavior change*. Elmsford, NY: Pergamon Press.

Johnson, J. M., & Pennypacker, H. S. (1980). *Strategies and tactics of human behavioral research*. Hillsdale, NJ: Erlbaum.

Kazdin, A. E. (1976). Statistical analyses for single-case experimental designs. In M. Hersen & D. H. Barlow (Eds.), *Single-case experimental designs: Strategies for studying behavior change* (pp. 265–316). Elmsford, NJ: Pergamon Press.

Levin, J. R., Marascuilo, L. A., & Hubert, L. J. (1978). N = Nonparametric randomization tests. In T. R. Kratochwill (Ed.), *Single subject research: Strategies for evaluating change* (pp. 167–196). New York: Academic Press.

Walker, H. (1929). *Studies in the history of statistical method*. Baltimore, MD: Williams & Wilkins.

Woolf, H. (Ed.). (1961). *Quantification*. New York: Bobbs-Merrill.

4

The Nature and Functions of Experimental Questions

JAMES M. JOHNSTON AND H. S. PENNYPACKER

THE NATURE OF EXPERIMENTAL QUESTIONS

Scientific Behavior

Perhaps the most significant fact about experimental questions is that they do not exist independently of experimenters. Even saying that experimental questions are created by experimenters misses the mark by implying that something is being constructed that, like a house, is therefore separate from its creator.

Experimental questions are verbal behavior, and it makes no more sense to talk about them as created than it does of other operants such as walking, eating, or watching football games. As with other operants, these verbal response classes may exert control over much other behavior in both speaker and listener, especially when they exist in textual form. However, we must not confuse the written question with, for instance, the pot roast created by a chef. The pot roast existed before the chef cooked it; the question had no such status before the experimenter behaved. The experimental question is analogous to the chef's behavior of cooking the roast.

Although this clarification may seem somewhat overdone to some, if not entirely unnecessary, the behavioral nature of experimental questions often seems to get lost in discussions of research method. It is not so much that we do not know what questions are but that we forget to pursue the ramifications of this truth when talking about, teaching about, or actually developing experimental questions. Indeed, at least some of

JAMES M. JOHNSTON • Department of Psychology, Auburn University, Auburn, AL 36849.   H. S. PENNYPACKER • Department of Psychology, University of Florida, Gainesville, FL 32611.

the criticism that we have recently been giving ourselves (e.g., Birnbrauer, 1979; Deitz, 1978; Hake, 1982; Hayes, 1978; Hayes, Rincover, &
Solnick, 1980; Michael, 1980; Pennypacker, 1981; Pierce & Epling, 1980)
seems to be reducible to concerns with the directions of our research
literatures, clearly a consequence of our experimental-question-asking
behavior.

This bit of scientific behavior must therefore be assigned a substantial role in the health of the entire field, a position that the remainder
of this paper will certify. Such importance warrants the most thorough
consideration of this kind of verbal behavior that we can manage, and
that means that it must be thoroughly behavioral. A good place to start
is by describing more fully the behavior of interest.

References to question asking as the behavior of interest are somewhat misleading. They oversimplify by suggesting that it is only the
final utterance that we call an experimental question that is important.
Actually, quite a lot of verbal behavior precedes and occasions the official
statement of the question, and all of it must be the focus of our concern
(even though the phrase *question asking* will remain a convenient summary of the entire process). We describe this preparatory verbal behavior
as reading experimental reports, talking with colleagues and students,
and generally writing and talking about behavior and behavioral research.
Even after we begin to focus on a particular topic or general question,
we continue to engage in such behavior, although the sources of control
over it may grow increasingly narrow.

This verbal behavior will probably be the most difficult of all scientific behaviors for methodologists to study. Not only is there a great
deal of it in any single case, but the sources of control over it seem clear
only at a very general level. Much other scientific behavior is rule governed rather simply by comparison, although the resulting data are a
part of contingencies that are invaluable in guiding the experimental
repertoire. Let us now examine these sources of control, however superficially, in order to consider more fully the complexities of question-
asking behavior.

Sources of Control

Graduate Training. Often overlooked, graduate training is certainly
one of the most powerful and pervasive influences on question-asking
behavior, besides thoroughly permeating subsequent professional experiences. It is in graduate school that we are conceived: Through the
miscegenation of our professors, gestating as fetal behavior analysts, we
are finally thrust out of the ivy-covered womb, wearing only a scanty

dissertation—very much a neonate in a science still too prepubescent to guide authoritatively our early experimental steps.

We come to graduate school knowing relatively little about the field and leave with an extensive professional repertoire. Especially in this science, much of our culturally taught, preprofessional verbal repertoire about behavior is brought under fairly good control of a more limited range of social stimuli, and a specialized scientific language supplants it in a growing range of professional circumstances. This repertoire includes every aspect of how we view behavior, the various research literatures, the different facets of the field, and our role in it.

The experience also creates a variety of subtly powerful professional reinforcers that continue to control our repertoire indefinitely. Even well into post-graduate careers, many of our activities are at least influenced if not largely determined by the reinforcers acquired in our training history. Thus, certain activities are more reinforcing than others (research versus practice, for instance, or field research versus laboratory research). When considering the direction of our research programs, certain topics are clearly more appealing than others, as might be certain species or other subject characteristics.

Of course, our accumulating professional experiences in turn affect our repertoires and reinforcers, but probably never so thoroughly as our original graduate training does. In the present context, then, it influences the areas of literature we read, the ways in which we approach behavior as a subject matter for research, our preferences for subjects and research settings, the research ideas that we pursue, the directions in which we develop them, and the final form of our questions. It is difficult to imagine a more pervasive influence on our question-asking behavior.

Experimental Literature. One of the effects of graduate school is to make the literature of the field a powerful influence over many of our professional behaviors, especially those that lead to stating experimental questions. Of course, any single individual is familiar with only particular aspects of the field's experimental and nonexperimental literature. Even in a relatively small and young discipline such as ours, this is an unavoidable constraint. And yet, although this is a blessed relief to the overachievers among us, it is also unfortunate. The fact that we have been trained in and can keep up with only a few special areas of the field's entire literature often means that our appreciation of the subtleties of certain topics is balanced by our ignorance of much that other areas of literature have to say that might be relevant to our interests. Sometimes this may even be truer than it has to be, as when we do not seek out and read literature that by any standards is potentially relevant to our interests. When we avoid other literature merely because of species and setting differences, it is especially unfortunate. Even literatures that exhibit different conceptual and methodological perspectives have redeeming social value for the creative and thoughtful behavioral researcher who has acquired the full range of question-asking skills.

These skills include reading the studies in a literature critically, rather than unconditicnally accepting the author's directions. This means not just evaluating an experiment's method, but assessing its guiding question. The reader must ask if the experimental question is appropriate to the needs of the area. Appropriateness is not the highest standard, however; a study may be appropriate without being especially valuable. A more stringent criterion is whether the question is really the most important question for that topic, the one whose experiment provides data of major value to the field. If it is not, the process of reaching this conclusion will encourage the reader to decide just what that question is.

It is also important to examine a study's intended function in relation to its outcome. A study's stated purpose is sometimes at variance with its true function. This is likely to be the case when the procedures that constitute the experiment (especially those that define the independent and dependent variables) are not properly suited to the conceptual elements in the question. In more behavioral terms, this danger occurs when interpretative verbal behavior is under the control of the question and other influences and as a result is inadequately controlled by the procedures and the data. Such discoveries can provide the reader with an opportunity to consider whether the discrepancy suggests an experimental direction worth pursuing.

When the literature in question is not especially behavioral in its conceptual and methodological characteristics, the reader's task is somewhat narrower. The question then becomes, Is there a behavioral phenomenon or relation here that can be profitably pursued? If the answer is affirmative, then that literature has served its only important function—encouraging a skilled behavioral researcher to consider experimental questions about the true behavioral process at work underneath misleading description and inappropriate procedures.

Even literatures having nothing at all to do with behavior can be profitably perused by the inquisitive behavioral researcher who is alert to interesting experimental possibilities. The older natural sciences are not only excellent models in many respects for our own development, the directions of their research programs may also suggest innovative and valuable analogies for the study of behavior. For instance, the struggles of geologists to understand and predict seismic activity might lead one to wonder about how major behavioral disruptions, such as inner-city riots, could be studied and predicted with comparable empirical sophistication.

Of course, the biological science literature need not be examined analogously. Some of these specialities may be learning more about the variables influencing behavior than behaviorists are, although their independent variables are usually different from those preferred by behaviorists. These are especially valuable literatures for the skilled question asker.

Finally, familiarity with the field's literature contributes to the researcher's overall perspective about its general directions and needs. This sense of where the field is going and where it needs to go in turn greatly influences the researcher's reactions to particular studies. A newly published experiment does not lead all of its readers in the same direction, and certain of these directions will be more productive than others. The skilled question asker will consider not only the immediate and obvious consequences of a study but its larger context provided by the entire science.

Observing Behavior. Too slavish a reliance on archival literatures as a source of experimental questions carries its risks, however. Questions spawned by published studies naturally tend to pursue the general directions already established in the literature. This is not necessarily bad, of course, but it can lead to excessive attention to an increasingly tangential direction, as the literature's questions gradually shift to being more about the literature than about behavior. There is ample evidence for this tendency in psychology's history, leading Skinner to observe, "There are doubtless many men whose curiosity about nature is less than their curiosity about the accuracy of their guesses." (1938, p. 44).

A related risk from allowing the literature to dominate question asking is especially high in our young field. To the extent that the literature does not fully represent all possible aspects of behavior in all important contexts, it is less likely that new questions will search out and identify these unchartered areas. Almost by definition, the many and vast holes in our fledgling scientific literature are not clearly described or located; indeed we must presume that we are not even aware of the extent of our ignorance. This acknowledgement should therefore make us quite enthusiastic about other sources of control over our question-asking behavior.

It is a matter of balance. Our question asking must be controlled not only by the existing literature, but by our experiences with the subject matter itself. Behavior is a phenomenon that is always present in accessible and relevant forms, even if the researcher is the behaver. The complete behaviorist has acquired skills of observing behavior in very particular ways, and it has become reinforcing to do so. These skills are practiced very frequently during each day. For the behavioral researcher, there is no distinction between professional and personal in the style or temporal distribution of observations about behavior; they are all professional and occurring all of the time. More importantly, the well-trained behaviorist is always wondering. He or she wonders how and why about behavioral phenomena that range fully from exquisitely trivial to embarrassingly cosmic; although the wondering is not always in the form of formal experimental questions, it is at least comfortably close.

Questions with such origins might be suspected of being limited in substance and relevance, but this field is still sufficiently limited in size and scope that almost no otherwise sound experimental questions could fail to qualify for legitimacy. To the contrary, such questions are likely to be especially valuable for a long time to come in directing scientific attention to the entire roster of organism–environment relations. And because these questions are always asked with respect for the established facts, their answers will complement rather than detract from the existing literature. Our everyday but professional observations of behavior in these early years are an invaluable means of locating the key pieces of nature's behavioral jigsaw puzzle, which is still more hole than picture.

Existing Resources. It may seem obvious that the resources available for experimentation exert some influence on the nature of the question, but such influences may be stronger than is usually suspected. We most often think of resources as having a limiting effect on experimental ideas, and this is probably true. If an experimenter has a laboratory facility that is designed for a particular species, the experimenter will naturally try to develop questions that require that species and setting. If one has secure access to a population of subjects with certain characteristics (for instance, age, skills, deficits, gender, etc.), one is likely to design experiments that will take advantage of that population's availability. Of course, the limitations can be described negatively. The lack of certain equipment will probably discourage considering questions that would require it. Constraints in personnel or budget are also common influences on the experimental questions that are entertained.

Existing resources may also have a facilitating effect, however. Acess to a population of potential subjects with certain characteristics may encourage the researcher to search for sound experimental questions that can put them to good advantage. Similarly, particular equipment and other facilities may stimulate consideration of experimental questions that will make use of their capabilities.

The real issue, though, is less whether resources inhibit or facilitate asking experimental questions or how they do so than the nature of this influence on the appropriateness of the question in a larger context. When existing resources do dominate other influences in the development of a question, is the resulting study as valuable to the field's literature as questions with different etiologies? Of course, there is nothing about this source of control over question-asking behavior that guarantees inadequate or inappropriate studies; any single such effort may be quite illuminating or largely irrelevant. But when available resources such as subjects and settings override other considerations, such as the existing literature, perhaps we should examine the broader effects on the field's direction.

For example, the vast majority of behaviorists conducting research either work in field settings or, by virtue of their training and interests, have cultivated access to field settings populated by individuals with certain characteristics (elementary-school ages, mental retardation, etc.). Although the full array of other influences are also present, the features of subjects and settings have an unquestionably major impact on the experimental questions that define the bulk of the field's effort to study human behavior. It may be argued, however, that this creates a serious imbalance in the direction of the field's investigations in favor of technological rather than basic research—that we are asking "how" too often and "why" too infrequently. Whatever the merits of this particular contention, it illustrates the kind of risk that can accompany the influence of existing resources on experimental questions.

Protection from such risks comes from modulating the influence of experimental resources with the influence of the literature. Its guidance comes from the experimenter's skill at not only evaluating published studies but from evaluating the literature's broader strengths and weaknesses, its overall directions and, perhaps especially, its omissions. Experimental questions that are permitted by available resources must also be evaluated in these terms. The questions that can be pursued are not necessarily the ones that most need to be pursued. Conflicts may often be resolved by working to arrange the needed conditions, if only we can resist succumbing to the temptations of convenience. The obvious goal is that each experimental question be as useful as is possible, not only to a particular area of literature but to the discipline as a whole. However, *possible* should automatically imply special efforts to arrange ideal experimental conditions so that resources are not a limiting influence.

Experimental Contingencies. Substantial control over question-asking behavior also comes from an array of experimental contingencies that invariably accompany research. Each question and its resulting experiment serves particular functions in the narrow context of the investigator's research program, and in the somewhat broader context of some area of the field's literature. For instance, one question may lead to the next stage in a sequence of questions forming an evolving research program. Another may analyze the role of one component of a technological procedure. Still another might evaluate the effectiveness of an experimentally developed treatment program.

Although they are not usually thought of in this way, these functions served by questions and their experiments constitute contingencies that influence the researcher's development of experimental questions. As such, it is important to identify and appreciate their impact. The value of these often unnoticed contingencies comes from the fact that they encourage thematic research efforts (see Chap. 20 in Johnston & Pennypacker, 1980). In contrast to experiments that are relatively independent of other studies, experiments conducted in a thematic research style are carefully fitted into an existing mosaic of research literature and are designed to serve specific functions for it. Although experiments that are largely independent of the literature or even any local research may be excellent in every respect and quite useful, experiments designed for a particular role in relation to past research and future possibilities are likely to be even more valuable to the field. Their value comes from the systematically integrated literature that they leave behind. It is a literature with a minimum of holes or gaps and with important questions asked and answered as they arise.

These experimental contingencies thus tend to have very desirable effects on question asking, and our only concern is in how to create them in the first place. Once again, we must look to graduate training for their origins. It is through the formal and informal features of this training that these question-asking strategies are shaped and the literature is established as controlling stimuli. Once again, it would seem difficult to overstate the influence of the graduate school experience on question-asking skills.

Extraexperimental Contingencies. Another set of contingencies may have somewhat different effects. They can be generally described as extraexperimental in nature because they do not directly concern the details of the experiment, its role in the literature, or its possible influence on future research. Instead, these contingencies involve the relations between the nature of the question and the consequences of its answers that include the gains or losses for the experimenter that go well beyond narrowly scientific considerations. These include professional reputation, grants, patents, consulting contracts, books, tenure and promotions, access to a particular population or setting, and so forth.

The contingencies between these events and question-asking behavior can have considerable impact on the details of the question, as well as on the details of its resulting experiment. Unfortunately, the effects of such contingencies are not necessarily in the best interests of the field. They may lead to questions that are more self-serving than subservient to the needs of the literature, and it is not difficult to find such examples in all areas of the behavioral literature. Because it is unlikely that such extraexperimental contingencies can be eliminated or controlled (they exist for researchers in all sciences), the practical issue becomes that of how to train behavioral researchers so that other consequences are more powerful. The solution again lies in the subtleties of graduate training, a process whose careful examination might greatly benefit the discipline.

Personal History. Finally, there are a set of influences underlying all of these others that thoroughly pervade their effects. Although they may be lumped together under the rubric of "personal history," their etiology and nature are as unclear as this descriptor. Nevertheless, the experimental questions that we develop often seem to be partly influenced by subtle (or at least unidentified) aspects of our pre-and nonprofessional history. Given such uncertaintly about their nature, it may be wise to resist classifying these influences as predominantly good or bad in terms of the literature to which they eventually contribute, but a complete nosology must certainly recognize their existence.

It may partly be such influences that encourage a particular researcher to develop questions in directions that are new, different, or at variance with established directions. A close examination of this researcher's nonprofessional behavior might lead to similar descriptions of other activities. These influences may also join more professional variables in determining the general or even the specific type of problem or issue on which the researcher chooses to focus. One topic may be more reinforcing than another, not just because of graduate training or available resources, but because of influences that have nothing to do with one's profession.

Although such influences may be reasonably beyond intervention, they may not be entirely beyond personal recognition. Perhaps the best that we can do is to attempt to identify these historical effects on our question asking for whatever good might result. Even tentative detection affords the investigator with the opportunity of modulating their putative influence.

Basic versus Technological Directions

Certain sources of control over question-asking behavior come together to define an issue whose present importance may be a symptom of our young field's immaturity. At least it is an issue that does not seem to much concern the more fully developed sciences. It concerns the distinctions between basic and technological research and the direction in which a developing question tends to lean.

Not surprisingly, it is the research question itself that largely creates the distinction. The wide range of questions that the natural science of behavior pursues have in common a searching for the fundamental facts of behavior, a detailed identification of those variables that influence the organism–environment interaction. Research questions in the science ask about the basic nature of the relations between very specific variables and behavior and usually follow the answers with more questions beginning with "why." Perhaps their most consistent feature is that they are questions about behavior.

In contrast, the questions that direct technological research are generally about methods of controlling behavior.[1] Although this seems an easy distinction, it sometimes requires subtle discriminations in practice. The difficulty lies in the fact that basic research questions that ask about the influence of variables at the same time lead to statements about controlling behavior, whereas technological research questions (especially those that are asked in order to analyze the nature of a procedure's effects) may result in learning about some relatively fundamental influences on behavior. Instead of causing any distress, however, the occasional difficulty of this discrimination should be exciting. Research in the natural science and the more analytical portions of technological research should come together at many points in a symbiotic and synergistic alliance.

Most technological research inspires no such confusion, however; the focus on procedures for the useful control of behavior is usually obvious. The process of developing, analyzing, and improving technological procedures is an experimental venture in which the guiding questions labor in the strict service of practicality. Analysis for example, is usually at the level of understanding the relative contributions of the major components of a complex procedure. Only a minority of studies pursue a more detailed analysis of the mechanisms of action of certain critical components that might then reach the level of basic principles of behavior underlying their influence. Of course, a fair portion of technological research addresses the applied evaluation of procedures, and some fraction of this is likely not to be even superficially analytical.

Accepting for the moment the adequacy of this distinction's broad generalities, it is important because these sorts of differences in experimental questions lead to very different consequences for the field. Basic

[1]Technological application or practice may be further distinguished by the fact that it generally does not involve asking research questions at all.

science questions further the discovery of new variables and relations, though they may be of uncertain utility. Technological questions lead more narrowly toward application. Of course, both directions are proper and valuable, but only the mature, well-balanced, fully staffed, and adequately funded sciences can be indifferent to the proportion of its resources devoted to each. When a field is young with small and limited literatures describing only hesitant and undeveloped understandings of its basic phenomena as well as its ability to apply its principles with consistent and favorable results, it cannot be casual about this aspect of its questions. A small discipline with limited numbers of both basic and technological researchers as well as insufficient financial support must carefully consider the major directions of its growth in which its resources are expended.

In other words, a field of this tender age must try to predict the consequences of its research questions on its future development, and the relevant issues are far more complicated than this simple bifurcation suggests. For instance, should basic research use nonhuman species or human beings as subjects? Should laboratory scientists quantify relations in a deductive style or continue to search inductively for new relations and better understanding of present findings? Should technological researchers devote more effort toward trying out new procedures in order to meet societal demands, or must they insist on analyzing and fully understanding procedures before turning them over to practitioners?

These are clearly important issues that bear on a field's experimental directions. Although they may seem a bit abstract to the individual researcher considering the course of an experiment, this may only reflect our lack of sensitivity to them. It is difficult to imagine an experimental program in our field for which these concerns are not immediately relevant. It is not as if each researcher has to make a basic versus technological decision, of course; this would greatly misunderstand the complexity of the matter. It is more a matter of being acutely aware of the field's needs, both generally and for particular areas of literature, and then making sure that the experimental question that is developed properly serves those needs.

And what the field most generally needs is a balanced and wise use of its resources so that each study makes a significant contribution. As the discipline grows in size and maturity like the other natural sciences so that all of its directions are well identified and supported, these early issues will gradually evolve into simple matters of quality. Where a particular question falls on various continua, such as basic-technological, analytical-demonstrative, deductive-inductive, will then be quite secondary to its quality as a device for guiding the many decisions that create an experiment.

Developing and Phrasing Questions

It is not at all difficult to come up with experimental questions. Even the slightest familiarity with an area of literature will suggest numerous possibilities. At times it almost seems as easy as starting a sentence with "which," "why," "what," or "when" and ending with a question mark. Defending everything in between as a legitimate experimental question is rarely taxing in a field in which so little is known with any completeness and certainty. The process of acquiring this competency is easily observed in graduate students. The first-year student's fear of ever thinking of an experimental question is soon replaced by the second-year student's excitement at discovering them everywhere. Unfortunately, many never refine this elementary skill, and it is a rare graduate who is truly accomplished at deriving the best possible question for a topic.

This is clearly the goal: developing a question whose subsequent experiment will generate data that are more revealing and useful than those that any other question would have produced. In other words, in the context of any single area of literature some questions are simply better than others, and the process of comparing and refining and comparing again will eventually lead to one question that seems to be not only better than the rest but beyond improvement—at least to a single investigator. Along the way, perfectly sound questions may have been passed by in favor of something a little bit better. Does this strategy mean that they should never be dignified by experiment? Must we only pursue questions that attain this highest standard? Not at all. Not only may that researcher find certain of these questions worthy of later experimental attention, but other investigators may independently discover some of these to be their "best" questions. Each researcher's pursuit of this paragon will certainly not lead us all to the same single question.

The goal of developing the best possible question may be defended on at least two major grounds. First, the process of figuring out what that question is for a certain topic is inevitably a productive and profitable activity. It is hard to imagine that carefully sifting through existing studies, considering different research directions, comparing one question to another, and so forth would encourage mediocrity. Whether one researcher's final question is better or worse than another's, the field will gain from their efforts.

Second, as already pointed out, ours is a young science with a relatively small and sketchy experimental literature and extremely limited resources (especially research personnel). Worst of all, our survival as a discipline is in a number of ways far from assured. Under these conditions, we simply cannot afford for our research to be less than maximally productive for the field. Research is more than a form of parochial professional entertainment; it is our very core. It largely defines our field to both ourselves and others. It is the foundation of our offerings to the culture, and it is thus our primary justification for our existence as a point of view and an identifiable research community. Especially at this point in our history, our small research enterprise must aggressively lead the field by establishing new directions of investigation and application, discovering new variables and relations of unmistakable importance, and arguing persuasively with our competitors so that we grow by dominating other points of view and methods. Our research cannot be squandered on questions that are less than the best we can muster. We have so much to do and so little to do it with.

What makes one question better than another? What does an investigator do to develop the best possible question for a particular topic? The comparative criteria and verbal skills are many and difficult to articulate. It is obvious, for example, that the researcher must be thoroughly familiar with the immediately relevant literature, as well as its broader context in the field. The relations between published studies must be carefully evaluated for gaps and conflicts. Each study may have its weaknesses that suggest remedial efforts. However, these are just a few of the central and traditional ways of generating and assessing experimental questions, and they inadequately describe the complex verbal skills of the best researchers. For example, two different investigators may each be equally conversant with 20 experiments constituting a problem in the literature, as well as with the larger literature of which they are a part. And yet, it is unlikely that each will independently develop the same "best" question; indeed, their questions may not even be very similar. Even though both questions might be well worth experimentation (especially if they lead in divergent directions), a panel of the field's experts would probably have no real difficulty in predicting that one will be more valuable to the area than the other. Of course, the experts could be wrong, but the point is that familiarity with the literature and other such rules do not come very close to describing what makes one experimenter produce better questions than another.

Even less formal and traditional discussions seem inadequate. For instance, when we speak of familiarity with an area of literature, we are really referring to understanding exactly where its studies are leading, what the issues in that area are, and whether or not a somewhat different tack might be more illuminating. References to assessing our evolving questions by certain criteria vastly oversimplify the complex process of asking ourselves how a question can be improved, why one question is better than another, and why a question is truly the best possible for the present literature.

In fact, as the discipline whose responsibility it is to study scientific behavior, we have failed to do much more than dabble in it, and we pay the price when we try to teach others to be good researchers. The best established scientists can do is to write thoughtful but general discussions of research skills such as this and hope that fledgling behavior analysts model our best experimental efforts (while privately admitting that we may not always be the best models).

Part of the process of developing an experimental question involves its actual phrasing. This is far more than a trivial literary exercise. Forcing oneself to commit to paper a specific but one-sentence question is a revealing and educational task, and the process of developing an experimental question says a great deal about why it is being asked and what the investigator's real interests are.

Perhaps one of the most common discoveries about our own experimental planning or about the rationale that others offer for their experiments is that there really is no question or that its interrogatory style is largely artificial. This revelation suggests that interest lies more in demonstrating a suspected or known relation than in learning something new. Experimental demonstrations certainly have their place in science, but we should not delude ourselves about their true nature. They do not ask questions; they state contentions or predictions, and this usually leads in very different experimental directions than questions do.

Even when true questions are articulated, their phrasing may still reveal fundamental and widely divergent differences in the curiosities of their askers. For instance, many questions are not really queries about behavior. In reality, they may ask about a formal theoretical position or about an informal contention of the experimenter's or about an issue in the literature. Of course, it is not as if such questions encourage no discoveries about behavior; in fact, it usually takes a careful reading to detect their true fundamental direction because they typically express a behavioral relation. However, questions that are guided more by theoretical than behavioral curiosities may tend to generate experimental procedures and results that reveal somewhat less about behavior than would more behaviorally centered questions focused on the same phenomenon.

In a similar manner, questions that may at first appear to be about behavior may actually ask more about method. This is especially (and appropriately) the case in much technological research, although a portion of basic laboratory studies also has a procedural focus. Again, this is not so much a problem as a fact that needs to be recognized. Questions whose obvious dependence on behavior is bent towards an interest in methods of controlling behavior for the sake of control (whether for eventual experimental or technological ends) tend to generate experimental procedures and results that are at least slightly different from those that would follow questions with an unadulterated focus on behavior for the sake of explanation.

The importance of recognizing these often subtle themes in the phraseology of experimental questions that may otherwise appear to be more or less about behavior is, first, to encourage our honest admission about the real focus of our questions and, second, to reflect the true nature of our curiosities in the wording of questions that will serve as proper guides for subsequent experimental decisions. In other words, there are sound reasons for aiming basically behavioral questions in the directions of demonstration, theory, empirical issues, procedures, and so forth, but we must be fully aware of the nature of our true interests. If we are, then we can either redirect those interests more usefully or openly acknowledge them with questions that are unabashedly phrased to accomplish their mission. The point is to avoid deceiving or being deceived.

When the question's focus is fully on behavior, there is still room for substantial variety in phrasing, and this variety should not be ignored as poetic license. Consider the following examples:

1. Will a fixed-interval schedule of reinforcement generate positively accelerating patterns of responding (scalloping) in human subjects if they are instructed about the schedule contingency?
2. What are the relations between responding by human subjects under a fixed-interval schedule of reinforcement and contingency instructions?

At first glance, both questions may appear to post the same query, and in one sense they do. Yet, the differences between them suggest that their originators may well develop their experimental programs somewhat differently, and one direction may be more fruitful than the other. The first question appears to be fairly narrow in its interest; it wants to know if schedule instructions will produce scalloping. The answer will tend to be equally narrow—yes or no—and the wording of the question does not imply much concern with other answers, especially if they are complex. The question is, in fact, clearly positing a particular effect, and the inherent risk of this subtle version of hypothesis testing is the same as it was back in the heyday of hypothetico-deductive learning theory research. It is that experimental procedures will be bent in support of the investigator's expectations, however subtly and innocently. Whether or not this is the case, there is the further risk that data display and analysis will be similarly biased, making the researcher's interpretations less than veridical with the facts of nature and retarding the field's progress in this area.

The second question is, in contrast, open-ended; it posits no specific outcome. It simply asks what will happen to fixed-interval performance when contingency instructions are added. An important implication is that there are no expectations about the results. The fact that *relations* is plural further suggests receptiveness to complex or multiple effects. It may even be seen as encouraging a series of instructional manipulations probing for the fullest possible description of these relations.

In general, it may be most profitable to phrase questions in the least directive manner. Because all inferences are only about a relation between independent and dependent variables, the generic form, What are the relations between . . .? is a pretty good representative of this neutral posture, although other phrasings might be equally fair. When wordings predict or even lean toward particular answers, it is likely the reflected bias will also be manifest in experimental procedure, data analysis, and interpretation. The strategy of avoiding this directionality is based on the possibility that an investigator's efforts to develop an open and searching wording will alert the investigator to any biases and their procedural ramifications.

Although these scenarios may sound overly dramatic for the mere wording of a question, remember that it is the culmination of the investigator's training, reading of the literature, and all of the influences discussed in the earlier section on sources of control. When this background is combined with the question's functions in designing and conducting an experiment, the role of the question's phrasing can hardly be considered minor.

THE FUNCTIONS OF EXPERIMENTAL QUESTIONS

Guiding the Construction and Conduct of Experimental Procedures

The Strategy. A good experimental question is a limited and carefully worded expression of all of the investigator's best judgments about the direction and focus of that investigator's interests in a particular aspect of behavior. As such, it has enormous value as a guide for the innumerable decisions the researcher must make in order to create and manage an experiment that will satisfy those interests. Its direction may be strong or weak from one matter to another, but almost every decision the researcher must make can be usefully related to the experimental question.

Although this strategic statement has not been phrased in technical language, it is important to understand its behavioral translation. The experimental question is a bit of verbal behavior under the control of all of those variables just discussed. Those influences will exert their effects on the investigator's behavior of designing, conducting, and interpreting the experiment whether or not there is a formal question. However, all of the behavior that finally results in the statement of a question may also differentially modulate the influence of each of the variables on the experimental behaviors. In other words, the control over all subsequent experimental behavior does not lie just in a one-sentence bit of verbal behavior, but in all of the verbal behavior that led to it as well.

The relation between these procedural actions and the question is profoundly important. The obvious reason is that the experimental procedures are expected to provide answers to the particular question at issue. To the extent that the correspondence between question and procedures is less than perfect, the experiment will provide evidence that is less than fully relevant to that particular question. The problem emerges when this discrepancy is not recognized and the experimental evidence is innocently interpreted with reference to a question that it only partly illuminates. In such an event, the generality of the experimental relations may be quite good (though unnoticed), whereas the generality of the interpretations improperly tying them to the question may be comparatively poor. After all, when such discrepancies exist, it is the experimental procedures that speak to nature, not the question.

Psychology has long suffered from this problem. The correspondence between the constructs often at the core of its questions and the experimental procedures designed to reveal their operation has frequently been uncertain at best. The classic historical example of this problem is the research literature associated with the theories of learning promulgated by Clark Hull (1940, 1943) and others. However, the tradition has been well maintained throughout the full variety of contemporary psychological research.

Although the correspondence between the question and its experimental operations is not an inherent problem when the query is about behavior–environment relations, discrepancies are still quite common and probably as unnoticed as they usually are in other areas of psychology. These inconsistencies between question and procedure are easily created in myriad ways as the researcher makes the decisions that construct and conduct an experiment. A particularly frequent and obvious example is when the question asks about behavior (an intraorganism phenomenon) but measurement and data management procedures create data that represent the collated performance of a number of individuals. However, other examples, such as inadequate control of extraneous variables, are more subtle.

These risks may be minimized or even avoided entirely by recognizing and scrupulously honoring the question's functions in directing the creation and management of its experiment. The exercise is not always simple. It requires a thorough appreciation of the question's ramifications for the subject matter of behavior and a detailed understanding of every facet of research method. With these, however, the question becomes the touchstone of the experiment, guiding the investigator along an experimental route that can be exactly retraced when one brings the eventual inferences back to the question.

Selecting Subjects. In a crude chronological sense, one of the first decisions that the researcher must make is to determine the necessary characteristics of the experiment's subjects. The experimental question is obviously the source of subject selection criteria. Through its specification of independent and dependent variables, it will not only suggest major features such as species, age, or gender, but more detailed characteristics involving history, repetoire, and so forth. Although questions are often posed specifically for subjects with certain characteristics (at least species, for example), formal consideration of additional features may often be neglected. Careful examination of the question, however, will usually reveal other characteristics that might make certain individuals more suitable than others. For instance, a question addressing the effects of dietary variables on ruminating in profoundly mentally retarded individuals obviously requires these subject characteristics, but a more thorough reflection on the question's mission will also suggest avoiding those ruminating individuals who do so primarily because of anatomical anomalies.

The experimental question also dictates a certain degree of control, which in turn is likely to have substantial implications for subject selection. One aspect of control is simple availability; the question and its associated procedures will place certain requirements on the logistical aspects of each subject's participation. In a study designed to develop laboratory procedures for measuring the behavioral effects of psychotropic drugs in psychotic individuals, this might require the decision to use persons who are residing in an institution in favor of outpatients, who may be much less likely to attend consistently the necessary daily sessions.

The experimental question is likely to be especially eloquent about the control required by the independent variable and, by extension, all extraneous influences. The procedures that define the independent variable conditions of experimental phases will often impinge on the subject selection process because they require subjects who can be properly exposed to them. This may raise both logistical and ethical considerations.

Any influence that is not formally part of independent variable conditions is an extraneous variable, and this class of events must receive no less attention than the experimental treatments themselves. By implication, then, the experimental question requires subjects who will minimize problems in controlling extraneous variables. For example, it will probably be wise to avoid individuals whose behavior is highly controlled by powerful or pervasive extraneous influences that are difficult to eliminate or hold constant. A ubiquitous class of such influences in humans is self-verbal behavior—subjects talking to themselves during and between sessions in a way that effects their responding. If this is likely to be a disruptive influence (and it is not always so), it may be necessary to select nonverbal individuals as subjects, such as young infants or profoundly mentally retarded persons.

Choosing a Response Class. In a similar manner, the experimental question is a major influence on the desired characteristics of the response class that the investigator chooses. Some questions may leave little choice because they specify both subject population and response class; this is most likely to be true when the question's focus is on technology. On the other hand, when the question asks about relatively fundamental processes and suggests a laboratory or specially designed experimental environment, the response class decision can be quite open.

Whatever the direction of the question, there is usually more latitude here than is suspected. The traditionally obvious response class may not be necessary or even the best choice. Just because a laboratory setting will be used does not mean that button pushing or lever pulling are obligatory or ideal dependent variables. An interest in training techniques for building complex behaviors in mentally retarded individuals does not necessarily mean that existing training tasks and their related behaviors must serve in an experimental program. The researcher must consider the needs of the experimental question without preconceptions and choose a dependent measure accordingly.

In doing so, it is important to appreciate that the task is not merely to select a response class in the general sense of identifying and labeling one behavior out of the subject's entire repertoire. The real goal is to determine a list of qualities or characteristics that the target response class must exhibit and then either to identify a response class already in the subject's repertoire, which with the help of an arranged experimental environment will have those features, or to create such a response class by designing the experimental setting so that it produces behavior with the proper features. What qualifies any particular response class as desirable, then, are the details of its characteristics, and these are compiled partly by identifying what the question requires of a dependent variable.

Probably the most important example of response class characteristics that must be considered is its dimensional quantities. Every response class has the full variety, but certain of them are usually more appropriate targets for measurement than others, depending on the question and its associated independent variable conditions. One experiment may suggest frequency, but another may make duration, latency, or interresponse time more important. The underlying issue concerns how treatment-induced variability will be manifest in the response class. Although the answer may emerge only after examining data describing all of the dimensional quantities, certain questions and procedures may emphasize or eliminate particular aspects of responding. For example, an experimenter-controlled discrete-trials procedure may make frequency an insensitive or misleading choice. A different question and procedure may clearly focus interest on variability in the duration of responses.

Another influence on the choice of a response class is the independent variable conditions making up the experiment; however, because they are so intimately associated with the question, this is just another means by which the question directs the response class decision. Here the central (though not the only) concern is sensitivity; the response class must be sensitive to the independent variables manipulated from one phase to another. Sensitivity does not mean that the selected response must already be known to be strongly influenced by the experimental variables. If such a relation were certain, there might be little reason to ask the question. Sensitivity means that whatever the nature of the relations between treatment conditions and the response class, the subject's measured behavior will reflect them. Sensitivity would require, for example, that responding be able to exhibit an adequate range of variability. This would not be possible if under baseline conditions the chosen response occurred either very infrequently or very often, because it would be difficult to detect decreases or increases if such were the effects of the experimental condition.

One of the most common ways in which a response's sensitivity is limited is by powerful control by extraneous variables. This is especially a problem in nonlaboratory settings where there may be many extraneous variables that are difficult to control. Whether the effects on responding are from a single potent source or a number of shifting variables, the result obscures the clarity with which independent variable effects can be detected.

Of course, there are many other criteria guiding selection of the dependent variable (suitability for measurement, for instance), but they are not all directly tied to the experimental question. The question demands relevance to its theme, subservience to its detailed needs, and sensitivity to its independent variables. These demands are subtle, however, and good researchers have learned to read them carefully.

Designing Measurement Procedures. There are a great many important considerations in designing measurement procedures that have little or nothing to do with the experimental question (see Chaps. 8 and 10 of Johnston & Pennypacker, 1980, for a complete exposition). For example, the need for accurate transduction of the selected dimensional quantities of the target response class (or classes) does not vary from one question to another. Although the tactics by which this strategy is accomplished may vary considerably, they are guided by features of the response class, its setting, and logistical considerations.

The experimental question is not without its influence here, however. Its major impact is on decisions about the amount and distribution of observational time (sessions). The issue of how long and how often periods of measurement should occur is also related to the nature of the data, but the question plays its role by describing what independent-dependent variable relations are being examined. This specification contributes to these measurement decisions in obvious as well as subtle ways. The focus of the question may suggest weekday sessions in one case but 7 days per week measurement in another. It may allow relatively brief sessions, or it may require measurement throughout all waking hours.

For example, in a research program in which the senior author is involved concerning ruminating behavior in institutionalized profoundly mentally retarded individuals, most experimental questions require that measurement begin immediately after meals and continue for a half hour to an hour or more, depending on each subject's behavior. Furthermore, some questions permit such sessions after only one meal per day, whereas others require measurement after each meal. One experimental question concerning the effects of distributing the daily diet evenly throughout the day that was considered but not conducted would have necessitated continuous measurement throughout the entire waking day.

It is generally not difficult to divine the question's impact on this measurement decision. It merely requires thoughtful consideration about the nature of the relation that is to be the focus of the study. Some cautious and educated guessing about its characteristics and especially its temporal features will usually reveal the preliminary directions for these sampling decisions. They are only preliminary, of course, because accumulating data from early phases will both evaluate and, if necessary, redirect these decisions.

Selecting Independent Variables. The experimental question's influence on the choice of independent variables—the centerpiece of experimental procedure—is without peer as its most important methodological consequence. The question itself is mere verbal behavior; it is worthless until it leads to experimental action. The independent variables that are constructed into treatment conditions are the means by which we translate the language of the question into the language of nature. The critical issue is the adequacy of this translation. As pointed out earlier, the correspondence between the question and its independent variable conditions must be flawless in order for the resulting data to be fully relevant to the question. How, then, does the question guide the selection of independent variables that are properly related to it?

This may be the single most difficult question to answer in methodology.[2] The choice of independent variable conditions in science is often what leads us to describe certain researchers as brilliant or talented. Of course, this only certifies our ignorance of the variables controlling such decisions, and not until an experimentally derived understanding of this complex verbal behavior replaces discussions such as this will we be capable of routinely teaching this skill to students.

Absent such research, we can only speculate. Certainly, it helps to know as much about the relations of interest as the literature and personal experience will allow. It is particularly important to know what variables are already established as influential, the nature of their effects on the relation, and the mechanism of their action. Of course, this understanding of the extent of present knowledge is necessary for the framing of a good question in the first place, but it is equally valuable for considering the actual independent variable procedures that may create a relation with the dependent variable that will then answer the question.

---

[2]*Methodology* here refers to the study of method. This usage leaves the stem word available for unambiguous reference to experimental procedures.

In fact, this is the essence of the independent variable decision. What relation between behavior and environment will shed light on the experimental question? Candidates must then face the question of how or why each will be revealing. It is a bit like working backwards; given a certain question, what kinds of data will be required to answer it? In this search we should be wary of the tendency to become so attached to an early procedural idea suggested by the question that other possibilities are not developed and considered. Even properly specific experimental questions do not suggest only one way of producing answers. The first procedure thought of is unlikely to be beyond improvement, and a completely different procedure may be a better choice. The reference in this section to "decisions" the experimenter must make suffers the usual limitations of lay terminology by implying both too much and too little. In fact, the question should occasion a great deal of verbal behavior on these topics. Early ideas should be rigorously examined and contrasted to later ones. The goal is a process of a procedural evolution in which only the fittest survives, and this is possible only when all other relevant possibilities are identified, analyzed, and discarded as inferior.

In addition to this primary focus, an only slightly secondary consideration in selecting independent variable conditions concerns their relation to various extraneous variables. Extraneous variables are easily defined in relation to independent variables as "everything else," and their unfortunate role is to supply alternative explanations for what appear to be the effects of experimental conditions on responding. These extraneous influences may seem to come attached to either independent or dependent variables, but it is the relation that they cast doubt on. They are ubiquitous by definition and a major plague of experimental conduct and inference, though their diagnosis may be often made by editorial reviewers and peers rather than by the experimenters themselves.

The experimental question suggests the possibility of extraneous variables about as subtly as it does independent and dependent variables. Even though extraneous variables are defined as a consequence of the independent-dependent variable decisions, the question hints at possible culprits when it is used as a basis for speculation about alternative explanations that might be offered for the relation of interest. For example, if an experimenter is interested in the effects of a training procedure on the acquisition and maintenance of a particular skill by subjects, the question's focus should immediately suggest certain areas of concern. These might include elements of experimental procedure (i.e., measurement) that must be added to the training method in order to create an experiment, the behavior of those interacting with the subjects in order to administer the training method but which is not part of the method itself, and the subject's experiences between sessions that might affect their performance.

Creating Experimental Comparisons. Referring to experimental design in terms of creating experimental comparisons emphasizes the essential task that researchers face; they must arrange the presence or absence of selected independent variable conditions for every moment of experimental time in a way that provides a series of meaningful comparisons. The key word here is meaningful, and its definition originates with the experimental question.

If the question is really about behavior (an intraorganism phenomenon), then within-subject comparisons are unequivocally required. Whether a question is actually fundamentally about behavior may not be obvious, however. Many questions are only quasi-behavioral; they may clearly involve behavior, but only to the extent of requiring behavioral data in order to ask about populations of individuals. In such instances, between-groups comparisons may be quite appropriate, if not obligatory.

Questions are really about behavior when the inferences of interest are at the individual rather than the population level. Because behavior is a phenomenon that occurs only between individual organisms and their environments, questions that are intended to describe and explain these relations must be pursued with experimental designs that preserve the purity of the subject matter. This means (among other things) that the behavioral data must be uncontaminated by intersubject variability, and this is accomplished by creating comparisons between the presence and absence of treatment conditions in which the data under both conditions come from the same subject.

Given that this commitment has been made and that independent variable conditons have been as carefully chosen as can be before the data begin suggesting revisions in the protocol, the remaining decision concerns the temporal arrangement of conditions. The question's role here is again indirect. The concern about comparisons simply gets more refined. Now, it is not just a matter of the nature of experimental and baseline condition pairings, but which sequence of such comparisons will yield data that will be most useful in evaluating the propriety of the tentative upcoming comparisons. The question may also urge certain arrangements in order to provide evidence about extraneous influences (see Chap. 14 in Johnston & Pennypacker, 1980).

Both of these kinds of considerations were appropriate in the previously mentioned study of the effects of quantity of food consumed on ruminating behavior in profoundly retarded individuals. The first sequence of conditions alternated between the minimum and maximum food quantities possible in order to see if there was any relation (Rast, Johnston, Drum, & Courin, 1981). Having learned that there was, the experimenters subsequently provided arrangements that varied food quantity in ascending and descending parametric series in which phase changes were staggered across meals to see if there was any interaction effect (an extraneous influence). The experimental question concerning the existence and nature of the food quantity–rumination relation clearly suggested this sequence.

Data Analysis

The data result from bringing together the independent and dependent variables whose selection was earlier guided by the experimental question. It should be expected, then, that the question will exert some influence over the investigator's measurement and analysis of the data. The goals of graphic and quantitative manipulation of the data (conducted during and at the completion of the experiment) are three: (a) to modulate and supplement the original design and control decisions as the experiment progresses; (b) to identify and describe relations that answer the question, and (c) to discover relations that were not anticipated and may not even relate to the question. The first two goals can be accomplished only with the direct assistance of the question. It tells the investigator what relations to look for. These directions may sometimes be quite specific, but they are more often only general, leaving the experimenter considerable latitude to demonstrate skills in the fine art of data manipulation.

The third goal must not be lost in an effort to attain the others, however. If the data are examined with only the narrow focus of the experimental question, relations that it does not forecast may be missed or ignored. In other words, although the question is a major influence on data analysis decisions, it must not diminish the researcher's general curiosity. Experimental data must also be searched for any and all relations that exist, regardless of their relevance to the original question. It is this open and relatively unbiased search that results in serendipitous discoveries, and the history of science amply demonstrates that these are neither rare nor trivial. In fact, the entire research program on the effects of dietary variables on rumination is based on the serendipitous discovery of a relation between quantity of food ingested and rates of ruminating. This relation was not under study or expected, and it was not clearly revealed until graphs were constructed specifically to see if such a relation might be present.

Guiding Experimental Inferences

Experiments are conducted because they often result in interactions with natural phenomena that are reinforcing, both immediately to the researcher and eventually to other members of the culture. The control of independent variables over dependent variables described by the data that is a reinforcer for trained experimenters is also discriminative for a great deal of verbal behavior. In fact, our interpretive verbal behavior often tends to be predominantly under the control of graphic and quantitative arrangements of the data.

This is most unfortunate, although it is not widely recognized as a problem. It is a problem because there are other factors that must modulate the influence of the data, and the conditions under which they were produced is first on the list. This necessity is easy to appreciate in the case of measurement procedures, for example. Without considering the many characteristics of measurement operations that changed behavioral facts into behavioral data, one cannot unambiguously know exactly what each data point represents. The same dilemma exists for response class definitions, independent variable conditions, extraneous variable controls, and so forth. The responsibility is succinctly summarized by Johnston and Pennypacker (1980): "*In other words, the task is not just to interpret the data, but to interpret the entire experiment*" (p. 387).

After methodological constraints have been acknowledged, the interpreter's task is to translate nature's message back into the language of the culture. Because the procedures and their data that await translation originated with the experimental question, it is fitting that the question guide interpretative considerations. In other words, the experiment is related back to the question by searching for any answers that the procedures may have extracted from nature.

This may seem an obvious recommendation, but it is apparently easy to forget or ignore. Sometimes interpretive discussions make only passing reference to the original question before proceeding to other topics. When these themes seem to have only a general relation to the question and its experiment, such discussions can make the experiment appear to serve as no more than poetic license. In a variant of this interpretive style, the experiment is specifically related back to the question, but the question seems to generate more answers than procedures and data. Experiments designed and conducted under such motivations often exemplify an advocacy style of research, in which the interpretative agenda may be fairly well established before the experiment is conducted, if not conceived.

There are, however, two caveats to the strategy of relating experimental procedure and method back to the question. First, this is appropriate only if the procedures were properly related to the question in the first place. The necessity of this requirement was discussed earlier. Psychology has often had difficulty with the correspondence between the (often) theoretical elements of its questions and the empirical elements of its procedures, and neither our theories and concepts nor our procedures are yet so well developed and coordinated that we can afford not to scrutinize their relations in every instance. The danger, of course, is that experimenters and their peers will interpret the procedures and their data in the context of the question when they reveal little or nothing that bears on it. In such a case, the experiment might actually illuminate a different though unasked and unidentified question, whereas the question at hand was improperly encouraging its own set of inferences.

Second (and again), this sensitivity to the role of the original question in interpreting the experiment should not temper the enthusiasm with which we search for unanticipated inferential directions. In other words, although the question is a proper source of interpretative influence, it should not dominate the inferential process to the extent that relations not forecast or accommodated by it are not identified. These unexpected possibilities may complement or contrast with our preconceptions, but if the experiment was really performed to learn about behavior, then we will want to know everything that our procedures have teased from Nature.

Guiding the Development of the Science and the Culture

You can tell a lot about a science from its questions. Without any help from its methods or its findings, the past and present questions of a scientific discipline describe exactly where it has been and where it is in its evolution as a way of learning about some portion of the contingencies of Nature. They are more than merely revealing, however; because of their generative influence on method and the completeness of method's influence on data, questions guide the style and direction of a science's evolution.

This suggests that in addition to all of the more particular influences already detailed, the development of experimental questions should also consider their broader role in the growth of the science. This in turn requires some sensitivity to where the science (or area or literature within a larger discipline) is and where it needs to go. This understanding is aided by trying to answer a number of questions about our science as we formulate an experimental question. Are the directions already established in the literature good for the science's development? Are there more profitable directions in which to invest the field's resources? Are there unexplored areas that should be pursued? Are there particular themes that should be avoided? What effects might each particular experimental question have on the field as a whole?

Some of these considerations may be more easily appreciated in the context of an example, and the literature reporting experiments using human subjects under relatively controlled conditions will serve the point well. This specialty within the basic experimental branch of the science has always been a fairly restrained enterprise (Buskist & Miller, 1982; Nevin, 1982), although it may be expanding a bit recently. The vast majority of its studies are efforts to assess or extend the generality of laboratory findings obtained with nonhuman species to human beings. This is an important research direction, of course, and no criticism of it is implied. However, the basic animal literature in our field is generally aimed at identifying the most fundamental relations involved in the processes of conditioning. Although we certainly need to know about their extension to humans, there are many other directions that might be considered when asking basic questions about human behavior.

For instance, verbal and social behavior have been paid only slight attention by basic researchers, in dramatic contrast to their popularity in the rest of psychology and the social sciences and their obvious importance to the culture. There are also many fascinating patterns of human behavior whose scientific explanation would be of immediate technological benefit. Many of these are defined as pathological in function, but others are more broadly interesting. In addition, there are many variables whose influence on behavior does not depend on conditioning. Drugs, biochemicals, ingested and inhaled substances, diseases, injuries, homeostatic bodily processes, and geophysical influences suggest research directions not yet well represented in the small human experimental literature. Investigators interested in working with human subjects clearly have many research directions available to them. But although any good question deserves experimental attention, not every question will be equally valuable to the science. The entire science will profit if researchers in all of its specialties consider the impact of potential questions on the development of the discipline.

In a similar manner, possible experimental questions may be examined for the impact of their direction on the culture. This is not an uncommon consideration in science. Medicine in particular is often responsive to the needs of the culture in addition to the subtleties of its own literature. The subdisciplines of physics, chemistry, and biology are also generally sensitive to cultural problems or interests. After all, their investigators are also part of the culture and are influenced by their membership. In addition, federal, corporate, and nonprofit funding sources encourage the scientist to be aware of the relation between his or her experimental questions and the impact of their pursuits on everyday life. Science in the 20th century has become an indispensible part of the culture; we need it just to survive the complexities and problems that in part it has allowed us to create. As a culture we are only recently even beginning to appreciate fully the need for science to explain human behavior so that effective technologies can be developed. As we in the natural science of behavior undertake this responsibility, we must compose our experimental questions with a care that befits their consequences for the culture.

REFERENCES

Birnbrauer, J. S. (1979). Applied behavior analysis, service, and the acquisition of knowledge. *The Behavior Analyst, 2,* 15–21.

Buskist, W. F., & Miller, H. L. (1982). The study of human operant behavior, 1958–1981: A topical bibliography. *The Psychological Record, 32,* 249–268.

Deitz, S. (1978). Current status of applied behavior analysis: Science versus technology. *American Psychologist, 33,* 805–814.

Hake, D. F. (1982). The basic-applied continuum and the possible evolution of human operant social and verbal research. *The Behavior Analyst, 5*(1), 21–28.

Hayes, S. C. (1978). Theory and technology in behavior analysis. *The Behavior Analyst, 1,* 25–33.

Hayes, S. C., Rincover, A., & Solnick, J. V. (1980). The technical drift of applied behavior analysis. *Journal of Applied Behavior Analysis, 13,* 275–285.

Hull, L. L. (1940). *Mathematico-deductive theory of rote learning: A study in scientific methodology.* New York: Appleton-Century-Crofts.

Hull, L. L. (1943). *Principles of behavior: An introduction to behavior theory.* New York: Appleton-Century-Crofts.

Johnston, J. M., & Pennypacker, H. S. (1980). *Strategies and tactics of human behavioral research.* Hillsdale, NJ: Erlbaum.

Michael, J. L. (1980). Flight from behavior analysis. *The Behavior Analyst, 3,* 1–21.

Nevin, J. A. (1982). Editorial. *Journal of the Experimental Analysis of Behavior, 37,* 1–2.

Pennypacker, H. S. (1981). On behavioral analysis. *The Behavior Analyst, 4*(2), 159–161.

Pierce, W. D., & Epling, W. F. (1980). What happened to analysis in applied behavior analysis? *The Behavior Analyst, 3,* 1–10.

Rast, J., Johnston, J. M., Drum, C., & Courin, J. (1981). The relation of food quantity to rumination behavior. *Journal of Applied Behavior Analysis, 14,* 121–130.

Skinner, B. F. (1938). *The behavior of organisms.* New York: Appleton-Century-Crofts.

5

Some Factors Limiting the Applicability of Applied Behavioral Research

Descriptive Information in JABA Articles

R. WAYNE FUQUA AND JAN BACHMAN

INTRODUCTION

Despite recent controversy about the status and goals of applied behavior analysis research (e.g., Azrin, 1977; Baer, 1981; Deitz, 1978; Hayes, Rincover, & Solnick, 1980), most researchers hope that applied behavioral research might prove directly or indirectly applicable to the prevention and/or remediation of human problems. Thus, there is at least some expectation that research findings or conceptual understandings derived from that research will be applicable beyond the subjects, settings, and behaviors of the original research. The purpose of this article is to discuss some factors that may limit effective application of applied behavior analysis research and to suggest how these limitations might be overcome.

The applicability of a behavioral procedure depends on the reliability and generality of that procedure. When applied to research findings, reliability refers to the consistency of experimental results and is established when direct replications of an experimental procedure yield results that are qualitatively similar to the results previously attained with that experimental procedure (Johnston & Pennypacker, 1980; Sidman, 1960). Assessing the reliability of research findings presupposes that all important details of the original experiment can be accurately

R. WAYNE FUQUA and JAN BACHMAN • Department of Psychology, Western Michigan University, Kalamazoo, MI 49008.

replicated in subsequent research and clinical practice. If the research report does not contain complete and accurate descriptions of all relevant procedures implemented in the experiment, then attempts to directly replicate the procedures and assess the reliability of the results are impeded. The importance of procedural detail was recognized early in the history of applied behavior analysis when Baer, Wolf, and Risley (1968) discussed the technological dimension of applied behavior analysis.

> The best rule of thumb for evaluating a procedure description as technological is probably to ask whether a typically trained reader could replicate that procedure well enough to produce the same results, given only a reading of the description. (p. 95)

They emphasized the special importance of procedural description for the practitioner when they wrote, "Especially where the problem is application, procedural descriptions require considerable detail about all possible contingencies or procedures" (p. 95).

Attempts to apply a promising procedure based on an inaccurate or otherwise inadequate journal description of that procedure could produce disappointing or unexpected results much to the chagrin of the practitioner and perhaps to the detriment of the client. Furthermore, the failure to reproduce expected results in clinical application might be falsely attributed to faulty implementation of the procedure on the part of the practitioner or other behavior change agents (e.g., parents) or, worse yet, attributed to the general ineffectiveness of behavior modification techniques. Thus, the absence of adequate procedural detail to allow for replication of promising interventions poses not only scientific problems but ethical and public relations problems as well.

Inadequately described experimental procedures are most readily detected when direct replications of the procedure fail to reproduce the results of the initial experiment. Unfortunately, failures to reproduce an experimental effect rarely appear in technologically oriented journals where the implicit and often explicit criterion for publication is the production of socially significant behavior change. A practical alternative for assessing replicability of experimental procedures is to survey published articles for the presence of descriptive information that is theoretically important in replication attempts. This strategy has been profitably employed by Peterson and colleagues (Homer, Peterson, & Wonderlich, 1983; Peterson, Homer, & Wonderlich, 1982) to assess the adequacy of subject selection criteria and the consistency of independent variable implementation in applied behavior analysis research.

The applicability of behavioral research is in some cases limited by failures to establish the generality of that research. Generality refers to the "extent to which our interpretations of an experiment apply beyond the confines of their particular origin" (Johnston & Pennypacker, 1980, p. 396). Generality is typically established through systematic replications in which certain experimental factors (e.g., experimental setting, parameters of the independent variable, subject characteristics) are intentionally altered to determine if they are necessary for the reproduction of the results of prior research. Practitioners are especially concerned with the generality of behavior change procedures because practitioners must apply these procedures under conditions and with clients that differ from those with which the procedure was originally developed and validated. Questions about what interventions work with which clients under what conditions are utlimately questions about the generality of the interventions.

Much of the applied behavior analysis literature reports systematic replications across an impressive range of subjects, target behaviors, and procedural variations of the intervention and would thus seem to have established broad generality. Unfortunately, this conclusion would be misleading for at least two reasons.

First, limits to the generality (and understanding) of a behavior change procedure are most directly revealed in failures to reproduce an expected behavioral effect. Such failures suggest an incomplete understanding of the conditions necessary for producing the expected effect (Johnston & Pennypacker, 1980). As previously discussed, unsuccessful replication attempts are seldom published thus decreasing the probability of detecting procedures with limited generality. Even when a body of literature contains a number of studies with inconsistent results, there is some tendency for reviewers of that literature to accept the findings of the majority of research reports as representative of the "true state of nature" rather than taking each unsuccessful replication attempt as an indicator of an incomplete understanding of the conditions necessary for a procedure to produce a given effect.

Second, the nature of a series of systematic replications is more important in assessing the generality (and ultimately the applicability) of behavioral research than the sheer number of replications. This can best be explained by analogy. Assume that you are given the task of drawing a map of a country whose boundaries are unknown to you. Your only available research strategy is to travel around the countryside asking the residents, "Am I in country X?" With each affirmative reply you gain some information about the expanse of the country, but you can begin to describe the boundaries that define the country only after crossing the border into an adjacent country and receiving negative replies to your query. In a similar manner, a large number of successful replications provide useful information about the conditions necessary for a given effect but the most valuable information about the generality of a procedure is attained from research that systematically manipulates a variable until the limits of that variable's effectiveness are reached. It is through such analytic research that the necessary conditions that limit a procedure's generality are identified and answers to questions about "which intervention works with which clients under what conditions" are accrued.

The development of a body of literature that identifies the conditions necessary to obtain a given effect from any behavior change procedure will surely require a series of thematically related experiments conducted over a number of years. In the meantime, the applicability of applied behavior analysis research can be assessed from a descriptive point of view by simply pointing out factors in a study that are likely to limit the reproducibility of results. This tack was taken in the present study by evaluating experimental articles published in the *Journal of Applied Behavior Analysis* (JABA) along several dimensions likely to affect the generality of obtained results and the replicability of experimental procedures. This journal was surveyed because of its widely acknowledged methodological rigor; it seems unlikely that other applied behavioral journals would provide more complete descriptive information than JABA.

METHODS

The first two experimental articles in each of the four issues comprising a volume of JABA from 1968 (Vol. 1) to 1982 (Vol. 15) were scored for the presence or absence of certain descriptive information. An article was defined as experimental if it involved the manipulation of an independent variable. This definition excluded articles of a correlational or purely theoretical nature. When an article contained multiple experiments, each experiment was rated separately. The Methods section of each experiment was rated for the occurrence or nonoccurrence of descriptive information in a variety of discrete categories. A second observer independently rated the first two experimental articles in one randomly selected issue per volume (25% of total articles rated). Each experiment was scored for the inclusion of descriptive information related to the following broad categories: demographic characteristics of the subjects; psychological labels; descriptions of the subject's repertoire; descriptions of a subject's history with respect to the independent variable; and, certain descriptive information on the reinforcement contingencies operating in the experiment.

Demographic Characteristics

Age. The occurrence of an age description was scored if the age of a subject or the age range for a group of subjects was specified. An occurrence was also scored if descriptive information from which an age could be estimated (e.g., fourth-grade pupil) was reported. A nonoccurrence was scored if no age descriptors or only very general descriptors (e.g., adults) were specified.

Race. If the race of the subjects was specified (e.g., black, Caucasian, Latino), this category was scored as an occurrence. If no race descriptor or only a general descriptor was reported (e.g., minority) a nonoccurrence was scored.

Gender. An occurrence was scored if the sex of each subject was reported or the number of males (boys) and females (girls) in a group was specified.

Other. If demographic information other than that specified in the above categories was stated (e.g., place of employment or residence) this category was scored for an occurrence.

Subject Labels

Psychological Labels. A psychological-labels category was scored as an occurrence if a specific psychological label (e.g., paranoid schizophrenic, severely mentally impaired) was stated or if psychological test scores (e.g., IQ test scores) were reported from which a label could be inferred. A nonoccurrence was scored if no label was specified or a nonpsychological label was specified.

Other Labels. An other-labels category was scored as an occurrence if a label other than a psychological label was specified. This category included medical labels such as "hypertensive" and colloquial labels such as "disruptive, difficult to manage student." This category was also scored if test results (e.g., blood pressure) from which a nonpsychological label might be inferred (e.g., hypertension) were provided.

Repertoire Description

Prerequisite Behaviors. An occurrence was scored in the prerequisite-behaviors category if the experiment included a description of specific behaviors or skill levels that were necessary for the intervention to be implemented (e.g., the subject could follow three-step instructions). This category was also checked if the subject selection criteria specified certain behavioral characteristics that were judged to be prerequisites for implementation of the independent variable. The description of behavioral characteristics that were judged not to be prerequisites for the implementation of the independent variable or the failure to specify any prerequisites was scored as a nonoccurrence.

Other Behaviors. An other-behaviors category was scored when behavioral characteristics of subjects were described but they were not judged to be prerequisites to the independent variable implementation. Behaviors scored in this category typically provided some general information about the subject's daily activities or skill level (e.g., the subjects did homework in the group home) but were not directly related to the focus of the experiment (e.g., improving room cleaning through a self-monitoring system). A nonoccurrence was scored in this category if a repertoire description was not included or if only prerequisite behaviors were described.

Subject History with Respect to Independent Variables (I.V.)

History with I.V. An occurrence was scored in the history-with-I.V. category if a subject's history with the I.V. prior to the experiment was specified (e.g., previous exposure to token economy) or if the effectiveness of a specific element of the I.V. was described (e.g., the value of token reinforcement had been established as evidenced by . . .). If a history with the I.V. was not described or if the only history reported pertained to instructions regarding the I.V. a nonoccurrence was scored.

Instructions with Respect to the I.V. This category was scored if the experiment described instructions that could effect the "value" of the I.V. (e.g., when the red light comes on you will lose 5 cents of your earnings). A nonoccurrence was scored if the instructions included only a simple statement of the relationship between the dependent and independent variable and were judged as not likely to alter or establish the efficacy of the I.V.

Other Interventions. If prior or concurrent interventions that could effect the dependent variable of the current experiment were described, the other-interventions category was checked. A nonoccurrence was scored if no other interventions were described or if a prior intervention was described that was unrelated to the dependent variable under study.

Experimental Conditions

Contingencies of Reinforcement (C.O.R.) for Dependent Variable (D.V.) During Baseline. This category was scored if the antecedent and/or consequent stimulus changes for the dependent variable during the baseline phase were specified. Otherwise, a nonoccurrence was scored.

No Programmed C.O.R. for D.V. During Baseline. If the absence of programmed antecedent or consequent stimuli for the D.V. during baseline was actually specified this category was scored. Otherwise, a nonoccurrence was scored.

Description of C.O.R. for Behavior other than the D.V. If the antecedent or consequent stimuli for behaviors other than the dependent variable under study (e.g., incompatible or concurrent behaviors) were described an occurrence was scored in this category. Otherwise, a nonoccurrence was scored.

Reliability of I.V. Implementation. This category was scored if the experiment reported either the proportion of opportunities that the I.V. was actually implemented as described or if some statement assuring high accuracy of I.V. implementation was made. Otherwise, a nonoccurrence was scored.

RESULTS AND DISCUSSION

A total of 120 articles with 173 experiments were included in this survey. A second observer independently rated 51 of the 173 experiments (29.5%). Interobserver agreement percentages (agreements/agreements + disagreements × 100%) for each category ranged from 80% for the "other" category under subject demographics and for "description of C.O.R. for other than the D.V." to 98% for "age" and "gender." Because there were no discernible trends in the percentage of articles reporting any particular category across years, the data were summarized across years for each category. Figure 1 depicts the percentage of experiments providing descriptive information in each of the rated categories.

The data in Figure 1 should be cautiously interpreted. They do not imply that any particular article cannot be replicated. Nor does the inclusion of a descriptive category indicate the relevance of that category to any specific article. Surely, descriptive information in each category would prove inappropriate or irrelevant for many experiments. Nevertheless, it is instructive to examine the descriptive information included in JABA articles. In reviewing these descriptive categories, it is useful to evaluate their potential contribution to the reliability and generality of a literature by asking the following questions: "Would this information help me determine the applicability of these procedures and results in a particular situation or with a specific client?" and, "Would this information assist me in accurately replicating the procedure and attaining similar results?"

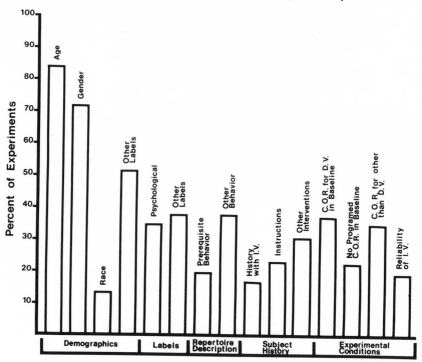

FIGURE 1. Percentage of experiments reporting descriptive information in each of the methodological categories specified.

Demographic Information. Demographic information on experimental subjects, especially age (88%) and gender (63%), is reported in a relatively high proportion of JABA articles. This is not surprising given the ready availability of such information and the long-standing tradition of including it in psychological research reports. There is little doubt that the age, sex, or race of a subject occasionally correlates with differential responding to an intervention and thus provides potentially useful information on the applicability of that intervention to subjects with similar demographic characteristics. Unfortunately, other factors correlated with these demographic characteristics are probably responsible for between-subject differences in experimental effects and thus are more useful in predicting the applicability of an intervention with other clients or subjects. For example, people of different ages often have different behavioral repertoires, different histories, and different physiological characteristics. Any or all of these factors may prove more useful than age *per se* in explaining differential treatment effects across subjects of different ages. Similar arguments can be made for gender and race.

Labels. Psychological labels are also reported in a sizable minority of the articles sampled (35.3%). The utility of diagnostic labels for the understanding, prevention, and treatment of psychological problems has been the topic of frequent conceptual and empirical evaluations (e.g., Ullmann & Krasner, 1975, Chap. 11; Zigler & Phillips, 1961). A review of these arguments is beyond the scope of this chapter. Suffice it to say that despite recent improvements in the reliability with which certain diagnostic labels are assigned, there remains substantial behavioral variability between individuals within the same diagnostic classification and for one individual across time and settings. The result is that diagnostic classification, psychiatric or otherwise, seldom provides adequate information about specific behavioral characteristics of experimental subjects that are relevant to treatment outcome. Thus psychological labels are of limited utility to a practitioner trying to determine if a behavioral procedure is likely to be effective with a particular client.

Repertoire Description. In many experiments the presence of prerequisite skills, such as instruction following, reading, or basic stimulus-discrimination skills can be inferred from a description of the subjects (e.g., normal adults). However, a sizable portion of articles used subjects, such as young children or the developmentally disabled, for whom the presence of specific prerequisite skills should not be taken for granted. Other experiments presupposed complex prerequisite skills (e.g., discrimination of assertive from aggressive behavior) whose presence cannot be assumed even with normal adults. It is quite possible that between-subject differences in treatment outcome could be related to different levels of prerequisite behaviors for the subjects. A published description of prerequisite skills or subject selection criteria (see Homer *et al.*, 1983) would be of substantial benefit to practitioners in determining the appropriateness of a given intervention for a particular client or in identifying the prerequisite skills to be trained for clients lacking such skills. Unfortunately, only a small portion (20%) of experiments described behaviors that could be construed as prerequisites for the reported intervention.

Subject History. A relatively small percentage of articles (17%) described the subject's history with respect to the independent variable. Failure to describe an experimental history appears to be a serious oversight, given the potential significance of historical variables in determining the value of experimental stimuli for the subject (Michael, 1982). For example, differential social attention appears to have a paradoxical punishing effect rather than the predicted reinforcing effect for some children (e.g., Budd, Green, & Baer, 1976). These findings suggest the need for further analysis of the role of conditioning history in establishing the reinforcement value of social attention. If common historical variables emerge among these children then practitioners should be wary of implementing procedures based on the presumed reinforcing effects of social attention for children with similar histories.

Detailed instructions to subjects represent a special and significant history. A sizable minority (27%) of rated studies describe or reprint the instructions given to subjects. That instructions can influence experimental outcomes is readily apparent. Instructions have been shown to affect a wide variety of behaviors ranging from human fixed-interval responding (Poppen, 1982) to the topography of cigarette smoking (Frederickson & Simon, 1978). Furthermore, instructions may play an important role in establishing the motivational properties of stimulus changes as exemplified by instructions given subjects in biofeedback research regarding the "value" of changes in tonal pitch or a physiological readout. The importance of instructions in establishing the motivational properties of stimuli becomes most obvious when for some reason instructions fail to establish certain stimuli as reinforcers and alternative motivational stimuli must be considered (e.g., Kohlenberg, 1973). Given the variety of behaviors influenced by instructions, it only seems prudent to standardize and describe instructions given to subjects. Even though some factors, such as the subject's history with respect to the accuracy of instructions, may influence an individual's response to instructions (Galizio, 1979), reprinting or, at minimum, describing instructions would surely assist in replicating experimental procedures and probably promote the reproduction of experimental effects.

One other aspect of a subject's history, prior exposure to other interventions, also merits comment. A brief description of prior interventions, successful or otherwise, for the behavior of interest would prove useful for many of the reasons previously discussed in relation to the motivational aspects of specific stimuli. Furthermore, a person's prior therapy experience may influence not only that person's expectancies regarding the therapeutic process and ultimate outcome but also may influence the degree to which a "therapeutic relationship" is established with the researcher or practitioner. Although terms such as *expectancy* are seldom operationally defined and have a questionable role as causal variables, they do refer to potentially operational variables, such as the subject's prior history or self-statements about that history, which could influence the outcome of any particular intervention. Thus, when known, this aspect of a subject's history also merits brief description, as it may relate to differential treatment effects across subjects and provide both useful predictive information for the practitioner and leads for future research. However, rather few studies (31%) provided information concerning interventions to which subjects had been previously exposed.

Experimental Conditions. A sizable minority (37.6%) of the articles sampled described the contingencies of reinforcement (C.O.R.) for the dependent variable during baseline conditions. Twenty-three percent of the articles did however stipulate the absence of programmed C.O.R. during baseline. Unfortunately, all behaviors, even those with no experimenter-programmed contingencies, have events that occur prior to and subsequent to their occurrence and thus in this broad sense can be said to have C.O.R. even if inconsistent across time. If our sample is representative of the remaining JABA articles, we can expect approximately 60% to lack a complete description of the C.O.R. for the dependent variable during baseline. This is in marked contrast to the standard practice of describing the C.O.R. that define the nominal intervention or independent variable. The specification of experimenter-arranged or naturally occurring contingencies during baseline is important for at least two reasons. First, many interventions for existing behaviors are superimposed over existing C.O.R. that maintain the behavior during baseline. The effects of such interventions may interact with the existing C.O.R. to produce results that are not characteristic of that intervention when superimposed over different C.O.R. for the dependent variable. For example, a smoking cessation intervention may produce different effects, depending on whether or not a client's smoking is controlled primarily by avoidance of withdrawal symptoms or by social modeling and social reinforcement. Knowledge of the controlling variables for the dependent variable during baseline provides a partial answer to questions regarding the conditions under which an intervention works and may thus allow practitioners to assess the similarity to the controlling variables for their clients and better predict treatment outcome based on these similarities.

Even when the C.O.R. maintaining baseline responding are discontinued with the introduction of the experimental intervention, there is still the possibility of sequence effects in which the outcome of an experimental intervention varies depending on the immediately prior condition. The behavioral literature abounds with examples of sequence effects (e.g., responses to placebos in behavioral pharmacology research) and they need not be further discussed except to say that baseline conditions could be involved in sequence effects and thus merit description and control.

Approximately one-third (35%) of the rated articles described the C.O.R. for behaviors other than the D.V. This percentage seems relatively low given the existence of an extensive experimental literature documenting interactions between concurrent behaviors (for reviews see Catania, 1966; de Villiers, 1977). The relevance of concurrent behavior analyses, more specifically the matching law, to therapeutic endeavors has been discussed elsewhere (McDowell, 1982). Suffice it to say that the existence of concurrent behaviors, especially those that contact the same class of consequences as the dependent variable, can greatly influence the impact of the independent variable on the behavior of interest. Such concurrent behaviors should be described because they may be a source of between-subject variability and thus provide information that would help a practitioner predict the effect of that intervention with a particular client.

Finally, 20% of the articles reported procedures to insure that the independent variable was reliably and accurately implemented. Based on a larger sample of JABA articles, Peterson et al. (1982) attained a similar percentage (23%). These values are distressingly low given that an obvious requirement for reproducing the results of a study is that the treatment evaluated therein was implemented as described.

Overall, it appears that a relatively large percentage of rated articles provide descriptive information of limited value (e.g., age), whereas they fail to provide other kinds of descriptive information of greater potential value for those interested in replicating procedures in experimental and clinical applications. It is also worth noting that only 2 of the 173 experiments evaluated in this survey reported as many as six of the nine "valuable" categories included under "Repertoire Description," "Subject History," and "Experimental Conditions." It is impossible to directly evaluate the long-term effects of such omissions, but the omission of important procedural details could surely have an adverse effect on the reliability and generality of an experimental literature. Needless to say, a scientific literature whose reliability and generality were compromised (or unassessed) would not only limit the applicability of technologies emanating from that literature but would also have serious epistemological ramifications for that science.

The reliability and generality of applied behavioral research might be enhanced in several ways. First, failures to reproduce the results of prior experiments in direct replication attempts should be disseminated through professional publications. Such failures are most likely a result of one of the following situations, each of which is of vital importance to the development of a science and technology: (a) prior results were flukes and those interventions will not reliably produce the expected results; (b) all important procedural details have not been accurately replicated perhaps because of inaccurate or inadequate descriptions in the original research; (c) important but unidentified differences exist between the original research and attempts to apply or replicate the research; or, (d) the prior research was fraudulent. It should be noted that replication failures are most noteworthy when they involve interventions that were previously accepted as effective and when there is some attempt to determine empirically the cause of the failure to reproduce the expected results.

Second, researchers should attempt to identify and analyze those factors that are necessary for attaining a given effect with a particular intervention. Most, if not every, intervention will have some limitations on its generality, thus the identification of factors capable of "making or breaking" an intervention is of vital importance to the health of behavior analysis as a science and as a technology. The relative merits of such analytic research has been extensively discussed (e.g., Deitz, 1978; Hayes *et al.*, 1980; Johnston & Pennypacker, 1980) and will not be repeated here except to point out, as does Baer (1981), that a balance between analytic research and technological application research is highly desirable.

Finally, improvements in the descriptive information published in articles would do much to promote replications. This suggestion, like the previous two, is not without costs. First, the objective information for some of the descriptive categories may be difficult to attain, forcing a researcher to rely on anecdotal reports. Although objective data about a descriptive category are preferable to anecdotal reports, we feel that anecdotal reports, if acknowledged as such, are preferable to no descriptive information and should be included if the cost of attaining more objective information is prohibitive.

Second, journal space is expensive and the inclusion of additional detail might necessitate an increase in subscription costs or a reduction in the total number of articles published in each issue of a journal. A less expensive alternative would be for journals to require researchers to provide detailed descriptive information (perhaps including standardized flow charts or state diagrams of experimental procedures) that would not appear in the article, but could be purchased by interested parties from an information service or from the journal itself. Regardless of the costs of these alternatives, we feel that the potential benefits to researchers, practitioners, and ultimately to the consumers of behavioral technology would readily justify the efforts.

REFERENCES

Azrin, N. H. (1977). A strategy for applied research: Learning based but outcome oriented. *American Psychologist, 32,* 140–149.

Baer, D. M. (1981). A flight of behavior analysis. *The Behavior Analyst, 4,* 85–91.

Baer, D. M., Wolf, M. M., & Risley, T. R. (1968). Some current dimensions of applied behavior analysis. *Journal of Applied Behavior Analysis, 1,* 91–97.

Budd, K. S., Green, D. R., & Baer, D. M. (1976). An analysis of multiple misplaced parental contingencies. *Journal of Applied Behavior Analysis, 9,* 459–470.

Catania, A. C. (1966). Concurrent operants. In W. K. Honig (Ed.), *Operant behavior: Areas of research and application.* (pp. 213–270). New York: Appleton-Century-Crofts.

Deitz, S. M. (1978). Current status of applied behavior analysis: Science versus technology. *American Psychologist, 33,* 805–814.

de Villiers, P. A. (1977). Choice in concurrent schedules and a quantitative formulation of the law of effect. In W. K. Honig & J. E. R. Staddon (Eds.), *Handbook of operant behavior* (pp. 233–287). Englewood Cliffs, NJ: Prentice-Hall.

Frederickson, L. W., & Simon, S. J. Modifying how people smoke: Instructional control and generalization. *Journal of Applied Behavior Analysis, 11,* 431–432.

Galizio, M. (1979). Contingency-shaped and rule-governed behavior: Instructional control of human loss avoidance. *Journal of the Experimental Analysis of Behavior, 31,* 53–70.

Hayes, S.C., Rincover, A., & Solnick, J. V. (1980). The technical drift in applied behavior analysis. *Journal of Applied Behavior Analysis, 13,* 275–285.

Homer, A. L., Peterson, L., & Wonderlich, S. A. (1983). Subject selection in applied behavior analysis. *The Behavior Analyst, 6,* 39–45.

Johnston, J. M., & Pennypacker, H. S. (1980). *Strategies and tactics of human behavioral research.* Hillsdale, NJ: Erlbaum.

Kohlenberg, R. J. (1973). Operant conditioning of human anal sphincter pressure. *Journal of Applied Behavior Analysis, 6,* 201–208.

McDowell, J. J. (1982). The importance of Herrstein's mathematical statement of the law of effect for behavior therapy. *American Psychologist, 37,* 771–779.

Michael, J. (1982). Distinguishing between discriminative and motivational functions of stimuli. *Journal of the Experimental Analysis of Behavior, 37,* 149–155.

Peterson, L., Homer, A. L., & Wonderlich, S. A. (1982). The integrity of independent variables in behavior analysis. *Journal of Applied Behavior Analysis, 15,* 477–492.

Poppen, R. (1982). The fixed-interval scallop in human affairs. *The Behavior Analyst, 5,* 127–136.

Sidman, M. (1960). *Tactics of scientific research.* New York: Basic Books.

Ullman, L. P., & Krasner, L. (1975). *A psychological approach to abnormal behavior* (2nd ed.). Englewood Cliffs, NJ: Prentice-Hall.

Zigler, E., & Phillips, L. (1961). Psychiatric diagnosis: A critique. *Journal of Abnormal and Social Psychology, 3,* 607–618.

6

Interobserver Agreement

History, Theory, and Current Methods

TERRY J. PAGE AND BRIAN A. IWATA

INTRODUCTION

Research in applied behavior analysis often involves the measurement of behavior under conditions precluding the use of precision mechanical recording equipment often found in experimental laboratories. As a result, it has been necessary to rely on human observers to record data that reflect some characteristic of the behavior observed; rate, duration, magnitude, or latency measures, for instance.

The use of human observers has proved advantageous to the field in at least two respects. First, it has allowed researchers to conduct analyses across a wide range of settings. Although much of the initial research began in controlled situations (e.g., institutions and classrooms), the focus has since expanded to encompass such diverse areas as behavioral medicine and community psychology. Research in these and other areas would not have been practical without the flexibility possible with human observers. Human observers can be stationed in virtually any location to observe and record data, whereas the use of mechanical recording devices is limited by the necessary power supply. Second, regardless of the setting in which behavior is observed, human observers can more readily detect and record diverse response classes and topographies. Mechanical recording devices traditionally have allowed access to very circumscribed behaviors. For example, Lindsley (1960) studied lever pulling responses of psychotic patients and found

TERRY J. PAGE and BRIAN A. IWATA • Division of Behavioral Psychology, The John F. Kennedy Institute, Johns Hopkins University School of Medicine, Baltimore, MD 21205.

mechanical recording a practical method of recording and analyzing data. However, many dependent variables currently under study do not result in products readily scored by mechanical devices, or are process measures for which mechanical recording would not be possible.

Despite the advantages of using human observers, drawbacks are apparent. Mechanical recording devices, when their use is practical, allow for the concurrent measurement of a larger number of behaviors for a more extended period of time than is possible with human observers. More importantly, with human observers there is always the possibility that data are collected inaccurately or inconsistently.

In response to the problem of human error, researchers have included an index of interobserver agreement, or reliability, when reporting results. Such an index serves as a statistical summary of the extent to which independent observers agree on the occurrence and nonoccurrence of predetermined classes of behaviors. Indexes that show at least 80% agreement between observers are usually considered sufficient to suggest that obtained data are accurate and reliable. Acceptable-agreement indexes permit an experimenter to conclude that observed changes in behavior are likely due to alterations in responding rather than changes in the way an observer applies an observational code.

Reporting indexes of observer agreement is now a necessary component of applied behavior analysis research. Indeed, a technology of assessing and calculating agreement has developed in the past 10 years. There are, however, several areas of confusion and misunderstanding associated with the use, reporting, and interpretation of agreement indexes.

First, there are different methods of calculating and reporting agreement. Initially, agreement indexes often took the form of correlation coefficients, but in recent years additional methods of computing agreement have been reported. At present, there are many different methods by which an experimenter may assess, calculate, and report agreement (Kelly, 1977). These methods vary widely in their precision, sensitivity, and the information they provide.

Second, it is quite possible that obtained agreement indexes may not exceed those figures expected on the basis of chance alone (Harris & Ciminero, 1978; Harris & Lahey, 1978; Hopkins & Herman, 1977; Johnson & Bolstad, 1973; Yelton, Wildman, & Erickson, 1977). In such cases, internal validity of a study should be questioned. Although it is possible to calculate chance agreement for any observational system, and several researchers recommend doing so, many reports in the literature fail to acknowledge this source of confounding.

Third, agreement may be reported on different levels of the dependent variable under study. Which level is chosen for the calculation of agreement again results in differing degrees of sensitivity and information (Hartmann, 1977; Johnson & Bolstad, 1973).

Fourth, there are many factors inherent in the typical observation system that can confound agreement scores. Phenomena such as observer bias and drift, observer expectancy, complexity of the observation code, predictability of observed behavior, and experimenter feedback to observers can affect agreement.

The purposes of this chapter are to (a) provide a historical perspective of current interobserver agreement methods, (b) illustrate the basic methods of assessing and calculating agreement indexes, (c) provide a critical review of problems associated with these indexes, and (d) discuss further considerations in the design of interobserver-agreement methods.

HISTORICAL PERSPECTIVE

The concept of reliability, or interobserver agreement, in applied behavior analysis is closely related to that of reliability in the field of psychological tests and measurement. Testing instruments designed to quantify some characteristic of behavior often serve as the basis for predicting performance at a future time or under different circumstances, and aid in several areas of decision making: (a) selection/rejection of individuals, (b) classification of individuals, (c) evaluation of treatments or programs, (d) verification of scientific hypotheses.

In addition to reliability, other concepts, such as accuracy, objectivity, and validity, are important in any discussion of measurement. Each is briefly outlined below in terms of its importance to the fields of psychological testing and behavior analysis.

Reliability. The *reliability* of a test refers to its consistency in measuring performance. With all tests, there will be some variation in a person's performance from one testing session to another. Although some of the variation will be the result of actual differences in the level of responding, some will be the result of errors in the testing instrument that vary from one measurement to the next. A reliability coefficient, in the form of a statistical index, expresses what proportion of variation observed across two or more administrations of a test is due to natural differences in the performance of the person tested, rather than error in the testing instrument. Thus, an index of reliability serves as a quantitative expression of a test's consistency.

There are at least four commonly used methods of assessing the reliability of a measuring instrument. One, referred to as *test–retest* reliability, provides a coefficient of a test's stability, or consistency across time. To obtain a measure of test–retest reliability, a test is given to a person (or group) and then readministered at a later time. Responses from the two administrations are then compared item by item for consistency. Error in the testing instrument is determined by differential performance in the two administrations and is reflected in the index of reliability.

A second type of reliability, referred to as *parallel-test*, or *alternate-forms*, provides a measure not only of stability, but also equivalence, or the consistency of the items comprising a test. Although similar in logic to test–retest reliability, alternate-forms reliability involves the administration not of the same test at different times, but of different (parallel) tests, at the same time. The two parallel tests are designed to measure the same skill, but are composed of different test items. Scores on the two tests are compared for consistency.

Another type of reliability that yields a coefficient of equivalence is *split-half reliabilty*. Here, a test is divided into two equal parts (e.g., odd and even numbered items), and a comparison is made between the answers to questions in the two parts. When performances on the two halves are highly correlated, reliability of measurement is assumed.

Another way in which reliability can be described is with *Kuder–Richardson* reliability (cited in Helmstadter, 1964). A test is arranged such that items become increasingly more difficult, under the assumption that a person administered the test will reach a point before which all items will be correctly answered, and after which all items will be incorrectly answered. A test yielding such ideal performance would be given a rating of perfect reliability according to the criteria of Kuder–Richardson. The degree to which answers conform to this criterion determines the degree of reliability achieved.

Recently in the applied behavior analysis literature there has been a trend away from the use of the term *reliability*, with *interobserver agreement* more frequently used in its place. It is sometimes said that reliability is more applicable to traditional testing instruments than the measurement procedures used in applied behavior analysis. In testing, the instrument is assessed in terms of its reliability across either different testings or time. With each of the four types of reliability discussed, the amount of variation in performance is presumed to be kept to a minimum: either from one testing to another with the same instrument (test–retest), or from one test to a different, parallel test (alternate forms), or from one half of a test to the other half (split-half), or among different levels of complexity within a test (Kuder–Richardson). Due to the variability inherent in most applied target behaviors, particularly across experimental conditions, the utility of assessing the reliability of an observational instrument, in the traditional sense, seems questionable. As Baer (1977) pointed out, traditional reliability procedures have addressed whether a psychological test measures anything at all, with the result being that the essence of reliability is the homogeneity of the items combined to produce a given score. Baer (1977) argued that with behavior analysis studies there is no reason to believe that even trials or observation intervals within an observation session will be homogeneous.

However, it is possible to consider interobserver agreement scores as a type of alternate forms reliability. When observer agreement is assessed, the two observers can be considered analogous to the two parallel forms of a testing instrument used in determining alternate forms reliability. The resulting index of interobserver agreement is a summary statistic of equivalence or the extent to which the two observers independently measured the same behavior. The information provided is quite similar to that obtained from an alternate forms reliability coefficient.

Another type of traditional testing reliability that is directly related to measurement systems in applied behavior analysis is test–retest reliability. An observer's ability to measure ongoing behavior can be subjected to a similar analysis by having an observer rescore behavior from a videotape at a later time. The extent to which the two observations are in agreement is a measure of stability and is, thus, analogous to a coefficient of test–retest reliability. However, the importance of assessing such agreement may be limited, due to the usual variability in responding. Because the behavior under study will likely vary from its baseline level to one resulting from some intervention, it is important to show high interobserver agreement across an entire experiment, that is, to show that the measurement instrument is consistently reliable across different levels of responding.

Objectivity. An important characteristic of any test that purports to measure and predict human behavior is its *objectivity*, or the extent to which two independent test examiners can evaluate a person's performance and arrive at similar conclusions. If examiners using the same measuring instrument draw differing conclusions and predictions from the same test performance, the instrument is not objective. When the individual examiner's subjective interpretations enter into decision making, the reliability of a prediction is determined largely by the expertise or intuitive skills of the examiner rather than by test performance itself.

The Rorshach test, as used in psychoanalytic assessment, is an example of a measuring instrument with a low degree of objectivity. The same set of responses by an individual can be interpreted by different experts, with differing inferences and predictions made concerning an individual's behavior. An example of a highly objective measuring instrument would be the Graduate Record Examination, used to screen applicants to graduate school. An individual's responses to test questions can be scored by several examiners, with all most likely arriving at the same numerical score.

Because of its emphasis on the manipulation of observable and measurable aspects of human behavior, applied behavior analysis is also concerned with the objectivity of measurement instruments. Specifically, the degree to which at least two independent observers can objectively apply the same set of behavioral definitions to ongoing human behavior, or its artifacts, is of great importance (Baer, Wolf, & Risley, 1968) and is directly addressed by interobserver agreement indexes. Acceptable agreement between independent observers increases confidence that behavioral definitions in an observation system are objective.

Validity. Another term important to the field of psychological testing is *validity*, or the degree to which a testing instrument measures what it purports to measure. For example, a test designed to measure a child's readiness for school must assess exactly those behaviors that contribute to successful school adjustment in order to be valid. If the test measures instead many behaviors presumed important to adjustment but not critical, and fails to measure those actually necessary, it will not be a valid predictor. Although the validity of measurement instruments is important in applied behavior analysis, the issue is primarily relevant to the broader question of social validity (cf. Kazdin, 1977a) and does not bear directly on interobserver agreement.

Accuracy. Although it is sometimes presumed that acceptable indexes of interobserver agreement guarantee acceptable accuracy, such is not the case. It is important to know that observers are scoring behavior accurately with regard to the definitions used in the observation system, but typical methods of assessing interobserver agreement fail to address the question. It is quite possible for two observers to be consistently in perfect agreement, and yet be inaccurately applying response definitions. This problem, inherent in any attempt to assess agreement, is covered more thoroughly in discussions of observer bias and observer drift (e.g., Kazdin, 1977b).

Although it is true that high interobserver agreement does not guarantee accuracy, a well designed observation system, with careful attention to sources of confounding, can suggest accuracy. When the possibility of observer bias and drift are controlled (cf. Kazdin, 1977b), agreement can be considered to reflect accuracy.

INITIAL ASSESSMENT TECHNIQUES

Early in the development of applied behavior analysis, primarily three methods of assessing interobserver agreement were emphasized. All three, correlation coefficients, total agreement, and interval agreement, have since been found deficient in one or more aspects and are now rarely used alone when other more stringent indexes of agreement are available. Each is discussed here in terms of the information it provides, with particular attention to problems that can arise when attempting to use it.

Correlation Coefficients. One of the earliest methods of quantifying interobserver agreement involved the use of correlation. A statistical summary of the relationship between two variables, a correlation coefficient provides information on the extent to which two observers' scoring shows similar patterns. The most common type of coefficient presented has been the product–moment calculation.

The formula for calculating a product—moment correlation is

$$r = \frac{\Sigma(d_x)(d_y)}{N\sigma_x\sigma_y}$$

where x represents the scores from one observer and y the scores from the second observer; d_x and d_y are deviations of each score from its mean, N is the number of sessions over which the correlation is computed, and σ_x and σ_y are the standard deviations of the x and y scores, respectively (Hilgard & Atkinson, 1967).

Table 1 provides a hypothetical example of a product–moment computation based on the numbers of responses (or some other measure such as trials or percent of intervals) recorded by two observers during each of five sessions. Given d_x and d_y, the deviations of individual observers' scores from their means, the right hand column shows the products of these deviations and its sum (102), which is divided by the product of the number of sessions (5) and the standard deviations of the two observers' scores (4 and 6, respectively). For the data shown in Table 1, the resulting product–moment correlation is .85 (cf. Cronbach, 1960, and

Table 1. Computation of a Product–Moment Correlation

Sessions	Observer 1 x	Observer 2 y	(d_x)	(d_y)	$(d_x)(d_y)$
1	71	39	6	9	54
2	67	27	2	−3	−6
3	65	33	0	3	0
4	63	30	−2	0	0
5	59	21	−6	−9	54
Sum	325	150	0	0	102
Mean	65	30			

$x = 4; y = 6.$

$$r = \frac{\Sigma\,(d_x)(d_y)}{N\sigma_y\sigma_y} = \frac{102}{5 \times 4 \times 6} = .85$$

Gehring, 1978, for slightly different methods of calculating product–moment correlation coefficients).

There are three major problems with using correlation coefficients. First, it is possible to obtain high coefficients when one observer consistently scores more occurrences of behavior relative to a second observer. Even if the discrepancy between observers is quite large, high correlations can be obtained if the difference is consistently in one direction. The computation shown in Table 1 provides an example. The two observers' scores were widely discrepant, yet similar trends in the reported data of the two observers produced a coefficient of .85. Because a coefficient of .80 is usually considered minimally acceptable, the hypothetical observers whose data are shown in Table 1 would be considered to be in sufficient agreement on the occurrence of the behavior under study, even though their scores are quite different for each of the five sessions.

Second, with correlation coefficients there is no indication of whether or not observers agreed on the same exact occurrences of behavior. Because observers' data summed across an entire session are used as the basis for calculation, perfect correlation will be obtained as long as the observers have the same number of occurrences. Two observers could each score a total of 20 responses during a 10 minute session; although Observer 1 scored all 20 responses during the initial 5 minutes and Observer 2 scored all 20 responses during the final 5 minutes, a perfect correlation would be obtained even though the observers never agreed on the occurrence of a single response.

A third problem with correlation coefficients is that as the range of the dependent variable under study becomes greater, higher correlation coefficients become more probable. If a behavior occurs at a low rate, for example 10 times per session, two observers must agree rather closely for an acceptable correlation coefficient to be obtained. If the same behavior occurs at a higher rate, say 100 times per session, observers need agree less frequently to obtain an acceptable coefficient.

Total Agreement. A more rigorous method of calculating agreement than correlation coefficients, total agreement was another of the initial attempts at quantifying observer reliability. Also known as *Type I reliability*, an index of total agreement describes the extent to which two observers record the same number of occurrences of behavior.

Figure 1 provides an example of calculating total agreement. Hypothetical data are shown for two observers who have recorded occurrences of a behavior during a session comprised of 20 time intervals or trials. Observers marked "B" on the data sheet in any interval during which behavior was observed; blank or empty intervals denote the nonoccurrence of behavior. For example, during Interval 1 both observers recorded the behavior as occurring, and during Interval 2 neither observer scored the behavior as occurring.

In calculating total agreement, one must sum the number of responses scored by each observer across the session, divide the smaller number by the larger, and then multiple the quotient by 100. Thus, calculating total agreement based on the observation sheets in Figure 1, the percent agreement would be $6/6 \times 100 = 100\%$.

One advantage of total reliability over some form of correlation coefficient is that it is more sensitive to discrepancies in the overall level of responding. Observers must agree closely on the actual number of occurrences of the behavior in order to obtain a high index of total agreement. Thus, total agreement avoids the problem with correlation coefficients in which an acceptable index may be obtained despite one observer consistently overestimating the other. A second advantage is the computational simplicity of total agreement compared with that of correlation coefficients.

However, total agreement does have a serious weakness. As with correlation coefficients, total occurrences of behavior are used as the basis for computing agreement, and there is no assurance that two observers ever agreed on the same occurrences of behavior. The records shown in Figure 1 provide an illustration of this problem. Total agreement was shown to be 100%, and yet when the records are examined more closely it can be seen that correspondence between the two observers occurred in only two of the 20 intervals (Intervals 1 and 19).

Interval Agreement. A third method of calculating agreement has been termed *interval, overall, combined,* or *Type II reliability.* The interval statistic is more sensitive than either the correlation coefficient or total

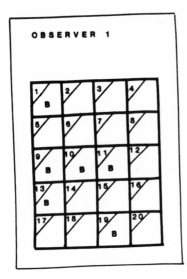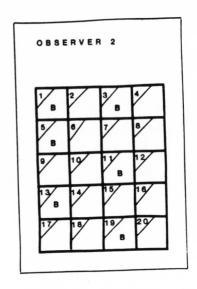

1. Total Agreement:

$$= \frac{S}{L} \times 100$$

$$= \frac{6}{6} \times 100$$

$$= 100\%$$

2. Interval Agreement:

$$= \frac{A}{A + D} \times 100$$

$$= \frac{16}{16 + 4} \times 100$$

$$= 80\%$$

3. Occurrence Agreement:

$$= \frac{A_{occ}}{A_{occ} + D} \times 100$$

$$= \frac{4}{4 + 4} \times 100$$

$$= 50\%$$

4. Nonoccurrence Agreement:

$$= \frac{A_{non}}{A_{non} + D} \times 100$$

$$= \frac{12}{12 + 4} \times 100$$

$$= 80\%$$

FIGURE 1. Simulated data sheets for two observers recording the occurrence of behavior within each of 20 observation intervals. Intervals in which a behavior was observed by either observer are marked *B* on the respective observer's data sheet. Also shown are calculations for the basic agreement indexes (total, interval, occurrence, and nonoccurrence), based on a comparison of the data sheets shown.

agreement, and has become the standard method of reporting agreement in behavior analysis research (Kelly, 1977).

The only requirement that must be met in order to calculate interval agreement is that there be discrete intervals or trials for which agreements and disagreements can be scored. The observation sheets in Figure 1 provide an example of this. Because the hypothetical recording session is divided into 20 intervals, it is possible to score each interval in terms of agreement or disagreement between the two observers. For example, an agreement would be scored for Intervals 1 and 2 because in Interval 1 the observers agreed that the behavior occurred, whereas in Interval 2 they agreed that the behavior did not occur. In Interval 3, though, a disagreement would be scored because the observers disagreed on the occurrence of behavior, Observer 2 scoring the behavior and Observer 1 leaving the observation sheet blank for that interval. In addition to a situation in which a session is divided into intervals, interval agreement can be calculated when discrete trials are scored by observers. Here, each trial is examined and an agreement or disagreement scored between observers.

When calculating interval agreement, the total number of agreements between observers is divided by the number of agreements plus disagreements, and the quotient is multiplied by 100. Using the observers' records shown in Figure 1, interval agreement is $16/(16 + 4) \times 100 = 80\%$. Observers 1 and 2 agreed on the occurrence or nonoccurrence in 16 intervals (1,2,4,6,7,8,11,12,13,14,15,16,17,18,19,20) and disagreed in four intervals (3,5,9,10).

The preceding calculations highlight the more stringent nature of interval agreement compared to correlational measures and total agreement. By using the same observer data as those used to compute a total index of 100%, an interval index of 80% was obtained. The greater sensitivity to agreement on specific behaviors can be attributed to the focus on discrete intervals or trials. In order to obtain a high index of agreement with the interval calculation, observers must agree on the occurrence of behavior within short intervals, increasing the likelihood that they are scoring the same episodes of behavior. This is in contrast to correlational measures where observers need not even agree on total occurrences, and total agreement where observers need never agree on specific occurrences. Because of this characteristic of interval agreement, it has replaced total agreement as the preferred statistic when discrete intervals or trials make its application possible.

Despite advantages of the interval statistic over correlation and total indexes, interval agreement does have one inherent weakness. The statistic can be affected dramatically by extreme rates of the dependent measure. When a behavior occurs very infrequently, say during one or two of 20 observation intervals, there will likely be a high index of agreement due to the large number of intervals in which observers agreed that the behavior did not occur. In such a case, a high percentage of agreement may be a spurious representation because the observers rarely (or perhaps, never) agreed on the occurrence of behavior. A similar problem exists where behavior occurs very frequently. Agreement can be spuriously high because of the large number of agreements on occurrence. This problem with interval agreement is discussed in more detail in the section on chance agreement.

Exact Agreement. Another method of assessing agreement that is more stringent than the initial techniques has been termed *exact agreement* (Repp, Dietz, Boles, Dietz, & Repp, 1976). A requirement for calculating exact agreement is that observers record the frequency of some behavior within discrete intervals or trials.

When calculating exact agreement, an interval is scored as one of agreement only when both observers have recorded the same exact number of instances of behavior. Figure 2 illustrates such a calculation, and is based on hypothetical observers having scored the actual frequency of behavior within each interval by making a tally for each corresponding occurrence. Because of the different observation method shown in Figure 2, that is, tallying frequencies within each interval, it is possible to calculate an exact agreement index. As can be seen, the observers agreed on the exact frequency of behavior in the first interval only, yielding an exact agreement index of $1/(1 + 19) \times 100 = 5\%$.

Exact agreement is more sensitive to agreement on specific instances of behavior than other indexes (e.g., total and interval agreement). However, because the criterion for agreement is so stringent, it is often difficult to demonstrate high agreement between observers, as Figure 2 illustrates. As shown above, an exact agreement index of 5% is obtained from the data shown in Figure 2. Yet, because the observers agreed in all but four intervals (3,8,12,16) that at least some behavior occurred, the resulting index of interval agreement would be $16/(16 + 4) \times 100 = 80\%$.

A variation of exact agreement has been described by Bailey and Bostow (1979) and termed *block-by-block agreement*. As with exact agreement, the calculation of this index is possible only when observers have recorded the frequency of occurrence within time intervals (as illustrated in Figure 2). When calculating block-by-block agreement, an index of total agreement is computed for each interval, by dividing the smaller of the two observers' scores by the larger. The resulting quotients are

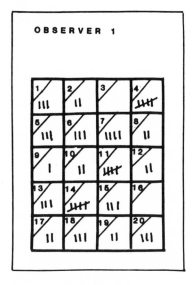

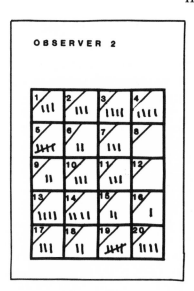

Exact Agreement:

$$= \frac{A_{freq}}{A_{freq} + D} \times 100$$

$$= \frac{1}{1 + 19} \times 100$$

$$= 5 \%$$

FIGURE 2. Simulated data sheets for two observers recording the frequency of one behavior within each of 20 observation intervals. For each interval, the frequency of occurrence is indicated by the number of hatch marks. Also shown is the calculation for an exact agreement index based on a comparison of the data sheets shown.

then summed and divided by the number of observation intervals, with the quotient then multiplied by 100. As shown in Figure 2, block-by-block agreement for the hypothetical observers' records is 10.72/20 × 100 = 54%.

An advantage of block-by-block over exact agreement is that it avoids the extremely stringent criterion for agreement inherent in the calculation of the latter statistic. And when its use is possible (i.e., frequency of responding is recorded within time intervals), a block-by-block index affords a more rigorous estimate of agreement than the alternative of computing an index of total agreement.

THE CHANCE AGREEMENT PROBLEM

Early in the development of behavioral observation methodology, a major drawback with the use of an interval agreement index was identified by Bijou, Peterson, and Ault (1968). The problem is rooted in the fact that the statistic changes as a function of extreme rates of occurrence in the behavior under study. The problem can be characterized as part of a more general phenomenon in which obtained agreement may actually be less than that which would be expected between two observers due to chance. For example, two observers randomly scoring data sheets can be expected to agree some percent of the time due to chance alone, with the level of chance agreement being directly affected by the rate of the behavior under study. When a behavior occurs at a very low rate, chance agreement increases dramatically due to the large number of potential agreements on nonoccurrence, and when the behavior occurs frequently, chance agreement increases due to the potential agreement on occurrence. The problem of chance agreement has received considerable attention recently, with differing solutions proposed by different authors.

Bijou *et al.* (1968) were the first to describe chance agreement and suggest that researchers report two indexes of agreement—one considering only agreements on occurrence of behavior, and one considering only agreements on nonoccurrence. However, no guidelines or details were provided regarding how the calculations would be made or in what ways they would be used by researchers and consumers.

Johnson and Bolstad (1973) used the term *base-rate problem* in their discussion of chance agreement, with "base-rate" referring to the actual rate of behavior under study. These authors suggested a formula by which chance agreement may be calculated, taking into consideration the base-rate of the dependent measure. The calculation consists of squaring the base rate of each behavior scored (or in the case of a behavior dichotomized as occurring or not occurring, squaring the totals of these categories), and then summing the values. Referring to Figure 1, it can be seen that Observer 1 scored behavior as occurring 30% of the time (i.e., in six intervals), and as not occurring the remaining 70% (14 intervals). Thus, chance agreement would be computed as follows:

$$\text{Agreement} = .30^2 + .70^2$$

$$A = .09 + .49$$

$$A = .58$$

Therefore, given the scoring pattern shown in Figure 1, an agreement index of 58% could be expected due only to chance. Johnson and Bolstad (1973) suggested that an index of chance agreement always be calculated and reported along with the obtained index of interobserver agreement. Consumers would then be able to judge whether obtained agreement exceeds chance agreement and, if so, to what degree.

Hawkins and Dotson (1975) provided a more in-depth analysis of the chance agreement problem and presented a solution, consistent with that of Bijou *et al.* (1968). Hawkins and Dotson (1975) proposed reporting an index of agreement only on occurrence when the behavior is observed at a low rate, and reporting an agreement index only on nonoccurrence when the behavior is observed at a high rate. The former index has been termed *scored-interval agreement* (Hawkins & Dotson, 1975), *occurrence agreement* (Bailey & Bostow, 1979; Bijou *et al.*, 1968; Hopkins & Hermann, 1977), *response intervals only agreement* (Repp *et al.*, 1976), and *effective percentage agreement-occurrence* (Hartmann, 1977). The latter has been called *unscored-interval agreement* (Hawkins & Dotson, 1975), *nonoccurrence agreement* (Bailey & Bostow, 1979; Bijou *et al.*, 1968; Hopkins & Hermann, 1977; Johnson & Bolstad, 1973; Kelly, 1977), and *effective percentage agreement-nonoccurrence* (Hartmann, 1977). In this chapter, the indexes will be referred to as *occurrence agreement* and *nonoccurrence agreement*, respectively.

As with interval agreement, the only requirement for computing either occurrence or nonoccurrence agreement is that observation sessions are divided into intervals or discrete trials within which behavior is scored. Thus, the observation records shown in Figure 1 can be used to illustrate the calculation of these indexes.

Occurrence Agreement. When calculating occurrence agreement the computation is the same as that used for calculating interval agreement, that is, number of agreements is divided by agreements plus disagreements and multiplied by 100. The definition of what constitutes an agreement is different, however. When tallying agreements, only those intervals (or trials) during which both observers scored an occurrence of behavior are counted. Those intervals during which neither observer scored an occurrence of behavior are not included in the calculation. For example, Figure 1 shows that observers agreed on occurrence during only four intervals (1,11,13,19), and disagreed during four intervals (3,5,9,10). The other 12 intervals were scored by both as nonoccurrences. Thus, agreement on occurrence is 4/(4 + 4) × 100 = 50%.

Nonoccurrence Agreement. When calculating nonoccurrence agreement, only those intervals in which observers agreed that behavior did not occur are counted as agreements, and intervals in which both scored an occurrence are not included. In Figure 1 it can be seen that observers agreed on nonoccurrence in 12 intervals (2,4,6,7,8,12,14,15,16,17,18,10) and disagreed in the same four intervals noted when calculating occurrence agreement. Thus, nonoccurrence agreement is 12(12 + 4) × 100 = 75%.

The preceding calculations illustrate the utility of occurrence and nonoccurrence agreement indexes when a target behavior occurs at extreme rates. Occurrence agreement is more conservative than interval for low rate behaviors because the many intervals during which there is agreement on nonoccurrence are not included in the calculation. Nonoccurrence agreement, on the other hand, is a more conservative index for high rate behaviors because intervals with agreement on occurrence are discarded.

The calculations shown in Figure 1 provide a comparison between occurrence agreement and interval agreement. For the low-rate behavior shown, interval agreement is 80%. Yet when occurrence agreement is calculated, an index of 50% is obtained. With such low-rate behaviors, occurrence agreement yields a more rigorous reflection of the extent to which observers actually agree. Because occurrence and nonoccurrence indexes yield a more stringent index of agreement, they have been suggested as appropriate indexes for studies in which low- and high-rate behaviors, respectively, are examined. However, there are three problems with reporting either index alone. First, there are no accepted guidelines for what constitutes a low- or high-rate behavior. Kratochwill and Wetzel (1977) suggested a "rule of thumb" that occurrence agreement be reported when behavior is recorded as occurring less than 20% of the time, and nonoccurrence agreement be reported when behavior occurs more than 80% of the time. For behaviors occurring at intermediate rates, Kratochwill and Wetzel (1977) suggested reporting interval agreement (although they referred to this latter statistic as "total agreement," the calculation is that of interval agreement). This suggestion is by no means a widely accepted guideline, and which index to report is left to the discretion of the individual researcher.

A second problem exists in the fact that, taken alone, neither occurrence nor nonoccurrence agreement reflects agreement on the total observations made. Thus, with either statistic alone, consumers never are given the complete picture of agreement between observers.

A third problem occurs because of the change in behavior across experimental conditions that occurs in behavioral research. Typically, a behavior occurring at an excessively high (or low) rate is exposed to some intervention designed to change its rate to a more acceptable low (or high) level of occurrence. Thus, with a behavior occurring at a low rate during baseline, occurrence agreement would be suggested as the most accurate index of observer agreement. But if the intervention successfully increases the rate of behavior, occurrence agreement would be spuriously high during intervention.

Mean Occurrence–Nonoccurrence Agreement. Because of the problems associated with reporting either occurrence or nonoccurrence agreement alone, Hawkins and Dotson (1975) suggested calculating the mean of the two, and reporting that statistic as an index of agreement. The requirement for using this statistic is the same as that for using occurrence or nonoccurrence agreement, that is, intervals or discrete trials, within which agreements and disagreements can be scored. The calculation of mean occurrence–nonoccurrence agreement involves computing occurrence and nonoccurrence agreement separately, and then determining the mean of the two. For the data shown in Figure 1 mean occurrence–nonoccurrence agreement is 63%.

The advantages of mean occurrence-nonoccurrence agreement are that it addresses the problems described earlier with using either occurrence or nonoccurrence agreement alone. First, it circumvents the problem of when to report occurrence and when to report nonoccurrence agreement. By reporting the mean of the two, the question of which to report becomes academic. Second, because agreements on both occurrence and nonoccurrence are used in the calculation, it reflects agreement on the total observations made. Third, it could serve as a useful statistic across different experimental conditions, even if behavior changes in rate.

Despite its advantages, mean occurrence–nonoccurrence agreement does have at least two inherent weaknesses. First, it is to some extent affected by extreme rates of behavior in much the same manner as interval agreement. This is particularly so for situations in which no, or very little agreement is obtained on behaviors occurring at extreme rates. For example, if two observers agreed that behaviors occurred in 18 of 20 intervals, but never agreed on nonoccurrence, the occurrence agreement would be $18/(18 + 2) \times 100 = 90\%$, nonoccurrence would be $0/(0 + 2) \times 100 = 0\%$, and the resulting mean of the two would be 45%. In this example, and in similar situations, the mean index may provide an unrepresentatively poor reflection of agreement.

Second, a mean occurrence–nonoccurrence index is a statistic one step further removed from the actual data obtained. The result of using such statistical abbreviations can be a loss of information, and may result in undesirable effects on the experimenter and the consumer.

Hopkins and Hermann (1977) also discussed chance agreement, and presented the following solutions to the problem. Their first recommendation was that researchers report interobserver agreement as suggested by Bijou *et al.* (1968) and Hawkins and Dotson, (1975), that is, report agreement on occurrence and nonoccurrence separately, or the mean of the two. Their second recommendation was that researchers calculate and publish indexes of chance agreement, against which obtained indexes could be compared. The formula suggested by Hopkins and Hermann (1977), although slightly different than that proposed by Johnson and Bolstad (1973), yields a similar statistic. According to Hopkins and Hermann (1977), chance agreement equals:

$$\frac{(O_1 \times O_2) + (N_1 \times N_2)}{T^2} \times 100$$

where O_1 and O_2 are the number of intervals in which Observer 1 and Observer 2 recorded the behavior as occurring, N_1 and N_2 are the number of intervals in which Observer 1 and Observer 2 recorded the behavior as not occurring, and T is the total number of intervals for which the observers' records were compared. The formula yields the agreement index that would be expected due to chance alone, given the rate of occurrence recorded by the two observers. However, the formula yields a more accurate estimate of chance agreement than the one suggested by Johnson and Bolstad (1973), because it takes into account the rates of behavior recorded by both observers (O_1 & O_2 in the formula). The formula of Johnson and Bolstad (1973) assumes that two observers have recorded behavior as occurring in approximately the same number of intervals.

To illustrate the calculation of Hopkins and Hermann (1977), chance agreement for the observers' records shown in Figure 1 would be determined as follows:

$$\frac{(6 \times 6) + (14 \times 14)}{20^2} \times 100 = 58\%$$

The obtained index, 58%, is identical to that yielded by the calculation of Johnson & Bolstad only because both observers recorded the same rates of behavior. Had one observer recorded fewer or more intervals of behavior than the other, a different index of chance agreement would have been obtained.

Yelton, Wildman, and Erickson (1977), although providing an analysis of the chance agreement problem similar to that of Bijou *et al.* (1968),

Hawkins and Dotson (1975), and Hopkins and Hermann (1977), suggested a slightly different solution. Yelton et al. (1977) suggested calculating and reporting a statistic indicating the exact probability that the obtained number of agreements, or higher, would have occurred due to chance. The formula, which is based on probability theory, is considerably more complex and time consuming to apply than those suggested by Johnson and Bolstad (1973) and Hopkins and Hermann (1977). The formula is

$$\sum_{Z=A}^{y} \times \frac{Y!}{Z!(Y-Z)!} \times \frac{X!}{(X-X)!} \times \frac{(N-X)!}{((N-X)-(Y-Z))} \times \frac{N-Y)!}{N!}$$

where A is the number of agreements on occurrence, N is the number of intervals, X is the number of occurrences recorded by Observer 1, and Y is the number of occurrences recorded by Observer 2. (When labeling observers, the recorded frequency of behavior for Observer 1 must be equal to or greater than that of Observer 2.)

Yelton et al. (1977) argued not only for the above calculation, but also that calculations be made for any possible greater number of agreements. For example, again referring to Figure 1, a calculation would be made based on the obtained four agreements between observers. In addition, though, calculations must be made assuming five, and then six agreements, because both observers recorded six occurrences, making it possible for them to agree up to six times.

The formula suggested by Yelton et al. (1977) has at least three disadvantages and has not seen widespread use. First, it is quite time consuming to perform manually. Although the authors mention the availability of a computer program that circumvents the complexity of calculation for researchers having access to a computer, the complexity involved in manual computation speaks against its use. Second, a basic understanding of probability theory is necessary to understand the logic of the statistic. Third, the statistic is quite far removed from the actual data (i.e., the frequency of agreements between two observers), further complicating interpretation.

Hartmann (1977) has suggested yet another method of calculating interobserver agreement in which chance agreement is taken into account. He recommended reporting a correlational-like measure, Kappa (K), a statistic developed by Cohen (1960). Kappa reflects the proportion of agreements, with correction for agreements due to chance. The formula is: $(P_o - P_c)/(1 - P_c)$, where P_o is the proportion of obtained agreements, and P_c is the proportion of chance or expected agreements. For the observers' records shown in Figure 1, the calculation of Kappa is

$$\frac{(0.8 - 0.58)}{(1.0 - 0.58)} = .52$$

Problems associated with Kappa are similar to those noted with the Yelton et al. (1977) formula: Its interpretation requires greater sophistication in statistics than do more conventional indexes, and the statistic is far removed from the actual data on observer agreement. However, this statistic is much easier to calculate than the Yelton et al. (1977) formula, and it has become more frequently reported in the literature to express agreement.

Harris and Lahey (1978) suggested a variation on reporting occurrence and/or nonoccurrence agreement. These authors produced three arguments to advise against occurrence and nonoccurrence index. First, occurrence and nonoccurrence indexes may overcompensate for chance agreement by discarding all agreements on unscored or scored intervals, respectively. Second, as mentioned, neither index alone is appropriate in experiments where rates of behavior vary across conditions. Third, the reporting of both occurrence and nonoccurence is an unnecessary inconvenience for the research consumer (cf. Kratochwill and Wetzel, 1977).

As an alternative, Harris and Lahey (1978) suggested a variation of a statistic reported by Clement (1976). The Clement (1976) formula is $(A \times B) + (C \times D)$, where A is the number of agreements on occurrence divided by the number of intervals marked by the primary observer; B is 1.00 minus (the number of occurrences marked by the primary observer divided by the total number of intervals); C is the number of agreements for nonoccurrence divided by the number of nonoccurrences marked by the primary observer; D is 1.00 minus (the number of nonoccurrence marked by the primary observer divided by the total number of time samples).

The formula yields a weighted mean of indexes of occurrence and nonoccurrence agreement. Weight is assigned to the two indexes according to the rate of the behavior observed. The statistic thus circumvents the problems with occurrence and nonoccurrence indexes identified by Harris and Lahey (1978). However, Harris and Lahey (1978) cited two weaknesses in the Clement (1976) formula. First, A and C should include the number of intervals marked by either observer rather than only the primary observer. Second, B and D should be the mean of occurrences and nonoccurrences, respectively, recorded by both observers rather than just the primary observer. Harris and Lahey (1978) suggested the following formula as a more appropriate measure than the one proposed by Clement (1976).

Weighted Agreement = $(O \times U) + (N \times S) \times 100$, where O is the occurrence agreement score, that is, the number of agreements on occurrence divided by the number of agreements on occurrence plus the number of disagreements; U is the mean proportion of unscored intervals, that is, the proportion of intervals not scored by Observer 1 plus the proportion of intervals not scored by Observer 2 divided by two; N is the nonoccurrence agreement score, that is, the number of agreements on nonoccurrences divided by the number of agreements on nonoccurrence plus the number of disagreements; S is the mean proportion of scored intervals, that is, the proportion of intervals scored by Observer 1 plus the proportion of intervals scored by Observer 2 divided by two. Using the observer's records shown in Figure 1, we can determine the weighted agreement to be

$$\left(\frac{4}{4+4}\right)\left(\frac{.70 + .70}{2}\right) + \left(\frac{1.2}{12+4}\right)\left(\frac{.30 + .30}{2}\right) \times 100 = 58\%$$

Although based on sound statistical logic, the weighted agreement mean has not been widely adopted in applied behavior analysis research, and the utility of the statistic remains to be demonstrated.

Repp *et al.* (1976) made a comparison of interval, occurrence, and nonoccurrence indexes similar to Hawkins and Dotson, (1975), but went further by analyzing total and exact agreement as well. Also, in addition to comparing the various methods of assessing agreement, length of the observation interval was varied, with resulting effects on agreement examined. Based on the results of their comparisons, Repp *et al.* (1976) drew five conclusions. First, total and interval agreement were similar, with interval actually yielding higher agreement with three of the five response classes examined. Second, interval agreement produced indexes averaging 14% higher than exact agreement for all five responses classes. Third, total agreement was an average of 12% higher than exact agreement with four of the five response classes. Fourth, occurrence agreement was consistently lower than interval agreement, with a difference of 7% between the two response classes. Fifth, as the length of the observation interval increased, the difference between interval and exact agreement increased, with exact agreement decreasing whereas interval indexes increased.

Birkimer and Brown (1979) compared interval agreement with occurrence, nonoccurrence, and occurrence-nonoccurrence agreement. Surprisingly, these authors recommended interval agreement over the other three indexes. Their rationale centered around weaknesses of the other methods. One problem identified by Birkimer and Brown (1979) concerns the way in which occurrence and nonoccurrence indexes are affected by the rate of the behavior. Assuming a constant rate of disagreement between two observers, say during 10% of intervals observed, occurrence (nonoccurrence) agreement decreases as the rate of behavior decreases (increases). For example, given 100 observation intervals during a session in which observers disagreed 10 times or 10%, if there were 40 agreements on occurrence, occurrence agreement would be $40/(40 + 10) \times 100 = 80\%$. If, however, observers agreed on occurrence during only 20 intervals, and still disagreed on 10% of the intervals, occurrence agreement would be $20/(20 + 10) \times 10 = 67\%$. As Birkimer and Brown (1979) indicated, interval agreement is algebraically a direct function only of rate of disagreement, and thus yields a constant index of agreement, given a constant rate of disagreement, regardless of the rate of behavior. This aspect of occurrence agreement can be troublesome in applied research where an experimenter attempts to reduce the frequency of a high-rate behavior. Acceptable agreement may occur during baseline, but as the rate of behavior decreases, agreement may decrease to unacceptable levels even though the percent of disagreement remains constant.

Another strategy for dealing with chance agreement is to report three agreement indexes together—interval, occurrence, and nonoccurrence. Although this method has yet to be formally proposed, several studies have reported agreement in this fashion (e.g., Page, Iwata, & Neef, 1976; Powell, Martindale, & Kulp, 1975; Rapport, Murphy, & Bailey, 1982). Reporting all three indexes may have sufficient advantages to recommend its use. First, it effectively controls for chance agreement. If all three indexes are acceptable (i.e., above 80%) the possibility of chance agreement exceeding obtained agreement can be ruled out. Second, the problem of which index to report under different rates of behavior is avoided. Third, the three indexes together are appropriate across experimental conditions, even when the rate of the dependent variable changes. Fourth, agreement is shown on all data, rather than excluding certain intervals as is the case with occurrence or nonoccurrence alone. Fifth, unlike some complex statistics, these three indexes are not far removed from the actual data.

BASIC CONSIDERATIONS IN REPORTING AGREEMENT

Applied researchers are faced with four interrelated decisions in assessing and reporting interobserver agreement. The first decision involves which of several indexes of agreement to report (Hartmann,

1977; Johnson & Bolstad, 1973). The second concerns specification of the unit score over which agreement should be assessed (Hartmann, 1977; Johnson & Bolstad, 1973). The third decision involves which time span agreement scores will be summed across (Hartmann, 1977; Johnson & Bolstad, 1973). A fourth question is whether or not to co-plot data from reliability observers with that of the primary observer in graphic presentations of dependent variables (Birkimer & Brown, 1979; Hawkins & Dotson, 1975; Kratochwill & Wetzal, 1977).

Agreement Index. The first decision, choice of an index of agreement, involves considering the many issues previously discussed. Unfortunately, an all-inclusive rule is difficult to formulate in light of the number of recommendations in the literature and the absence of objective evaluative criteria (Cone, 1979). However, the following recommendations would seem to meet minimal standards and yet leave room for individual preferences. First, when possible, observation methods should be designed to allow for the calculation of interval-by-interval (or trial-by-trial) agreement as opposed to total (or correlation) agreement. For example, when designing a frequency data-collection system, it would be preferable to have observers record frequencies within short time intervals rather than tally frequencies for an entire observation session. By imposing the shorter time intervals, the calculation of exact or block-by-block agreement is possible, yielding a more rigorous estimate of interobserver agreement.

Second, when the dependent variable occurs at extreme rates it is necessary to supplement the primary agreement index with some summary statistic addressing chance agreement. Each of the many proposed solutions has advantages and disadvantages, and it is beyond the purview of this chapter to nominate one as the most appropriate.

Unit Score. Indexes of agreement should be reported for the unit score according to which the dependent variable is presented (Hartmann, 1977). Often applied studies have examined very circumscribed, narrowly defined target behaviors. For example, the prime dependent measure in a litter control study by Powers, Osborne, and Anderson (1973) was the number of filled trash bags deposited in a marked container, and agreement was reported on that measure. However, researchers have sometimes examined changes in a behavior that is a composite score of a number of more discretely defined classes of behavior. Johnson and Bolstad (1973) argued that in such cases, it is appropriate to report agreement on the composite score rather than the specific behaviors comprising the composite. Johnson and Bolstad (1973) suggested that although an index of agreement on observers' composite scores does not guarantee that independent observers recorded the same behaviors, such information is not important; overall occurrence of the composite behavior over a given period is of primary interest. However, other researchers have calculated agreement in terms of specific responses that are components of a larger, composite target behavior. Koegel, Russo, and Rincover (1977), for example, reported agreement in terms of a composite behavior, correct teaching responses, but when calculating agreement, assessed to what extent observers agreed on the more specific behaviors of which correct teaching behaviors consisted.

Time Span. Hartmann (1977) identified two different time spans over which agreement may be calculated. The first, which he called session reliability, involves calculating agreement for an entire session (or occasionally for longer temporal periods, such as treatment conditions.) With the second, called trial reliability, agreement is calculated for observers' scores during recording intervals or trials. Thus, *session* reliability includes correlation coefficients and total agreement, and provides information on the generalizability of the session scores of a given observer. *Trial* reliability, on the other hand, refers to agreement on individual trials, and may take the form of interval, occurrence, nonoccurrence, mean occurrence–nonoccurrence, or exact agreement.

As with the determination of the unit score over which agreement will be assessed, agreement should be assessed for at least the time span over which the dependent variable is calculated and reported. However, as indicated earlier, it would seem preferrable to always report agreement on the molecular level of analysis provided by trial reliability, even though session reliability may be more closely in line with the dependent measure reported. The disadvantages of the session reliability statistics have been discussed earlier in this chapter, and argue strongly against their use as an aid in assessing interobserver agreement.

Coplotting. Graphic presentation of the actual data collected by a second observer, that is, the reliability assessor, has been suggested by several writers. Hawkins and Dotson (1975) argued that only when such data are offered for visual inspection, rather than in the form of a derived statistic, can consumers adequately judge the true extent of agreement between observers. Presentation of a second observer's data would allow evaluation of differences in observer's scores across experimental conditions, and thus provide more opportunity for detecting observer bias or drift.

Birkimer and Brown (1979) proposed co-plotting as part of a solution to the problem of chance agreement. In addition to coplotting the second observers' data, Birkimer and Brown (1979) proposed plotting disagreement percentages and the limits of chance disagreement ranges.

Kratochwill and Wetzel (1977) also discussed the advantages of coplotting observers' scores, enumerating five benefits to the researcher. First, there is the detection of behavior. On occasion, a second observer will record behavior unnoticed by the primary observer; only through coplotting can these data have an effect on the behavior of the experimenter. Second, an advantage of coplotting is that it forces a researcher to have contact with the actual data rather than merely looking at statistical summaries of agreement. The more closely an experimenter interacts with data, the more likely it is that important relationships suggesting other experimental questions will be observed (cf. Michael, 1974). Third, an evaluation of absolute differences in observers' data is more readily available through coplotting. The direction of differences can be seen for any given observer, and adjustments then made in an observation system. Fourth, there is the benefit of the detection of threats to internal validity. Coplotting would reveal whether the primary observer consistently reported more (or less) occurrence of a behavior when a second observer was present. Fifth, a benefit identified by Kratochwill and Wetzel (1977) concerns sophistication in statistics. Paraprofessionals, parents, clients, and others who might be asked to reliably observe and graph data might be more likely to understand and attend to observer agreement if it were coplotted rather than in summary statistic form.

Kratochwill and Wetzel (1977), however, disagreed with Hawkins and Dotson on the merits of coplotting. They agreed that coplotting can be useful for the researcher, but identified limitations regarding benefits to consumers. First, a disadvantage is the anticipated expense on the part of researchers. Second, there is a concern that misrepresentation of experimental effects could result from the exclusive use of visual analysis of graphical displays.

Other reservations exist regarding the merits of coplotting. One is that individuals may confuse observer agreement with believability of experimental effect (Hartmann, 1979; Kratchowill, 1979). Another issue concerns the lack of standard criteria regarding the judgment of how much discrepancy between observers will be accepted (Hartmann, 1979; Kratochwill, 1979). A third concern is the complexity introduced to any graphic data display when data from a second observer are added (Kratochwill, 1979).

Coplotting has advantages and disadvantages. However, as with other suggestions regarding agreement methods (Birkimer & Brown, 1979; Harris & Lahey, 1978; Yelton et al., 1979), its functional utility remains to be seen. Since the recommendations by Kratochwill and Wetzel (1977) and Birkimer and Brown (1979), the strategy has seen only very limited application.

SUMMARY AND CONCLUSIONS

The documentation of sufficient agreement between independent observers continues to be a necessary component of research in which human observers are used in the collection of data. A historical perspective suggests that the general scope and specific methods for assessing agreement are closely related to the traditional concept of reliability in the field of psychological testing.

The most commonly reported indexes of agreement are product–moment correlation, total, interval, occurrence, nonoccurrence, and more recently, Kappa. Each statistic provides different information due to the specific nature of agreement emphasized by the calculation. Those indexes shown to be more sensitive to changes in agreement on specific instances of behavior (trial reliability) are preferred over those sensitive to changes over a larger time span (session reliability).

A major problem in the assessment of agreement is the issue of chance agreement. Independent observers will agree a certain proportion of observations due only to chance; the specific proportion of chance agreements can be directly related to the rate of occurrence of the behavior under study. Several methods of controlling for chance agreement have been suggested. However, although it is apparent that researchers should design reliability methods so as to take into account the problem of chance agreement, there appears to be little consensus on which of the several proposed suggestions should be adopted.

Other considerations in reporting agreement regard the level of the dependent variable on which agreement is reported, the time span over which agreement is calculated, and whether to coplot the data collected by a reliability observer.

REFERENCES

Baer, D. M. (1977). Reviewer's comment: Just because it's reliable doesn't mean that you can use it. *Journal of Applied Behavior Analysis, 10,* 117–119.
Baer, D. M., Wolf, M. M., & Risley, T. R. (1968). Some current dimensions of applied behavior analysis. *Journal of Applied Behavior Analysis, 1,* 91–97.
Bailey, J. S. & Bostow, D. E. (1979). *Research methods in applied behavior analysis.* Tallahassee, FL: Copy Grafix.
Bijou, S. W., Peterson, R. F., & Ault, M. H. (1968). A method to integrate descriptive and empirical field studies at the level of data and empirical concepts. *Journal of Applied Behavior Analysis, 1,* 175–191.
Birkimer, J. C., & Brown, J. H. (1979). A graphical judgmental aid which summarizes obtained and chance reliability data and helps assess the believability of experimental effects. *Journal of Applied Behavior Analysis, 12,* 523–533.

Clement, P. G. (1976). A formula for computing inter-observer agreement. *Psychological Reports, 39,* 257–258.

Cohen, J. A. (1960). A coefficient of agreement for nominal scales. *Educational and Psychological Measurement, 20,* 37–46.

Cone, J. D. (1979). Why the "I've got a better agreement measure" literature continues to grow: A commentary on two articles by Birkimer and Brown. *Journal of Applied Behavior Analysis, 12,* 571.

Cronbach, L. S. (1960). *Essentials of psychological testing.* New York: Harper & Row.

Gehring, R. E. (1978). *Basic behavioral statistics.* Boston, MA: Houghton Mifflin.

Harris, F. C., & Ciminero, A. R. (1978). The effect of witnessing consequences on the behavioral recordings of experimental observers. *Journal of Applied Behavior Analysis, 11,* 513–521.

Harris, F. C., & Lahey, B. B. (1978). A method for combining occurrence and non-occurrence interobserver agreement scores. *Journal of Applied Behavior Analysis, 11,* 523–527.

Hartmann, D. (1977). Considerations in the choice of inter-observer reliability estimates. *Journal of Applied Behavior Analysis, 10,* 103–116.

Hawkins, R. P. & Dotson, V. A. (1975). Reliability scores that delude: An Alice in Wonderland trip through misleading characteristics of interobserver agreement scores in interval recording. In E. Ramp & G. Semb (Eds.), *Behavior analysis: Areas of research and application* (pp. 359–376). Englewood Cliffs, NJ: Prentice-Hall.

Helmstadter, G. C. (1964). *Principles of psychological measurement.* New York: Appleton-Century-Crofts.

Hilgard, E. R., & Atkinson, R. C. (1967). *Introduction to psychology.* New York: Harcourt, Brace, & World.

Hopkins, B. L., & Hermann, J. A. (1977). Evaluating interobserver reliability of interval data. *Journal of Applied Behavior Analysis, 10,* 121–126.

Johnson, S. M., & Bolstad, O. D. (1973). Methodological issues in naturalistic observation: Some problems and solutions for field research. In L. A. Hamerlynck, L. C. Handy & E. J. Mash (Eds.), *Behavior change: Methodology, concepts and practice* (pp. 7–67). Champaign, IL: Research Press.

Kazdin, A. E. (1977a). Assessing the clinical or applied importance of behavior change through social validation. *Behavior Modification, 1,* 427–451.

Kazdin, A. E. (1977b). Artifact, bias and complexity of assessment: The ABC's of reliability. *Journal of Applied Behavior Analysis, 10,* 141–150.

Kelly, M. B. (1977). A review of observational data-collection and reliability procedures reported in the *Journal of Applied Behavior Analysis, 10,* 97–101.

Koegel, R. L., Russo, D. C., & Rincover, A. (1977). Assessing and training teachers in the generalized use of behavior modification with autistic children. *Journal of Applied Behavior Analysis, 10,* 197–205.

Kratochwill, T. R., & Wetzel, R. J. (1977). Observer agreement, credibility, and judgment: Some considerations in presenting observer agreement data. *Journal of Applied Behavior Analysis, 10,* 133–139.

Lindsley, O. R. (1960). Characterization of the behavior of chronic psychotics as revealed by free operant conditioning methods. *Diseases of the Nervous System,* Monograph Supplement, *21,* 66–78.

Michael, J. (1974). Statistical inference for individual organism research: Mixed blessing or curse? *Journal of Applied Behavior Analysis, 7,* 647–653.

Page, T. J., Iwata, B. A., & Neef, N. A. (1976). Teaching pedestrian skills to retarded persons: Generalization from the classroom to the natural environment. *Journal of Applied Behavior Analysis, 9,* 433–444.

Powell, J., Martindale, A., & Kulp, S. (1975). An evaluation of time-sample measures of behavior. *Journal of Applied Behavior Analysis, 8,* 463–469.

Powers, R. B., Osborne, J. G., & Anderson, E. G. (1973). Positive reinforcement of litter removal in the natural environment. *Journal of Applied Behavior Analysis, 6,* 579–589.

Rapport, M. D., Murphy, H. A., & Bailey, J. S. (1982). Ritalin vs. response cost in the control of hyperactive children: A within-subject comparison. *Journal of Applied Behavior Analysis, 15,* 205–216.

Repp, A. C., Dietz, D. E., Boles, S. M., Dietz, S. M., & Repp, C. F. (1976). Differences among common methods for assessing interobserver agreement. *Journal of Applied Behavior Analysis, 9,* 109–113.

Yelton, A. R., Wildman, B. G., & Erickson, M. T. (1977). A probability based formula for calculating interobserver agreement. *Journal of Applied Behavior Analysis, 10,* 127–131.

7

Simulation Research in the Analysis of Behavior

ROBERT EPSTEIN

INTRODUCTION

The more interesting some instance of human behavior, the more difficult it is to analyze (perhaps that's why we call it interesting). And where objective analysis is difficult, fictions turn up. Consider the following cases: at age one, most children react to their mirror images as if they are seeing other children; by age two, most children react as if they are seeing themselves. How can we account for the change? Does it help to say that the child has developed a "self-concept"?

Virtually all human beings acquire language and, by age five, have rich vocabularies. They also seem capable of emitting an infinite number

This chapter is dedicated to the memory of Don F. Hake who had agreed to write the chapter on simulations for this volume. His death in August 1982 made this impossible. Dr. Hake was a pioneer in the study of cooperative behavior with human subjects and would surely have discussed some of his innovative work in this area. Rather than try to anticipate what he might have said, I have concentrated more on my own work. I urge the interested reader to consult some of Professor Hake's writings directly (e.g., Hake, 1982; Hake & Olvera, 1978; Hake & Vukelich, 1972, 1973). Portions of this chapter were included in an invited address entitled "The Self-Concept and Other Daemons," which was given at the 8th annual meeting of the Association for Behavior Analysis, Milwaukee, May, 1982 (Epstein, 1982b, Epstein & Koerner, 1986).

ROBERT EPSTEIN • Cambridge Center for Behavioral Studies, 11 Ware Street, Cambridge, MA 02138. Research reported herein was supported in part by National Science Foundation grant BNS-8007342 to Harvard University, National Institutes of Health grant MH32628 to the Foundation for Research on the Nervous System, and by a Grant-in-Aid of Research from the Sigma Xi Society.

of different sentences. How can we explain this? Does it help to say that we are born with "language organs" or that a set of "cognitive rules" is guiding us?

A 2-year-old girl is faced with the proverbial "marble-under-the-couch" problem: She stretches toward the marble but cannot reach it. After repeated attempts, she looks around the room and reaches suddenly for a nearby magazine. She casts about with it until she knocks the marble out from under the couch. Do we shed light on this behavior by attributing it to "insight" or "reasoning"? If not, what contribution, if any, can we make?

An audience of cognitive psychologists has listened with adoration to a prominent colleague. A member of the audience, known for his wit, raises his hand, stands, and deadpans, "But how is this relevant to *pigeons*?" There is a swell of laughter and some applause. Could we predict who would laugh? Does it help to say that someone has a "sense of humor"? (Did *you* laugh?)

These and many other instances of complex behavior in people are difficult to analyze for several reasons. First, they are all multiply determined at the time they occur. Sofa, marble, magazine, toys, television, and so on, strengthen many behaviors, and the child's own behavior changes the environment and hence changes the probability of subsequent behavior. Second, they are the result of complex environmental histories and, presumably, biological factors. Language is acquired haphazardly over a period of years, and, though speaking and speaking grammatically may not be systematically taught, it is more effective than not speaking or speaking ungrammatically; in other words, children are exposed from birth to subtle and complex "contingencies of reinforcement" that support speaking and speaking grammatically. Modeling, instructions, and physical maturation also undoubtedly make important contributions. Third, they are all typically human phenomena; problem solving, language, wit, the behaviors that come under the rubric of *self-awareness*, and so on, are all relatively rare in nature; the study of non-human organisms is not as informative as it is for simpler behavioral phenomena. And finally, because the histories are complicated and the phenomena relatively unique to humans, it is difficult, if not impossible, to explore them through experimentation.

Similar problems are faced in many domains of scientific inquiry. Complexity (say, in meteorology), the importance of events in the remote past (say, in evolutionary biology), inaccessibility (say, in astronomy), or ethical considerations (say, in neurology) often prevent direct study. Fortunately, methods have evolved which allow at least some tentative analyses. This chapter concerns one of the most powerful of such methods—the simulation—and its application in the analysis of complex human behavior.

ONE HUNDRED BABIES

B. F. Skinner once told me that an Indian (Asian) tried to induce him to move to India by offering him 100 babies with which to do research. As appalling as the offer may sound, without those babies some of the most interesting questions in the analysis of behavior can never be anwered definitively.

Let us say, for example, that you are interested in the origins of language. If you took an extreme nativist position, you might assert that spoken language would emerge even if a child were never exposed to it—as, presumably, would walking. How would you test such an assertion? You might wait for a naked child to appear at the edge of the woods, but you would have a long wait and could never be certain of the child's history. The handful of feral children that have turned up have not shed light on the issue; the so-called "wild boy of Burundi," for example, was indeed mute but turned out to be brain damaged, autistic, and profoundly retarded (Lane & Pillard, 1978).

More definitive answers could come only from carefully conducted deprivation studies. One would have to raise some children from birth without exposing them to language (taking care, somehow, to deprive them of nothing else). A positive result would be extremely informative: If the children came to make sounds that had characteristics of known languages, your hypothesis will have been supported. Perhaps nonlinguistic sounds of certain frequencies were responsible; we could control for that possibility with still other children. A negative result would be less informative: Perhaps we inadvertently deprived the children of something besides the sound of language.

According to Salimbene, a medieval historian, the Roman emperor Frederick II conducted such an experiment in the 13th century:

> His . . . folly was that he wanted to find out what kind of speech and what manner of speech children would have when they grew up, if they spoke to no one beforehand. So he bade foster mothers and nurses to suckle the children, to bathe and wash them, but in no way to prattle with them or to speak to them, for he wanted to learn whether they would speak the Hebrew language, which was the oldest, or Greek, or Latin, or Arabic, or perhaps the language of their parents. . . . But he laboured in vain, because the children all died. For they could not live without the petting and the joyful faces

and loving words of their foster mothers. (quoted in Ross & McLaughlin, 1949, p. 366)

We are better off, some people say, not knowing the answers to certain questions. This issue aside, we can know the answers to certain questions in the analysis of behavior only by employing extreme and entirely unacceptable methods of the sort Frederick (the one with the "K") was said to employ. For all practical purposes, then, we can never develop definitive accounts of certain complex human behaviors (though it is a useful exercise to devise the necessary methods).

This sad pronouncement applies to all of the examples of complex behavior I gave above, as well as to countless others. You may suspect, for example, that a child can not efficiently solve the marble-under-the-couch problem unless the child has already learned—perhaps through shaping, modeling, instructions, or some combination of these—both to grasp objects and to make contact with objects using other objects. Again, how would you test such a hypothesis? Simply testing a child who lacks such skills before and after you have established those skills would not be adequate, for you would still somehow have to control for prior learning.

It is a truism that all scientific pronouncements are tentative. But some are far more tentative than others. If we could carefully control and monitor all of the conditions that we believed to be relevant to the emergence of some behavior—genes, learning experiences, nutrition, and so on—we could establish with greater confidence the contributions of each. In cases in which we cannot, for some reason, experiment directly, we must resort to indirect methods. Which brings us to the laboratory simulation.

SIMULATIONS IN THE SCIENCES

As is the case in the analysis of behavior, the most interesting questions in the natural sciences are the most difficult to analyze. The origin of the universe, of life, and of species is still attributed by many to a deity, and not only is it impossible to disprove such a theory, it is equally impossible to prove an alternative. Scientists bring diverse methods and information from many fields to bear on such questions. One helpful method is the simulation. Consider some examples: in the 1950s the biologists S. L. Miller and H. C. Urey tested a theory of the origin of life by simulating some of the conditions believed to be typical of primitive earth. The "soup" they prepared contained no organic materials at first but soon yielded both amino and hydroxy acids, important precursors of life as we know it (Miller & Orgel, 1973). They did not *prove* that the theory was correct; they merely proved its *plausibility*. In recent years, new geological and other data have revised our conception of earth's primitive atmosphere. New theories of the origin of life are tested in laboratory simulations like Miller and Urey's (e.g., Pinto, Gladstone, & Yung, 1980). As is true in any domain of science, the dominant theory at any point in time will usually be the one that accounts for more data—in this case, a steady accumulation of data in several fields.

Recently evidence was presented that supports a rather fantastic explanation for the mass extinction of dinosaurs and other organisms that occurred on earth 65 million years ago. Some now believe that a large asteroid struck the earth and kicked up enough dust to darken the skies for several months, thus destroying vital food chains (Alvarez *et al.*, 1984). Critical evidence comes from laboratory simulations of large-body impacts (Kerr, 1981). Again, such simulations do not prove the theory, but, in conjunction with the fossil record and other geological data, they lend credence to it.

The computer has become one of the most powerful tools of simulation research. If the variables controlling some phenomenon are sufficiently understood so that it can be described in formal terms—so that laws in the form of equations or algorithms can be stated—the computer can be used to plot the course of extremely complex systems that involve many such phenomena. With accurate equations and parameters, the behavior of such systems can be predicted. Such is the basis of long-term prediction in meteorology, astronomy, and other sciences. In recent years, computers have been used successfully to predict the course of chemical reactions by utilizing laws of chemical and physical processes (Edelson, 1981). Computer simulations have also been used for many years in the social sciences—in economics, cognitive psychology, game theory, political science, and so on—but, as the introduction to a book on the subject points out, "the researcher must know a great deal about the real system before he can presume to simulate it" (Dawson, 1962, p. 14); where basic principles are still under investigation and formal statements are crude and simplistic, computer simulations are probably premature. It is true that you can, by accelerating processes or varying parameters, use computer simulations to discover things you did not know, but your results will be no better than the equations with which you started.

Most of the simulations I have mentioned have been attempts at faithful reproductions of certain phenomena in all their complexity— "causality-based description[s] combining the underlying fundamentals of the many components of . . . highly complex system[s]" (Edelson, 1981, p. 981). But as Edelson points out, the language of simulation and modeling is used in diverse ways. Some simulations mimic phenomena in relatively arbitrary ways. At one extreme are models that look or behave like something but whose resemblance is superficial and which have no predictive value. The circus animal that wears glasses and turns the pages of a book appears to be a reader but does not do these things for the same reasons a person does and is not affected by the words on each page as a person is.

The language of simulation is usually reserved for models that are at least predictive. Even predictive models, however, may have varying degrees of similarity to the object. An engineering text (Murphy, 1950) makes some useful distinctions, adapted somewhat for this discussion: A *true simulation* faithfully reproduces all significant characteristics of some phenomenon; Miller and Urey attempted a true simulation. An *adequate simulation* reproduces only some significant characteristics. A *dissimilar simulation* bears no apparent resemblance to the object but is still predictive. An electrical circuit, for example, can simulate characteristics of a vibrating mechanical system. Virtually all computer simulations fall in this category.

The computer simulation requires its own analysis, for though it bears no apparent resemblance to its object, it can represent formally any number of the object's characteristics. If it faithfully represents all significant characteristics—say, in the case of the marble problem, critical experiences, current stimuli, relevant principles of behavior, and so on— we might call it a *true computer simulation*. Edelson's (1981) simulations of chemical reactions fall in this category. If it behaves appropriately and is predictive but uses algorithms that may be unrelated to those that characterize the object—say, it produces various solutions to the marble problem simply by calling them up from memory—we might call it a *dissimilar computer simulation*, and so on.[1]

What follows is an example of what was intended as a true simulation of an instance of complex human behavior.

[1] I have heard such programs called, respectively, "simulation-mode" and "performance-mode." Weizenbaum's (1966) famous ELIZA program, which simulates a therapist, would be an example of the latter. Though it engages in fairly natural exchanges, no one would claim that it does so because it incorporates "true" models of language or therapy.

"SELF-AWARENESS" IN THE PIGEON

A variety of behavior is said to indicate that a person has a "self," "self-awareness," "self-knowledge," or a "self-concept." People tell you what they are thinking and where it hurts; at some point children recognize photographs of themselves and their reflections in a mirror; children will apparently imitate videotapes of themselves longer than videotapes of others; and so on (Gallup, 1968; Kagan, 1981; Lewis & Brooks-Gunn, 1979). Little progress has been made in accounting for such behavior. Kagan (1981) suggested that physical maturation is the key. Lewis and Brooks-Gunn (1979) and Gallup (e.g., 1979) attributed it to the development of a cognitive entity called the "self-concept."

Behavior with respect to one's mirror image is said to be a "compelling" example of the development of self. Such behavior is said to progress through a series of four stages, first noted by Dixon (1957). At first a child shows little or no reaction. When a few months old it begins to react as if it is seeing another child—by laughing, touching, and so on. The third stage, which Dixon (1957) called a period of "testing" or "discovery," is critical: Children often stare at their reflections while they make slow, repetitious movements of the mouth, hand, leg, and so on. Finally, by about age 2, most children react as if they are seeing themselves, at which point they are said to be "self-aware" (Amsterdam, 1972; Lewis & Brooks-Gunn, 1979). Amsterdam (1968, 1972) devised an objective test of such behavior: a child had to use a mirror to locate some rouge that had been smeared on its nose (which, presumably, it could not see directly). Chimpanzees, after extensive exposure to mirrors, also come to exhibit such behavior, though monkeys apparently do not, and it is claimed that only humans and the great apes are capable of it (cf. Epstein & Koerner, 1986). How can one account for the change?

This is another one of those origins problems. Without the 100 babies, one can use only indirect methods to determine the possible role of experience, physical maturation, and so on. The Miller and Urey approach could be used as follows: Suppose that success in the mirror test is due to some rather simple learning experiences, ones which chimps and children actually have before they are successful in the test (Gallup, 1970; Lewis & Brooks-Gunn, 1979). Perhaps they must acquire two behaviors—touching themselves where they must touch during the test, and locating objects in real space given only mirror images. One could test such a theory by establishing such behaviors in organisms that would normally be incapable of success in the mirror test and seeing whether they were then successful.

Epstein, Lanza, and Skinner (1981) did so with pigeons. Pigeons were taught over a period of a few days (a) to scan their bodies for blue stick-on dots and peck them and (b) to peck certain positions on the wall and floor of their chamber given only the brief flash of a blue dot in a mirror. A blue dot was then placed on each pigeon's breast and a bib placed around its neck in a way that made the dot invisible to the pigeon but visible to others when the bird stood fully erect (Figure 1). Each of three birds was observed for 3 minutes in the absence of a mirror and 3 minutes in its presence. Independent observers judged few or no "dot-directed" pecks during the first period and an average of 10 per

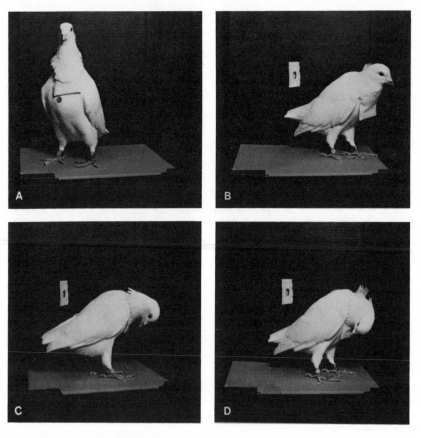

FIGURE 1. "Self-awareness" in a pigeon. (A) A dot is visible just below the bib with the bird standing fully upright. (B) The bird faces the mirror at right. The bib makes it impossible for the bird to see the dot directly. (C,D) The bird repeatedly moves toward and pecks the position on the bib which corresponds to the dot he has seen in the mirror.

bird in its presence. Even though no reinforcers were delivered during the test and though the birds had never before worn blue dots when exposed to the mirror, it seemed that each pigeon was now able to use a mirror to locate a spot on its body which it could not see directly. We thus proved the plausibility of our hypothesis, just as Miller and Urey had proved the plausibility of one theory of the origin of life.[2]

THE COLUMBAN SIMULATIONS

There are at least four classes of behaviors that have resisted analysis—covert behaviors (thoughts, feelings, images); complex, typically human behaviors that are difficult to trace to either environmental or biological factors (language, the behavior that comes under the rubric of "self," problem-solving behavior); behavior controlled by temporally remote stimuli (which leads some people to speak of "memory"); and novel behavior ("creativity," "productive thinking") (Epstein, 1985a). As I noted above, complexity, inaccessibility, the importance of events in the distant past, ethical considerations, or some combination of these factors makes it difficult to study such phenomena directly.

The self-awareness experiment was one of several simulations I have conducted with B. F. Skinner and others to try to investigate such recalcitrant behaviors; the project came to be called the "Columban [from the *Columba livia*, the taxonomic name for pigeon] Simulation Project" (Baxley, 1982; Epstein, 1981).

Rationale. The rationale, briefly stated, for this work is as follows: if you have reason to believe, based on principles of behavior established in the laboratory and information about a person's past, that certain experiences were responsible for the emergence of some mysterious behavior, you provide support for this conjecture if, after providing an animal that does not normally exhibit such behavior with these experiences, the animal exhibits similar behavior (Epstein, 1981). You can thus use animals to shed light on the possible contributions of certain environmental histories in the emergence of certain mysterious behaviors in humans. If your simulation is successful, you have not *proved* that the conjecture was correct—that the environmental history you identified is responsible for the emergence of the behavior in humans;

---

[2]Normal children and chimpanzees seem to be unique in that mere exposure to the contingencies of reinforcement that govern mirror use is sufficient to establish appropriate behavior (cf. Mans, Cicchetti, & Sroufe, 1978). Why the same does not occur with monkeys is a matter for further research.

rather, you have provided a plausible account of the behavior—what some philosophers call a "plausibility proof."

Adequacy. The adequacy of a simulation depends on a number of factors, and the set of pertinent factors varies with the domain of the simulation. The adequacy of the Columban simulations rests on five criteria, not all of which are met by all of the simulations.

First, if one makes use of certain techniques of conditioning or appeals to certain principles of behavior, the applicability of these techniques and principles to people must be shown. The greatest strength of the Columban simulations lies in the demonstrated generality of behavioral phenomena, such as chaining, discrimination, generalization, extinction, and so on, to scores of species, including *Homo sapiens.*

Second, the topography of the behavior in the simulation should resemble the topography of the simulated behavior; that is, the result should look right. In the self-awareness experiment, the pigeon's beak clearly moves toward a mark on its body that it cannot see directly; limbs aside, the behavior looks much like that of a chimp or child being subjected to the same test.

Third, the function of the behavior in the simulation should resemble the function of the simulated behavior; that is, the behaviors should occur for roughly the same reasons. Say we could get a pigeon to make a pecking movement toward the center of its breast simply by tugging on a tail feather. If we learned that during the mirror tests the tail feathers of our birds were being tugged, we would dismiss the results as uninformative. In fact, the birds pecked at their breasts because they had been taught to scan their bodies for blue dots and peck them and, as the various control conditions showed, because they spotted a blue dot in the corresponding position in the mirror. They did not peck simply because a mirror had been uncovered (uncovering the mirror while a bird wore a bib but no dot did not result in breast-directed behavior). And they did not peck simply because they felt the dot or saw it directly (dot-directed pecks did not occur in the absence of the mirror).

Fourth, the more structurally similar the organism is to a human, the more adequate the simulation. The more dissimilar the organism, the greater the likelihood that the result is due to an interaction between the conditioning you have provided and peculiarities of that organism. Ideally, of course, one would test humans themselves. Chimpanzees would probably be the next best candidates. Pigeons are hardly ideal, but one can do much worse (see below). Pigeons are used, not because of significant structural overlap with humans, but for other reasons, to be discussed in the final section of this chapter.

Fifth, and most important, it is critical that humans have had the experiences you have identified; the more evidence you have that this is so, the more adequate your simulation. The self-awareness simulation is strong here in one respect and weak in another. As noted above, there is considerable evidence that chimps and children have acquired both of the repertoires we identified before they are successful in the mirror test; chimps and children are unique in that they can learn to use mirrors through mere exposure to the contingencies of reinforcement which govern mirror use (Epstein, 1985a; Epstein & Koerner, 1986).

Examples of other Columban simulations follow:

SYMBOLIC COMMUNICATION

Savage-Rumbaugh, Rumbaugh, and Boysen (1978) reported what they claimed to be the first instance of "symbolic communication" between nonhumans—two chimpanzees. Though extensive training was necessary to establish the simple exchange, the authors attributed it, not to the training, but to the "knowledge," intentions, and flow of information between the chimps. An account in terms of conditioning would have been a clearer statement of what had been achieved. We made the point by setting up a similar exchange between two pigeons (Epstein *et al.*, 1980). After 5 weeks of training, one pigeon would, loosely speaking, "inform" another about a hidden color by pecking the corresponding black-on-white letter (Figure 2). We claimed in the published report that a similar history of conditioning could account for "comparable human language." Though the exchange does not measure up as a serious simulation, we have no reason to doubt the validity of the claim.

THE SPONTANEOUS USE OF MEMORANDA

In the symbolic-communication experiment one pigeon had functioned as a kind of speaker; it "said something about" a hidden color. The other was a kind of listener; it waited for and made use of a symbol provided by the speaker. We reversed the positions of the birds and trained each in the opposite role. Then we removed the restraining partition and, without any further training, placed each bird alone in the chamber so that it had access to both panels at once. Having learned to behave as a speaker and a listener in this situation, would it somehow talk to itself?

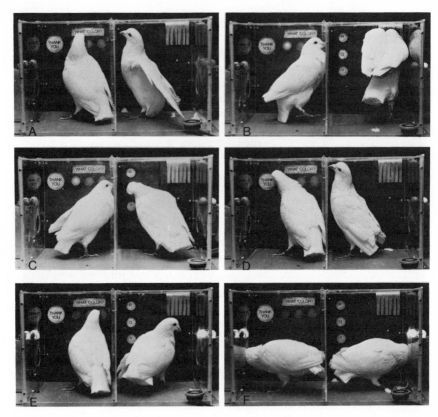

FIGURE 2. Typical communication sequence. (A) Jack pecks (and thus illuminates) the WHAT COLOR? key. (B) Jill thrusts her head through the curtain and pecks the color illuminated there (red, green, or yellow). (C) Jill pecks the corresponding letter (in this case, G for green), as Jack looks on. (D) Jack pecks THANK YOU, which operates Jill's feeder, as Jill looks on. (E) Jack pecks the corresponding color (in this case, green), which operates his feeder. (F) Both birds eat. The color keys below the WHAT COLOR? key are yellow, red, and green, respectively. The symbol keys are black-on-white.

After a few minutes, each bird came to display repeatedly the same stable sequence of responses. Elements of the speaker and listener repertoires came together to produce new, functionally distinct behavior that can reasonably be called memorandum-making. A bird would thrust its head behind the curtain on the right side of the panel and peck the hidden color, then peck and thus illuminate the corresponding black-on-white letter, behaving as a speaker. Then it would cross to the left-hand panel, often *look back* at the illuminated letter, and then peck the corresponding color (Figure 3). It appeared that the birds were using

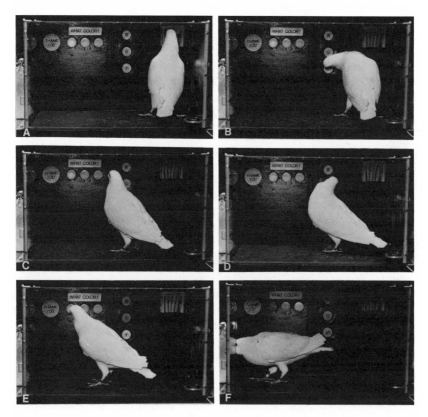

FIGURE 3. Use of a memorandum. (A) Jack pecks the color hidden behind the curtain. (B) Though doing so is not required, he pecks the corresponding letter (in this case, Y for yellow), which illuminates it. (C) He walks to the color keys. (D) He looks back at the illuminated letter. (E) He pecks the yellow key, which operates his feeder. (F) He eats.

the symbol keys as humans use memoranda, in this case to bridge the delay between the sight of the hidden color and the opportunity to peck the corresponding color key on the left-hand panel. We conducted a series of tests over a 5-month period that convinced us that the birds were indeed using the symbol keys as memoranda (Epstein & Skinner, 1981).

We had witnessed what has come to be called *the spontaneous interconnection of repertoires*. Previously established behaviors can come together in new situations to produce new sequences of behaviors, behaviors that have new functions, or behaviors that have new topographies. The spontaneous interconnection of repertoires is one of four probable sources of novel behavior in humans and the one, most likely, which accounts for novel behavior of the sort we usually consider the most mysterious (Epstein, 1985a).

"INSIGHT"

We have simulated a classic problem from Köhler's classic *The Mentality of Apes* (1925). Köhler placed a banana out of reach in one corner of a room and a small wooden crate about 2 1/2 m from the position on the floor beneath it. After a number of fruitless attempts by all six chimpanzees in the room to jump for the banana, one of them (Sultan) paced rapidly back and forth, then suddenly moved the box half a meter from the position of the banana "and springing upwards with all his force, tore down the banana" (Köhler, 1925, p. 41). The solution appeared in about 5 minutes. Köhler attributed the behavior to a mental process—the "insight" of the chimp.

We made some reasonable guesses about the origins of this behavior. Two repertoires seemed necessary: climbing on objects to reach other ones, and pushing things around. Because a pigeon normally does neither, it seemed an ideal candidate to test an environmental account of the chimp's "insight." We taught a pigeon (a) to push a small box toward targets at ground level and (b) to climb on a box fixed beneath a toy banana and then to peck the banana. We also placed it in the chamber with the banana alone and out of reach until brute force attempts to peck the banana (by flying and jumping) had extinguished. With the two repertoires established, we hung the banana out of reach in one corner of the chamber and placed the box in another corner—a new situation for the bird, not unlike the one that faced the chimps.

The bird performed in a manner that is remarkably chimp-like (and, perforce, human-like). It paced and looked perplexed, stretched toward the banana, glanced back and forth from box to banana and then energetically pushed the box toward it, looking up at it repeatedly as it did so, then stopped just short of it, climbed, and pecked (Figure 4). The solution appeared in about a minute for each of three birds (Epstein, 1981; Epstein, Kirshnit, Lanza, & Rubin, 1984). We have conducted controls that show that the climbing and pushing repertoires are necessary for the solution and have shown how different environmental histories contribute to success in the problem (Figure 5).

Based on these and other experiments, a tentative, moment-to-moment account of the performance can be given in terms of empirically

FIGURE 4. "Insight" in a pigeon. (A,B) The bird looks back and forth from banana to box. (C) It pushes the box toward the banana. (D) It climbs and pecks.

validated principles of behavior. At first stimuli are present which control both the climbing and pushing repertoires, and thus behaviors with respect to both the banana and the box appear, a phenomenon that may be labeled *stimulus matching*. The behavior we interpret as a sign of perplexity is probably the result of competition between the repertoires; the bird stretches toward the banana, looks over at the box, looks back at the banana, and so on. Behavior with respect to the banana quickly disappears primarily because of the recent history of extinction of "brute force" behavior; the pushing repertoire quickly gains in relative strength. Why the animal pushes *toward* the banana is a complicated matter. A process akin to what some call *functional generalization* (as opposed to generalization based solely on common physical characteristics) seems to be involved: Birds that have been trained to push toward a target but not to peck the banana do not push toward the banana in the test situation but do push toward the banana when subsequently trained to peck it.[3] In other words, the birds push toward the banana for the "right

[3] I am not, for two reasons, entirely happy with the term *functional generalization*. First, it implies an explanation, though at best it simply *describes* a spread of effect between stimuli which is not based on common physical characteristics. I *explain* the bird's behavior by

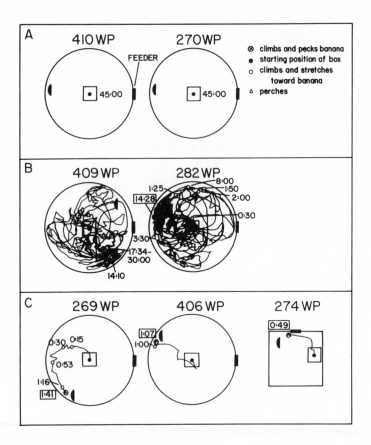

FIGURE 5. The contributions of various experiences to success in the "insight" experiment were assessed by conducting the test with birds that had different training histories. For example, birds that had been trained to peck the toy banana but never to climb did not climb when the banana was placed out of reach above the box (not pictured). Birds that had been trained to climb and peck but never to push did not push the box in the test situation (Panel A). Birds that had been trained (a) to climb and peck and (b) to push the box aimlessly for long periods of time pushed the box over much of the floor space of the chamber. The birds rarely looked up while pushing. One of the birds stopped pushing in the appropriate place and climbed and pecked the banana after having pushed for more than 14 min (Panel B). Birds that had been trained (a) to climb and peck and (b) to push the box toward a green spot placed at random positions along the base of the chamber "solved the problem" efficiently and in a manner suggestive of human problem-solving behavior (Panel C). For all of these animals, brute force attempts to reach the banana by jumping and flying were extinguished before the test. Another bird was tested that had been trained to climb and push toward the spot but whose "brute force" behavior had not been extinguished. It jumped and flew toward the banana for several minutes but eventually "solved the problem." Times are shown in minutes and seconds.

reasons"—because they have learned directional pushing and because some history of reinforcement has made the banana "important." The bird stops pushing in the right place because of a phenomenon called *automatic chaining:* In the course of pushing toward the banana, it sets up for itself at some point a stimulus (box-under-banana) that controls other behavior (climbing and pecking). It therefore stops pushing, climbs, and pecks (Epstein *et al.*, 1984; cf. Epstein, 1985b).

Other topics that have been investigated include learned and spontaneous imitation, cooperation, competition, reaction time as a measure of "mental processes," and "morality."

TOOL USE AND RESURGENCE

In one variation of the insight experiment, an element of what many would call "need" was introduced: The banana was placed within reach and pecking it was reinforced; the box was available in another part of the chamber, but the pigeon did not push it until it "needed to"—until the banana was raised (Au & Epstein, 1982).

In another experiment, a pigeon was confronted with a variation of the marble-under-the-couch problem: The pigeon, which had previously learned to push a box toward targets, appeared spontaneously to use a flat, hexagonal box as an extension of its beak—that is, as a tool—to touch a small metal plate that was out of reach behind a Plexiglas wall. (Pecking the plate had been reinforced when the plate was within reach.) Again, it did so only when it "needed to"—when the plate was no longer within reach. The details are noteworthy: The pigeon first stretched repeatedly toward the metal plate. After about 30 sec, it pecked weakly at the hexagonal box. It stretched again a few times toward the plate and then began somehow to look confused and even pensive. It pecked at the wall and floor. It looked back and forth from the box to the plate. Suddenly, after about 90 sec, it began to push the box directly toward the Plexiglas wall. When the box was under the wall, the pigeon lost control of it for a few seconds. It looked again at the plate, made

referring to its history (both pecking the banana and pushing toward the spot have been reinforced) and the current circumstances. Why such a history affects the bird in this way is a matter for the physiologist. The term has also been defined more narrowly than I have used it. Consider Bruner, Goodnow, and Austin (1961): "The problems of specifying the properties of objects that mediate a common categorizing response become less arduous when the category is a functional or utilitarian one. Rather than an internal state rendering a group of things equivalent, now equivalence is based on an external function. *The objects of a functional category fulfill a concrete and specific task requirement*—'things large enough and strong enough to plug this hole in the dike' " (p. 5, italics added).

some adjustments, and then pushed the box solidly against the plate and pecked it repeatedly (Epstein & Medalie, 1983).

A simple principle, called *resurgence,* can account for the behaviors that one might attribute to "need" in the experiments described above: *When, in a given situation, some response is extinguished, other responses that were reinforced under similar circumstances tend to recur* (Epstein, 1983, 1985c). Loosely put, when one response no longer pays off, an organism reverts to a response that used to pay off under similar circumstances. Thus, when the metal plate was moved out of reach, pecks to it were quickly extinguished. Older behavior—box pushing—got stronger as the first repertoire got weaker. As was the case in the insight experiment, the behavior from which we inferred confusion was probably produced by competition between the repertoires as they varied in strength (though the two repertoires were made available here through resurgence, not stimulus matching). Research is in progress which supports a general principle of resurgence, applicable not only to problem solving but to several anomalous findings in the literature on conditioning (Epstein, 1983, 1985c; cf. Enkema, Slavin, Spaeth, & Neuringer, 1972; Epstein & Skinner, 1980; Estes, 1955; Lindblom & Jenkins, 1981; Mowrer, 1940; O'Kelly, 1940; Sears, 1941).

The simulations have, as should be the case with any fertile program of research, raised more questions than they have answered: for example, is the interconnection of repertoires a random process? Would irrelevant repertoires have an equal chance of resurging in a problem-solving situation? The program has also provided a methodology for answering such questions.

COMPUTER SIMULATIONS OF COGNITIVE PROCESSES

Psychologists do not generally do the kind of simulation previously described. More common is the computer simulation—and not of behavior or of physiology, but of mental processes (e.g., Kosslyn & Schwartz, 1977; Newell & Simon, 1972; Simon, 1981). For example, Winograd's (1972) robot SHRDLU uses a sophisticated model of language processing to decipher the commands it is given. Anderson's (1972) FRAN is based on a model of human associative memory and can replicate some standard results of verbal learning experiments. Newell and Simon's (1972) General Problem Solver solves a limited class of logical problems (for example, in chess and mathematics) with human-like uncertainty. How do the Columban and computer simulations compare?

Adequacy. Computer simulations of cognition are inadequate in several respects. They live up best to the second criterion described earlier. The topography of the behavior of a computer is presumably its output; in a successful simulation the computer presumably produces output (protocols, diagrams, latencies, and so on) that resembles either some property of human behavior (e.g., latency) or some product of human behavior (e.g., a protocol). The function, however, of the behavior of a computer would seem to have little in common with that of human behavior. A computer's behavior is almost always rule-governed; that is, it is controlled by instructions. The behavior of organisms, on the other hand, is often multiply determined and, in particular, is often contingency-shaped (Skinner, 1966); that is, it is determined by the consequences of past behavior. A CRT that simulates a mental image (e.g., Kosslyn & Schwartz, 1977) does so because of a set of instructions that someone entered into the computer; whereas college sophomores respond in certain ways in a mental-imagery experiment because they have learned to speak English, because they have been given certain instructions and been asked certain questions, because they have been shown certain stimuli, and so on.

Computers and people would seem also to have little common structure. The anatomy and physiology of a pigeon are certainly closer to the anatomy and physiology of a person that are those of a computer. As Edelman (1982), a biologist, put it

> We are not clockwork machines, and we certainly are not possessed of brains that are like digital computers. We are part of that seamy web of natural selection which has itself evolved a selection machinery called our brain. (p. 48)

Because they are also products of evolution, presumably the same could be said of pigeons.

Finally, the history that one identifies in a Columban simulation—the origins of the behavior—is one that might indeed be possible for a human. No one would claim, however, that computer simulations of mental processes uncover anything about the origins of human behavior; it would be absurd to assert that a man behaves in certain ways because someone input a program into him.[4]

---

[4]A related argument is often made, but I think it is incorrect. Occasionally a program is equated with a kind of inner agent. Writes Edelman (1982), "In recent times, the brain has been looked at as a kind of computer. The difficulty with that view has to do not so much with the theory of computation as with the famous ghost that haunts all considerations of the brain, namely, the homunculus. Who, in fact, is telling whom what to do? Who is writing the program?" (p. 22). According to Skinner (1969), "There is a

Computer simulations of cognition, in short, may be plausible in the way they mimic human behavior but are adequate on no other grounds.

Other Problems. There are other reasons for objecting to computer simulations of cognition as tools for understanding human behavior or brain function (cf. Epstein, 1981). Even prominent cognitive psychologists have found reasons to object (e.g., Miller, 1981; Neisser, 1976).

Computer models of cognition are, virtually without exception, unconstrained by physiological data. They are not models of the brain (though such models have been developed—consider Edelman & Reeke, 1982). Some cognitivists defend this merely on the grounds that little is known about the nervous system; others go so far as to assert that physiological data are irrelevant to the study of cognition. You can, they say, discover the "software" that runs the brain—the "rules," the "instructions," the "organization"—without knowing anything about the hardware (consider Fodor, 1981; Simon, 1969). This assertion has several flaws.

First, it rests on a faulty characterization of software. Some cognitivists would have us believe that computer software does not actually exist in the computer—that it is the mental world of the machine.[5] But computer software has physical status—it is in no sense mental, metaphysical, or even particularly abstract. It usually exists as a magnetic

---

homunculus in any machine built and instructed by men" (p. 61). But a program is a far cry from a little man inside the head; it is, as I discuss below, simply part of the structure of the computer which is critical to certain controlling operations—analogous, perhaps, to synaptic states in the brain. Cognitivists are not so naive as to think that there are homunculi in the head; the very attraction of the computer as a model of human intelligence is that the computer, once programmed, needs no helping hand to behave intelligently. The fact that the programmer is human is irrelevant to their position. An unprogrammed computer might be limited in its behavior, but so is the feral child; they were each produced and programmed by outside agents—mainly, people. An inner agent is no more necessary to the analysis of one than it is to the analysis of the other. The cognitivist is concerned only with whether or not the program is a good representation of the mental world, not with the origin of the representation.

[5]Simon (e.g., 1969) and others would have us believe that cognition stands in relation to the brain as molecular physics does to quantum mechanics—that is, that it is at a "higher level" of analysis. But unlike the "levels" at which we observe physical phenomena in biology, chemistry, physics, and their various subdivisions, cognition is rather difficult to locate. Just where and what is it? The word *level* is hardly a solution to the mind–body problem; nor should it justify scientific inquiry into the metaphysical. As I have noted elsewhere, the prayer of a cognitive scientist as he sits down before his computer terminal must go something like this: "Oh, Mind, if I have one, please reveal to me today the proper set of Rules—if there are any."

array or a pattern of high and low voltages in a physical device. With the proper equipment and a translation table, one could literally read off one's software directly from the device. How a given pattern controls the operation of the machine and eventually produces certain output could in principle be established by running the machine very slowly—by "single stepping" it. In this sense, one might call the DNA of living cells "software"—highly compact, *physical* information that is critical in certain controlling operations. The "software" of the brain—a superfluous concept—can be found *in* the brain.[6]

Second, as any programmer can tell you, one can write a large number of different programs to do the same job (consider Moore, 1959). The issue has been brought to the attention of cognitive psychologists by Anderson (1978), who argues that pictorial and propositional accounts of mental imagery and indeed "wide classes of different representations" can be made to yield identical behavioral predictions and therefore that we can never decide between such models on the basis of behavioral data alone. The argument has been made in a different way in Quine's (1969) classic essay, "Ontological Relativity," in which he shows that an infinite number of mutually incompatible theories—not translatable one into the other—can be generated to account for the same data. Computer models of cognition will, in other words, most likely be dissimilar computer models.

Third, even granting that we could somehow deduce the existence of one and only one program by studying merely the behavior of our machine, the program would tell us nothing about the hardware—what it is made of, how to repair it, how to improve it, whether it uses Jacobson junctions or some other sort of gates; we would still have to start from scratch to learn where and how the program exists in the machine and how the machine works. In other words, Anderson's (1978) argument applies as well to hardware as it does to software. Even if it were possible to discover *the* program in cognition, it would tell us nothing about the brain.

[6]Where software ends and hardware begins is not always clear. ROMs, for example, are storage devices from which one can only read. They are preset with instructions or data during manufacture. Is a ROM hardware or software? Hardware that contains software? More important, the instructions need not be represented in a magnetic array; they could literally be "hard wired": The modern equivalent of wires, relays, resistors, capacitors, and diodes, properly connected, could fulfill the same function that the program fulfills. One can have either a software or hardware "spooler," a hardware or software "latch," a hardware or software timer, and so on. In general, there is a hardware equivalent for every software function and vice versa.

Fourth, wanting to discover the program when you are working with a computer—though perhaps a thankless task—is not an unreasonable means for understanding its behavior, because a program is what you use to control a computer; it makes no sense to ask about its phylogenic or ontogenic histories. But we can control organisms only by manipulating the environment, genes, or the body; as I have indicated above, we will never be able to change line 455 in an instruction set in the mind. In that sense, computer models of mind can provide only the most trivial and ineffectual understanding of behavior, for they yield no means to control it.

Fifth, existing computer models encompass fairly narrow domains of human behavior, and there is little overlap between models. Models of attention, memory, imagery, language, perception, and so on, often have little in common, and Boden (1977, p. 444) has argued that more comprehensive simulations are in principle unattainable. Ironically, in the 17th century Descartes proposed a model of human functioning that was far more comprehensive than any existing computer model; he used his famous hydraulic metaphor to try to account for the emotions, thought, perception, sensation, and skeletal movements. His model was entirely hypothetical, of course, which made his task somewhat easier than that faced by today's computer modelers.

Sixth, as I have noted previously, rules may be entirely the wrong approach for representing human functioning. The behavior of a computer is truly rule governed. Its every action is governed by an instruction (LOAD, JUMP, POP, If A THEN B), and the instructions are stored in some form in the machine. Human behavior, too, can be governed by instructions: someone tells us where to turn ("Turn at the next corner"), or we read a recipe from a cookbook ("Add three eggs"), or we recite a rule that we have memorized as an aid to better performance ("Slow and steady wins the race"). But it is easy enough to envision intelligent systems that make no use whatsoever of rules, and no rules whatsoever need be stored in us—even the rules we recite aloud—for us to behave as we do.

Must an organism be equipped with a library of words, images, instructions, maps, and so on, to behave effectively in the world? Absolutely not. But clearly an organism is changed by its exposure to such things—changed in such a way that subsequent behavior will be different. An undergraduate exposed to a photograph in an imagery experiment on Monday will behave differently to similar photographs on Tuesday. How might we account for such a change without resorting to the representation and storage metaphors? What is the minimum picture we might paint?

Say that when some neuron (or group of neurons, or synapse, or group of synapses, or circuit, etc.) in a rat's (or undergraduate's) brain is in a certain state—call it the active state—the rat tends to flex its leg when exposed to the flash of a red light. And say further that this cell is normally inactive but that we can make it active simply by pairing the flash of a red light with the application of a shock to the rat's leg. *Voilà.* We can, by this operation, change the rat so that, in the future, when it is exposed to the flash of a red light, it will flex. Note that when the rat is so changed, it contains no rule about the new relationship that has been established between an environmental event and an event in its behavior. True, we could describe the relationship with a rule: "When you see a red flash, flex." But the cell is not such a rule; nor does it contain one. The active cell is in no sense analogous to the computer instruction; at best, it is analogous to a "flag" in a computer memory. But a flag is a far cry from an instruction. And the cell is not the red light, either, nor an encoding of it. It is simply the simplest possible manifestation of change in an organism which can effect subsequent behavior in meaningful ways.

As Epstein (1981) has noted, the stimulus that produces a change in us need not in any fashion produce a change that corresponds to the stimulus, for *to produce a change* is not necessarily *to produce a correspondence.* The change sometimes manifests itself, of course, in behavior that in some sense corresponds to the stimulus, but the nature of the change is simply not yet known.

Information Processors. The major problem lies with the assertion, which somehow always remains unanalyzed, that humans are "information processors"; that the human brain (or mind?) is an instruction-driven symbol system; that, in short, we work like computers. An *American Scientist* article is flagged, "*When considered as a physical symbol system,* the human brain can be fruitfully studied by computer simulation of its processes" [italics added]. Newell and Simon (1972) assert, "programmed computer and human problem solver are both species belonging to the genus IPS [Information Processing System]" (p. 870). It is true that programs can be written that get computers to behave in some (usually trivial) respects like people do. But one commits an error of logic in asserting from that fact and in the absence of other evidence that computer simulations of "cognitive processes" shed light either on the brain or on human behavior.

The major flaw in modern cognitive science can be reduced to a single syllogism, one that pervades the literature in this field. From Premises (1) and (2) below, an invalid inference is drawn:

Premise 1: All computers are entities that are capable of behaving intelligently.
Premise 2: All computers are information processors.
Conclusion: All entities that are capable of behaving intelligently are information processors.

In other words, all A (computers) are in the set B (entities that are capable of behaving intelligently); all A are in the set C (information processors); therefore, B is contained in C; or

$$[(A \supset B) \cap (A \supset C)] \supset (B \supset C)$$

Sometimes a more modest assertion is made: Because all D (human beings) are in B, all D must be in C (Figure 6); or *Homo sapiens* is a "species belonging to the genus IPS"; or

$$[(A \supset B) \cap (A \supset C) \cap (D \supset B)] \supset (D \supset C)$$

Note that although these expressions are false and the conclusions invalid, the conclusions may still be "true." Symbol manipulation may be the basis of all intelligent behavior (B $\supset$ C) or at least all human behavior (D $\supset$ C). But, as things stand, there is no evidence to support these conclusions; in other words, they are drawn (incorrectly) entirely from the premises. There is ample reason, on the other hand, to be skeptical about a characterization of people in terms of programs and symbols.

As long as the primary assertion of cognitive science remains unsupported by independent evidence, computer models of mind will tell us only the obvious—how we can get information-processing systems to behave like people.

PIGEONS

Why pigeons? As in most laboratory sciences, one starts one's investigations with the materials at hand. Pigeons have been used for many years in behavioral psychology because they are inexpensive, highly resistant to disease, and easy to handle; because they often live 15 or even 20 years in captivity; because their visual sensitivity is similar to that of humans; and because many of the behavioral processes that have been identified in pigeons have been shown to be applicable to humans

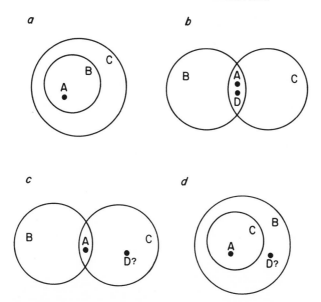

FIGURE 6. Venn diagrams that represent variants of the syllogism described in the text. A is the set of all computers. B is the set of all entities that are capable of behaving intelligently. C is the set of all information processors (for our purposes, the set of all entities whose behavior is governed by an instruction-driven symbol system). And D is the set of all human beings. An assertion that pervades the literature in cognitive science is that B is contained in C (Diagram a). A more modest assertion, implied by the first, is that D, the set of all people, necessarily lies in the intersection between B and C (Diagram b). Neither assertion is supported by evidence, however, and there is ample reason to be skeptical of both assertions. Though A is contained in both B and C, and though D is contained in B, the membership of D in C is uncertain (Diagram c). One could also argue that all Cs are contained in B (that all information processors are capable of behaving intelligently), but D might still lie outside of C (Diagram d).

and other animals. Pigeons, unexpectedly, proved to be good candidates for the Columban simulations precisely because they are so different from people. Because there is little physical resemblance and because the history and current conditions controlling a pigeon's behavior are apparent or at least accessible, one is less tempted to anthropomorphize than one might be with more human-like animals. The tendency to anthropomorphize in work with chimpanzees has been costly. It has, on the one hand, led to many instances of overinterpretation to which ethologists, linguists, and psychologists alike have objected (e.g., Chomsky & Premack, 1979; Epstein, 1982a; Epstein, Lanza, & Skinner, 1980;

Sebeok & Umiker-Sebeok, 1980; Terrace, Petitto, Sanders, & Bever, 1979), and it has obscured an account of the conditions that actually produce complex behavior in chimpanzees.

A point mentioned briefly earlier is worth emphasizing. It would be fatuous to assert that human behavior and pigeon behavior necessarily have the same causes. A history of conditioning that leads to the emergence of novel, interesting, human-like behavior in pigeons is not necessarily responsible for comparable human behavior; conditioning may not even be necessary for the human's achievement. The account becomes increasingly plausible, however, as one establishes the generality of behavioral principles, as one demonstrates that humans have indeed had certain experiences, and so on. Though pigeons are a good starting point for the investigation of certain complex human behaviors, one should hardly limit one's investigations to pigeons.[7]

CONCLUSIONS

Frederick II was a competent scientist, though irresponsible by current standards. We who are less bold can still shed light on the emergence of some otherwise mysterious human behaviors. Where a direct attack is impossible, we can construct plausible accounts of the emergence of certain complex human behaviors through careful simulations. Such simulations have so far revealed the possible role that certain complex histories of conditioning play in the emergence of novel behavior and have called attention to several behavioral processes that have received relatively little attention in laboratory praxics.

REFERENCES

Alvarez, W., Kauffman, E. G., Surlyk, F., Alvarez, L. W., Asaro, F., & Michel, H. V. (1984). Impact theory of mass extinctions and the invertebrate fossil record. *Science, 223,* 1135–1141.

---

[7]Hake (1982) and others have noted, as I did early in the chapter, that some domains of human behavior seem to be so uniquely human that animal studies can shed little light on them. Where, however, such behavior is derivable from simpler behaviors or general processes, animal studies can still be useful. Studies that employ animals to explore complex, typically human behavior are growing in both number and scope; animals studies have been proposed to study even subtle verbal processes (consider Catania, 1980). I do not think we yet fully appreciate what animals can tell us about complex behavioral phenomena.

Amsterdam, B. K. (1968). *Mirror behavior in children under two years of age.* Unpublished doctoral dissertation, University of North Carolina, Chapel Hill, NC.

Amsterdam, B. K. (1972). Mirror self-image reaction before age two. *Developmental Psychobiology, 5,* 297–305.

Anderson, J. R. (1972). FRAN: A simulation model of free recall. In G. H. Bower (Ed.), *The psychology of learning and motivation, Vol. 5* (pp. 315–378). New York: Academic Press.

Anderson, J. R. (1978). Arguments concerning representations for mental imagery. *Psychological Review, 85,* 249–277.

Au, R., & Epstein, R. (1982, April). *Problem solving in the pigeon.* Paper presented at the 62nd annual meeting of the Western Psychological Association, Sacramento, CA.

Baxley, N. (Producer). (1982). *Cognition, creativity, and behavior: The Columban simulations* [Film]. Champaign, IL: Research Press.

Boden, M. (1977). *Artificial intelligence and natural man.* New York: Basic Books.

Bruner, J. S., Goodnow, J. J., & Austin, G. A. (1961). *A study of thinking.* New York: Wiley.

Catania, A. C. (1980). Autoclitic processes and the structure of behavior. *Behaviorism, 8,* 175–186.

Chomsky, N., & Premack, D. (1979, November). Encounter: Species of intelligence. *The Sciences, 23,* pp. 7–11, 23.

Dawson, R. E. (1962). Simulation in the social sciences. In H. Guetzkow (Ed.), *Simulation in social science: Readings.* Englewood Cliffs, NJ: Prentice-Hall.

Dixon, J. C. (1957). Development of self-recognition. *Journal of Genetic Psychology, 91,* 251–256.

Edelman, G. M. (1982). Through a computer darkly: Group selection and higher brain function. *Bulletin of the American Academy of Arts and Sciences, 36,* 20–49.

Edelman, G. M., & Reeke, G. N., Jr. (1982). Selective networks capable of representative transformations, limited generalization and associative memory. *Proceedings of the National Academy of Sciences, 79,* 2091–2095.

Edelson, D. (1981). Computer simulation in chemical kinetics. *Science, 214,* 981–986.

Enkema, S., Slavin, R., Spaeth, C., & Neuringer, A. (1972). Extinction in the presence of free food. *Psychonomic Science, 26,* 267–269.

Epstein, R. (1981). On pigeons and people: A preliminary look at the Columban Simulation Project. *The Behavior Analyst, 4,* 43–55.

Epstein, R. (1982a). "Representation" in the chimpanzee. *Psychological Record, 50,* 745–746.

Epstein, R. (1982b). The self-concept and other daemons (abstract). *Behaviour Analysis Letters, 2,* 300–302.

Epstein, R. (1983). Resurgence of previously reinforced behavior during extinction. *Behaviour Analysis Letters, 3,* 391–397.

Epstein, R. (1985a). Bringing cognition and creativity into the behavioral laboratory. In T. J. Knapp & L. Robertson (Eds.). *Approaches to cognition: Contrasts and controversies.* Hillsdale, NJ: Erlbaum.

Epstein, R. (1985b). The spontaneous interconnection of three repertoires. *Psychological Record, 35,* 131–141.

Epstein, R. (1985c). Extinction-induced resurgence: Preliminary investigations and possible implications. *Psychological Record, 35,* 143–153.

Epstein, R., & Koerner, J. (1986). The self-concept and other daemons. In J. Suls & A. Greenwald (Eds.), *Psychological perspectives on the self, Vol. 3.* Hillsdale, NJ: Erlbaum.

Epstein, R., & Medalie, S. (1983). The spontaneous use of a tool by a pigeon. *Behaviour Analysis Letters, 3,* 241–247.

Epstein, R., & Skinner, B. F. (1980). Resurgence of responding during the cessation of response-independent reinforcement. *Proceedings of the National Academy of Sciences U.S.A., 77,* 6251–6253.

Epstein, R., & Skinner, B. F. (1981). The spontaneous use of memoranda by pigeons. *Behaviour Analysis Letters, 1,* 241–246.

Epstein, R., Lanza, R. P., & Skinner, B. F. (1980). Symbolic communication between pigeons (*Columba livia domestica*). *Science, 207,* 543–545.

Epstein, R., Lanza, R. P., & Skinner, B. F. (1981). "Self-awareness" in the pigeon. *Science, 212,* 695–696.

Epstein, R., Kirshnit, C., Lanza, R. P., & Rubin, L. (1984). "Insight" in the pigeon: Antecedents and determinants of an intelligent performance. *Nature, 308,* 61–62.

Estes, W. K. (1955). Statistical theory of spontaneous recovery and regression. *Psychological Review, 62,* 145–154.

Fodor, J. A. (1981). The mind–body problem. *Scientific American, 244,* 114–123.

Gallup, G. G., Jr. (1968). Mirror-image stimulation. *Psychological Bulletin, 70,* 782–793.

Gallup, G. G., Jr. (1970). Chimpanzees: Self-recognition. *Science, 167,* 86–87.

Gallup, G. G., Jr. (1979). Self-awareness in primates. *American Scientist, 67,* 417–421.

Hake, D. F. (1982). The basic-applied continuum and the possible evolution of human operant social and verbal research. *The Behavior Analyst, 5,* 21–28.

Hake, D. F., & Olvera, D. (1978). Cooperation, competition, and related social phenomena. In A. C. Catania & T. A. Brigham (Eds.), *Handbook of applied behavior analysis: Social and instructional processes* (pp. 208–245). New York: Irvington.

Hake, D. F., & Vukelich, R. (1972). A classification and review of cooperative procedures. *Journal of the Experimental Analysis of Behavior, 18,* 333–343.

Hake, D. F., & Vukelich, R. (1973). Analysis of the control exerted by a complex cooperation procedure. *Journal of the Experimental Analysis of Behavior, 19,* 3–16.

Kagan, J. (1981). *The second year: The emergence of self-awareness.* Cambridge, MA: Harvard University Press.

Kerr, R. A. (1981). Impact looks real, the catastrophe smaller. *Science, 214,* 896–898.

Köhler, W. (1925). *The mentality of apes.* London: Routledge & Kegan Paul.

Kosslyn, S. M., & Schwartz, S. P. (1977). A data-driven simulation of visual imagery. *Cognitive Science, 1,* 265–296.

Lane, H., & Pillard, R. (1978). *The wild boy of Burundi: A study of an outcast child.* New York: Random House.

Lewis, M., & Brooks-Gunn, J. (1979). *Social cognition and the acquisition of self.* New York: Plenum Press.

Lindblom, L. L., & Jenkins, H. M. (1981). Responses eliminated by noncontingent or negatively contingent reinforcement recover in extinction. *Journal of Experimental psychology: Animal Behavior Processes, 7,* 175–190.

Mans, L., Cicchetti, D., & Sroufe, L. A. (1978). Mirror reactions of Down's Syndrome infants and toddlers: Cognitive underpinnings of self-recognition. *Child Development, 49,* 1247–1250.

Miller, G. A. (1981). Cognitive science [review of *Perspectives on cognitive science*]. *Science, 214,* 57.

Miller, S. L., & Orgel, L. E. (1973). *The origins of life on earth.* Englewood Cliffs, NJ: Prentice-Hall.

Moore, E. F. (1959). The shortest path through a maze. *Proceedings of an international symposium on the theory of switching* (pp. 285–292). Cambridge, MA: Harvard University Press.

Mowrer, O. H. (1940). An experimental analogue of "regression" with incidental observations on "reaction-formation." *Journal of Abnormal Psychology, 35*, 56–87.

Murphy, G. (1950). *Similitude in engineering.* New York: Ronald.

O'Kelly, L. I. (1940). An experimental study of regression. I. The behavioral characteristics of the regressive response. *Journal of Comparative Psychology, 30*, 41–53.

Neisser, U. (1976). *Cognition and reality: Principles and implications of cognitive psychology.* San Francisco: Freeman.

Newell, A., & Simon, H. (1972). *Human problem solving.* Englewood Cliffs, NJ: Prentice-Hall.

Pinto, J., Gladstone, G., & Yung, Y. (1980). Photochemical production of formaldehyde in Earth's primitive atmosphere. *Science, 210*, 183–185.

Quine, W. V. (1969). *Ontological relativity and other essays.* New York: Columbia University Press.

Ross, J. B., & McLaughlin, M. M. (Eds.). (1949). *The portable medieval reader.* New York: Viking.

Savage-Rumbaugh, E. S., Rumbaugh, D. M., & Boysen, S. (1978). Symbolic communication between two chimpanzees (*Pan troglodytes*). *Science, 201*, 641–644.

Sears, R. (1941). Non-aggressive reactions to frustration. *Psychological Review, 48*, 343–346.

Sebeok, T. A., & Umiker-Sebeok, D. J. (Eds.). (1980). *Speaking of apes: A critical anthology of two-way communication with man.* New York: Plenum Press.

Simon, H. (1969). *The sciences of the artificial.* Cambridge, MA: M.I.T. Press.

Simon, H. (1981). Studying human intelligence by creating artificial intelligence. *American Scientist, 69*, 300–309.

Skinner, B. F. (1966). An operant analysis of problem solving. In B. Kleinmuntz (Ed.), *Problem solving: Research, method, and theory* (pp. 225–257). New York: Wiley.

Skinner, B. F. (1969, April). The machine that is man. *Psychology Today,* pp. 20–25; 60–63.

Terrace, H. S., Petitto, L. A., Sanders, R. J., & Bever, T. G. (1979). Can an ape create a sentence? *Science, 206*, 891–902.

Weizenbaum, J. (1966). ELIZA—A computer program for the study of a natural language communication between man and machine. *Communications of the Association for Computing Machinery, 9*, 36–45.

Winograd, T. (1972). *Understanding natural language.* New York: Academic Press.

8

The Graphic Analysis of Data

BARRY S. PARSONSON AND DONALD M. BAER

INTRODUCTION

Graphic data presentation, visual data analysis, and single-subject designs have each achieved a unique prominence in the experimental and applied analysis of behavior. In combination, they have allowed the direct, responsive, and individualized behavior-control procedures that characterize the functional analysis of behavior as no other strategy could have done (Baer, 1977; Michael, 1974; Skinner, 1956).

The analytic function of the graph in behavior analysis apparently grew out of the successful development of the cumulative recorder as an instrument for plotting data in a form from which the rate of responding, and the pattern over time of the rate of responding, could be seen instantly, sensitively, and directly. Thus, reliable control of that behavior could also be seen in the same way, in that the prevailing experimental variables, and their replications, were easily plotted over the same time span. Whatever their correlation with the behavior might be was obvious. Thus, the graph served as a comprehensive yet simple means of recording, storing, representing, communicating, and above all, analyzing behavioral data.

Typically, functional relationships between experimental variables and the behaviors under study were affirmed or denied through that same visual inspection of just that graph. Manifestly, that worked well, as can be seen by inspecting any issue of the Journal of the Experimental Analysis of Behavior (1957 through the present) and the Journal of Applied Behavior Analysis (1968 through the present)—for a start. In consequence, virtually all ongoing research and intervention decisions, all

BARRY S. PARSONSON • Department of Psychology, University of Waikato, Hamilton, New Zealand.   DONALD M. BAER • Department of Human Development, University of Kansas, Lawrence, KS 66045.

assessments of meaning and importance, and all conclusions about relationship have continued to be based largely on the visual analysis of graphs. Obviously, that can continue; not so obviously, but true enough, it need not continue. The question is whether it should (Baer, 1977).

HOW SENSITIVE IS VISUAL ANALYSIS?

If changes in graphed data are to be seen as such, they need to be relatively large—so large that the visual analysis of data tends to be less sensitive than statistical analysis of the same data. This relative insensitivity may have certain remarkable advantages for behavior analysis, especially for applied behavior analysis (Baer, 1977; Parsonson & Baer, 1978).

Insensitivity as Conservatism

Insensitivity ought to generate more conservative judgments that behavior has changed in correlation with experimental variables. Some studies of visual analysis suggest that this is indeed the case. For example, Glass, Willson, and Gottman (1975) found that visual judgments were often more conservative than statistical tests (and later emphasized the times when they were not—Gottman & Glass, 1978). Similarly, Jones, Weinrott, and Vaught (1978) showed that visual judgments tended to be as sensitive as time-series analyses only when autocorrelation was low and experimental effects, if any, were too slight to prove statistically significant; thus they concluded that graphic analysis at least typically was more conservative than time-series analysis.

Some analysis of this discrepancy may have been indicated in a study by Wampold and Furlong (1981); they found that students with only a little experience in visual data analysis tended to respond primarily to the absolute size of changes between experimental conditions. (Thoroughly trained behavior analysts will respond to a great deal more than that, as we intend to show in this chapter.) Reacting only to the absolute amount of behavior change is probably a conservative tactic (at best), but (as the researchers noted) it is then easily influenced inappropriately by the size and range of the units used in the ordinate of the graph. Similarly, in arguing the case for time-series analysis as an aid to the interpretation of behavior-analytic data (rather than as its essence), Hartmann et al. (1980) contended that the one instance in which this statistical procedure could usefully supplement visual analysis is when an experimental effect is small or otherwise difficult to detect.

All of this research and argument seems to imply that time-series analysis is usually less conservative than visual analysis. The proper question then becomes one of determining when conservatism is good strategy and when it is poor strategy.

Conservatism and Trouble

Conservative judgments are probably less troublesome for behavior analysis, and especially for applied behavior analysis. If statistical procedures are less conservative, then they are more likely to produce Type I errors (i.e., inappropriate rejection of the null hypothesis, thereby asserting that an experimental relationship exists when in truth none does) than visual analysis of the same data would. Convention in conventional behavioral science recommends rejection of null hypotheses at the 5% level of confidence—when the chance of making a Type I error is no more than 1 in 20 (which is the same as saying it is as high as 1 in 20). That means that the most probable long-term outcome of this tactic is a false affirmation of an experimental relationship in 1 of every 20 replications of the generalized experiment in which there is in fact no relationship to be found. Thus any obtained significant result might be significant only by chance, and because a number of replications sufficient to show its pattern of about 1 in 20 is unlikely, a certain uneasiness about which 5% of any statistically analyzed literature to disbelieve arises. By contrast, at least one immediate replication of an apparent experimental effect is a virtual requirement in applied behavior analysis (Baer, Wolf, & Risley, 1968), and in laboratory-based behavior analysis the number of immediate and protracted replications is usually so large as not to be worth counting. (In applied behavior analysis, obvious ethical considerations militate against repetitive replications conducted merely for the sake of proof.)

The adoption of statistical significance as the criterion of a successful experiment may lead to the virtual abandonment of replication as a scientific tactic; it may also lead to editorial policies that reject studies that are "only" replications of already published studies, and studies with "only" nonsignificant results. Indeed, just this seems to have happened in those areas of psychology that traditionally rely on statistical analysis (Craighead, Kazdin, & Mahoney, 1975; Lubin, 1957; McNemar, 1960; Stirling, 1959).

The emphasis on publishing statistically significant findings, and the professional importance of such publications to researchers, probably encourage efforts to enhance nearly significant results. Typically, nearly significant results are made significant either by finding a statistical test that after all will give significant results from the current data, or by increasing the amount of that data until a statistically significant result emerges. Those tactics probably increase the probability of Type I errors and of statistically significant results that are nonetheless nearly bereft of extractable importance or meaning, either theoretical or pragmatic. If statistically significant findings inhibit rather than facilitate further replications (Bakan, 1967), more Type I errors will go undetected or unquestioned than otherwise would be the case. Thus, Type I errors are a problem because they are difficult to detect, they inhibit further research explorations in their immediate area, and they invariably complicate our supposed understanding of what, without them, had been a simpler (and truer) set of relationships.

By contrast, a Type II error (i.e., accepting a null hypothesis when it should have been rejected, thereby ignoring a probably slight relationship that in fact exists at least sometimes) represents a conservative decision: it fails to clutter our current understanding of an area with relationships that are too often small, variable, specialized to sharply limited conditions, and, in metaphor, tricky. Eventually, all such relationships must be understood within an area; initially, however, they are probably exactly the right relationships to miss if our understanding of the area is to be nurtured at the critical early stages of its development. Of course, the chance probability of Type II errors typically goes uncalculated (varying with every alternative hypothesis that could be entertained about the magnitude of the relationship that we are failing to affirm), the only way to detect the Type II error is to examine a series of direct or close replications. Interestingly, direct or close replications are common in the behavior-analytic literature (especially the applied behavior-analytic literature); as a consequence, Type II errors do eventually emerge as such in that field, but later, when they are more useful and less destructive; however, the frequency of those direct replications often leads critics of the field to label it as "boring."

The Contribution of Insensitivity

The relative insensitivity of visual analysis, with its consequent bias against weak, unstable, and specialized variables (variables that are effective only under narrowly delimited conditions), has functioned as a filter: it has allowed the identification mainly of those variables whose effects are evident despite the insensitivity of their measurement. This has yielded two important contributions to behavior analysis. First, because in the early development of the field, it was mainly the powerful and pervasive variables with widespread effects on the behaviors under study that were discovered and harnessed; the field developed rapidly— it consistently encountered convincing, reinforcing demonstrations of the significance of those variables across a wide range of behaviors and settings. Second, when application beyond the well-controlled confines of the laboratory began, these were the only variables that could not only survive to be seen as functional, but in addition could accomplish strong enough outcomes to be worthy of application. Again, that was both convincing and reinforcing, not only for the act of application, but for the goodness of the underlying analysis. Perhaps validating variables as potent was a good strategy in discovering those variables that ought to be postulated as theoretically fundamental.

So far, we have argued that the graphic analysis of single-subject designs has certain extraordinary advantages: It is ongoing and continuous, and thus allows—indeed, prompts—flexible, responsive, and functional programs that manifest every descent into ineffectiveness almost immediately; and it assesses its effects conservatively, thereby allowing mainly the discovery of the kind of variables that are essential and conducive to a socially useful technology of behavior. It is now time to consider some thoughtful criticisms of graphic analysis.

OBJECTIONS TO VISUAL ANALYSIS

It has been argued that graphic analysis alone may be unsatisfactory, because agreement among judges using graphic analysis alone, at least when sampled in a certain way, seems low (De Prospero & Cohen, 1979; Gottman & Glass, 1978; Jones et al., 1978). Furthermore, agreement between graphic analysis and time-series analysis of the same data has also been sampled (again under certain, rather specialized conditions), and it too has been found to be low (Gottman & Glass, 1978; Hartmann et al., 1981; Jones et al., 1978). Both forms of disagreement have been attributed to the characteristics of the data being evaluated: poor agreement between graphic analysis and time-series analysis is said to be largely a consequence of serial dependency (Jones et al., 1978); low interjudge agreement was argued by De Prospero and Cohen (1979) to be the consequence of four data characteristics—both pattern and degree of mean shift, within-phase variation, and trend, all of which can interact to influence judgment about the meaning of graphic data. Each of these arguments merits more detailed consideration.

Discrepancies between Graphic Analysis and Statistical Analysis

Visual judgments about the significance of graphed data certainly are influenced by the characteristics of the data. But just as certainly, they are influenced by other factors, too. Comments by the judges in the De Prospero and Cohen (1979) study often related to presentation format and other extraexperimental aspects of the data display, many of them discussed by Parsonson and Baer (1978) in their graphics chapter's sections on controlling the type, format, and other presentation parameters of graphs. After all, the interpretation of graphic data is not merely an exercise in rationality, but rather is an exercise in the stimulus control of the judge's behavior, which implies that all functional sources of controlling stimuli must be assessed. Because some of these variables are perforce omitted from statistical analyses (and perhaps vice versa), lack of agreement between graphic and statistical analyses is thus not surprising.

And some more of the disagreement noted between the two techniques may have resulted from the nature of the tasks given to the judges in these studies. Those judges may well have found the brief given them by the researchers so limiting, compared to their usual research situation for making comparable judgments, that they were unable to apply their usual analytic procedures effectively. Again, if the problem is seen not as one limited to a rational reaction to the characteristics of only the data visible so far, but instead as a thoroughly behavioral response to all stimulus-control aspects of the data presentation, then the experimental situation in which these judges were asked to respond may well be considered an unusual and artificial one, and the principles of stimulus control allow (but do not demand) a prediction of behavior disrupted somewhat from its usual pattern.

In many studies of the behavior of judges examining graphed data, that behavior is examined in response to the portrayal of a baseline of behavior followed by some degree of change associated with a hypothesized experimental intervention—in other words, the judges see an AB design. An *a priori* analysis of single-subject designs does indeed suggest insistently that the AB configuration is the logical structural unit of such designs. However, we argue here that the AB configuration is in fact not the functional behavioral unit of interpreting such designs. Most students of experimental behavior analysis are taught that the minimal unit for interpretation is either an ABA or BAB configuration, and preferably an ABAB; or it is a combination of two AB's in multiple-baseline fashion. Certainly the published literature of the field rarely offers the reader anything less than that for interpretation. Research offering only

AB configurations may presume to be operating at the level of design units, but we doubt strongly that it is: Those are less than units for the behavior of drawing a conclusion about a relationship from such a data display. In other terms, those are less than units of the stimulus-control functions that have been established to operate in such judgments. If so, small wonder that judges disagree then—they have had no training in that stimulus situation (at least, we believe, they should have had none).

De Prospero and Cohen (1979), Jones *et al.* (1978), and Sharpley (1981) all argue that any problems of inconsistency across comparisons of data would be overcome by using statistical analyses, because those analyses would always produce the same result, and hence the same conclusion. But would they?

First, the assumption of perfect reliability may not hold for time-series analyses. In such analyses, the problem of incorrect model identifications (a process, curiously, that is often done by mere visual judgment) is especially severe with series shorter than 50 observations (Zinkgraf & Willson, 1981). Very short series (baselines) are, of course, the most common in applied behavior-analytic studies. Many researcher–practitioners consider longer ones unethical, in that they would represent a time of subject–client disadvantage that the researcher-practitioner was presumably able to remedy early, but refrained from doing so for nothing more urgent than statistical-model considerations. Westra (1979), examining the behavior of judges trained to identify the correct model for time-series analyses, reported that they could do so correctly in only 60%–70% of the series involving 50 observations generated by computer to have known characteristics. Yet in applied behavior analysis, a baseline of 50 observations would be considered very, very long—possibly, depending on circumstances, unethically long.

Second, there is no evidence that, if statistical procedures were always used to analyze data, everyone would agree on which statistical procedure was the most appropriate for a given set of data. Ledolter (1983), reviewing a recent book by Gottman (1981) on time-series analysis, offers a striking glimpse of the world of difficult, unclear, and occasionally arbitrary decisions that underly necessary choices just within the time-series domain. An examination of the relevant literature suggests strongly that any sample of behavior analysts applying statistical procedures to the analysis of graphic data (e.g., Edgington, 1980, 1982; Kazdin, 1976; Kratochwill, 1978; Kratochwill & Brody, 1978; Kratochwill & Levin, 1980; Wolery & Billingsley, 1982) would show as much inconsistency and disagreement as have any of the samples of them reacting to AB versions of graphic analyses so far.

164   BARRY S. PARSONSON AND DONALD M. BAER

Thus, the safest conclusion available is that lack of concurrence
between graphic and statistical analyses of the same data do not testify
to the inaccuracy of graphic analysis, but rather to the difference of
graphic analysis from statistical analysis, in that their relative accuracy
is unknown: when users disagree on which statistical model to apply
to data, they are disagreeing fundamentally on which will be most accurate—and they are still disagreeing.

Discrepancies between Judges

Interjudge agreement in graphic analysis is desirable, but can be
overvalued. In our current absence of established, formal procedures
and standardized criteria to guide graphic analysis, perhaps the amount
of agreement reported in these studies was surprisingly high—and, if
higher, would have been alarmingly high. The stimulus conditions under
which these judgments were made seem comparable to asking an observer
team to record behaviors for which they have been given no behavioral
definitions (e.g., "record intervals of happiness"). When observers agree
under those circumstances, it bespeaks a private agreement among them
that is controlling measurement, yet is probably unknown to them, to
the researcher who is to interpret its results, and to the audience who
will later study any report of those results. Until very recently, training
students to interpret graphic data has been implicit and probably quite
haphazard. Indeed, this is exactly the situation reported by De Prospero
and Cohen (1979): they asked graphic-data judges an open-ended question about what evaluative criteria they used, and also asked how often
each of them was used. The judges' answers revealed that a wide variety
of criteria were applied, and inconsistently at that, even within judges.
Such behavior ought to cause such judges to disagree.

The best response to low interjudge agreement about graphic data
is first to analyze agreement and disagreement as a behavioral process,
rather than to retreat in panic to some arbitrarily regularized statistical
model, the crucial decisions within which the great majority of us would
never understand (cf. Ledolter, 1983)—those, too, are essentially private
agreements. De Prospero and Cohen (1979) have already offered us a
picture of disagreement, its behavioral components, some of its controlling stimuli, and the obvious inference that there are more stimulus
controls yet unknown to us. We often respond to such problems by
finding the environmental conditions that will allow us to impose a
different and more thorough control. In this case, that will mean finding
the training techniques that will bring all judges into agreement. That
is the sort of problem that we have solved before, and very likely can

solve in this case, too. We can create some standardized set of criteria, teach them to future graphic-data judges in well chosen exemplars covering the diversity of cases that we know they are likely to encounter, and set up the common-stimulus conditions and schedules that are likely to prove useful for the generalization and maintenance of that new class of skills. In short, we can impose interjudge agreement, very likely; but the strategic question is, should we? Or, to what extent should we? In the process of setting up the training program necessary to impose interjudge agreement, we would probably discover that we do not always agree on what the standardized criteria are to be, and do not always agree on all the exemplars to which they should be applied for appropriate generalization. That might very well set the occasion for a subsequent discovery, which is that we do not wish to agree *that* much: we value some of our differences in standards; we each value our freedom to believe or disbelieve a given interpretation of a set of data; and we will begin to review what we know about countercontrol if it appears that we shall need to defend that freedom. In that context, we may well remember that graphic analysis maximizes exactly that freedom, by presenting only lightly treated, nearly raw data to the entire audience (not just to the researcher). The audience is then relatively free (certainly, freer than when confronted with a set of means and a statement of confidence at the .05 level) to make different interpretations, look into the fine grain of the data, and perhaps start down a new line of research, or balk at what now seems to them an overinterpreted and thus eventually useless line. Discrepancy between judges tends, observably, to be more local than generalized: Sufficient replications, especially direct replications, eventually make clear whether some behavioral phenomenon works. The argument is not that graphic data analysis allows that to happen but statistical analysis does not; the argument is only that graphic data analysis allows that more readily—so much more readily as to prompt it. This discernment of a possible virtue in disagreement about the interpretation of data has increased recently in a variety of disciplinary approaches to the problem (cf. Tukey, 1977).

FINE-GRAINED GRAPHIC ANALYSIS

Many research publications in applied behavior analysis seem to attend only to the gross features of their graphic data. Sometimes, they ignore aspects of their data that might well have led to changes in the experimental procedures during the study, or at least to an enhanced assessment and discussion of their present results, either of which could increase the value of the work. Even relatively subtle changes in trend, level, or stability of a data line within or between various conditions can sometimes provide valuable prompts to an alert researcher. This form of ongoing data analysis is best done graphically because that allows and supports alertness. Familiarity with the experimental procedures, the preceding data, the subjects, the target behaviors, the environment, and the appropriate experimental literature also are relevant to the analysis, but they operate equally well for researchers using statistical analysis—later. It is the subtle but potentially important changes that may be masked even by simple statistical treatment of ongoing data, such as averaging, collapsing, or coalescing data before analyzing them, that graphic analysis preserves to provoke researchers at every point in the unfolding of their behavioral analysis.

Data Characteristics Relevant to Graphic Analysis

Graphic analysis will function best if it is always done thoroughly. It was a concern for that thoroughness that influenced our initial argument on this topic: we attempted to list the stimuli in graphic data that ought to control analytic behavior in their onlookers (Parsonson & Baer, 1978), and to list them as comprehensively as we could, according to the theorem that thorough stimulus controls produce thorough behavior. We found that at least 10 characteristics of graphic data can function in their analysis and interpretation. We describe them again here, this time in the context of fine-grained analysis and relative to some variety of single-subject designs within which they may operate, to better emphasize their contribution.

The data in Figure 1 were invented so that one figure could illustrate all of the points necessary to this demonstration. These fictitious data represent the results of an equally fictitious program. The program used a combination of reversal and multiple-baseline designs to analyze the effectiveness of some procedures intended to teach two 5-year-old children to cross the street safely. Assume that the children's parents served as their teachers; assume that street-crossing behavior was scored according to a reliable and valid 10-point recording code defining each of the behaviors necessary to systematically cross streets safely. The two children learned by completing to criterion a sequence of these behaviors, each preceded by demonstrations, instructions, and the say-do and do-say exercises of correspondence training aimed at giving verbal behavior about safe street-crossing control over the actual behaviors of crossing streets. During their training, correct crossing, accurate reporting of

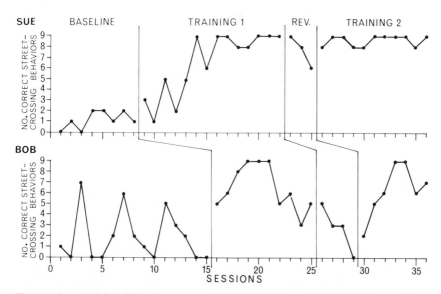

Figure 1. Invented data illustrating some components of a fine-grained graphic data analysis.

correct-crossing behaviors, and appropriate promises to cross correctly all resulted in consistent descriptive praise from the parent–teachers.

Consider Sue's baseline data in Figure 1. A slow increasing trend in her likelihood to cross safely is seen. In an 8-point baseline, that might be attributed to chance variation; on the other hand, it is visible, and interpretation later will depend on what changes can be seen relative to this baseline. Thus, it does not really matter whether the baseline is truly increasing; what matters is that any intervention applied after this baseline must produce increases that contrast to this apparent trend. A researcher concerned with whether this baseline is truly increasing simply must collect and inspect more of it, without intervention. A researcher whose concern is only to evaluate the effectiveness of the intervention poised for imposition on this baseline might well decide to proceed after these eight points: even if Sue's street-crossing behavior is improving without that intervention, it is doing that so slowly that any useful intervention will produce effects clearly contrasting to it—and any intervention that cannot produce effects better than that need not be validated as functional, anyway: it will have no use in a pragmatic world, because we know that we can do better than that. If there were some question that the skills of safe street crossing could be taught, or that the behaviors included in this curriculum are the skills of safe street-crossing, then even a very slowly effective training program might be of some value to the research, especially if it were the only program that the researcher could devise. In that case, it would become important to examine a longer baseline, to see if it would prove appropriate for contrasting the slow effects of that program with what was happening anyway. The researcher might eventually conclude that this degree of untaught improvement would make it impossible to see the slow improvement that the experimental intervention was expected to accomplish, and might then abandon this subject as a subject, in favor of another with a truly stable, low baseline.

It is, of course, the stability of baseline that is at issue here—the first of the data characteristics that need to be discriminated in graphic analysis. The researcher who produced Figure 1 clearly had decided that Sue's baseline was stable enough to proceed; obviously, the researcher intended to do better than the baseline trend with the intervention to be applied. An imprudent researcher might have looked selectively at the last five points of Sue's baseline and thought that stability could be seen there, that the trend had ended, and that one or two correct behaviors in any sequence of street-crossing was all that would be seen from Sue in the foreseeable future. We suggest that such a tactic would truly be imprudent: There is as much reason to think that the last three points of Sue's baseline are, by chance, uncharacteristically low as there is to think that the first three points of her baseline are uncharacteristically low. That is, the amount of data that must be discounted to conclude that the baseline has stabilized without trend is the same as the amount that must be discounted to assume that a slight upward trend is operative. Extraexperimental knowledge about Sue and this kind of behavior might favor one of those conclusions more than the other; but the data do not support one better than the other.

Imprudently selective judgments about stability might well be decreased in a researcher by a relevant training program. We have argued elsewhere (Baer & Parsonson, 1981) that one such training program is to calculate the least-squares linear regressions of many such baselines, so as to learn what a mathematical algorithm's steadily dependable diagnosis of trend will do with such data paths. In our experience, that program has salutory effects: In the process of examining perhaps 50 to 100 successive linear regressions, graphic analysts become very adept at seeing the regression line quite accurately before it is calculated; thus the program is automatically self-terminating. They become more conservative in assessing stability as well; in people who are going to deal with the characteristically very short baselines of applied behavior analysis, this is a much safer bias than its opposite. Thus, they tend to collect slightly longer baselines than previously, which is usually a good research tactic, even if a little troublesome in clinical contexts. Furthermore, protracted experience with the calculation of linear regressions eventually produces a certain scepticism about the technique, which it merits: Most regressions, when calculated and imposed on the data baseline, look like a correct summary of the baseline (and in the early stages of this training program, sometimes seem to be a revelation about aspects of the baseline that had not been appreciated before)—but some look wrong, even when their arithmetic is correct. These are the ones that teach us that the least squares solution to linear regression conceals a bias, one that gives disproportionately strong effect to the most deviant points in a data path (a result of using the square of their deviation as their contribution to the calculation of the regression line). We recommend the temporary use of linear regression as nothing more than a training program, not as something to be done in every case, certainly not as something to be believed, and most especially not as something to be analyzed for the statistical significance of its difference from other regression lines of other conditions (even though it can be). In short, a linear regression is something worth being able to see, but nothing more than that.

Sue's data show that training resulted in a period of initially unstable improvements that fairly quickly became stable, maximally safe street-crossing performances. These data show 2 more of the 10 data characteristics that should control graphic analysis. *Variability within a phase* is exemplified by the initial variability of the Training 1 phase, followed by the stable data of its last seven sessions. *Changes in level between phases* is illustrated by a pattern indicative of a *delayed* change in level between the original baseline and the final level of the Training 1 phase. In combination, these two characteristics suggest that the training program eventually is successful, but that there is some problem in its early steps. Perhaps, an inadequate task analysis or an overly optimistic assessment of the subject's entry-level skills, or both, create such variability in the initial training components of the program. Whatever the cause, the efficient acquisition of these skills, which certainly should be possible, has not been accomplished. If a fuller understanding of this problem is sought, further experimental analysis will be necessary. But the graphic data have delivered their message, whether or not the researcher chooses to act on it.

A three-session reversal was attempted after the first training phase. These 3 data points are all within the range established by the first training phase, and overlap the points of the final, stable sessions of that phase. None of them is even close to the baseline range. Then there is no reason to see them as different from those points. True, their trend is perfectly downward—but it is not at all difficult for a mere 3 points to have a perfect trend in some direction simply by chance, and since these started at the measurement ceiling for this performance, the only possible appearance of trend will be downward. We can see now that 3 points are simply too few to establish anything, if they have these values; we can see that especially clearly because the data for the second training phase are present as well: These 3 reversal points simply do not establish that the behavior characteristic of the two training phases is any different from the 3 points of it shown during the reversal that procedurally separated them. No great change in level is apparent at the resumption of Sue's training. The initial point in Training 2 is very similar to 2 of the 3 points during the preceding reversal. It is easier to see sessions 9 to 36 as one smooth process of training than to interpret them as two training phases functionally broken by a three-session reversal. Yet in truth, the latter interpretation might be the more accurate one. Because of the brevity of the reversal period, we shall never know.

The researcher who terminated this reversal after those 3 points presumably saw them as sufficiently informative at the time; probably, the researcher was overly influenced by the supposed downward trend of these points. Had the researcher been properly under the control of changes in level between phases, the need for a sufficient number of data points to accurately evaluate a trend, and the scepticism inherent in overlap in the data points of supposedly different phases, the reversal would have been extended for more sessions, and a more definitive conclusion would probably have become obvious. Thus, four of the data characteristics that ought to control graphic analysis should have been at issue in this case. Unfortunately, only one of them—trend—seems to have been, and as a result, the data are nearly useless. We do not know if a longer reversal would have shown that the safe street-crossing performances still depended on the procedures of the first training phase, or instead had become functionally independent of those procedures, such that they would have been maintained at high levels indefinitely in the absence of those procedures. "Trapping" of that behavior into a natural community of reinforcement is not impossible. (What if Sue later reported that both her teacher and the crossing guard now sometimes commented admiringly on her careful street-crossing behaviors?) Indeed, we do not even know if the overall and desirable change in Sue's safe street-crossing should be attributed at all to the Training 1 and Training 2 phases that she encountered. The ambiguity of the reversal gives us no experimental control of what we now can only suspect to be a training effect in Sue's new behavior. Only by considering Sue's case as a multiple-baseline design with Bob's can we gain some confidence that the Training

1 phase, at least, was functional in changing these behaviors of both children.

Then we had better look at Bob's data. His baseline points are especially meaningful in terms of the important hypotheses that they support just by themselves. All but 3 of these points fall within the 0 to 3 range. However, the remaining 3 points are quite high on the possible scale—they are, in fact, already within the range that training will attempt to achieve. Baseline data that overlap with the levels to be expected from the intervention are an instance of another data characteristic that should control graphic analysis: *variability between phases.* This situation suggests that a variable as potent as the intervention occasionally operates in the baseline condition. Perhaps it is the same variable as the intervention, controlled by agencies other than the researcher; perhaps it is different from the intervention, but has the same effect. Either possibility is an important message from the data to the researcher. An investigation of baseline, to see what it contains that sometimes accomplishes what the researcher intends to accomplish later with a specific intervention, may show the researcher an even better intervention than the researcher is planning. It may show that the subject does not require the shaping of these behaviors, in that they already occur in good form during baseline, if only the right stimulus controls are present. Then the intervention might better concentrate on extending those stimulus controls to more dependable ones, rather than wasting time on skill-shaping. But first they must be studied, to see what they are. (Perhaps we shall learn that Bob's class was given a talk on safe street crossing by a police-education officer on the day of the 1st high point, his teacher had reminded the class of those rules on the 2nd, and he had walked home with Sue on the 3rd. That would tell us how easy it would be to achieve control over these behaviors in Bob; we should think in terms of stabilizing some of the effective stimulus controls.)

Bob's data illustrate another data characteristic that should control graphic analysis: *change in trend across adjacent phases.* His baseline has no systematic trend, but in the first half of the Training 1 phase, a clear and immediate upward trend is obvious. Such abrupt changes often are considered "good" data, because they are visually impressive, suggest the operation of potent variables, and are easy to interpret. But the function of graphic data is not to be good so much as it is to be true. If the variables operating are that potent, then the data should say so; but if the data say differently, that means only that the variables are not as desirable as the researcher had hoped—but it still means that the data are doing their job of telling the researcher how this intervention works. As long as they do that, they should be considered very good data indeed. Researchers should prize them for their function, and not confuse good data with good interventions. Besides, not all interventions can be immediately and dramatically effective, yet for some problems, they still may be very good interventions—especially when they are the only effective interventions that we know. In short, it is prudent not to be under the exclusive control of abrupt changes in trend across adjacent phases, or abrupt changes in level between adjacent phases.

After six sessions of smoothly increasing trend, Bob's Training 1 data show a sudden increase in variability and a change in trend. *Change in trend within phases* is another relevant data characteristic that should control some analytic behavior in the researcher. Such increased variability, and especially a change in trend back toward baseline levels, in the middle of what until then had seemed an effective intervention, are almost surely the early signals of a developing loss of control. Thus, analytic questions about control should be asked. Has the reinforcer lost its effectiveness? Satiation is possible, but not common with descriptive praise given on such brief schedules. Can we hypothesize some competing contingencies or stimulus controls? If so, they may prove amenable to being included in this intervention. If they prove to be unalterably counterproductive, we must find a way to exclude them from the environment. Figure 1 shows that none of this hypothesizing was acted on, if it was done; the Training 1 phase would have been otherwise extended for some internal experiments along these lines. The absence of that leaves us without a functional analysis of much of this intervention. It had stable effects in Sue's case—if those effects are to be attributed to it. We need some confidence about Bob's case to be able to make that attribution in Sue's case, because Sue's baseline was not analyzed by its reversal, and the addition of Bob's could have accomplished a minimal multiple-baseline analysis. But now we see that Bob's case is in doubt as well: It too will not be analyzed by the reversal programmed into it, because the behavior was already reversing at least four sessions prior to the programmed reversal of the Training 1 procedures. Behavior during the reversal looks continuous in trend with the trend of those preceding four sessions. Only by ignoring all events following Session 21 can we point to a minimal multiple-baseline analysis indicating that Training 1 procedures are responsible for Sue's and Bob's changes from baseline levels in safe street crossing.

May we ignore all events subsequent to Session 21? Certainly we can. If our behaviour is under the control of demonstrating that our Training 1 procedures are an effective safe-street-crossing curriculum, ignoring all data subsequent to Session 21 may be strongly reinforced. And what happened after Session 21 clearly cannot alter the facts of what happened before Session 21. However, it may alter our evaluation of what happened before Session 21. What if our behavior is under the control of finding out the truth about this curriculum, rather than under the control of showing that it is an effective curriculum? That seems to be a better function for a researcher. It will constantly refer us to all the data characteristics that affect graphic analysis. *Evaluating the overall pattern of the data in a design* is another of those data characteristics that ought to affect graphic analysis. Part of evaluating the overall pattern of the data is *comparing across similar conditions:* asking whether behavior during a reversal to baseline conditions looks like the behavior of the baseline condition, and asking whether the behavior during the Training 1 phase looks like the behavior during the Training 2 phase. Making those comparisons suggests strongly that the overall pattern of the data of Figure 1 is full of losses of control; it ought to similarly fill us with caution about extracting out sessions 1 to 21 to serve as a multiple-baseline demonstration of the effectiveness of the Training 1 procedures. If neither baseline can be brought under the simple control of reversal procedures, why should we trust those lone two aspects of the data that do happen to fit the minimal multiple baseline as establishing a training effect?

The failure to extend the reversal in Sue's case, and the failure to extend the Training 1 condition in Bob's, so as to pursue internal experiments aimed at explaining the loss of control apparent there, now can be seen to have been very costly failures: they tend to invalidate the total pattern of the data, yet that need not have happened. Extension of Sue's reversal by only three or four more sessions might well have demonstrated clear experimental control by the Training 1 procedures. What if, in Bob's case, we had begun examining his social environment, looking for competing variables, and found anecdotal evidence that some of Bob's male peers had teased him for his caution in street crossing, and were beginning to exclude him from their group as a "sissy"? What if we found that the quite variable recovery of training effects during the Training 2 phase was closely associated with his walking home with Sue on those days when the other boys excluded him from their group, thus bringing him under the control of her safe-street-crossing model on those days? The entire process then would seem quite clear. An intervention into Bob's peer group, aimed at recruiting the other boys to support rather than deride safe street crossing, might have recovered thorough control of Bob's behavior by the Training 1 and Training 2 procedures. The literature of the field contains several examples of just such interventions; they might well have been done in this case, too, appearing as miniexperiments in the extended Training 1 phase for Bob, and, if successful, probably obviating any loss of control during the subsequent Training 2 phase.

Data Characteristics Inherent in Particular Single-Subject Designs

The data characteristics just discussed may appear in virtually any single-subject design; many operate within any condition of any of these designs. But there are other characteristics of graphic data that should control our analytic behavior, too; these are closely correlated with specific designs. In essence, they are patterns of data that ought to be seen in such designs, if the analysis is clear; when they fail to appear, or appear in distorted forms, that sets the occasion for potentially valuable questions about the processes operating in these data.

Incomplete Reversals. When a reversal design returns procedurally to its baseline condition after the first experimental intervention, but the data do not recover the level or form that characterized them during the baseline, and clearly are not likely to do so even if the reversal is protracted, that signals an incomplete analysis. An incomplete analysis is one that manipulated a variable capable of altering the behavior under study, and also manipulated one or more other similarly capable variables, no doubt inadvertently. The procedural reversal after the first intervention is meant to discontinue the variable knowingly manipulated in the first intervention, and it usually succeeds in doing so: The researcher knows the procedures utilized in the experiment to turn on that variable, and so knows how to turn it off. But if other variables were inadvertently activated, the researcher probably knows neither what they are nor how to discontinue them. They tend to remain in operation, consequently; the signal that they are still operating is the failure of the behavior to recover its baseline level or form. Figure 2A illustrates such a case. This deviation from the classic form usually seen in the ABAB design invites the researcher to look for the extra variables that were activated by the intervention, and then investigate their functions. At least, a more complete understanding of this behavior and its relationship to some of its controlling variables will result. In addition, the researcher may gain useful knowledge about how variables may be chained together in the environment, such that activating one also activates others not previously known to be sensitive to those procedures, as for example in social "trapping" (Baer & Wolf, 1970). Systematic replications, perhaps in multiple-baseline designs, almost surely will be required to separate these cases from coincidences—that is, from cases in which the experimental variable deliberately manipulated in the first intervention was in fact ineffective, but by coincidence was implemented at the same time

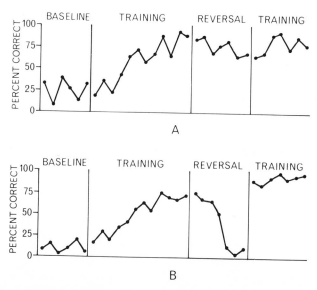

Figure 2. Some data characteristics of reversal designs: (A) failure to obtain a reversal to baseline; (B) postreversal intensification.

that another, effective variable happened to occur in the relevant environment. In that case, there should be a total failure to reverse the behavioral change under study. Otherwise, only a partial failure may well be seen. But distinguishing between these two possibilities is not always simple. Figure 2A has been drawn to represent a difficult case: does its reversal display a small trend toward baseline, or is it a picture of total failure to recover the baseline level despite a reversal to baseline procedures? Situations like that of 2A need longer periods of reversal to resolve this kind of ambiguity.

  Postreversal Intensification. Reversal occasionally is observed to be followed by an intensification of the form of behavior change that had been produced by the intervention preceding the reversal. The second training phase in Figure 2B illustrates this effect. Such an effect might result from enhanced discrimination of the essential stimulus components of the setting controlling the behavior under study; alternatively, it might represent better differentiation of the response components themselves, as when pigeons exposed to very high ratio schedules apparently learn a more efficient form of pecking that they continue to use thereafter, even when returned to lower ratios. The presumption is that both of these kinds of processes may be activated by alternating conditions of baseline and intervention. These are only hypotheses, of course, but they are in principle researchable hypotheses. The form of the reversal design allows graphic data patterns like this to provoke such hypotheses.

Untreated Baselines Parallel Treated Baselines. In multiple-baseline designs, a data characteristic that should control some additional analytic behavior is trends in previously untreated baselines. Figure 3A represents a case in which an untreated baseline changes in much the same form and degree as does a treated baseline, and at just about the

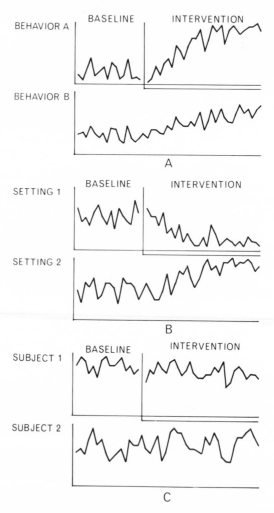

Figure 3. Some data characteristics of multiple-baseline designs: (A) data trend in the untreated baseline parallels that of the intervention data; (B) data trend in the untreated baseline contrasts with that obtained in the intervention data; (C) there is no discernible intervention effect.

same time. This may represent (a) stimulus or response generalization from the treated baseline to the previously untreated baseline; (b) it may testify to the fact that the second baseline is somehow chained to the first, or maintained by the first; or (c) it may be a case in which the experimental variable is not the functional variable, but instead was merely programmed coincidentally with a more general environmental change that affected both baselines similarly. Further analysis, then, might well include the interpolation of a reversal in only the first baseline, followed by reinstatement of the intervention there, to accomplish an ABAB design on that baseline; assessment of course would concurrently examine both baselines. No control of either baseline, or control of the treated baseline but not the untreated baseline, or identical control of both baselines by these procedures would do much to indicate some differential likelihood of each of the three possibilities cited.

Untreated Baseline Shows Contrast with Treated Baseline. Figure 3B illustrates a treatment effect in the first baseline and a contrasting change in the untreated baseline. If these are systematically reciprocal changes, rather than coincidental ones, they at least resemble the phenomenon called "behavioral contrast," in its laboratory versions (Reynolds, 1961). Gross and Drabman (1981) have reviewed applied training studies that systematically reflect this phenomenon, and suggest that their nontraining settings may be equivalent to the untreated component of the multiple schedule in contrast typically, which is studied in the laboratory. Unfortunately, although the laboratory studies of contrast describe it well, and have begun to specify the conditions under which it will be seen, they have not yet explained it. Thus, tying applied multiple-baseline designs to it by invoking the same label (contrast) does not actually contribute to the analysis of those applied cases (nor to the laboratory cases). In fact, the applied cases sometimes seem amenable to explanatory possibilities that could not be operating in the laboratory studies. Figure 3B, for example, could represent a case in which an intervention has decreased the behavior of the first baseline, which has opened new opportunities for responding previously filled by that behavior; thus, the behavior of the second baseline now fills that environmental gap. Hinson and Staddon (1978) have described an apparently similar phenomenon as representing "interim responses"; another example is seen in data shown as Figure 2 in a Rollings, Baumeister, and Baumeister study (1977), which is discussed somewhat differently by them. We cite these not as explanations, but as examples of the need to pursue further experimental manipulations when the baselines of our designs offer these nonclassic, unpredicted, but surely meaningful patterns. Again, a good start would be to program a reversal and then a reinstatement of the intervention in the treated baseline.

No Experimental Control. Figure 3C reminds us that not all experimental variables are functional, by showing us the classic graphic pattern of no experimental control. It also reminds us of two other kinds of analytic behavior to display under these conditions: (a) we should be willing to recognize noncontrol when we see it, and (b) we should remember that these baselines are now available for yet another intervention, one that may be functional—but if it is, we must also remember that it was preceded by the first intervention. The fact that the first intervention caused no changes in the behavior(s) under study does not mean that it does not interact in some way with the next or any later intervention. It could have sensitized the behavior or the organism to be more sensitive to a later intervention than would otherwise have been the case; or it may have desensitized the behavior or the organism to a later intervention. In general, as AB designs that show no effect of B turn into A/B/C designs, that might then turn into A/B/C/D designs, etc., the possibility of interactive order or sequence effects explodes into more and more numerous and complex possibilities. Here is a case in which there are no data patterns to signal specific analytic behaviors in the researcher; instead, it is a design pattern that provides the signal. Any design that, when summarized in our conventional acronyms, emerges as an A/B/C/D/E . . . design, tells us that we are making the best of some surprising failures to be effective (B, C, D, etc.) by economically going on with the same subject and baseline to try E, and then F, if necessary, and then G, if necessary, and so on. It also tells us that we have invited a large number of potential order or sequence effects to interact with whatever we find effective, finally, and so we should avoid such designs when simple relationships or thorough explanations are desired. However, when a multiple-baseline design has somehow allowed one of its baselines to become an A/B/C/D/E . . . design, a useful way of cutting through some of the complexity in deciding whether the most recent intervention's effectiveness depends on any or all of those conditions that preceded it is to program the most recent intervention into one or more of the remaining untreated baselines of the design. If the design is a multiple baseline across subjects, then the complexities of A/B/C/D/ E . . . in one baseline cannot affect the operation of (say) E on the next baselines (in AE designs). However, if these are within-subject multiple-baseline designs, then a complex history of A/B/C/D/E . . .in one of the subject's baselines certainly could affect and interact with an apparently simple later intervention into another of that same subject's baselines.

Loss of Control in Multielement Designs. The multielement design, strongly advocated by Ulman and Sulzer-Azaroff (1975), is essentially a very fast-moving reversal design: It alternates its conditions very frequently, compared to the usual reversal design, but otherwise is identical to the prototypic reversal design. The advantage of alternating conditions very rapidly is that historical events and confoundings interact equally with all of the alternating conditions; thus, any trends that those events or processes can introduce into the baselines under study will appear uniformly in them all, and the difference attributable to the experimental conditions can always be examined at any point in those historical processes. Such designs are not troubled by processes like maturation, seasonal changes, aftereffects of illnesses, holiday periods, etc. The disadvantage of the design is that it is impossible to study in it any process that cannot tolerate being interrupted if its effect is to emerge, or any process that requires a good deal of time for its effects to disappear once the process has ended. The graphic analysis of a multielement design typically is a graph of the behavior under study, appearing as a number of concurrent baselines that are, of course, not truly concurrent but instead are simply interleafed very frequently. A different baseline illustrates the time course of the behavior under each condition operating in the design. Figure 4 offers a simple example of a behavior under frequently and regularly alternating baseline and treatment conditions; baseline conditions prevail during morning sessions, and treatment conditions during afternoon sessions, with two sessions held each day. (A probably better design would have had baseline conditions in the morning every other day, with treatment conditions in the morning on in-between days.) Figure 4 also illustrates an eventual loss of control: After the treatment has decreased the behavior under study relative to its level in baseline conditions, the behavior begins to decrease in the baseline conditions as well, falling finally to levels just as low as the treatment was able to effect. Apparently, the effects of the treatment have generalized, finally, to the untreated baseline condition. Although control has been lost, many analysts would agree that enough control was shown early in the process to allow a strong conclusion that the treatment was effective, and that either some sort of generalization of its effects finally has occurred in the baseline condition, or that some

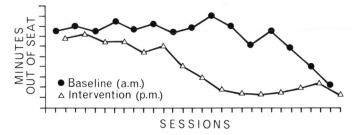

Figure 4. Loss of experimental control seen as a baseline data trend intersecting the final intervention level in a multielement design.

confounded event is reducing all responding of this type. Inserting a reversal condition into the treatment baseline, in place of the treatment condition, would do much to analyze this loss of control, as would analysis of the baseline conditon for any contingencies operating there to reduce this behavior. Figure 4 also shows us that the initial effect of the treatment was slow. Perhaps this treatment should be expected to reduce that behavior only slowly; on the other hand, when a pattern like this is seen in a multielement design, it is always worth asking whether the design has created the effect. If the treatment condition were not interrupted every day with a baseline condition that might undo much of its effects, would it produce its effects much more rapidly? Answering this question will require leaving the multielement design, at least for some time. Because multielement designs are still fairly rare in the literature of applied behavior analysis, responding to this kind of data pattern with an analysis of the possible interaction of the design with the effects of the treatment studied within the design would be well worthwhile. The susceptibility of multielement design to such effects in the realm of application has been noted only recently (Shapiro, Kazdin, & McGonigle, 1982); in the laboratory, the possibility has long since been noted (e.g., Sidman, 1960, p. 325).

Quick and Slow Acquisition in Changing-Criterion Designs. The changing-criterion design is a relatively new, little used variant of the reversal design. It establishes a baseline, then programs an intervention, and then, rather than reversing to baseline conditions, "reverses" to an intensification of a key parameter of the intervention; once behavior has changed and stabilized in answer to this intensification, the design repeats the process as often as analysis and a good applied outcome jointly dictate. Figure 5 displays a minimal changing-criterion design, one that imposes only three successive levels of its key parameter. Step 1, the first level of the intervention, clearly seems to have initiated a behavior

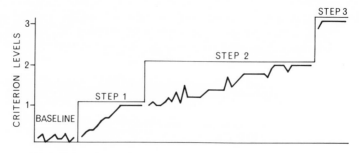

Figure 5. Changing-criterion design data that illustrate slow and variable acquisition (Steps 1 and 2) and rapid acquisition (Step 3).

change—unless it has been programmed coincidently with some other environmental event controlling that behavior. Proof that this is not the case will be gained by establishing similar changes in response to Step 2 and Step 3, later in the design. But if that is the graphic pattern that is to function as analysis and proof, it must be clear that the behavior systematically changes in answer to each new step, and having been changed by one step, remains unchanged until the next step is imposed. Thus, when acquisition of change is slow in response to a step, as is the case for Step 1, and especially for Step 2, a convincing graphic analysis requires that the behavior be allowed to stabilize and remain stable for a correspondingly long time before the next step is imposed, so that we shall be able to see that the next behavior change is in response to the next step imposition, and not something that was likely to happen in that way at that time anyhow. The researcher who produced the data of Figure 5 apparently was somewhat under the control of this requirement—but we might prefer that the behavior had been allowed to show stability at the conclusion of the Step 1 change for 5 to 10 more sessions, and at the conclusion of the Step 2 change for 10 to 15 more sessions: It would not be difficult to see the data path of behavior change as one process, not two, from the initiation of Step 1 to the initiation of Step 3. In general, Figure 5 illustrates one of the limitations of the changing-criterion design, namely, that when its behavior changes turn out to be slow and variable, the design will require a great deal of time, not all of which may seem clinically and ethically justified, waiting for a convincing graphic before the next desirable step change. Thus Figure 5 also suggests, as did some aspects of Figure 1, that an imperfect task analysis is operating in this study. Step 1 perhaps asks too much of its subject; Step 2 almost surely does. In contrast, Step 3 is mastered so promptly that we may suspect it to be nearly redundant; it might well have been intensified a little further in its behavior-change demands. Thus, the data of Figure 5 strongly recommend an analytic turn into task analysis, or a more accurate assessment of the subject's entry skills, or both, before continuing the experimental analysis of the steps as they exist now, at least for this subject.

Format and Context Characteristics Relevant to Graphic Analysis

A number of factors other than data and design can influence graphic analysis. These include the formats of graphic presentation (cf. Parsonson & Baer, 1978, pp. 116 to 119, 150 to 152 for illustrative examples), and the analyst's considerations about the procedures, meaning, and importance of the research—in short, its scientific and social context (cf. De Prospero & Cohen, 1979).

Scale Variables. Several aspects of the graph's measurement scales can influence graphic analysis. Scale captions, because of their necessary brevity, may convey inadequate or misleading information. Special care must be taken with multiple-scale graphs, which often enough show that treating one behavior fairly leads to overstatement or understatement of the changes in another. In general, ordinate (vertical-axis) scale divisions disproportionately larger than abscissa (horizontal-axis) scale divisions tend to exaggerate behavior changes, leaving an impression of large effects when, in truth, perhaps only small ones occurred. Conversely, disproportionately small ordinate scale divisions diminish behavior changes perhaps to less than their true importance. Abbreviations of the ordinate scale by excluding from its range the apparently unused portions at its low end tend to overemphasize behavior changes; this practice is especially troublesome when such scale abbreviations are not clearly indicated on the scale itself or acknowledged in the caption of the graph. Relative behavior change can be confused in bar graphs, too, in all these ways, and in addition by placing the zero point of the ordinate disproportionately high above the level at which each bar begins visually. (Yet, placing the zero point exactly on the line at which all bars begin their upward extent confuses the case of a zero score with a missing-data session. The problem is not simple to remedy by prescription, but good intentions usually will find a solution.)

Data-Path Variables. A profusion of data paths on one graph is likely to be confusing, unless they rarely overlap or intersect. The use of very different symbols for each line and each line's data points is essential. Multiple-scale graphs are easily misinterpreted by identifying the wrong data path with each scale; the stimulus controls to prevent this are worth careful planning and subsequent empirical checks prior to publication. Data paths that extend unbroken across all experimental conditions are more difficult to interpret, and their actual behavior changes are more likely to be underemphasized, than will be the case with data paths that break with each change in experimental conditions. Data-smoothing procedures (e.g., collapsing daily points into 2-day means or weekly means) can drastically change the meaning of a data path; thus data smoothers need to consider carefully if the changed meaning is fair, accurate, and desirable to the scientific community as a whole. When data smoothing conveys the same message as unsmoothed data, but more clearly and readily, then the scientific community ought to be, and usually is, grateful. (But reviewers often ask to see the unsmoothed data, and only after that agree that it should be smoothed—when it should.) The inclusion of horizontal lines at the mean level achieved in each experimental condition can serve as a useful summary of the effects of that condition; unfortunately, it also can and often does function to obscure trends within conditions, and sometimes those trends say that the mean difference between adjacent conditions was not the result of the difference in those two conditions. (The arguments against averaging data lie at the heart of the logic of single-subject design; thus, it should not be surprising that averaging is still likely to be misleading even within a single-subject design.)

Intraexperimental Contexts. Graphic analysis can be influenced by the extent to which the study, not just its data, meets the criteria of an applied behavioral analysis (e.g., those proposed by Baer *et al.*, 1968). Relevant procedural considerations can include the significance of the problem under study; the adequacy of its definitions, samplings, and observational techniques; the technique of reliability assessment and the level of reliability achieved, relative to the importance of the behavior being studied and the known ease or difficulty of measuring it reliably; the appropriateness of the intervention procedures to the problem under study; the probing or programming of desirable generalization of the effects achieved directly in the study; and the extent to which the audience agrees with the researcher about what the study proves or could prove (cf. De Prospero & Cohen, 1979). Often enough, these characteristics probably influence not so much the audience's belief in what has been shown as the audience's belief that the study is important enough to present to the field, so as to enable each person in the field to make an individual judgment about what it proves. In other words, judgments about intraexperimental contexts often lead naturally to judgments about extraexperimental contexts.

Extraexperimental Contexts. According to De Prospero and Cohen (1979), some judges in their study reported considering factors such as their assessment of the potential clinical, social, and applied significance or importance of the graphic results they were studying. Some said that their assessments of what the data showed were influenced by the "frequency of research previously compiled in an area" (p. 578). A number of commentators in behavior analysis have agreed that the issue of importance, significance, or value is and should be a functional part of behavior analysis, including the evaluation of its research (e.g., Hugdahl & Ost, 1981; Kazdin, 1977; Risley, 1970; Wolf, 1978). However, when studying the behavior of behavior analysts, especially as scientists convinced or not convinced by a given course of data and design, it may be important in the future to distinguish cleanly and sharply between any individual's personal belief in the meaning of a given study and that individual's belief that the study merits presentation to the field. Perhaps many of us, when serving as reviewers of research, have been willing to recommend publication so that a study could be presented to the field for judgment, grounds being that it held possibilities that could make it exceptionally important, even though we ourselves had found it to be unconvincing. Thus, if you really want to know how we behavior analysts evaluate data, you must be sure to ask us the right questions.

APOLOGIA

We believe that the fine-grained graphic analysis of data, responsive to all the stimulus controls that we have outlined here (and no doubt to more that future experience will clarify and justify), provides researchers and research audiences with information and analytic power that cannot be matched by statistical analysis, or, indeed, in any other way. (The obverse is also probably true.) We believe that the graphic analysis of an ongoing graphic data presentation interacts powerfully with single-subject design to produce a responsive, functional, accurate, and analytic approach to the scientific investigation of behavior, just as argued so long and so effectively by Skinner (e.g., 1956) and Sidman (1960).

REFERENCES

Baer, D. M. (1977). Perhaps it would be better not to know everything. *Journal of Applied Behavior Analysis, 10*, 167–172.

Baer, D. M., & Parsonson, B. S. (1981). Applied changes from steady state: Still a problem in the visual analysis of data. In C. M. Bradshaw, E. Szabadi, & C. F. Lowe (Eds.), *Quantification of steady-state operant behaviour* (pp. 273–285). Amsterdam: Elsevier/ North Holland Biomedical Press.

Baer, D. M., & Wolf, M. M. (1970). The entry into natural communities of reinforcement. In R. Ulrich, T. Stachnik, and J. Mabry (Eds.), *Control of human behavior (Vol. 2): From cure to prevention* (pp. 319–324). Glenview, IL: Scott, Foresman.

Baer, D. M., Wolf, M. M., & Risley, T. R. (1968). Some current dimensions of applied behavior analysis. *Journal of Applied Behavior Analysis, 1*, 91–97.

Bakan, D. (1967). *On method: Toward a reconstruction of psychological investigation.* San Francisco: Jossey-Bass.

Craighead, W. E., Kazdin, A. E., & Mahoney, M. J. (1976). *Behavior modification: Principles, issues, and applications.* Boston, MA: Houghton Mifflin.

De Prospero, A., & Cohen, S. (1979). Inconsistent visual analysis of intra-subject data. *Journal of Applied Behavior Analysis, 12*, 573–579.

Edgington, E. S. (1980). Random assignment and statistical tests for one-subject experiments. *Behavioral Assessment, 2*, 19–28.

Edgington, E. S. (1982). Non-parametric tests for single-subject multiple schedule experiments. *Behavioral Assessment, 4,* 83–91.

Glass, G. V., Willson, V. L., & Gottman, J. M. (1975). *Design and analysis of time-series experiments.* Boulder, CO: University of Colorado Press.

Gross, A. M., & Drabman, R. S. (1981). Behavioral contrast and behavior therapy. *Behavior Therapy, 12,* 231–246.

Gottman, J. M. (1981). *Time-series analysis: A comprehensive introduction for social scientists.* Cambridge, England: Cambridge University Press.

Gottman, J. M., & Glass, G. V. (1978). Analysis of interrupted time-series experiments. In T. R. Kratochwill (Ed.), *Single-subject research: Strategies for evaluating change* (pp. 197–235). New York: Academic Press.

Hartmann, D. P., Gottman, J. M., Jones, R. R., Gardner, W., Kazdin, A. E., & Vaught, R. (1980). Interrupted time-series analysis and its application to behavioral data. *Journal of Applied Behavior Analysis, 13,* 543–559.

Hinson, J. M., & Staddon, J. E. R. (1978). Behavioral competition: A mechanism for schedule interactions. *Science, 202,* 432–434.

Hugdahl, K., & Ost, L. G. (1981). On the difference between statistical and clinical significance. *Behavioral Assessment, 3,* 289–295.

Jones, R. R., Weinrott, M. R., & Vaught, R. S. (1978). Effects of serial dependency on the agreement between visual and statistical inference. *Journal of Applied Behavior Analysis, 11,* 277–283.

Kazdin, A. E. (1976). Statistical analyses for single-case experimental designs. In M. Hersen & D. H. Barlow (Eds.), *Single-case experimental designs: Strategies for studying behavior change* (pp. 265–316). Oxford: Pergamon Press.

Kazdin, A. E. (1977). Assessing the clinical or applied importance of behavior change through social validation. *Behavior Modification, 1,* 427–452.

Kratochwill, T. R. (Ed.). (1978). *Single-subject research: Strategies for evaluating change.* New York: Academic press.

Kratochwill, T. R., & Brody, G. H. (1978). Single-subject designs: A perspective on the controversy over employing statistical inference and implications for research and training in behavior modification. *Behavior Modification, 2,* 291–307.

Kratochwill, T. R., & Levin, J. R. (1980). On the applicability of various data analysis procedures to the simultaneous and alternating treatment designs in behavior therapy research. *Behavioral Assessment, 2,* 353–360.

Ledolter, J. (1983). The study of time-series data. [Review]. *Contemporary Psychology, 28*(2), 157–158.

Lubin, A. (1957). Replicability as a publication criterion. *American Psychologist, 8,* 519–520.

McNemar, Q. (1960). At random: Sense and nonsense. *American Psychologist, 15,* 295–300.

Michael, J. (1974). Statistical inference for individual organism research: Mixed blessing or curse? *Journal of Applied Behavior Analysis, 7,* 647–653.

Parsonson, B. S., & Baer, D. M. (1978). The analysis and presentation of graphic data. In T. R. Kratochwill (Ed.), *Single-subject research: Strategies for evaluating change* (pp. 101–165). New York: Academic Press.

Reynolds, G. S. (1961). Behavioral contrast. *Journal of the Experimental Analysis of Behavior, 4,* 57–71.

Risley, T. R. (1970). Behavior modification: An experimental-therapeutic endeavor. In L. A. Hamerlynk, P. O. Davidson, & L. E. Acker (Eds.), *Behavior modification and ideal mental health services* (pp. 103–127). Calgary, Alberta: University of Alberta Press.

Rollings, P. J., Baumeister, A. A., & Baumeister, A. A. (1977). The use of overcorrection procedures to eliminate the stereotyped behaviors of retarded individuals. *Behavior Modification, 1,* 29–46.

Shapiro, E. S., Kazdin, A. E., & McGonigle, J. J. (1982). Multiple-treatment interference in the simultaneous- or alternating-treatments design. *Behavioral Assessment, 4,* 105–115.

Sharpley, C. (1981). Visual analysis of operant data: Can we believe our eyes? *Australian Behaviour Therapist, 8,* 13–21.

Sidman, M. (1960). *Tactics of scientific research.* New York: Basic Books.

Skinner, B. F. (1956). A case history in scientific method. *American Psychologist, 11,* 221–233.

Stirling, T. D. (1959). Publication decisions and their possible effects on inferences drawn from tests of significance—or vice-versa. *Journal of the American Statistical Association, 54,* 30–34.

Tukey, J. W. (1977). *Exploratory data analysis.* Reading, MA: Addison-Wesley.

Ulman, J. D., & Sulzer-Azaroff, B. (1975). Multi-element baseline design in educational research. In E. Ramp & G. Semb (Eds.), *Behavior analysis: Areas of research and application* (pp. 377–391). Englewood Cliffs, NJ: Prentice-Hall.

Wampold, B. E., & Furlong, M. J. (1981). The heuristics of visual inference. *Behavioral Assessment, 3,* 79–92.

Westra, D. P. (1979). Testing interventions in the interrupted time series quasi-experiment: The reliability of Box-Jenkins noise model specification with short series. *Dissertation Abstracts, 39*(11), 5621-B.

Wolery, M., & Billingsley, F. F. (1982). The application of Revusky's R_n test to slope and level changes. *Behavioral Assessment, 4,* 93–103.

Wolf, M. M. (1978). Social validity: The case for subjective measurement, or How applied behavior analysis is finding its heart. *Journal of Applied Behavior Analysis, 11,* 203–214.

Zinkgraf, S. A., & Willson, V. L. (1981). The use of the Box-Jenkins approach in causal modelling: An investigation of the cost of misidentification of selected stationary models. In O. D. Anderson & M. R. Perryman (Eds.), *Time series analysis* (pp. 651–653). Amsterdam: North Holland.

9

Autocorrelation in Behavioral Research

Wherefore Art Thou?

BRADLEY E. HUITEMA

INTRODUCTION

Every now and then a mathematical solution to a general data analytic problem becomes available to researchers working in diverse fields. These solutions are often initially developed by mathematical statisticans and subsequently presented to research workers by methodologists who recognize the apparent usefulness of such procedures to specific content areas. This is the case with time-series intervention models that were initially presented by Box and Tiao (1965). Their classic paper has been followed by many extensions and simplified treatments of the essential ideas associated with these models and methods of analysis.

Two expository papers on the application of time-series analysis to behavioral data have been written by Jones, Vaught, and Reid (1975) and Jones, Vaught, and Weinrott (1977). Unfortunately, errors in these papers have led these authors (and many others) to recommend time-series analysis as the basic method required in the statistical analysis of behavior modification data. This recommendation is not justified, and many aspects of their description of time-series analysis require correction.

The major purpose of this chapter is to describe the two basic errors in the previous literature and to explain why time-series analysis is not generally required in the statistical analysis of the type of single subject research published in, for example, the *Journal of Applied Behavior Analysis* (JABA). The chapter is broken down into three sections. The first is a review of two basic points used to justify time-series analysis that have been presented by Jones *et al.* (1977). The second describes the

BRADLEY E. HUITEMA • Department of Psychology, Western Michigan University, Kalamazoo, MI 49008.

problems with this presentation of time-series analysis. The third section contains the outcome of an extensive study of single subject data that clearly answers the question of crucial importance in deciding whether time-series analysis of behavior modification data is necessary: Are the residuals of the ANOVA model autocorrelated?

TWO MAIN POINTS JONES *ET AL.* (1977) USE TO JUSTIFY THE USE OF TIME-SERIES ANALYSIS

Time-series intervention models are frequently recommended in place of the simple analysis of variance (ANOVA) model when there is clear evidence that the residuals of the ANOVA model are autocorrelated. If the residuals of the ANOVA model are highly autocorrelated, the conventional F test is considered invalid because the probability of Type I error (concluding that there is an intervention effect when, in fact, none exists) can be much higher than the nominal value. Because autocorrelated residuals can have such drastic effects on the validity of the ANOVA F test, it seems desirable that one should understand the nature of data having this characteristic and obtain valid information on the extent to which behavioral data actually do have autocorrelated residuals. Jones *et al.* (1977) cite logic and data to support the use of time-series methods. Their appeal to common sense can be seen in the following quote:

> An autocorrelation indicates the extent to which scores at one time point in a series are predictive of scores at another time point in the series. . . . The reason that one should expect serial dependency is simply that people and their environments do not behave or function randomly over time. . . . In fact, it could be argued that serial dependency *should always* be found in repeated measurements for individual subjects. (p. 154, italics added)

Jones *et al.* (1977) go on to data to support intuition. They state that in their study of a sample of typical JABA data

> twenty of the 24 experiments (83%) had significant lag 1 autocorrelations, ranging from 0.40 to 0.93. Nine of the 20 significant autocorrelations were greater than 0.70. Clearly, then, serial dependency is a relatively common property of behavioral scores obtained in operant experiments. (p. 154)

PROBLEMS WITH THE JONES *ET AL.* (1977) POINTS

The two major points, that (a) JABA data should be autocorrelated because it is logical to expect them to be so, and that (b) JABA data are in fact autocorrelated, need to be examined very carefully.

Let us first consider the basis for the conclusion that JABA data should be autocorrelated. There are essentially two weak ways to bolster this suggestion: (a) by assumption, and (b) by citing authorities who refer to content areas removed from JABA-type studies.

Assumption

It is reasonable to assume that data from a single subject will be autocorrelated simply because data points collected across time intuitively seem likely to be tied to each other or to be serially dependent. That is, it just seems to make sense that data points collected across time will be related to each other more than would data points coming from different subjects. However, the justifications cited by Jones *et al.* (1977) for assuming serial dependency are not correct—for reasons described later in this section.

Authority

It is stated by most authorities on time-series analysis that autocorrelation or serial dependency is a characteristic of time-series data. According to Box and Tiao (1965): "In practice successive observations usually (would) be dependent" (p. 181). Glass, Wilson, and Gottman (1975) state that "*most* time series do not consist of independent observations" (p. 74, italics added).

It is of interest to examine the type of time-series data to which Box and Tiao and Glass *et al.* refer. Box and Tiao (1965) allude to examples of economic indicators and the daily output of a chemical process. In more recent work (Box & Tiao, 1975; Tiao, Box, & Hamming, 1976), they deal with environmental problems using atmospheric ozone concentration as an outcome measure. The Glass *et al.* statement appears to be largely based on an analysis of 116 series of

> social or behavioral indices. . . . The series reflect a variety of things observed (e.g., a person, a city, a nation) and a varied range of applications: alpha brain waves, crime rates, examination scores, students time spent studying, learning curves, etc. (p. 115–116)

Only 25% of these studies did not appear to require the estimation of autoregressive or moving average parameters for appropriate time-series analysis. The number of JABA-type studies included in the 116 series was not reported.

Data

The issue of whether JABA data are *in fact* autocorrelated is perhaps more relevant to behavioral psychologists than whether data from other substantive areas are autocorrelated. Although no large-scale analyses of the statistical structure of JABA data have been previously published, the work of Jones *et al.* (1977) is frequently cited as proof of the existence of serial dependency in most JABA studies. An analysis of the conceptual, computational, and sampling problems associated with this and related papers is presented next.

Incorrect Conceptualization of Autocorrelation

The statements of Jones *et al.* (1977) quoted earlier suggest that: (a) if observations are not autocorrelated, then (b) people are behaving randomly over time and (c) the prediction and control of behavior is thus nonexistent. Situation (a) does not, however, logically lead to conclusions (b) and (c). The purpose of this section is to explain why this is the case.

There are several terms repeatedly employed in the previously cited paper that should be closely examined if the justification for the argument of this chapter is to be understood: prediction, residual, and interrupted (intervention) time-series model.

Prediction. Let us first consider the notion of prediction. The baseline data presented in Figure 1 have been contrived in such a way that each observation has almost the same value (the slight differences are so small that they can not be seen in the graph). In a sense, this is a

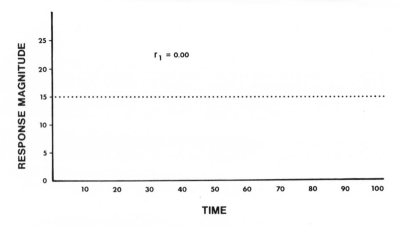

Figure 1. Realization of a stationary baseline process, not autocorrelated.

representation of an ideal baseline; it is based on many time periods, no trend or drift is present, and there is almost no variability across time. It is a realization of a stable stationary process. The autocorrelation coefficient associated with these data is zero. Nevertheless, it is possible to predict the value of the observation Y at time t with essentially no error given the mean of the series or of any point in the series. This result suggests that there is a problem with the notion that data yielding an autocorrelation coefficient of zero are not predictable.

Next consider the case where there is obvious variability in the series. Figure 2 contains the baseline data from a study reported by Baer, Rowbury, and Baer (1973). The autocorrelation coefficient associated with these data is about zero (.02). Notice, however, that the data in Figure 2 are quite different from the data contained in Figure 1—even though the autocorrelation or degree of serial dependence is effectively zero in both cases. Because more variability is present in Figure 2, it can be seen that the use of the mean to predict the score at a specific time does not generally yield highly accurate predictions. The fact that the predicted value generally differs somewhat from the actual value does not mean that there is nothing systematic about the behavior or that the behavior is not at all predictable. Notice that the data tend to hover around the mean of 37.6; they clearly do not hover around, say, 97 or 5.

If zero autocorrelation does not mean that the behavior is completely unpredictable, what does it mean? It simply means that, in general, the squared difference between the observed score at time t and the predicted score at time t is just as large when a prediction equation employing both the mean and the score at $t - 1$ is used as when only

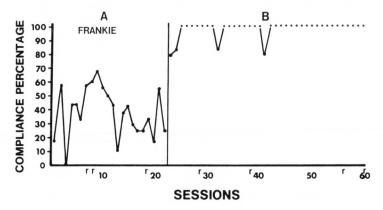

Figure 2. Nonautocorrelated baseline data with substantial variability. *Note.* From Baer, Rowbury, and Baer, 1973. Copyright 1973 by the *Journal of Applied Behavior Analysis.* Reprinted by permission.

the mean is used as the predicted value. In other words, with zero autocorrelation, knowledge of the behavior at time $t - 1$ provides no unique contribution in predicting the behavior at time t. This does not mean that the behavior is unpredictable.

The data contained in Figure 3 are similar to the baseline data of Figures 1 and 2 in that they can be characterized as stationary in level. That is, there is no general upward or downward drifting or trend. They are similar to the data of Figure 2 in that there is considerable variability around the mean. Unlike the data of the first two figures, however, the residuals of the data contained in Figure 3 are perfectly autocorrelated. The autocorrelation coefficient is -1.0. This suggests that the residual at time period t is completely predictable from knowledge of the residual at time period $t - 1$. In addition, if *both* the mean and the residual at $t - 1$ (or the observation $Y_t - 1$) are known, it is possible to perfectly predict the observation at time period t (i.e., Y_t).

Residual Autocorrelation. The discussion of autocorrelation in the preceding unit consistently referred to the autocorrelation of the residuals of the model. As can be seen in the previous quotes, Jones *et al.* (1977) refer to the autocorrelation or serial dependency of the "scores." Does it make any difference whether the residuals $(Y_t - \overline{Y}) = E_t$ or the raw scores Y_t are employed in computing the autocorrelation? That depends. If the data consist of a series of scores from a *single* phase of a study, as was the case in all examples of the previous section (i.e., the baseline data contained in Figures 1–3), it makes no difference. That is, if the data consist of the scores obtained in, for example, only the baseline phase of a study, the autocorrelation coefficient will be exactly the same whether it is computed on the raw scores or the residuals. This occurs because the residuals are obtained by simply substracting a constant (the series mean) from each raw score. It can be shown mathematically that adding a constant to or subtracting a constant from the scores in a phase

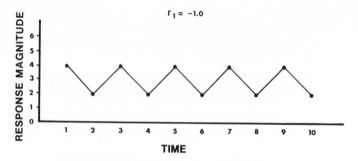

Figure 3. Perfectly negatively autocorrelated residuals.

of a series will not affect the autocorrelation for that phase. If more than one phase is involved in a time series, there is a crucial difference between the autocorrelation of all the raw scores (observations) combined and the autocorrelation of all the residuals of the ANOVA model.

Interrupted Time-Series Model. A time-series model is simply an equation that relates observations at time t to the previous history of the series. It appears that the failure to explicitly describe an interrupted (intervention) time-series model has led to (or is at least associated with) the incorrect computational recommendations contained in Jones *et al.* (1975), Jones *et al.* (1977), and others.

If it is kept in mind that a time-series model is supposed to adequately describe a time series, it should seem reasonable that the model must contain a term for the intervention effect if such an effect may be present. Consider all of the data in Figure 2. It is clear that the total time-series can be broken down into a preintervention series and a postintervention series, and that an intervention effect appears to have occurred after the preintervention phase. It follows that a model of the total series should in some way describe the preintervention series, the intervention, and the postintervention series. There should, then, be terms to describe the preintervention process, the intervention, and the postintervention process. The following first order autoregressive *intervention* model does this.

Preintervention (baseline) portion of the model:

$$Y_t = L_{\text{pre}} + a_1 (Y_{t-1} - L_{\text{pre}}) + E_t$$

$$\text{for } 2 \leq t \leq n_{\text{pre}}$$

Postintervention portion of the model:

$$Y_t = L_{\text{pre}} + I + a_1 [Y_{t-1} - (L_{\text{pre}} + I)] + E_t$$

$$\text{for } n_{\text{pre}+2} \leq t \leq N_{\text{total}}$$

where L_{pre} is the level of the preintervention phase, I is the intervention effect, a_1 is the within-phase lag 1 autocorrelation which is assumed to be the same within each phase, and E_t is the residual of the model.

For simplification, neither the first observation of the preintervention phase ($Y_{1\ \text{pre}}$) nor the first observation of the postintervention phase ($Y_{1\ \text{post}}$) has been modeled. (The full model can be found in Box & Tiao, 1965.) The postintervention portion of the model is similar to the preintervention portion, but a term has been added to represent the extent to which the level of the series has been affected by the intervention. Notice that the specification of the intervention model in two explicit portions leaves no doubt about the nature of the residuals of the model. This model makes it clear that there are two sets of residuals. One set of residuals is associated with the preintervention portion of the model, and a second set of residuals is associated with the postintervention portion of the model. A residual in the preintervention portion is simply the value of a preintervention observation minus the sum of the terms in the equation excluding the residual term. That is,

$$E_t = Y_t - [L_{\text{pre}} + a_1(Y_{t-1} - L_{\text{pre}})]$$

A residual for the post-intervention portion of the series is:

$$E_t = Y_t - [L_{\text{pre}} + I + a_1(Y_{t-1} - (L_{\text{pre}} + I)]$$

If there is zero autocorrelation within phases, the model can be simplified to the point that the preintervention and postintervention residuals are simply deviations around the means of the pre- and post-intervention processes. It turns out that these residuals are the same residuals that are associated with the 1-factor ANOVA model. These residuals are of major interest in time-series experiments.

Incorrect Computation of Autocorrelation Function

A major reason for computing the autocorrelation coefficient is to evaluate whether the independence assumption associated with the 1-factor ANOVA model is met. If the autocorrelation coefficient (or, more appropriately, the whole autocorrelation function) is not statistically significant, it is concluded that the independence assumption is met and ANOVA F or the equivalent two-sample t test can be justified for testing the difference between the level of the baseline data and the level of the post-intervention data. Two questions are relevant here: (a) What is the ANOVA model when time-series data are involved? (b) What "scores" are employed in the computation of the appropriate autocorrelation coefficients?

There appears to be much confusion in the behavioral literature on the answer to the second question; this is probably because the answer to the first question is often not well understood. An answer to these questions is attempted next through the use of a data set that has been employed previously in expository articles on time-series analysis.

Figure 4 contains data from Hall *et al.* (1971). Data from the baseline 1 and praise-a-favorite-activity phases were employed in a time-series analysis by Jones *et al.* (1975). They describe the computation and interpretation of the autocorrelations as follows:

> So we calculated autocorrelations for these data, combining the scores from both phases into one time series of 41 data points. . . . For these Hall *et al.* (1971) data, The lag 1, 2, 3 and 4 correlations were .96, .94, .92 and .89, respectively. These extremely large correlations are conclusive evidence of serial dependency in this behavioral time series, and hence the assumption of independence among replicates required by the *t*-test is clearly violated. (p. 167)

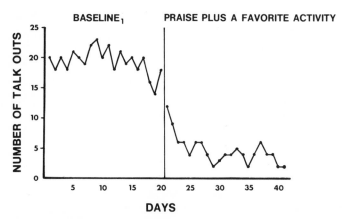

Figure 4. Empirical example of data illustrating very high but irrelevant total autocorrelation. *Note.* The data are from Hall *et al.*, 1971. Copyright 1971 by the *Journal of Applied Behavior Analysis*. Reprinted by permission.

Unfortunately, this computational procedure and the interpretation are incorrect; the major error here is computing the autocorrelations on the *combined* preintervention and postintervention observations treated as a single time-series. The autocorrelations that result from this procedure are completely irrelevant to the independence assumption of interest. Let us take a close look at the independence assumption and the appropriate method of computing the autocorrelations before returning to the Hall *et al.* data.

In the case of the independent sample ANOVA model it is crucial to understand that the estimated residuals associated with this model are deviations of preobservations and postobservations from the estimated pre- and postintervention means, respectively. The mathematical assumption of concern with this model is that the model residuals are not autocorrelated. Hence, the estimated residuals of this model must be entered into the autocorrelation formula in order to evaluate whether the assumption of independence is met. It is quite ambiguous to refer to residuals or to the independence assumption if the model is not clearly defined. One must ask, "independence of what?" Likewise, it is not sufficient to state that the residuals are serially dependent or autocorrelated unless the model, and consequently the estimated residual, is defined. If the ANOVA model is understood, there is no question about how the residuals are defined and estimated.

Jones *et al.* (1975), in their analysis of the Hall *et al.* data, computed the autocorrelations on the single series of combined pre- and postintervention raw scores. The coefficients they obtained are irrelevant to the issue of whether the independence assumption of the independent sample t or ANOVA F is met because the computation is not consistent with the assumption. Because the assumption is that the residuals of the ANOVA F (or independent sample t) model are independent, it follows that one should test the independence of these residuals. This is accomplished by computing and testing the statistical significance of the autocorrelation function based on the residuals of the ANOVA model. Because there is one set of residuals for the preintervention data and a second set of residuals for the postintervention data, one computes a separate autocorrelation function for each phase.

If there is a common autoregressive structure for the pre- and postintervention phases (as is assumed under many intervention models), it is appropriate (if the step function intervention model is valid) to then compute a weighted average of the separate pre- and postautocorrelation functions to obtain a single "best" estimate that is based on all available data. Note, however, that even though this approach utilizes data from all observations in the total series, it is not the same as computing a "total" autocorrelation function as Jones *et al.* (1975) have done by treating the total data set as a single series. The distinction between these two approaches is similar to the distinction between the within-group and total variance estimators in the analysis of variance.

Recall that the pooled within-group variance estimator in ANOVA (which is generally called the within-group mean square) is not affected by differences between means, but the between-group variance estimator (generally called the between group mean square) and the total variance estimators *are* affected by differences between means. Hence, among these three variance estimators (pooled within-group, between-group, and total), the only one that is unbiased in the case of unequal population means is the pooled within-group estimator. Essentially the same rationale holds in attempting to estimate the autocorrelation function. If the estimate is based on a pooled within phase approach, the intervention effect will not (given no change in the autoregressive structure and a step function effect) affect the estimated autocorrelation function of the residuals of the model. If, however, the total autocorrelation function is computed, the intervention effect will bias this estimate. The nature of the bias is quite predictable.

If there is no autocorrelation among the residuals of the ANOVA model, the effect of the intervention is to produce positive total autocorrelation. Notice in Figure 5(a) that the lag one autocorrelation is zero for the preintervention data as well as for the postintervention data. When no intervention effect is present, the total autocorrelation (based on combining preintervention and postintervention data into one series

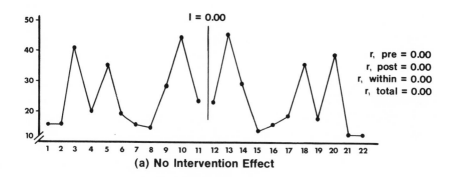

(a) No Intervention Effect

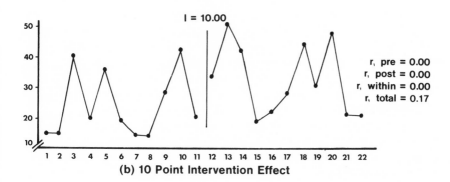

(b) 10 Point Intervention Effect

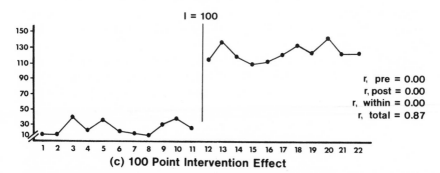

(c) 100 Point Intervention Effect

Figure 5. Total autocorrelation as a function of intervention effects for data with zero autocorrelation of ANOVA residuals.

with N_{total} = 22) is also zero. In Figure 5b, when a 10-point intervention effect is introduced between the pre- and postintervention phases, the within-phase autocorrelation estimates are still zero, but the total auto-correlation coefficient is 0.17. When the intervention effect is set at 100 points, the total autocorrelation is 0.87 and, of course, the within-phase estimates are still zero.

There is no question about whether the within-phase estimates (which normally are pooled to yield a single within-phase estimate if they do not differ significantly) or the total estimate should be employed in deciding whether the ANOVA model independence assumption is met. This is because the within-phase residuals are the residuals relevant to the ANOVA model. The implicit model underlying the computation of the total autocorrelation is $Y_t = L + E_t$ for the total series. This model is not relevant here.

A more dramatic example of the difference between the within phase and the total coefficients can be seen in Figure 6a. The autocorrelation within phase is -1.0 (perfect negative). When there is zero intervention effect, the autocorrelation computed on the combined preintervention and postintervention data set (N_{total} = 20) is -1.0. The result of introducing a 10-point intervention effect is shown in Figure 6(b). Whereas the within-phase autocorrelation is still -1.0, the total autocorrelation jumps to a positive .84. If the intervention effect is set at 110 points, as is shown in Figure 6(c), the total autocorrelation is .90. Once again, it is the within-phase information that is relevant because the residuals of the ANOVA model are residuals within phases.

It is hoped that the contrived examples have clarified the basic rationale for computing autocorrelations on the residuals of this model. At this point the skeptical reader may question whether real rather than contrived data similarly yield large discrepancies between total and within-phase coefficients. Consider the previously mentioned data of Hall *et al.* (1971).

The autocorrelations for lags one through four for these data are contained in Table 1. The large discrepancies between the within-phase and total estimates are apparent. Box–Pierce tests of significance on the autocorrelation function are not significant for the pooled within phase estimates but are clearly significant for the total estimates.

As a second empirical example of the correct and incorrect methods of computing the autocorrelation function, let us return to the data of Baer *et al.* (1973) contained in Figure 2. It was pointed out earlier that the lag one autocorrelation (computed on either raw scores or residuals from the mean) for the baseline data is .02. If the lag one autocorrelation is computed for the second portion of the total series, a coefficient of

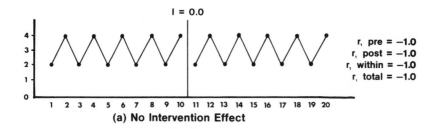

(a) No Intervention Effect

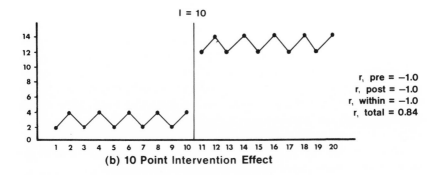

(b) 10 Point Intervention Effect

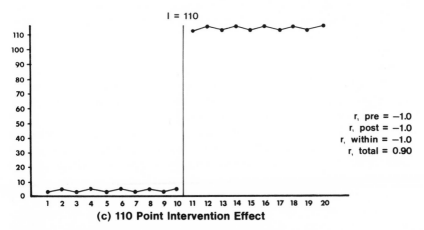

(c) 110 Point Intervention Effect

Figure 6. Total autocorrelation as a function of intervention effects for data with perfect negative autocorrelation of ANOVA residuals.

Table 1.   Empirical Example of the Difference
between Within-Phase and Total Series
Autocorrelations

Phase			
Pre-	Post-	Pooled within	Total
$r_1 = .28$	$r_1 = .49$	$r_1 = .38$	$r_1 = .96$
$r_2 = .30$	$r_2 = .13$	$r_2 = .21$	$r_2 = .94$
$r_3 = .09$	$r_3 = .07$	$r_3 = .08$	$r_3 = .92$
$r_4 = .10$	$r_4 = .04$	$r_4 = .07$	$r_4 = .89$

.19 is obtained. A weighted average of these two within-phase coefficients is .13, which is clearly not statistically significant; there is no reason
to state that autocorrelation among the residuals of the ANOVA model
is present. Further support of this conclusion is provided by Box–Pierce
tests on various lags of the autocorrelation function; probability values
associated with this test are greater than .60—insufficient evidence to
conclude that the residuals are serially dependent. Now let us combine
the data from the two phases into a single series and compute the lag
one autocorrelation from this combined (total) series. The result is a
coefficient of .82, which is clearly statistically significant. As was the
case with the Hall *et al.* data, this coefficient is completely irrelevant for
purposes of testing the assumption of the independence of the residuals
of the ANOVA model.

It can be seen in the two empirical examples just cited that the
autocorrelation coefficients based on the residuals of the ANOVA model
differ from the irrelevent coefficients based on the data of combined pre-
and postintervention phases. Consider next the autocorrelations associated with the whole set of studies cited by Jones *et al.* (1977) as proof
of the existence of the need for time-series analysis. Table 2 contains the
within-phase residual lag one autocorrelation coefficients for these studies. The frequency distribution of the coefficients contained in Table 2
can be seen in Figure 7. Interestingly, the mean (unweighted) autocorrelation coefficient is *zero*, and only one of the coefficients is statistically
significant of the 5% level! These data obviously do not support the
contention that the residuals of the ANOVA model are autocorrelated
with JABA data. A much more thorough empirical analysis of the statistical structure of JABA data is presented in the next section.

Table 2.   Within-Phase Lag One Autocorrelation Coefficients for Studies
Cited in Jones *et al.* (1977)

Study	Phase	n	r_1
Boren & Colman (1970)	1	14	.05
(Figure 1)	2	9	−.06
	3	10	.01
	4	5	−.51
(Figure 2)	1	15	.17
	2	9	.15
	3	5	−.05
	4	13	−.19
(Figure 3)	1	10	−.21
	2	5	−.27
	3	9	.46
(Figure 4)	1	15	−.13
	2	20	.47*
Ingram & Andrews (1973)	1	8	−.23
(Figure 1)	2	5	−.43
Dependent variable S	3	4	−.64
	4	3	−.04
	1	8	.40
Dependent variable M	2	5	.29
	3	4	.13
	4	3	−.17
(Figure 2)	1	8	.18
Dependent variable S	2	6	−.12
	3	4	−.25
	4	3	−.05
	1	8	.29
Dependent variable M	2	6	.48
	3	4	−.24
	4	3	−.67

Continued

Table 2. (*continued*)

Study	Phase	n	r_1
(Figure 3)	1	8	.25
Dependent variable S	2	6	−.05
	3	4	−.66
	4	3	−.17
	1	8	.52
Dependent variable M	2	6	.50
	3	4	−.04
	4	3	−.00
Phillips *et al.* (1971)	1	34	.06
	2	20	.14
	3	19	.01
	4	16	.24
Baer *et al.* (1973)	1	10	.06
	2	20	−.07
Subject: Hannah	3	14	.04
	4	6	−.46
	5	10	−.05
	1	18	.02
	2	11	−.17
Subject: Charlotte	3	4	.25
	4	13	−.02
	5	14	−.20
Subject: Frankie	1	22	.02
	2	38	.19
Wincze *et al.* (1972)	1	7	.34
	2	7	.14
	3	7	.48
	4	7	.23
	5	7	−.15
	6	7	.20
	7	7	−.65
	8	7	.26

*$P < .05$.

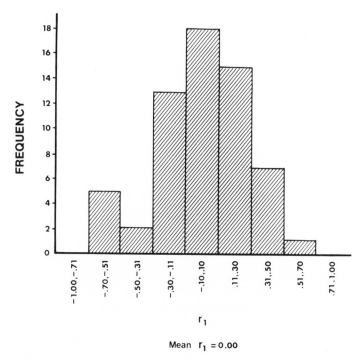

Mean r_1 = 0.00

Figure 7. Frequency distribution of within-phase lag one autocorrelation coefficients for data cited in Jones *et al.* (1977).

THE STATISTICAL STRUCTURE OF JABA DATA

An extensive investigation of *all* JABA data published from the first issue (1968) to 1977 was undertaken to provide a clear picture of statistical structure of this type of behavioral data. The methodology employed in this study follows.

Sampling

All graphed data from every issue of JABA were included in the sample of studies with the exception of those graphs containing five or fewer baseline observations, no individual data points, impossible or difficult to interpret data, baseline data with all observation values equal to zero, or histograms.

A total of 441 data sets met the criteria for being included in the sample. Because each data set contained more than one phase, there were 1,748 phases involved in the analysis. Conventional drafting equipment was employed to aid the transformation[1] of graphed representations to numerical values. In a small number of studies, tables of raw data were already included. A reliability check on the adequacy of the transformation procedure was then carried out.

Reliability

A subsample of 16 data phases was randomly selected from the 1748 available phases for use in estimating the reliability of the procedure used to obtain numerical values from the graphs. A second researcher obtained numerical values for the data points from these 16 phases, using the same procedure that had been employed by the researcher responsible for the original transformation. Hence, two sets of scores were available (one from each researcher) for each of the 16 data phases; Pearson correlation coefficients were then computed between the two sets of scores. The range of the 16 correlation coefficients (one for each of the phases in the subsample) was .99 through 1.00. This outcome supports the adequacy of the method of transforming the graphed points to numerical values.

Data Analysis

Autocorrelation coefficients for lags one through four associated with each phase of each data set were computed using program CORREL (Bower et al., 1974). In the case of very short phases, autocorrelation coefficients for all four lags were not computable. A short summary of the major findings of these analyses is presented next.

FINDINGS

The findings are presented in the following order: (a) frequency of the number of observations contained in graphed data, and (b) autocorrelation coefficients for each phase and lag.

[1]The author is indebted to Suzanne M. Girman for accomplishing this tedious task and other important aspects of this investigation.

Frequency of Number of Observations

The distribution of the frequency of the number of observations contained in the first phase (i.e., initial baseline) is presented in Figure 8. It can be seen that the frequencies for the graphed data sets included in the right-hand part of the distribution are based on the 441 data sets included in the originally defined sample. This distribution is truncated below six observations because no graphs with fewer than six baseline (phase one) data points were selected for analysis. The frequencies associated with the left-hand portion of the figure are based on the 440 data sets excluded from the originally defined sample. That is, there were 440 data sets in the JABA articles published through 1976 that had fewer

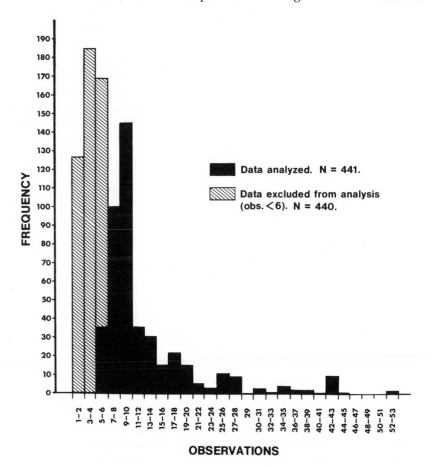

Figure 8. Frequency distribution of baseline observations.

than six baseline observations. By combining the information from the sampled and excluded graphs, one can obtain a more representative estimate of the typical number of baseline observations. The mean and median frequencies based on the combined graphs are approximately 7.9 and 5.5, respectively. The modal frequency is between 3 and 4. The number of observations contained in phases two through 10 (not reported here) tend to be even smaller.

The purpose of describing the frequency of observations in the detail presented here is to make clear that the typical behavior modification study is, in fact, characterized by very few observation points. This characteristic of behavior modification data has important implications for methods of statistical analysis of such data.

Autocorrelation

The frequency distribution of the lag one autocorrelation coefficients based on phase one (baseline) data from the 441 graphs sampled is contained in Figure 9. The mean and standard deviation of this distribution of r_1 are presented at the bottom of this figure. If there were no autocorrelation in the theoretical population of graphs from which these graphs were selected, the expected mean autocorrelation would be 0.00. The obtained value is -0.01, which is, of course, almost exactly the expected value. This obtained autocorrelation coefficient is not significantly different from 0.00 in either a practical or a statistical sense. (A more detailed analysis of these data can be found in Huitema, 1985.)

CONCLUSIONS

This chapter is critical of previously published expository papers on the application of time-series intervention analyses to behavior modification data. These papers have been widely read and cited in major methodology texts (e.g., Hersen & Barlow, 1976; Kazdin, 1980, 1982) that have a strong influence on research procedures employed in our science. It is suggested that Occam's razor be applied in the selection of models to be retained in the methodological armamentorium employed by research workers in the field of applied behavior analysis. The application of complex ARIMA intervention time-series models to data obtained in the typical behavioral study appears to be generally unnecessary. ARIMA models provide an elegant solution to a putative problem that does not seem to exist.

Because the typical applied behavior analysis study does not reveal autocorrelated residuals under the ANOVA model, many problems are

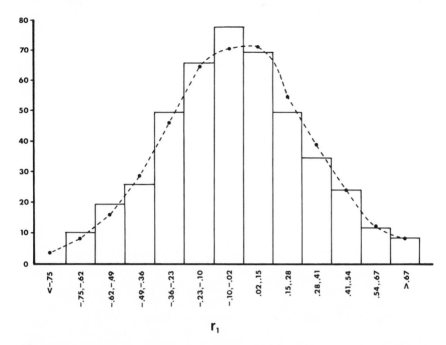

Figure 9. Frequency distribution of 441 baseline autocorrelation coefficients from JABA data: (———) observed frequency; (--•--) theoretical frequency expected with population autocorrelation equal to zero; $\bar{r}_1 = -0.01$; standard deviation of $r_1 = .31$.

simplified. If the baseline and intervention phases are reasonably stable (within conditions), a comparison of means may provide useful information. A test on the difference among means can be carried out using conventional ANOVA. Other simple procedures (not described here) are appropriate when more complex patterns are encountered.

REFERENCES

Baer, A. M., Rowbury, T., & Baer, D. M. (1973). The development of instructional control over classroom activities of deviant preschool children. *Journal of Applied Behavior Analysis, 6,* 289–298.

Boren, J. J., & Colman, A. D. (1970). Some experiments on reinforcement principles within a psychiatric ward for delinquent soldiers. *Journal of Applied Behavior Analysis, 3,* 29–37.

Bower, C. P., Padia, W. L., & Glass, G. V. (1974). *TMS: Two Fortran IV programs for the analysis of time-series experiments.* Boulder, CO: Laboratory of Educational Research, University of Colorado.

Box, G. E. P., & Taio, G. C. (1965). A change in level of a non-stationary time series. *Biometrika, 52,* 181–192.

Box, G. E. P., & Taio, G. C. (1975). Intervention analysis with applications to economic and environmental problems. *Journal of the American Statistical Association, 70,* 70–79.

Glass, G. V., Willson, V. L., & Gottman, J. M. (1975). *Design and analysis of time series experiments*. Boulder, CO: Colorado Associated University Press.

Hall, R. V., Fox, R., Willard, D., Goldsmith, L., Emerson, M., Owen, M., Davis, F., & Porcia, E. (1971). The teacher as observer and experimenter in the modification of disputing and talking-out behaviors. *Journal of Applied Behavior Analysis, 4,* 141–149.

Hersen, M., & Barlow, D. H. (1976). *Single case experimental designs: Strategies for studying behavior change*. Oxford: Pergamon Press.

Huitema, B. E. (1985). Autocorrelation in applied behavior analysis: A myth. *Behavioral Assessment, 7,* 109–120.

Ingham, R. J., & Andrews, G. (1973). An analysis of a token economy in stuttering therapy. *Journal of Applied Behavior Analysis, 6,* 219–229.

Jones, R. R., Vaught, R. S., & Reid, J. B. (1975). Time series analysis as a substitute for single subject analysis of variance designs. In G. R. Patterson, I. M. Marks, J. D. Matarazzo, R. A. Myers, G. E. Schwartz, & H. H. Strupp (Eds.), *Behavior change 1974* (pp. 164–169). Hawthorne, NY: Aldine.

Jones, R. R., Vaught, R. S., & Weinrott, M. (1977). Time-series analysis in operant research. *Journal of Applied Behavior Analysis, 10,* 151–166.

Kazdin, A. E. (1980). *Research design in clinical psychology*. New York: Harper & Row.

Kazdin, A. E. (1982). *Single case research designs: Methods for clinical and applied settings*. New York: Oxford University Press.

Phillips, E. L., Phillips, E. A., Fixsen, D. L., & Wolf, M. M. (1971). Achievement Place: Modification of the behaviors of pre-delinquent boys within a token economy. *Journal of Applied Behavior Analysis, 4,* 45–49.

Tiao, G. C., Box, G. E. P., & Hamming, W. J. (1975). Analysis of Los Angeles photochemical smog data: a statistical overview. *Journal of the Air Pollution Control Association, 25,* 260–268.

Wincze, J. P., Leitenberg, H., & Agras, W. S. (1972). The effects of token reinforcement and feedback on the delusional verbal behavior of chronic paranoid schizophrenics. *Journal of Applied Behavior Analysis, 5,* 247–262.

10

Statistical Analysis and Single-Subject Designs

Some Misunderstandings

BRADLEY E. HUITEMA

INTRODUCTION

In the beginning there were no statistical analyses of operant experiments. It was like a breath of fresh air for many psychologists when, many years ago, Skinner (1963) said:

> Statistical methods are unnecessary. . . . When a variable is changed and the effect on performance observed, it is for most purposes idle to prove statistically that a change has indeed occurred. . . . rate of responding and changes in rate can be directly observed . . . The effect is similar to increasing the resolving power of a microscope: A new subject matter is suddenly open to direct inspection. (p. 508)

This viewpoint struck a responsive chord among those researchers who recognized that psychology (along with several other sciences) appeared to be becoming overly mathematized in an effort to gain scientific respectability. My contact with colleagues in the physical sciences leads me to believe that statistically oriented psychologists have indeed had a positive impact on the image of psychology as a science. It has been pointed out to me by several consulting statisticians at various universities that the level of sophistication of the typical psychological experiment to which they are exposed exceeds the typical level found in most other disciplines. This, of course, is gratifying to hear and it tends to encourage those of us involved in the teaching of research

BRADLEY E. HUITEMA • Department of Psychology, Western Michigan University, Kalamazoo, MI 49008.

methodology to continue extolling the virtues of complex designs and the wonders of statistical analysis. But even the inveterate statistician has to admit that the case for data analytic simplicity promoted by operant psychologists is, at least, worth considering. After all, there has been much emphasis among many statisticians on graphic data display for the past decade (e.g., Andrews, 1976; Bachi, 1978; Barabba, 1980; Beniger & Robyn, 1978; Bertin, 1980; Gnanadesikan, 1973; Hartwig & Dearing, 1979; Tufte, 1983; Tukey, 1977; Wainer, 1974).

At the same time, behavior modifiers have recently reconsidered the case for statistical analysis. Predictably enough, many psychological statisticians (e.g., Glass, Willson, & Gottman, 1975; Gottman, 1981; Gottman & Glass, 1978; Horne, Yang, & Ware, 1982) have concluded that behavior modification experiments would benefit from statistical inferential tests, whereas several behavior modification methodologists (e.g., Baer, 1977; Michael, 1974) have evaluated statistical analysis as harmful to the development of the discipline. Even though both camps have presented convincing position papers that contain useful points, flaws and misunderstandings permeate both sides of the argument; these should be pointed out. The purpose of this chapter is to do so.

NINE COMMANDMENTS

It appears that the major errors in the most frequently cited work concerning statistics and operant experiments would have been avoided if the authors had followed the nine methodological commandments presented in the following sections.

I. Thou Shalt Not Confuse the Design with the Analysis

Ever since Sidman's *Tactics of Scientific Research* was published in 1960, operant psychologists have described their experiments as being characterized by (a) repeated or continuous data collection across time on (b) a single subject whose data are (c) analyzed by visual inspection. These characteristics are said to differ from those of the traditional nonoperant experiment, which are: (a) one observation on each member of (b) two or more groups whose data are (c) analyzed by methods of statistical inference (generally hypothesis tests). Until recently, it was presumed by operant methodologists that any single-subject experiment necessarily involved the collection of data across time and a visual analysis. Conversely, it has been presumed that group designs require "an excessive dependency on the significance test, since such experiments cannot be reacted to in any other way" (Michael, 1974, p. 27). There is a problem, however, with these descriptions of single-subject and group experiments.

The basic flaw is that three dimensions of experiments have been confounded. That is, the classification of an experiment as *single subject* or *group* has been confounded in much of the methodological literature with the classifications of analytic procedure and the number of observations on each subject. Many operant methodologists (e.g., Sidman, 1960) use the term "statistical design" to refer to a one-shot group experiment that is statistically analyzed; but notice in Figure 1 that the classification of experimental design (single subject versus group) is independent of both the classification according to the number of observations obtained from each subject (one versus multiple observations) and the type of analysis (visual versus statistical). It can be seen in this figure that all combinations of the three classification dimensions are possible. Although most single-subject designs fall in Cell A and many group designs fall in Cell H, this pattern is not necessary.

It should be recognized that even though this three dimensional representation may clarify some of the previously confounded issues, the cells are not necessarily mutually exclusive. An experiment can be analyzed visually and statistically, the behavior of an individual subject in a repeated measurement group design can be isolated and analyzed separately, and a single complex experiment can contain both repeated measurement and nonrepeated factors. Some of the most frequently made distinctions between designs vanish or blur upon inspection.

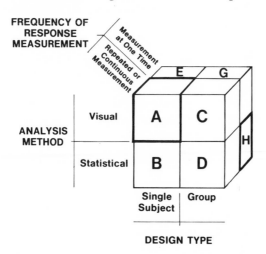

Figure 1. Three frequently confounded dimensions of research methodology.

The general issues associated with visual and statistical analyses are the same with single-subject and group designs. Hence, the suggestion that group designs can only be reacted to using a significance test is equally true (or false) for single-subject designs.

II. Thou Shalt Not Confuse the Effect Size with the Statistical Significance of the Effect

An article appears in the behavioral and social science literature every 3 or 4 years restating the point that statistical significance is not the same thing as practical significance, clinical significance, or the size of the effect. Alas, it seems that this is still not understood. In general, statisticians are doing a horrible job of communicating this very important point. The failure to make this distinction is a problem in several widely read papers on the argument of whether to use statistical methods in analyzing behavior modification data.

Baer (1977) argued against the use of statistical analysis by claiming that (a) researchers who use individual-subject designs and visual analysis make fewer Type I errors (claiming an effect when none is present) than those who use group designs with statistical analysis and (b) the reason the visual analysis researchers make fewer Type I errors is because they identify only those effects that are large and useful whereas statistical analysis identifies effects that are weak and of questionable usefulness. There are several problems with these points.

First, in arguing that a basic advantage of visual analysis over statistical analysis is the identification of only large effects, Baer suggests that the purpose of both types of analysis is to identify only large, important effects. That is, he seems to imply that a statistical analysis is flawed when it identifies an effect that is trivial in size or importance. This is debatable. The purpose of a significance test is not to identify only large and important effects.

If one is interested in evaluating the size of an effect in an individual-subject design it is reasonable to eyeball the level of behavior under different experimental conditions. In the case of a group design, it is equally reasonable to evaluate the size of the treatment effects by eyeballing the level of behavior under different experimental conditions. That which is eyeballed is similar with both types of design. In the case of an individual-subject design it is the graphed data under different conditions and, in the case of a group design, it is the plotted frequency distribution of the data under the different conditions. If the single-subject data are stationary the researcher may find it helpful to compute the mean or median level under each condition; likewise, the computation of the mean or median level associated with each treatment in a group design may help the researcher visualize the size of the apparent effect.

Clearly, the size of the effect can be conveyed by the visual representation of the data or by the difference between simple descriptive measures of level; this is true for single-subject and group designs. The typical inferential test statistics such as t or F and the associated probability values are not measures of the size or importance of the effects. An example may be helpful. Suppose the data in Table 1 were collected in several different two-group experiments all employing the same response measure. Compare the outcome of Experiment 1 with that of Experiment 2. Notice that the size of the estimated effect (a 3-point *mean* difference) is exactly the same in both experiments. The t values and the corresponding probability values are, however, far different.

Next, compare the results of Experiments 3 and 4. The t and probability values are the same in these experiments but the size of the estimated treatment effects are far different. Last, compare the results of Experiments 5 and 6. Here the size of the estimated effect is much smaller in Experiment 6 than Experiment 5, but the t value associated with this small difference is much larger than the t value associated with Experiment 5. If the researcher follows convention in the interpretation of the t tests the smaller estimated effect of Experiment 6 will be declared statistically significant, whereas the larger estimated effect of Experiment 5 will not.

The point of these examples is that test statistics and probability values should never be interpreted as descriptive measures of the size of the effects of experimental treatments. Information concerning the size of the effect is easily obtained from graphs, data plots, descriptive statistics, and confidence intervals, but not from significance tests. This holds for single-subject and group designs.

Baer's view that significance tests often identify small effects is correct; empirical data to support this conclusion abound. Likewise, few will argue with the point that bigger is better when it comes to treatment effects. But I do not agree with the conclusion that visually analyzed single-subject designs are associated with large effects because they are not as sensitive as statistically analyzed group designs.

III. Thou Shalt Not Confuse Conclusions Based on Speculations with Those Based on Meaningful Data

The main reason I am unconvinced that visual analyses of single-subject designs fail to identify small effects is the same reason I am skeptical of the effectiveness of laetrile in treating cancer—there are no meaningful data to support such a conclusion. It is doubtful, for several

Table 1. Experiments Illustrating the Inconsistency between the Size and the Statistical Significance of an Effect

Treatment		Treatment	
A	B	A	B
Experiment I		*Experiment II*	
12	9	19,12,15	12,16,16
15	12	12,22,19	19,9,14
17	14	17,17,22	12,19,9
19	16	12,15,15	19,16,9
22	19	17,22,19	12,14,14

3.0 ←	Effect size	→ 3.0
1.25 ←	*t* Value	→ 2.33
.25 ←	Probability value	→ .03

Experiment III		*Experiment IV*	
2	11	20	40
5	6	25	30
4	8	10	55
9	10	45	50
5	10	25	50

4.0 ←	Effect size	→ 20.0
2.76 ←	*t* Value	→ 2.76
.03 ←	Probability value	→ .03

Experiment V		*Experiment VI*	
11	98	15	17
31	22	16	17
5	45	14	17
12	92	15	18
1	3	15	16

40.0 ←	Effect size	→ 2.0
2.05 ←	*t* Value	→ 4.47
.11 ←	Probability Value	→ .002

reasons, that such data will ever exist. First, the independent and dependent variables employed in single-subject and group designs are not generally the same. This, of course, may be interpreted as support for those who argue that the independent variables identified in behavior modification experiments are highly effective (i.e., yield large effects). The problem with such an interpretation is that there are reasons other than the type of design and analysis that can explain why behavior modifiers often employ variables with larger effects.

Perhaps we have an example of confusing correlation with cause here. Baer (1977) argued that only large effects are identified in behavioral studies because visual analysis is sensitive to only large effects. An alternative explanation is that those researchers who report large effects using visual analysis are reinforced for submitting results of such effects to certain journals whether they are expected or not. Others who report smaller (but less redundant) results are perhaps less likely to get such data published in the same journals. Because editorial policy of one journal may be to accept only single-subject studies reporting large effects, whereas another journal will accept studies reporting any effects at all (based on statistically significant group results), maybe editorial policy rather than type of design and analysis explains the difference some believe exists in the size of effects associated with these different designs.

This interpretation should not be construed as either support for one editorial policy over another or as an argument against single-subject designs. It is eminently reasonable to disseminate information on treatments that repeatedly yield large effects and it is often highly practical and convincing to use single-subject designs. But it should be kept in mind that there are situations where small differences can be very important; single-subject designs should not be labeled impotent for the identification of such effects.

There is a second reason that I question the conclusion that visually analyzed single-subject designs are less powerful (i.e., less sensitive to effects when they are present) than statistically analyzed group designs. There are drastic differences within the two types of design on the parameters that affect power. The amount of data and the variability within and between conditions largely determine the identification of effects. This is true for single-subject and group designs and for visual and statistical analyses. A quick look at the data from a few dozen single-subject experiments will reveal vast differences from study to study on the amount of variability within conditions. Similarly, the within-group variability in group designs differs a great deal from study to study. This is true even when the independent and dependent variables are similar. I doubt that it is worthwhile to make general statements of the differential sensitivity of single subject and group designs when such large differences exist within the two design types.

Because there are no meaningful comparative studies on the sensitivity issue, opinions differ. Sidman (1960) argues forcefully that

> a feature of intrasubject replication, is the reliable demonstration of smaller effects than would be possible otherwise. A small effect obtained in a group-type experiment is likely to be washed out in intersubject variability. (p. 91)

Hence Sidman's conclusion is that single-subject designs are more sensitive than group designs, whereas Baer concludes that single-subject designs are less sensitive.

A close reading of Sidman's classic methodological work makes it clear that his approach to single-subject experimentation strongly encourages tracking down and controlling those variables that determine much of the baseline variability. After reasonable stability of the baseline data is observed, conditions are changed. But the fact remains that much variability is not controlled in both human and animal research. When control of baseline variability is high the sensitivity to small intervention effects is high; poor control leads to low sensitivity.

In those single-subject studies where baseline variability is practically nil, one might find much higher sensitivity than with the typical group design using the typical sample size, the typical heterogeneity of within-group behavior, and the typical data analysis (e.g., a t test).

Let us say a specific single-subject experiment is twice as powerful as the typical group experiment in this case. If any of the "typical" group design characteristics change, the relative sensitivity also changes. Suppose an analysis of covariance is run rather than a conventional t. A well-chosen covariate could easily reduce the error variance to a quarter of the original size; the sensitivity of the analysis of the group design would dramatically increase. A change in any of the other characteristics of the group design could likewise result in a large change in sensitivity. Because there are many characteristics of both group and single-subject designs that affect sensitivity, no general comparison of the two is possible. Besides that, the questions answered with those different designs are not generally the same; this makes comparisons between them meaningless.

IV. Thou Shalt Not Confuse Statistical Significance with Replication

The meaning of the term *statistical significance* appears to be almost universally misunderstood. I have no data on this, but I would venture the guess that the term's use is bungled as often as that of the term *behavior modification.* Statistics books and statistics professors always tell us what it is, but what appears to be needed is an understanding of what it is not. Suppose a two-group experiment is run with 10 subjects in each group, a mean difference of 7 points is obtained, and the *t* test on this difference is associated with a probability value of exactly .05. I will list five points concerning the interpretation of this outcome; the first one has already been mentioned but it cannot be overemphasized:

1. The probability value of .05 does not provide direct information on the size of the effect.
2. The probability value of .05 does not provide a direct answer to the question of how often a result can be expected to be replicated (i.e., the results do not mean that the chances are 95 out of 100 that the outcome will be replicated if the experiment is run again).
3. The result of the significance test does not mean that the chances are 95 out of 100 that the difference between population means is 7 points.
4. The result of the significance test does not mean that the probability is .05 that the population mean difference is zero.
5. If the study is run again and a nonsignificant outcome is obtained (p > .05) in this second study, this does not necessarily mean that the two studies are inconsistent. (See Experiments 1 and 2 in Table 1 for an example of this.)

The value .05 does answer to the following question: If there are 10 subjects in each group, what is the probability of obtaining a difference between the two sample means of 7 or more points given zero difference between the population means? Notice that the probability value refers to neither the notion of a large effect nor to the chance of obtaining the same outcome if replication is attempted. Rather, we have a simple statement of conditional probability.

Such a statement provides useful information about the results of an experiment if it is correctly interpreted, but it is not ultimate proof. While discussing the .05 level of statistical significance almost 60 years ago, Fisher (1926, p. 504) pointed out that "A scientific fact should be regarded as experimentally established only if a properly designed experiment rarely fails to give this level of significance." Clearly Fisher acknowledged the great importance of replication. A significant test statistic (or a confidence interval) can supply some confidence that a direct replication on the same subject would not show zero effects. Such a test would not be the same as a direct replication, but it is relevant evidence. It should be obvious, however, that direct replication is a much more straightforward and convincing way to answer the question of whether the intervention effect can be replicated. This, of course, is a reason behavioral methodologists should argue against the use of A/B designs and promote, for example, A/B/A/B designs.

V. Thou Shalt Not Perform an Analysis That Is Inconsistent with the Design

The general class of statistical procedures most frequently recommended for single-subject behavioral data is time-series intervention analysis. Every reference I have encountered that recommends these procedures presents an approach for evaluating the effect of an intervention in the context of two phases. Glass et al. (1975); Gottman (1981); Gottman and Glass (1978); Hartmann et al. (1980); Horne et al. (1982); Jones, Vaught, and Reid (1975); and Kazdin (1976), all describe time-series intervention models for data sets containing two phases. The A/B or two-phase design is not the type of design encouraged or even tolerated by most single subject methodologists. Virtually every treatment of single subject research designs (e.g., Hersen & Barlow, 1976; Kazdin, 1982; Risley & Wolf, 1972; Wolf & Risley, 1971) discourages the use of this very weak design. The bread and butter designs for applied behavior modification studies are, of course, variants of reversal- and multiple-baseline designs, not A/B designs.

Some expository treatments of time-series analysis present data from typical behavioral designs, but then select only the data from the first two of several phases for analysis. For example, two excellent textbooks on time-series analysis (Glass et al., 1975, and Gottman, 1981) present graphed A/B data from Hall et al. (1971). This study was not based on an A/B design; data from five phases are contained in the original figure. These data phases contain important information concerning the intervention effects and they should not be ignored.

Jones, Vaught, and Weinrott (1977) have presented data from behavioral studies containing several phases and have recommended that they be analyzed using ARIMA time-series methods. Their general recommendation is to run an ARIMA t on each pair of adjacent phases. For example, in describing their analysis of a study by Wincze, Leitenberg, and Agras (1972), they state: "comparing the level in each phase with the level of the preceding phase produced only one statistically significant change in level, between Phases 6 and 7 ($t = 2.36$; $df = 12$; $p < 0.05$)" (p. 163). The problem of inflated Type I error associated with multiple comparisons within a single experiment is well known in group designs; the same issue is relevant here. That is, the probability of one or more test statistics (i.e., ARIMA ts) in this study being incorrectly declared significant is far greater than the nominal alpha of .05. It is closer to .30.

There is a second problem in following the recommendation to run a test on each pair of adjacent phases. This is the problem of low power. Each test on adjacent phases uses only the data in those two phases. Information contained in the other phases is ignored and consequently the power of the test to detect effects is much lower than would be the case if all the data were employed simultaneously (as is the case with the analysis of variance applied to multiple groups). Time-series models can be built to include multiple interventions, but they are not generally mentioned in the literature proposing statistical analysis to applied behavioral data.

This problem of ignoring data because the analysis does not fit the design is not limited to reversal designs. Consider the multiple-baseline data contained in Figure 2. A visual analysis of these data (from Baer, Rowbury, & Baer, 1973) makes use of the information gleaned from inspecting the behavior of all three subjects simultaneously. All subjects contribute important data concerning the intervention effect. The analyses suggested by Jones et al. are separate ARIMA t tests on the data from each subject. Once again, this analytic approach is not consistent with the design and, as with the reversal design, the consequences are increased probability of making a Type I error and low power (i.e., high probability of Type II error).

Hence, the recommendation to employ separate ARIMA t tests on either adjacent pairs of phases (in the case of reversal designs) or on each subject (in the case of multiple-baseline designs) is questionable if decision errors are considered. Although these two types of errors are dwelled on by statisticians, they are not necessarily the only errors committed. There is another class of errors that must be considered.

VI. Thou Shalt Not Commit Type III Errors

The researcher who employs simple inferential test procedures with group designs generally has a fairly good idea of the nature of the descriptive statistics or parameter estimates associated with such analyses. For example, it is well known that the conventional independent sample t test is associated with the difference between two sample means and that this difference is an estimate of the difference between two population means μ_1 and μ_2.

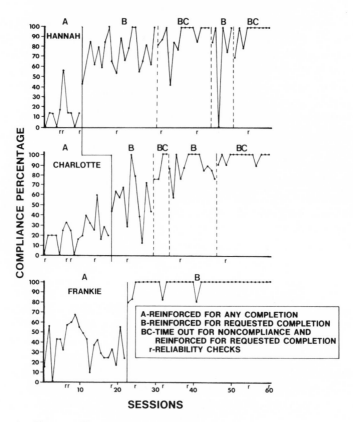

Figure 2. Illustrative data from Baer, Rowbury, & Baer (1973).

Until recently researchers tended to avoid computing certain complex analyses because they did not understand the associated mathematics or the need for such procedures. It has probably been a good
thing that the authors of advanced statistics books routinely wander off
into hyperspace never to be understood again. But mathematical intim-
idation and tedious number crunching sessions are no longer effective
in preventing the computation of esoteric statistics. Computer software
is now available to allow us to compute easily the most complex analysis
imaginable. But, as any Apple should know, to compute is not to
understand.

Because researchers can now easily obtain sophisticated analyses
without reading detailed descriptions of their purpose and meaning, it
is not unusual to encounter computer output and, ultimately, published
results that contain correctly computed complex inferential statistics (e.g.,

a significance test such as Wilk's lambda for a multivariate analysis of variance) but no clear description of the comparison that has been estimated. The problem here is not that of misinterpreting the meaning of a probability value. Rather, there is a misinterpretation of the nature of the comparison that is tested. When this occurs we have a Type III error.

What does this have to do with the analysis of behavioral experiments? It appears to me that the output of most intervention time-series programs is almost always misinterpreted. Unfortunately, the existing books on the topic and the documentation associated with time-series programs are often of little help. The problem is with the meaning of the estimated intervention effect. I will use the output of program TSX (written by Bower, Padia, & Glass, 1974) to illustrate the issue. Although somewhat inefficient, this excellent program is widely used and familiar to many researchers in the behavioral and social sciences who have been exposed to ARIMA (Autoregressive Integrated Moving Averages) intervention models through Glass *et al.* (1975).

The data contained in Figure 3 are from one of two subjects who participated in a study described by Komechak (1974) on the control of anxious thoughts. The first phase is the baseline period and the second

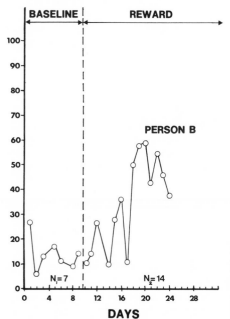

Figure 3. Graph used by Gottman and Glass (1978) to illustrate the inconsistency between visual and statistical methods of analysis. *Note.* Copyright 1978 by Academic Press, Inc. Reprinted by permission. (Data from Komechak, 1974.)

phase is the period during which the subject was rewarded for maintaining anxiety-free thoughts.

These data were employed by Gottman and Glass (1978) in a study comparing visual analysis with time-series analysis on conclusions reached. They asked 13 graduate students to inspect Komechak's data and to judge whether an intervention effect was present "at the point of intervention of reward" (p. 199). They then computed an ARIMA intervention analysis. The model employed was a step-function first-order integrated moving averages or (0,1,1) process. Their results are presented in Table 2.

Gottman and Glass conclude that this study demonstrates the discrepancy between the conclusions reached using visual as opposed to statistical analysis. At first glance it seems reasonable to concur. After all, 11 of 13 judges concluded that there was an effect, whereas the statistical analysis clearly led to the conclusion that there was not an effect. There are, however, two problems with this demonstration.

The first problem is that several attempts to replicate this study have yielded visual analysis results that are essentially the reverse of those reported by Gottman and Glass. The second problem is that the outcome of the statistical analysis they performed is widely misunderstood. The first problem has been discussed elsewhere (Huitema, 1979); the second one is the topic of this section—the insidious and generally unknown problem of Type III error associated with the interpretation of some ARIMA intervention time-series models.

The Gottman and Glass statistical analysis of the Komechak data strongly argues that there was no intervention effect. But exactly what is the effect estmated by the statistical analysis?

I have asked this question of a dozen or so graduate students and colleagues who have attended various workshops on intervention time-series analysis over the past 5 years. These workshops have been offered

Table 2. Outcome of Gottman and Glass (1978) Study on Visual and Statistical Analyses of Komechak (1974) Data

Visual analysis	Statistical analysis
Question asked: Is there an intervention effect at the point of intervention of reward?	Question asked: Is there sufficient evidence to reject the hypothesis that the step-function intervention effect is equal to zero?
Outcome: Yes. The proportion of judges who decided that there is an intervention effect is 11/13 = .85	Outcome: No. There is insufficient data to reject H_0: $\delta = 0.0$ ($t = .2$; $p = .83$)

by many highly qualified instructors to a wide variety of research work-ers. The common theme of these workshops is how to evaluate inter-vention effects. Indeed, the participants do learn how to use computer software that provides descriptive and inferential information on inter-vention effects. For example, those who were exposed to program TSX can identify the delta hat $\hat{\delta}$ statistic and the associated t value. When I have asked students what the delta hat statistic is, the reply has been, "The size of the intervention effect" or "The treatment effect." Those students who had recently read one of four applied texts on time-series intervention analysis stated that the effect, in the case of stationary data and a step-function intervention, is the difference between the level of the baseline phase data and the level of the postintervention phase data.

When I presented the Komechak data contained in Figure 3 to the students and asked, What is the level of the baseline phase and what is the level of the postintervention phase?, the typical response was that the "level" of a phase is simply the mean of the data points in that phase. Hence the estimated effect was frequently interpreted to be the differ-ence between the arithmetic mean of the baseline data and the arithmetic mean of the postintervention data. If these means are computed for the Komechak data the estimated effect is $(34.36 - 13.71) = 20.65$. This difference is statistically significant ($p < .01$) when analyzed with a con-ventional independent sample t test. (The difference is also statistically significant when analyzed with appropriate correction for the hetero-geneous variances.)

If we carry out the ARIMA $(0,1,1)$ intervention time-series analysis recommended (and computed) by Gottman and Glass on the Komechak data, we will discover that the estimated intervention effect is nowhere near the 20.65 point difference between the means. Rather, it is 2.46. It is this difference that is associated with the nonsignificant time-series t test Gottman and Glass report, and it is this difference that is not under-stood by the typical student and research worker.

The typical reaction of those who have seen these graphed data and both the mean difference (20.65) and $\hat{\delta}$ (2.46) is, "How can this be?" The explanation can be seen in Figure 4. Notice the length of the spikes in the top row (a) relative to those in the second row (b). The spikes in the first row represent the weights attached to each observation in the computation of the phase means. It can be seen that each observation within a phase is weighted equally in the computation of the phase mean. The spikes in the second row represent the approximate weights used in computing the values that yield $\hat{\delta}$. The weight for each obser-vation depends primarily on the moving average parameter estimate $\hat{\theta}$ and the number of time periods separating the observation from the intervention.

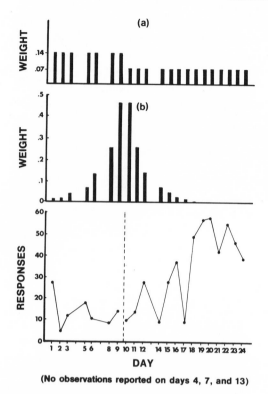

Figure 4. Weight functions associated with (a) independent sample t test and (b) ARIMA (0,1,1) intervention model applied to Komechak data.

Notice in Figure 4 that the weights fall off very rapidly with these data. This, of course, means that data points more than four or five steps removed from the introduction of the intervention are essentially ignored in the computation of the intervention effect $\hat{\delta}$. The currently available applied time-series texts do a fine job of describing the matrix manipulations involved in obtaining the correct estimates, but this is not adequate for most researchers who attempt to conceptualize the $\hat{\delta}$ statistic.

I believe that every description of an ARIMA intervention model should convey the point that $\hat{\delta}$ is (a) essentially the difference between two weighted means and (b) that the weights depend on the model and the nature of the data. Better yet, intervention time-series computer programs should provide a plot of the weights associated with the pre- and postintervention data or a table of such weights. If one were to examine these weights for every analysis run, the influence of various moving average and/or autoregressive statistics on the estimated effect would be apparent; to many the estimates would be surprising. This is not the place to provide a complete treatment of the issues of interpretation of $\hat{\delta}$ under different ARIMA models, but they are many. In several cases it provides an answer to a question that is likely to be very different from the question the researcher thinks is being answered; note that this situation meets our definition of a Type III error.

VII. Thou Shalt Not Ignore the Nature of the Data

It has been pointed out in Sections V and VI that the ARIMA time-series models most frequently recommended to applied behavior modification researchers are generally inconsistent with the designs of this area and are frequently misinterpreted. In this section, I will ignore those problems and concentrate on the structure of the within-phase data.

The basic justification for employing ARIMA intervention models rather than more conventional (and simpler) procedures is the problem of autocorrelated residuals. Time-series data in some areas of chemistry, economics, engineering, physiology, political science, psychology, and sociology have been found to contain substantial residual autocorrelation. Because applied behavioral data are also collected across time, it has been presumed that time-series analysis is required.

Recent evidence (Huitema, Chapter 9) indicates that the earlier warnings concerning autocorrelation problems were premature. There are three reasons for questioning the previous recommendations to employ ARIMA time-series models.

First, the early studies (e.g., Glass *et al.*, 1975) of behavioral data that seemed to require autoregressive, moving average, and differencing parameters were not typical applied behavior analysis studies. They were social or behavioral data, but not generally the type of data published in, for example, the *Journal of Applied Behavior Analysis* (JABA).

Second, the early studies of autocorrelation in data from JABA (e.g., Jones *et al.*, 1977) contained computational errors that distorted the autocorrelation estimates. Third, none of the papers and texts that recommend the use of ARIMA and related models with applied behavioral studies acknowledge the extent to which exceedingly short phases characterize these studies. For example, Horne *et al.* (1982) recently stated that the data set in their time-series paper was typical of applied behavior analysis data. It contained two phases; the first contained 66 observations and the second contained 74.

The typical (modal) number of baseline observations per phase in the *Journal of Applied Behavior Analysis* is about four. The longest baseline phase contained in 881 data sets published in this journal through 1976 is about 50. Approximately 95 percent of the baseline phases contain 20 or fewer observations. Studies with more than 10 baseline observations comprise only 19% of this sample. Phases past the initial baseline tend to be even shorter.

The importance of sample size in ARIMA time-series analysis is discussed in the next section. Before moving on to that section, one last point should be made concerning the nature of behavioral data. They often do not meet the statistical definition of a time-series. Notice in Figure 3 that there are 9 days in the first phase, but only 7 observations. Because these observations were not obtained at equally spaced time intervals this is not, strictly speaking, a time-series. This is often the case with behavioral data. The extent to which one should worry about this issue depends on the amount of missing data, the structure of the complete process, the ARIMA model employed, and whether the pattern of missing data in all phases is similar.

VIII. Thou Shalt Not Quash Small Sample Warnings

The first textbook treatments of time-series models recommend 50 to 100 observations as a minimum for carrying out ARIMA analyses. More recently there have been suggestions that fewer observations are satisfactory. For example, Hartmann et al. (1980) suggest that "under some circumstances, substantially fewer than 50 observations may be appropriate" (p. 555). As support for this recommendation they point out that the Glass et al. approach is quite powerful with as few as 20 baseline and 20 postintervention observations when it can be assumed that a simple ARIMA model fits. Similarly, Gottman (1981) states that

> The complaint that a lot of points are necessary in time-series analysis is equivalent to the case of analysis of variance. Indeed, more points usually permit one to identify more sophisticated models that provide a better fit to the data and make it easier to detect smaller departures from the process after intervention. (p. 58)

There are two basic problems with the arguments of Hartmann et al. and Gottman. The first is concerned with the reason for large data set recommendations and the second concerns the consequences of ignoring small N warnings.

The major reason for the conventional recommendation to employ ARIMA models only with large data sets is not power or sensitivity to intervention effects. The reason is model identification. It appears that the $N = 50$ minimum suggested in both the earlier mathematical statistics references and the more recent applied texts (e.g., McCleary & Hay, 1980) is justified. Westra (1978) has shown that model identification is very risky with fewer than 50 observations per phase.

I have no quarrel with the point that small data sets are appropriately analyzed if a specific model can be assumed to fit *a priori*. But the procedures recommended by Hartmann *et al.* and Gottman involve building a model for each data set *de novo*. Hence the issue of relevance is not the power of a known model; rather, the issue is whether the correct model can be identified.

The second issue is tied to the model identification problem. Once a model has been identified it is reasonable to ask, What are the consequences of employing this model if it is, in fact, incorrect? I believe that insufficient attention has been directed toward this problem. Let me explain my concern using the Komechak data as an example.

Recall from Section VI that there were seven observations in the preintervention phase and 14 observations in the postintervention phase. Gottman and Glass (1978) identified the model as (0,1,1), whereas I suggested that a white noise or (0,0,0) model seemed to be reasonable. (It might be of interest to some readers to mention that the p values associated with the Box–Pierce test on the residuals of the two models are .19, pre, and .76, post, for the (0,1,1) model, and .56, pre, and .30, post, for the (0,0,0) model). I will not argue that I am right and they are wrong; there are insufficient data for an unambiguous identification. If the major consequence of disagreement on model identification was no more severe than a difference in power (as Gottman seems to suggest) I would not be concerned with the small N issue. Unfortunately, the consequences are more severe.

The major problem is that the size (and even the direction) of the estimated change in level can be drastically different under various ARIMA models. Recall that the analysis of the Komechak data under the (0,0,0) model results in an estimated effect almost 10 times the size of the estimated effect under the (0,1,1) model. Several other time-series models also yield large and statistically significant effects for this data set. The basic point of this example is that model identification is not a minor problem.

When several different ARIMA models seem to fit the data we have model ambiguity. This is handled by some researchers by simply taking a position on a specific model and then reporting the outcome of that model. I would like to argue for a less rigid approach for those intent on using ARIMA analysis. The results of all plausible models should be reported when the most appropriate model is not clear. This means that more analyses will be required with small data sets because this is the situation in which the greatest ambiguity is present.

If the results of multiple models differ greatly the inconsistency will make the point that ambiguity exists. The amount of ambiguity will generally be inversely related to the amount of data available.

I do not want to give the impression that small data sets and model ambiguity always result in large discrepancies between estimated effects. Glass *et al.* (1975) analyzed data from Hall *et al.* (1971) and identified an ARIMA first order moving averages model (0,0,1). Alternatively, Gottman (1981, p. 56) suggests that a white noise (0,0,0) model is appropriate for these data. The t value and estimated intervention effect are $t = 16.52$, $\hat{\delta} = 14.40$ under the (0,0,1) model and $t = 20.64$, $\hat{\delta} = 14.64$ under the (0,0,0) model. (These values do not correspond exactly to Glass *et al.* and Gottman results because they eliminated the last data point from the second phase.) Notice that the two different models yield almost the same estimated effect. When results from several different models converge, the outcome is clear. This is not unusual when the various analyses are all based on certain simple models.

Up to this point, I have pointed out that there are many problems in the use of time-series analysis. Does this lead me to conclude that the statistical analysis of behavioral data is a waste of time? No.

IX. Thou Shalt Not Commit Political Suicide

Most applied behavior analysis researchers are quite content with visual analysis. The simplicity, flexibility, and directness of this method are apparent. Why then should one consider the statistical method to supplement (not replace) the visual method?

The arguments generally offered in support of the statistical approach are (a) statistical methods allow the identification of small but potentially important effects that might be ignored in a visual analysis, (b) statistical methods can evaluate intervention effects when there is instability and/or trend during the baseline phase, and (c) statistical methods are more objective than visual methods. I have presented my position on the first point in Section III. My responses to the other points are that (a) visual methods can also be used to evaluate intervention effects when instability and/or trend is present and (b) objectivity can vanish when it is necessary to identify an ARIMA model on the number of data points available in the typical applied behavioral study.

The main reason for mentioning the three typical arguments in favor of statistical methods is not to present counterarguments. Rather, the reason is to suggest that these arguments miss the most important point: credibility.

The field of behavior analysis has gone through a developmental sequence that has resulted in a high degree of insularity. Those within the field frequently comment on the obvious advantages of integration, communication, and mutual admiration that goes along with having our own professional organizations and journals. But some of us have more interest in making a social impact outside our conclaves than in telling each other of our activities. Those of you making better mousetraps don't only have to convince each other; you need to convince potential consumers. To accomplish this it may be helpful to both speak the same language and travel in the right circles.

I get the impression that mellowspeak is buying our graduates a lot more cooperation than is behaviorese. Likewise, I am convinced that most administrators, program evaluators, granting agencies, researchers (in many areas including education, psychology, business, political science, and the medical sciences) and journal editors greatly prefer formal statistical methods of analysis to visual analysis alone when statements are made concerning the effects of treatments and programs.

Some time ago I was standing in a colleague's office when he opened a rejection letter from a granting agency. His comment was, "These guys don't even know what I'm talking about." Precisely. The proposal had been submitted to an agency that had not previously funded applied operant work. It was pointed out in the letter that the methodology section was weak—no statistical analysis was proposed. Just as the terms alpha, beta, delta, phi, and theta sound like Greek to the behaviorist, the terms *ABA, ABAB,* and *BABB'A* sound like babble to the nonbehaviorist. Statistical tests have very high credibility to most people in most fields; to act otherwise is to commit political suicide. Whether justified or not, this seems to be the way it is. To ignore this is often to ignore one of the most important constructs in the belief system of your audience. If an audience is convinced that a researcher has something worthwhile to say on the basis of statistical significance alone, consider how impressed it will be when both statistical significance and a very large visually apparent effect is presented.

My suggestion then, is to employ statistical as well as visual methods when you are attempting to communicate with a nonbehavioral audience that is likely to be influenced by the presentation of statistical tests. Infiltration works. Besides that, statistics make people feel good.

"Go on, Mrs. Pratt," says Mrs. Sampson, "Them ideas is so original and soothing. I think statistics are just as lovely as they can be." (O. Henry, "The Handbook of Hymen" as quoted in Weaver, 1963, p. 304)

SUMMARY

The literature on statistics in behavior-modification research contains papers that argue strongly for or against the use of statistical methods. The major papers that argue against such methods have: (a) confounded statistical analysis with experimental design, (b) confused statistical significance with the size of an effect, (c) confused statistical significance with replication and, (d) made untestable claims concerning the power of single-subject designs relative to group designs. The literature in support of statistical time-series analysis does not acknowledge: (a) the inconsistency between the proposed methods and the designs usually used in applied behavior analysis, (b) the inconsistency between the question answered by the analysis and the question the researcher often believes has been answered, (c) the inconsistency between the number of data points desirable for model identification and the number of data points actually available in the typical behavioral study, and (d) the inconsistency in the size of the estimated effects under different plausible ARIMA models. I believe that the strongest argument for employing statistical methods is credibility. Even though statistical tests are frequently misunderstood, they are considered an essential aspect of acceptable scientific evidence by a large segment of the scientific community.

REFERENCES

Andrews, D. F. Exploratory data analysis (1978). *International encyclopedia of statistics.* (pp. 97–107). New York: Free Press.
Bachi, R. (1976, August). *Graphical statistical methodology in the automation era.* Paper presented at the 136th annual meeting of the American Statistical Association, Boston, MA.
Baer, D. M. (1977). Perhaps it would be better not to know everything. *Journal of Applied Behavior Analysis, 10,* 167–172.
Baer, A. M., Rowbury, T., & Baer, D. M. (1973). The development of instructional control over classroom activities of deviant preschool children. *Journal of Applied Behavior Analysis, 6,* 289–298.
Barabba, V. (1980, May). *The revolution in graphic technology.* Paper presented at the Annual Meeting of the American Association for the Advancement of Science, San Francisco.
Beniger, J. R., & Robyn, D. L. (1978). Quantitative graphics in statistics: A brief history. *American Statistician, 32,* 1–11.
Bertin, J. (1980). *Graphics and the graphical analysis of data* (W. Berg, Trans.). Berlin: De Gruyter.
Bower, C. P., Padia, W. L., & Glass, G. V. (1974). *TMS: Two Fortran IV programs for the analysis of time-series experiments.* Boulder, CO: Laboratory of Educational Research, University of Colorado.

Fisher, R. A. (1926). The arrangement of field experiments. *Journal of the Ministry of Agriculture, 33,* 503–513.

Glass, G. V., Willson, V. L., & Gottman, J. M. (1975). *Design and analysis to time-series experiments.* Boulder, CO: Colorado Associated University Press.

Gnanadesikan, R. (1973). Graphical methods for informal inference in multivariate data analysis. *Proceedings of the International Statistics Institute Bulletin, 45,* 195–206.

Gottman, J. M. (1981). *Time-series analysis: A comprehensive introduction for social scientist.* Cambridge: Cambridge University Press.

Gottman, J. M., & Glass, G. V. (1978). Analysis of interrupted time-series experiments. In T. R. Kratochwill (Ed.), *Single-subject research: Strategies for evaluating change* (pp. 197–235). New York: Academic Press.

Hall, R. V., Fox, R., Willard, D., Goldsmith, L., Emerson, M., Owen, M., Davis, F., & Porcia, E. (1971). The teacher as observer and experimenter in the modification of disputing and talking-out behaviors. *Journal of Applied Behavior Analysis, 4,* 141–149.

Hartmann, D. P., Gottman, J. M., Jones, R. R., Gardner, W., Kazdin, A. E., & Vaught, R. S. (1980). Interrupted time-series analysis and its application to behavioral data. *Journal of Applied Behavior Analysis, 13,* 543–549.

Hartwig, F., & Dearing, B. D. (1979). *Exploratory data analysis,* London: Sage.

Hersen, M., & Barlow, D. H. (1976). *Single-case experimental designs: Strategies for studying behavior change.* New York: Pergamon.

Horne, G. P., Yang, M. C. K., & Ware, W. B. (1982). Time-series analysis for single-subject designs. *Psychological Bulletin, 91,* 178–189.

Huitema, B. E. (1979, May). *Graphic vs. statistical methods of evaluating data: Another look and another analysis.* Paper presented at the annual meeting of the Association for Behavior Analysis, Dearborn, MI.

Jones, R. R., Vaught, R. S., & Reid, J. B. (1975). Time-series analysis as a substitute for single subject analysis of variance designs. In G. R. Patterson, I. M. Marks, J. D. Matarazzo, R. A. Myers, G. E. Schwartz, & H. H. Strupp (Eds.) *Behavior Change 1974* (pp. 164–169). Hawthorne, NY: Aldine.

Jones, R. R., Vaught, R. S., & Weinrott, M. (1977). Time-series analysis in operant research. *Journal of Applied Behavior Analysis, 10,* 151–166.

Kazdin, A. E. (1976). Statistical analyses for single-case experimental designs. In M. Hersen & D. H. Barlow, *Single-Case experimental designs* (pp. 265–313). New York: Pergamon.

Kazdin, A. E. (1982). *Single-case research designs: Methods for clinical and applied setting.* New York: Oxford University Press.

Komechak, M. G. (1974). *The effect of thought detection on anxiety responses.* Unpublished doctoral dissertation. North Texas State University, Denton, TX.

McCleary, R., & Hay, R. A., Jr. (1980). *Applied time series for the social sciences.* Beverly Hills, CA: Sage.

Michael, J. (1974). Statistical inference for individual organism research: Mixed blessing or curse? *Journal of Applied Behavior Analysis, 7,* 647–653.

Risley, T. R., & Wolf, M. M. (1972). Strategies for analyzing behavioral change over time. In J. Nesselroade & H. Reese (Eds.), *Life span developmental psychology: Methodological issues* (pp. 175–183). New York: Academic Press.

Sidman, M. (1960). *Tactics of scientific research: Evaluating experimental data in psychology.* New York: Basic Books.

Skinner, B. F. (1963). Operant Behavior. *American Psychologist, 18,* 503–515.

Tufte, E. R. (1983). *The visual display of quantitative information.* Cheshire, CT: Graphics Press.

Tukey, J. W. (1977). *Exploratory data analysis.* Reading, MA: Addison-Wesley.

Wainer, H. (1974). The suspended rootogram and other visual displays: An empirical validation. *American Statistician, 28,* 143–145.

Weaver, W. (1963). *Lady luck: The theory of probability.* Garden City, NY: Doubleday.

Westra, D. P. (1978). *Testing interventions in the interrupted time-series quasi-experiment: The reliability of Box–Jenkins noise model specification with short series.* Unpublished doctoral dissertation, The University of South Dakota, Vermillion, SD.

Wincz, J. P., Leitenberg, H., & Agras, W. S. (1972). The effects of token reinforcements and feedback on the delusional verbal behavior of chronic paranoid schizophrenics. *Journal of Applied Behavior Analysis, 5,* 247–262.

Wolf, M. M., & Risley, T. R. (1971). Reinforcement: Applied research. In R. Glaser (Ed.), *The nature of reinforcement* (pp. 316–325). New York: Academic Press.

11

Ethical Standards in Behavioral Research

A Historical Analysis and Review of Publication Practices

NANCY A. NEEF, BRIAN A. IWATA, AND TERRY J. PAGE

INTRODUCTION

In a series of military experiments designed to ameliorate behavioral degradation under psychological stress, subjects were required to perform a task while being led to believe that they were in immediate danger of losing their life through a simulated plane malfunction (Berkun, Bialek, Kern, & Yagi, 1962).

In an effort to gain some insight into the blind submission of persons to Nazi authority under which millions of people were killed, a series of studies was conducted to assess obedience to the commands of a person in authority when the behavior demanded was contrary to the subject's beliefs, motives, and habits (Milgram, 1969). Specifically, these experiments involved an individual commanding naive subjects

NANCY A. NEEF • Division of Education, Johns Hopkins University, 100 Whitehead Hall, Baltimore, MD 21218. BRIAN A. IWATA and TERRY J. PAGE • The Division of Behavioral Psychology, The John F. Kennedy Institute, Johns Hopkins University School of Medicine, 707 North Broadway, Baltimore, MD 21205. Preparation of this manuscript was supported in part by grants from the Office of Special Education G00-800-1702 and G00-82-05409, the Maternal and Child Health Service, 000917-15-0, and The National Institute of Child Health and Human Development HD-16052.

to administer "electric shocks" to a confederate in the context of a learning task, in which subjects were told that they were inflicting a great deal of pain on the "victim," even to the point of endangering life. Almost 1,000 adults were exposed to the situation and, although a substantial number continued to administer the shocks, they demonstrated a great deal of emotional stress in doing so, including sweating, trembling, stuttering, groaning, and uncontrollable seizures.

In 1963, three doctors, with the approval of the director of medicine of Jewish Chronic Disease Hospital in Brooklyn, New York, injected "live cancer cells" into 22 chronically ill patients in order to detect the rate of antibody formation. The doctors did not inform the patients that live cancer cells were being used or of the purpose of the experiment, which was unrelated to their normal therapeutic program (Katz, 1972).

In 1954 in a court in Witchita, Kansas, the deliberations of juries in six civil cases were recorded by a group of law professors and social scientists with the approval of the judges involved. The jurors were not aware of the concealed microphones nor were the litigants informed of the research project (Katz, 1972).

In an attempt to determine the long-term effects of untreated venereal disease, the United States Public Health Service initiated a study in the 1930s of 400 black males who had syphilis. None of the subjects provided informed consent to participate in this government sponsored research. The study lasted for nearly 40 years, during which subjects were monitored but not treated (Tuskeegee Syphilis Study Ad Hoc Advisory Panel, 1973).

The controversy that ensued with each of these five well-publicized examples of experimentation with human subjects have highlighted a concern for ethical guidelines and constraints placed on research with human subjects. Each of these examples raises serious questions concerning informed consent, deception, concealment, invasion of privacy, protection from physical and mental stress, and possibly others. However, the experimenters in question undoubtedly felt their procedures to be necessary and unavoidable in exploring matters of considerable importance to their respective fields and in keeping with their ethical obligation to use their research skills to extend knowledge for the sake of ultimate human betterment (American Psychological Association, 1972). The issue, then, is not one of advocacy of ethical absolutes but of resolving conflicts between the ability of science to benefit society and the values that dictate concern for the individual. The purposes of this chapter will be to (a) review the development of standards to resolve conflicts in determining ethically acceptable research and, in doing so, to propose directions for the further development of such standards through a behavioral analysis; and (b) examine trends in legal and ethical standards as they relate to behavioral research involving aversive control.

HISTORICAL AND BEHAVIORAL ANALYSIS OF RESEARCH ETHICS

Ethically acceptable research has generally been considered to be that in which the theoretical and practical values maximize the probability of survival of humans as individuals and as a species and are sufficiently broad to justify the impositions it makes on the participants (American Psychological Association, 1972; Walker, 1963). Unfortunately, this definition creates more questions than it answers.

First, it requires that the ethics of an act be determined by its consequences, which can only be as reliable as the (experimenter's) scientific predictions of future events (Stuart, 1973; Walker, 1963). Second, it raises the question as to who is in the best position to determine whether the expected benefits of a given study outweigh the risks. The experimenter is typically an expert with the experience and knowledge to aid in the decision, but is vulnerable to control by other variables, such as the prestige of publication and advancement of the field. An external group of peers will also have knowledge and experience but may share some of the same biases as the experimenter (as demonstrated by the approval of the judges and lawyers in the Witchita Jury Recording case). Subjects have the right to govern their own fate, but their perhaps unwarranted suspicions or even awareness as participants are sometimes sufficient to stifle the advancement of knowledge. Obviously, this question demands a subjective judgment that can be influenced by the particular biases of the person or group responsible for making a decision regarding benefits and risks. In the Witchita Jury Recording case, hearings were held that led to the promulgation of a law prohibiting recording of jury deliberations. In the Jewish Chronic Disease Hospital Case (Katz, 1972), the Regents' decision was that patients should not be used in experiments unrelated to treatment unless they have given informed consent. These outcomes provide rules for very narrow circumstances but do not begin to cover the variety of situations encountered by researchers seeking to use human subjects in their work. Awaiting specific case-by-case ruling by courts does not seem to be a feasible alternative because it is a slow process involving specific situations, and codes and declarations are often too general to provide the necessary guidance (Stolz, 1977).

Generally, the three criteria for protection of subjects are informed consent, determination of the cost–benefit ratio, and validation by external professional peers (Stuart, 1973).

Informed Consent

Consent has as its base Western society's doctrines of individual freedom and self-determination, which are protected by common law. The development of consent as a legal term originated in therapeutic medical settings, in which its traditional function was to differentiate situations in which a doctor could be held liable for unauthorized "offensive touching" of a patient (Rosoff, 1981). The right to be free from physical intrusion by others has been supported by a number of court decisions indicating that the state cannot dictate or interfere in what happens to one's body unless it can demonstrate a compelling state interest for doing so (*Griswold v. Connecticut*, 1965; *Katz v. United States*, 1967; *Mackey v. Procunier*, 1973; *Roe v. Wade*, 1973; *Schloendorff v. Society*, 1914). The informed component has recently been established by the courts in their decision that a patient's agreement to a medical intervention is not valid or voluntary unless adequate information about the procedure, including collateral risks, has been provided (*Brady v. United States*, 1970; *Darrah v. Kite*, 1969; *Merriken v. Cressman*, 1973). Thus, in situations involving professional intervention, a stricter standard is required than in most commercial transactions. It becomes the professional's responsibility not only to obtain consent but to inform the consenting party of the resulting consequences. Though this standard has since been adopted for experimental situations, the law has not defined it well nor clearly determined its relevance for human experimentation. Issues such as the individual's capacity to consent and conflicts between the interest of the individual versus society are reflected in the number of exceptions to the rule of consent. In spite of the ambiguities inherent in the principle of informed consent, it is generally considered to be a criterion for grant funding (Department of Health, Education and Welfare, 1971) and university sponsored research. Because this obviously can serve as a controlling variable over researchers' behavior, it would seem useful to clarify the components of consent from a behavioral perspective.

The Nuremburg Code included voluntary consent of the human subject as a basic principle which must be observed in order to satisfy moral, ethical, and legal concepts in human experimentation. Behaviorally, this requirement of consent may be viewed as an individual's mediation of reinforcement or punishment; whatever reinforcement is to be obtained must be mediated by obtaining the person's permission to proceed with some action concerning that person (Vargas, 1977). The standards by which the granting of consent is deemed appropriate were specified by the Nuremburg Code as including the legal capacity of the subject to give consent; to be able to exercise "free power of choice without the intervention of any element of force, fraud, deceit, duress, over reaching, or other ulterior form of restraint or coersion"; to be provided with "sufficient knowledge and comprehension of the elements of the subject matter involved as to enable an understanding and enlightened decision," requiring that he or she be informed of the nature, duration, and purpose of the experiment, the method and means by which it is to be conducted, all inconveniences and hazards reasonably to be expected, and the effect upon his or her health or person that may possibly result from participation in the experiment, before an affirmative decision by the experimental subject can be accepted. Although such a criterion is not easily interpretable due to its references to internal states (e.g., "duress," "understanding," "enlightened"), it becomes possible to identify three components of consent, namely: (a) capacity to consent; (b) voluntary consent; and (c) informed (knowledgeable) consent (Martin, 1975).

Capacity to Consent. In the case of *Kaimowitz v. Michigan Department of Mental Health* (1973), the court held that capacity to consent requires that the subject "rationally understand the nature of the procedure, its risk, and other relevant information," which is consistent with legal tests to decide on the competence of an individual to stand trial. However, the law also recognizes that even if a person is found to be mentally handicapped by a court and committed to a hospital, no presumption can be made that the person is incompetent and that in the absence of a specific ruling, the individual still retains the right to manage his own affairs (*Winters v. Miller,* 1971). Defining the capacity to consent has been considered to be one of the most difficult issues in the regulation of applied behavior analysis research (Friedman, 1975). The goal of determining capacity involves facilitating self-control as opposed to paternalism, without sacrificing the best interests of the subject. Again, part of the problem arises from a criterion based on internal states (i.e., "rationally understand") and the absence of an objective, empirical standard; the issue of competence represents the least operationalized criterion for valid consent (Horner, 1979). An additional inadequacy of present guidelines stems from the fact that competency is as situation specific as it is person specific (Horner, 1979).

Several approaches have traditionally been used to define competency. One is based on whether the result of the subject's decision is one that a "reasonably competent man might have made" and whether one would be likely to make a decision contrary to one's physical and mental well-being due to mental illness (Friedman, 1975). Obviously, this offers little clarification and involves a catch-22 logic, because the reviewer of capacity could label a subject as incompetent on the basis of the subject's disagreement with the reviewer's own biased opinion and decision. A second approach defines competency as the capacity to reach a decision based on rational reasons, including the ability to understand the nature of the behavioral procedure and to weigh the risks and benefits (Friedman, 1975). Although some regard this as an improvement over the first definition, it becomes even more difficult to evaluate because it is based on an indirect process (i.e., pattern of thought) rather than product measure (i.e., decision *per se*) and does not escape subjective judgment. The third approach defines competency as the capacity to make a decision; if the client "adequately understands" the nature of the procedure, the risk and benefits, and possible alternatives, the client's decision is accepted (Friedman, 1975). Again, the criterion for a "sufficient understanding" remains unspecified. It has been acknowledged that decisions concerning capacity to consent or any other standard can be made only through a careful empirical study of operational results (Friedman, 1975).

It appears that the common element in each attempt to define capacity is the extent to which the subject understands the relevant information presented. In general, the listener (subject) understands what the speaker (experimenter) is saying when the listener says it for the same reasons, that is, when the same variable controls the response (Skinner, 1968). The subject understands in the sense that the subject can then formulate the contingencies described more exactly or respond to them more successfully (Skinner, 1974). In this sense, an analogy can be made to situations such as the classroom, for example, where the teacher is confronted with the problem of determining how well the student understands the material assigned. A sophisticated technology has been developed to assess this, such as test questions based on Bloom's (1956) taxonomy involving knowledge, comprehension, application, analysis, synthesis, and evaluation; these categories represent a hierarchy of understanding (Kryspin & Feldhusen, 1974). As applied to the issue of capacity to consent, the subject can be said to understand to the extent that the subject can answer similar questions based on the information presented, with a criterion most likely based on knowledge or comprehension levels (e.g., being able to name the risks involved, being able to give an example of a possible consequence of his or her participation in the experiment, etc.). Miller and Willner (1974), for example, have recommended use of a two-part consent form, the first part describing the experiment, with the second part asking key questions probing the subjects' comprehension of the explanation. Stuart (1978) has recommended the addition of a third part that would require the prospective participants to describe the experiment in their own words. He suggests that accurate answers and descriptions to salient questions about the specifics of the experiment would provide behavioral evidence that the subject understood the exact nature of the proposed investigation. The need for a behavioral assessment of the subjects' comprehension of an experiment is supported by several studies demonstrating that explaining the experimental procedure does not guarantee it has been understood, even by individuals whose competence would not ordinarily be suspect. For example, Epstein and Lasagna (1969) offered subjects three different levels of information about a proposed experiment and found that of the subjects provided with the most information, only 35% understood the experiment. More subjects (67%) understood the experiment when provided with the least amount of information. Stuart (1978) found through the use of a three-part consent form describing an experiment in various levels of detail that most of the college students agreeing to participate did not fully understand the experiment. Similarly, Gray (1975) found that 39% of the subjects who had signed forms agreeing to their subsequent participation in a drug experiment did not even know that they were research subjects, whereas most of the others did not understand important features of the research.

Minor children have traditionally been considered to be incompetent to give consent, and parents have given vicarious consent on their behalf. However, the effectiveness of parents as advocates of their children's best interests has been challenged (Friedman, 1975). For example, variables other than the best interests of the child, such as the interest of other children in the family, financial concerns, and others, may control the parents' decision. It has therefore been suggested that an institution using constitutionally intrusive behavioral procedures on children should solicit consent from both parent and child as well as a review of proposed procedures by a committee to guard against conflicts of interest (Friedman, 1975). Such a policy seems well advised in view of the unwillingness of courts to completely deny the competency of children for all purposes (*Relf v. Weinberger*, 1974). It has been noted elsewhere that a patient has a right to be fully and comprehensively informed, regardless of others' judgments concerning the patient's capacity of competency to render a valid consent (Croxton & Tropman, 1977).

Voluntary Consent. The second component of consent, voluntariness, requires that the subject's agreement to participate be: (a) free of coersion (defined behaviorally as the extent to which the consenting individual is in a position to manage his or her own contingencies); and (b) made with the understanding that at any time the consent can be withdrawn without negative consequence (Horner, 1979; *Knecht v. Gillman*, 1973). Voluntariness becomes a problem especially where the subject is incarcerated or involuntarily committed. This is illustrated by a court decision in the case of *Kaimowitz v. Michigan Department of Mental Health* (1973), which declared that because of the coercive environment and inherent inequality of the positions of involuntarily confined mental patients, they are not able to give informed consent. The court in *Kaimowitz* did not extend its conclusions to question the degree to which any behavior is truly voluntary given the effect of environmental events on behavior (Skinner, 1957, 1971). However, the court's observation that the extensive contingency control maintained by staff in an institutional environment precludes voluntary consent of incarcerated individuals was supported by subsequent events in this very case. While confined in a state hospital, the patient involved convinced two review committees that he genuinely and voluntarily desired to participate in a psychosurgery experiment, even if he was released, and insisted that his decision was not the result of coercion. However, when he was released from the institution after the statute justifying his commitment was held to be unconstitutional, he suddenly withdrew his consent to participate.

If the court's decision in *Kaimowitz* is interpreted to mean that an involuntarily confined patient may never be subjected to any treatment because he or she cannot have given truly voluntary consent, this would stifle efforts at normalization and the goal to restore personal autonomy to mentally handicapped persons. Furthermore, it would represent a failure to recognize degrees of voluntariness and would seem to imply that nonincarcerated persons act with unimpaired voluntariness (Friedman, 1975). Fortunately, the court in *Kaimowitz* did not intend to suggest that confined patients may never give a valid consent but rather was specific to experimental psychosurgery due to the potential risk as compared to benefits. Obviously, involuntary confinement is only one of many variables, albeit an important one, that may serve to limit voluntariness. Concern has been expressed, for example, about the use of students as volunteers in experiments conducted by their academic superiors, where voluntariness may be limited by at least the implied threat of loss of affection, decreased academic grade, or the belief that academic standing or future employment may be affected by failure to volunteer (Lasagna, 1969). Radical behaviorists would contend that informed consent must be considered to be a behavior that is environmentally controlled and, therefore, always subject to external manipulation. Ethical problems are, therefore, simply shifted from control of the problem behavior to control of the behavior of informed consenting (Krapfl & Vargas, 1977; Stolz, 1975). Such an argument fails to take into consideration that the behavioral approach, with its emphasis on environmental control, also assumes that people are able to learn behavioral principles and how their own behavior may be controlled by environmental events (Ulrich, 1967). Therefore, as public awareness increases, the problem of the experimenter engineering the subjects' consent should diminish (Stolz, 1975).

As with the issue of capacity to consent, a behavioral definition of uncoerced consent seems imperative. Some behaviorists have proposed that securing consent involves a hierarchy of protection according to the level of benefit, risk, validation status of the procedure to be used, and the degree to which the person can freely provide informed consent (Davison & Stuart, 1975). The hierarchy shown in Table 1 ranks the degree of consent that is required in relation to the variable factors, from 1, indicating that consent can be verbal, to 10, indicating that consent must be witnessed and approved by an outside review panel. For example, if the procedure offers high potential benefit to the subject, is well established, involves a low level of risk, and consent that is relatively free from coercion, then only verbal consent is required (1). On the other hand, if the procedure offers low potential benefit to the subject and

Table 1. Hierarchy of Consent Required According to the Level of Benefits, Validational Status of the Procedure, Risk, and Degree to Which Consent Can Freely Be Provided

Potential benefit to subject (vs. society)	Degree of novelty of procedure	Level of risk	Likelihood of free consent	Degree of consent required
High	Low	Low	High	1
Low	Low	Low	Low	2
High	Low	High	High	2
High	High	Low	High	3
High	Low	Low	Low	4
High	High	High	High	4
Low	High	Low	High	4
High	High	Low	Low	5
Low	Low	High	high	5
High	Low	High	Low	6
High	High	High	Low	7
Low	Low	Low	Low	7
Low	High	Low	Low	8
Low	Low	High	Low	9
Low	High	High	High	10

high potential benefit to society, is experimental, and involves a high level of risk, then a greater degree of consent is required that is witnessed and approved by an outside review panel (10).

It has been pointed out that the behaviorist should be particularly skilled at measuring the strengths of certain reinforcing stimuli in an attempt to measure coerciveness; behaviorists must examine an individual's suspected hierarchy of reinforcers and take appropriate precautions when especially strong reinforcers are used as a contingency for consent. In this sense, behaviorists may be in the best position to make a major contribution to law by concentrating their efforts toward developing an environment in which voluntariness is maximized (Croxton & Tropman, 1977). One way in which behaviorists may accomplish this is by educating the public and helping their subjects by making them aware of variables that may influence their decision (Stolz, 1975). Subtle aspects of control would be decreased if behavioral principles were more commonly understood.

> The more that is known about human behavior, the more it can be controlled. The more it is controlled, the more there is a requirement for countercontrol. The proper source of the countercontrol is in the hands of the public. A proper way to develop countercontrol in a democracy is to instruct the public in control technology, to teach them to recognize variables which control their own behavior. The long-term survival of the culture, the long-term good of the individual, and the long-term utility of behavior analysis itself will be best served by an enlightened public. (Krapfl & Vargas, 1977, pp. 326–327)

According to Maley and Hayes (1977), the most crucial variable affecting the use of the term *coercion* is the extent of control, involving both the strength of the contingencies and the narrowness of the control. Strong controls are those in which the probability of compliance is exceptionally great, such as with aversive stimulation. Narrowness refers to coercive controls that specify that only a limited range of behaviors may be reinforced (e.g., a robber threatening someone with a gun is considered to represent a coercive situation because the only options available may be surrendering one's money or securing the gun from the aggressor; however, if the aggressor pulls out a gun, declaring, "Do anything you want!" the situation could not be described as coercive).

Behavior analysts have made increasing use of contingency contracts to overcome some of the problems of informed consent. The effectiveness of this device is explained in terms of a "behavioral trap"; to establish the contract is a simple response but to then perform or refrain from the specified behavior may be more difficult (Mann, 1972). (A classic example of this is Homer's account of how Odysseus arranged to have himself tied to the mast of a ship before he passed the island of sirens to avoid succumbing to their temptations.) The commitment to accept the consequences, however, must be offered and accepted at a time when the reinforcing value of engaging in the contracted behavior (e.g., smoking) is strong. It has been suggested that the researcher should help the subject understand the implications of the agreement by, for example, providing the individual with an estimate, based on pilot work, of the probability that he or she would drop out of the program and forfeit the deposit (Stolz, 1975).

Knowledgeable Consent. The third component of consent is that the potential subjects must be informed as to the nature of the experiment to be conducted, including (a) their right not to consent; (b) their right to withdraw from the experiment at any time without prejudice; (c) the risks involved in the treatment; (d) the potential benefit of the procedure; and (e) the risks and benefits of alternative treatments (*Brady v. United States,* 1970; *Darrah v. Kite,* 1969; *Knecht v. Gillman,* 1973; *Merriken v. Cressman,* 1973). It has been pointed out that by ensuring that the subject understands the procedures and goals of a program, and even possibly by involving the individual in the program design, we increase the benefits to both the client and ourselves by facilitating the client's cooperation and avoiding false expectations or misunderstandings (Bitgood, 1975).

With the information element of informed consent, the subject would ideally be informed of all possible collateral risks of the treatment intervention. The problem is one of determining acceptable limitations on the scope of disclosing all remotely possible dangers in realizing this ideal. How much less than total disclosure will satisfy the demands of the law? Courts addressing this issue within a medical context have used criteria ranging from "enough information to meet standards of practice in effect in the community" (*Shetter v. Rochelle,* 1965) to all the information that the patient "reasonably needs to know to make an intelligent decision" (*Getchell v. Mansfield,* 1971). It is generally considered to be unnecessary to disclose risks that either "ought to be known by everyone" or that are known to the subject as a result of prior history with the particular intervention (Waltz & Scheuneman, 1970). From a legal standpoint, the traditional means of assessing the importance of information in the decision-making process is materiality: the task is to determine what risks are material or relevant in influencing the subject's decision to accept treatment. Two standards have been proposed for this purpose (Waltz & Scheuneman, 1970). The first is that only risks that would cause the subject to refuse treatment need to be disclosed. The problem with this is that (a) the experimenter has no way of determining precisely

which variables in an individual's complex history will control his or
her decision; and (b) this does not take into account that although a
single risk of a given magnitude may not cause a subject to refuse treatment, two or more such risks may cumulatively have that effect. The
second proposal is that any risk with the slightest potential influence
on the subject's decision should be disclosed, but this strategy may be
unrealistic. As a compromise, it has been suggested that experimenters
use their experience, solicited knowledge of the subject's history and
current circumstances to "exercise a sense of how the average, reasonable man would probably react." It is within the behaviorist's expertise
to adopt such a standard as objectively as possible through reference to
an empirical base (e.g., presenting information on previously documented hazards of the procedure in the literature, data on number of
others approached who declined to participate, and variables affecting
their decision, taking into account the experimenter's experience with
the potential subject's hierarchy of reinforcers). Stuart (1978), for example, found that as an experiment was described in increasing detail to
include the mention of use of aversive methods, fewer students vol-
unteered. Volunteerism was inversely related to the subject's belief that
participation would be dangerous. In addition, 18% of the students
believed that they would suffer if they did not participate in the experiment. Berscheid, Baron, Dermer, and Libman (1973) asked subjects if
they would participate in experiments such as those involving social
stress (Milgram, 1963). Subjects indicated they would not participate in
those studies they considered to be highly aversive though some reconsidered when the rationale of the experiment was explained.

Cost–Benefit Ratio

The second criterion used for protection of subjects is a comparison
of the expected benefits to the subjects and the importance of the information gathered to the possible risks. However, because risk-to-benefit
ratio is difficult to quantify, agreement is not always easily obtained
(Stolz, 1975). Various segments of society view the risks and benefits of
a given research project differently (Stolz, 1975), and the benefits to
participants and the benefits to others are often in conflict (Bitgood,
1975). As Vargas (1977) points out, there is nothing inviolate about any
right; and any universal right negates another. For example, the benefits
of right to life of a fetus may deny the benefits to a woman from her
right over her own body; refusing the right to euthanasia prohibits the
right to, and benefits from, escaping pain. Finally, the definitions of

risks and benefits themselves change over time as customs and knowl-edge change (Stolz, 1975). Weighing of potential risks objectively may also become obscured by the speculation of overzealous individuals who suggest remotely possible causal relations in the absence of empirical evidence (e.g., symptom substitution) (Bitgood, 1975). Computer tech-niques and statistical methods (e.g., probability theory) could be helpful in this respect by quantifying cost–benefit variables based on pilot work and previously documented information.

External Validation

A third recommended source of subject protection is review by a panel of external professional peers. It has been recommended that such committees should be composed of members who are from the imme-diate community, are competent behavioral programmers, have medical expertise, have legal expertise, or have experience with the population being served (Horner, 1979). Alternatively, lay persons from the com-munity could be selected to determine the ethics of an experiment in much the same way as a jury functions. Independent judgment by out-side evaluators does not, however, guarantee objectivity because it must be assumed that personal biases are no less operative among profes-sionals than among other persons (Stuart, 1973).

Recently, some behavior analysts have asserted that the appro-priateness of intervention programs is a subjective value judgment that only society is qualified to make; and they are, therefore, beginning to ask the specific consumer and the relevant community about the ethical acceptability of their procedures (Wolf, 1978). For example, in an effort to assess the acceptability of "contingent observation" as a treatment procedure (requiring the disruptive individual to stop playing and watch his or her appropriate playmates for a brief period of time), the exper-imenters delivered an anonymous questionnaire to each of the caregivers asking which of several procedures they preferred, which they felt was easier to use, and which they thought taught the children more about getting along with fewer problems in a group. In addition, they approached the children's parents, provided them with a description of the procedure, and invited them to express any opinions or objections to the center supervisor (Porterfield, Herbert-Jackson, & Risley, 1976). Thus, this attempt at social validation addressed the goals, procedures, and results of treatment.

Social validation, as with informed consent, determination of cost–benefit ratio, and validation by external professional peers is not infallible protection because, by using subjective data, we run the risk that the resulting verbal reports are unrelated to actual events and, therefore, misleading. Though the potential abuse of social validity measures has been acknowledged, this possibility should provide impetus for determining the conditions under which people can be assumed to best assess their own procedural preference (Wolf, 1978). We can lessen the discrepancy between subjective and objective data by refining our measurement systems to increase the probability that the consumer is not responding to variables we are not recording. We must also develop the means to teach people how to better observe their behavior and its environmental determinants and to make more accurate decisions (Wolf, 1978).

SURVEY OF RESEARCH PRACTICES AND CURRENT TRENDS

It is apparent from the above review of the development of ethical and legal standards in research that these practices are and will continue to be in a constant state of flux. Such ambiguity presents problems for the behavioral researcher as well as for others who must keep abreast of these changes in order to function within legitimate boundaries and protect themselves and the clients they serve.

For the professional researcher or practitioner, journals represent one of the main sources of validated treatment strategies. Prior to the publication of a code of ethics by the American Psychological Association in 1973, there was little interest in examining the extent of ethical conduct in the treatment of human subjects in the behavior therapy literature (McNamara & Woods, 1977). However, because these journal articles represent current treatment practices in the field and serve as models for others to follow in implementing treatment procedures, it seems important to assess changes and trends in these journals from an ethical and legal standpoint and to determine whether such trends are consistent with current legal and ethical guidelines. Although psychologists have generally maintained that they are more attentive to ethical standards in the conduct of research than students (Sullivan & Deiker, 1973), deceptive practices and coercive means of soliciting subjects, for example, are prevalent (Menges, 1973). Pappworth (1967) observed that violations of subjects' rights were still frequent in biomedical research in the mid-1960s, and Kelman (1970) noted that deception had become "a standard feature in psychological experiments . . . used without question . . . not as a last resort but as a matter of course" (pp. 66, 68). McNamara and Woods (1977) reviewed four psychological journals from

1971 to 1974 and found that there was little regard for the ethical standards established by APA.

One current issue of ethical and legal controversy concerns the use of punishment and aversive control (in fact, at the time of this writing, Division 16 of APA is attempting to generate support for passage of a resolution condemning the use of aversive control). When these procedures are used, it is important to take into account several factors.

1. Is the type of punishment used appropriate? The pain, discomfort, or loss of liberty imposed on the subject must be considered as well as whether the nature of the behavior to be eliminated justifies its use.

2. If aversive chemical, mechanical, or electrical stimulation is used, has it been demonstrated to be the least restrictive alternative? According to Martin (1975), "the test should be that aversive therapy might be used where other therapy has not worked." (p. 77)

3. Has consent been procured from the subject? According to Martin (1975), detailed consent must be obtained if treatment involves research, publication, follow-up, or electric shock. In spite of the importance of obtaining informed consent, a survey of four psychological journals from 1971 through 1974 revealed that only a mean of 28% of all studies explicitly noted that subjects were volunteers, a mean of 9% stated that participants were fully informed, and only a mean of 1% mentioned the procurement of written consent (McNamara & Woods, 1977).

4. Is the change in behavior as a function of treatment durable? The maintenance of behavior change as measured by follow-up data is an important variable to consider in assessing the effectiveness of treatment (Kazdin & Bootzin, 1972; O'Dell, 1974; O'Leary & Drabman, 1971; Tramontana, 1971). Keeley, Shemberg, and Carbonell (1976) reviewed three behavioral journals from 1972 to 1973 and found that only 8 out of the 146 studies analyzed presented objective data collected at least 6 months following the termination of treatment.

5. Is reinforcement provided for the acquisition of appropriate behaviors concurrent with punishment for inappropriate behavior? One of the most common arguments against the use of punishment is that it does not teach new behaviors (Azrin & Holz, 1966). Therefore, it seems important that with any punishment procedure, adequate measures be taken for teaching new, appropriate behaviors.

6. Is there a means for observing possible side effects as a function of punishment? The use of punishment may produce undesirable side effects, such as social disruption, emotional responding, or avoidance (Azrin & Holz, 1966). Furthermore, it is well documented in the experimental literature that behavior is a function of relative reinforcement

rather than absolute reinforcement, as demonstrated by behavior contrast and matching phenomena (Bradshaw, Szabadi, & Bevan, 1976). This holds implications for the use of punishment in that changes in the relative rate of reinforcement may produce undesirable changes in a nontarget behavior or in another situation. For example, Risley (1968) found that when a child's climbing on a bookcase was punished, this behavior subsequently varied inversely with climbing on the back of a chair. Willems (1974) similarly warned against such side effects and undetected changes in nontargeted behaviors that may accompany implementation of behavioral techniques. Thus, it may be necessary to take concurrent data on behaviors other than the target behavior so that undesirable changes may be detected and dealt with accordingly. However, a review of operant studies published in three behavioral journals between 1972 to 1973 indicated that only 8.9% reported response generalization measures (Keeley *et al.*, 1976).

7. Are possible limitations and disadvantages of the punishment procedure considered? Potential users of a particular punishment procedure should be informed of qualifications of either the specific results obtained or the procedure in general, in order to determine its suitability for use with a particular client (Bailey & Bostow, 1979).

The purpose of the present literature review was to determine the yearly trends in three major behavioral journals, as reflected by the studies they contain, with respect to these issues.

Survey Method

Three leading behavioral journals (Brady, 1973; Keeley *et al.*, 1976) were reviewed: *Journal of Applied Behavior Analysis* (JABA), 1968–1981; *Behaviour Research and Therapy* (BRT), 1968–1981; and *Behavior Therapy* (BT), 1970–1981. Articles included in the review consisted of experimental studies of a clinically important dependent variable in human subjects. The following types of articles were excluded from data calculations: (a) investigations of behaviors not typically relevant to clinical applications (e.g., energy conservation); (b) studies in which the data consisted solely of subjects' self report; (c) methodological or theoretical articles; (d) uncontrolled case studies that were essentially anecdotal in nature; (e) correlational studies; (f) follow-up studies; and (g) basic research.

The journals were surveyed first to determine the incidence of articles employing punishment compared to other procedures. *Punishment* was defined as the use of an operant procedure involving the presentation or removal of a stimulus contingent on a response that decreased the occurrence of that response. *Reinforcement* was defined as the use of an operant procedure involving the presentation of a stimulus contingent on either the absence of a target response or an incompatible response that was associated with a decrease in the occurrence of the target response. Thus, classical conditioning procedures were not included in these categories, regardless of whether or not the stimulus would be considered aversive, nor were studies in which the dependent variable was not defined to detect decreases in responding. Data were collected on the percent of articles per year from each journal involving the use of (a) punishment (either alone or in combination with reinforcement); (b) punishment combined with reinforcement; (c) punishment alone; and (d) reinforcement alone.

All punishment studies were further categorized in order to determine the relative frequency of use for various types of punishment. Data were collected on the percent of punishment studies involving: (a) chemical, mechanical, or electrical stimulation (e.g., ammonia capsules, lemon juice therapy, sensory extinction, shock, water mist); (b) overcorrection (e.g., contingent practice, restitution); (c) time out; (d) response cost; and (e) verbal reprimands.

All punishment studies were then analyzed in detail to assess research practices as they relate to human subjects considerations. Data were collected on the percent of articles involving punishment in which (a) it was noted that consent was obtained; (b) follow-up data were collected; (c) qualifications or limitations on the use of the punishment procedure were discussed; and (d) the possible occurrence of side effects was noted through empirical recording.

Finally, for the most restrictive procedures (May *et al.*, 1975)— chemical, mechanical, or electrical stimulation—data were collected on the percent of punishment studies in which (a) less restrictive alternatives were previously attempted; and (b) the punished behavior was immediately dangerous to the subject or others.

Survey Results

A total of 1,361 experimental studies were reviewed from the three journals, of which 23.5% (320) involved the use of operant procedures to decrease behavior. Articles in the latter group were further categorized according to general classes of procedures: of all articles reviewed, 17.7% (242) involved the use of punishment (either alone or in combination with reinforcement), 10.6% (145) involved the use of punishment combined with reinforcement, 7.1% (97) involved the use of punishment alone, and 5.8% (78) involved the use of reinforcement alone. These overall percentages suggest that punishment has been used more frequently than reinforcement as the sole means for decreasing behavior, and that when reinforcement has been used, it typically has been combined with one or more punishment techniques. However, the data do not show possible changes in these variables over time (and such changes might be expected in light of increasing concern over and restrictions on the use of punishment), nor do they reflect differences across research journals in the field that might be due to a number of factors, such as focus of the journal, editorial policy, etc.

Figure 1 provides a breakdown of the above data by journal and publication year. Panel A shows the percent of articles involving punishment procedures. BRT has published a smaller proportion of punishment studies (13.0%) than either JABA (18.7%) or BT (20.9%); however, a number of BRT articles containing aversive procedures were not included in the calculations, because the actual procedures employed were only vaguely related to punishment principles (Berecz, 1973). Panel A also reveals a gradual decline in the percent of punishment articles published in JABA across years; this trend is not evident for either BT or BRT.

In panels B and C, the data on punishment articles have been subdivided further to indicate whether or not reinforcement was also included as a part of the treatment. BRT has published a smaller proportion of articles containing punishment plus reinforcement and punishment alone (7.6% and 5.4%, respectively) than either JABA (10.8% and 8.1%, respectively) or BT (11.7% and 9.2%, respectively). In terms of trends, there appears to be a slight decrease across years in the percent of articles describing punishment procedures alone; however, this trend has not been consistent in any of the three journals during the 2 most recent survey years.

Panel D shows the percent of experimental articles using reinforcement alone to decrease a behavior. These articles account for a small portion of studies published in JABA (7.0%), BT (5.2%), and BRT (4.2%). Only BT seems to show an increase in this category across years, although the trend has fluctuated and has not been maintained as of the last 3 years.

Table 2 shows the percent of punishment studies in JABA, BT, and BRT using aversive chemical, mechanical, or electrical stimulation; overcorrection; timeout; response cost; and reprimands, across years. Overall, the most frequently reported procedures have been response cost (31.0% of all punishment studies), aversive chemical, mechanical, or electrical stimulation (28.1%), and timeout (28.9%), whereas overcorrection and reprimands have been used less frequently (16.5% and 12.8%, respectively). However, from 1975 through 1981 (the last 7 years of the

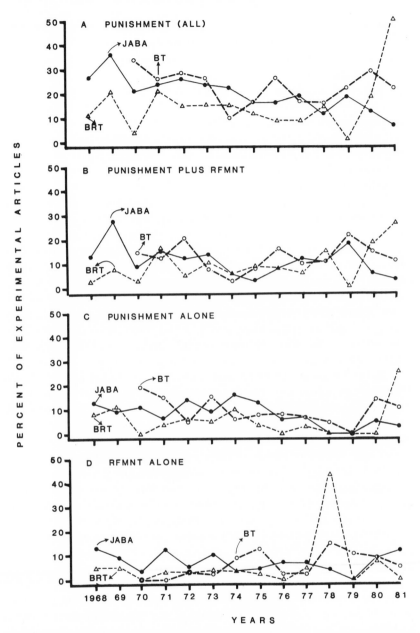

Figure 1. Percentage of experimental articles published in the *Journal of Applied Behavior Analysis* (JABA), *Behavior Therapy* (BT), and *Behaviour Research and Therapy* (BRT), employing punishment and reinforcement procedures to decrease a behavior, across years.

14-year survey), overcorrection has been most frequently reported procedure (31.0%), whereas aversive chemical, mechanical, or electrical
stimulation has been reported less frequently than all procedures except
for reprimands.

In terms of comparisons across journals, JABA published a smaller
percentage of punishment studies involving aversive chemical, mechanical, or electrical stimulation (22.6%) than BT (34.9%) or BRT (29.1%).
On the other hand, JABA published a higher percentage of studies using
either timeout or reprimands (36.0% and 16.9%, respectively) than BT
(23.5% and 7.9%, respectively) or BRT (15.8% and 12.8%, respectively).
BRT published a much higher percentage of overcorrection articles (47.6%)
than JABA (17.0%) or BT (23.6%), whereas BT published much lower
percentages of response cost articles (23.1%) than JABA (33.8%) or BRT
(37.2%).

The data in Table 2 also allow for a number of within-journal comparisons of the types of punishment articles published. For example,
assuming that aversive chemical, mechanical, or electrical stimulation is
considered the most intrusive of all punishment techniques, this method
of treatment has accounted for 50% or more of punishment articles
during a given year twice for JABA (1968, 1980), three times for BRT
(1968, 1971, 1978), and five times for BT (1970, 1971, 1973, 1974, 1980,
1981).

Table 3 shows the percent of punishment studies in JABA, BT, and
BRT in which authors mentioned that consent was obtained, follow-up
data were provided, qualifications or limitations of the procedure were
noted, and data were collected on possible side effects of treatment. The
provision of consent has been noted very infrequently across all journals
(21.8% of punishment studies overall), and less frequently in JABA (14.8%)
than in BT (22.8%) or BRT (27.9%). Furthermore, the yearly data indicate
no consistent increase in the reported provision of consent. During 3 of
the last 4 survey years, no punishment studies published in either BT
or BRT noted that consent was obtained; during the most recent year,
consent was not mentioned in any punishment article in any of the three
journals. Thus, the (reported) provision of consent has decreased in
recent years.

Follow-up data were reported in 43.7% of the punishment studies
surveyed, with BRT reporting a higher percentage (53.7%) than either
JABA (35.9%) or BT (42.5%). This category has varied considerably within
and between journals; however, data for the past 3 years suggest that
follow-up is taking on greater importance. During this period, 50% of
the punishment articles published in each of the journals have included
follow-up data.

Table 2. Percentage of Punishment Studies in JABA, BT, and BRT Using Specific Techniques

Technique	Journal	1968	1969	1970	1971	1972	1973	1974	1975	1976	1977	1978	1979	1980	1981
Aversive chem., mech., and elec. stimulation	JABA	50.0	9.0	14.3	28.6	0.0	23.1	25.0	42.9	0.0	15.4	33.3	25.0	50.0	0.0
	BT	—	—	57.1	63.6	37.5	50.0	66.7	16.7	16.7	11.1	0.0	0.0	50.0	50.0
	BRT	75.0	28.6	0.0	50.0	25.0	33.3	0.0	0.0	33.3	33.3	100.0	N/A	0.0	0.0
Overcorrection	JABA	0.0	0.0	0.0	0.0	0.0	7.7	25.0	0.0	28.6	15.4	0.0	25.0	0.0	50.0
	BT	—	—	0.0	0.0	0.0	0.0	0.0	50.0	25.0	66.7	50.0	100.0	16.7	25.0
	BRT	0.0	0.0	0.0	0.0	25.0	33.3	33.3	75.0	33.3	33.3	0.0	N/A	0.0	0.0
Timeout	JABA	12.5	45.5	28.6	57.1	45.5	53.9	33.3	14.3	57.1	23.1	33.3	25.0	25.0	50.0
	BT	—	—	28.6	18.2	37.5	20.0	33.3	16.7	33.3	11.1	25.0	0.0	33.3	25.0
	BRT	25.0	14.3	0.0	33.3	0.0	33.3	66.7	0.0	0.0	33.3	0.0	N/A	0.0	0.0
Response cost	JABA	25.0	36.4	57.1	14.3	72.7	23.1	41.7	28.6	28.6	46.2	0.0	25.0	25.0	50.0
	BT	—	—	14.3	9.1	37.5	50.0	33.3	50.0	25.0	0.0	0.0	0.0	33.3	25.0
	BRT	0.0	28.6	100.0	33.3	50.0	22.2	33.3	25.0	66.6	0.0	0.0	N/A	50.0	100.0
Reprimands	JABA	12.5	9.1	0.0	14.3	27.3	15.4	25.0	14.3	28.6	7.7	33.3	25.0	25.0	0.0
	BT	—	—	0.0	9.1	0.0	0.0	0.0	0.0	8.3	11.1	25.0	0.0	16.7	25.0
	BRT	0.0	14.3	0.0	33.3	0.0	11.1	33.3	0.0	0.0	0.0	0.0	N/A	50.0	25.0

Note. N/A = No punishment article published during the year.

Table 3. Percentage of Punishment Studies in JABA, BT, and BRT in Which Consent for Participation Was Obtained, Follow-Up Data Were Collected, Qualifications or Limitations in the Procedure Were Noted, and Potential Side Effects Were Assessed

Category	Journal	1968	1969	1970	1971	1972	1973	1974	1975	1976	1977	1978	1979	1980	1981
Consent	JABA	25.0	27.3	0.0	0.0	9.1	15.4	0.0	14.3	0.0	7.7	33.3	25.0	50.0	0.0
	BT	—	—	57.1	27.3	25.0	40.0	66.7	0.0	25.0	0.0	0.0	0.0	33.3	0.0
	BRT	75.0	28.6	100.0	50.0	25.0	11.1	66.7	0.0	66.7	66.7	0.0	N/A	0.0	0.0
Follow-up data	JABA	25.0	18.2	14.3	57.1	18.2	30.8	25.0	71.4	28.6	30.8	33.3	50.0	50.0	50.0
	BT	—	—	28.6	36.4	75.0	60.0	33.3	50.0	41.7	11.1	25.0	50.0	50.0	50.0
	BRT	100.0	57.1	100.0	33.3	50.0	56.6	33.3	25.0	66.7	66.7	100.0	N/A	50.0	50.0
Qualification	JABA	37.5	36.4	42.9	42.9	54.6	30.8	66.7	28.6	42.9	61.5	100.0	50.0	100.0	100.0
	BT	—	—	28.6	54.6	25.0	50.0	33.3	16.7	41.7	44.4	50.0	50.0	50.0	50.0
	BRT	25.0	28.6	0.0	50.0	75.0	33.3	66.7	50.0	33.3	66.7	100.0	N/A	0.0	0.0
Side effects assessed	JABA	50.0	45.5	42.9	14.3	36.4	38.5	50.0	14.3	28.6	38.5	33.3	100.0	25.0	100.0
	BT	—	—	28.6	27.3	0.0	10.0	33.3	16.7	25.0	33.3	0.0	0.0	16.7	0.0
	BRT	0.0	28.6	0.0	16.7	25.0	11.1	0.0	0.0	0.0	0.0	0.0	N/A	0.0	0.0

Authors pointed out procedural qualifications or limitations in 46.2% of the studies, with JABA articles more likely to include such information (56.8%) than those published in BT (41.2%) or BRT (40.6%). Recent trends appear somewhat divergent across journals, with JABA showing an increase to 100% during the last two years, BRT showing a decrease to zero during the same period, and BT remaining stable at 50%.

Very few attempts have been made to quantify the potential side effects of treatment. Data were provided in only 20.7% of the studies overall. JABA published a much higher percentage of such articles (40.9%) than BT (15.8%) or BRT (6.3%). In addition, although the yearly data show some fluctuation, empirical assessment of side effects seems to have become a standard feature of JABA articles, whereas the opposite might be said of BT and BRT.

The final set of data, presented in Table 4, pertains only to those studies employing aversive chemical, mechanical, or electrical stimulation. Across journals and publication years, 39.7% of these studies reported that alternative forms of treatment had first been attempted; 39.6% of the studies contained information suggesting that the behavior treated was dangerous to either the subject or others. JABA contained a higher percentage of studies reporting these two considerations (58.3%, 56.1%) than BT (48.2%, 37.7%) or BRT (12.5%, 24.9%).

Discussion

The data gathered in this survey are consistent with other sources (Kelman, 1970; Warwick, 1975) suggesting that adequate legal and/or ethical protection for subjects is not evident in a significant proportion of published psychological research. Although one might suspect that investigations designed specifically to reduce the frequency of a behavior would be more likely to employ ethical safeguards than other types of research with humans, the present data do not support such an assumption. In general, the following conclusions can be derived from the survey results.

1. For all three journals reviewed—JABA, BT, and BRT—a majority of studies attempting to effect a decrease in behavior employed one or more punishment techniques. Furthermore, there has been no consistent decrease in the use of punishment nor has there been any significant increase in the use of reinforcement in recent years. The frequent use of punishment in the literature does not necessarily reflect inadequate protection for human subjects, because a number of factors related to the target behavior, its situational context, and the focus of the study might justify the use of aversive procedures. The relative absence of

Table 4. Percentage of Studies Involving Aversive Chemical, Mechanical, or Electrical Stimulation in *JABA*, *BT*, and *BRT* in Which Less Restrictive Alternatives Were First Attempted, and the Target Behavior Was Immediately Dangerous to the Subject or Others

Category	Journal	1968	1969	1970	1971	1972	1973	1974	1975	1976	1977	1978	1979	1980	1981
Alternatives	JABA	25.0	100.0	0.0	100.0	N/A	33.3	33.3	0.0	N/A	100.0	100.0	100.0	50.0	N/A
First	BT	—	—	0.0	28.5	33.3	20.0	50.0	100.0	50.0	100.0	N/A	N/A	100.0	0.0
Attempted	BRT	0.0	0.0	N/A	0.0	0.0	0.0	N/A	N/A	0.0	0.0	100.0	N/A	N/A	N/A
Behavior	JABA	50.00	100.0	100.0	0.0	N/A	66.7	33.3	66.7	N/A	50.0	100.0	0.0	50.0	N/A
Dangerous	BT	—	—	0.0	57.1	33.3	20.0	50.0	0.0	50.0	100.0	N/A	N/A	67.7	0.0
	BRT	33.3	0.0	N/A	33.3	0.0	33.3	N/A	N/A	0.0	0.0	100.0	N/A	N/A	N/A

Note: N/A = no articles published in year.

differential reinforcement procedures, however, cannot be justified as easily. This is especially important in view of data indicating that the combined use of punishment plus reinforcement is likely to be more effective than either procedure used alone (Azrin & Holz, 1966; Bostow & Bailey, 1969; Favell, McGimsey & Jones, 1978; O'Leary, O'Leary, & Becker, 1967; Wahler, Winkel, Peterson, & Morrison, 1965; Wolf, Risley, & Mees, 1964). The acquisition and maintenance of behavioral alternatives to the punished response also would seem to require the use of positive reinforcement at some point during the course of treatment. Thus, from the standpoint of treatment selection, the survey results are most discouraging.

    2. Data on the types of punishment employed suggest a general decrease in the use of aversive chemical, mechanical, and electrical stimulation across years, a trend that is consistent with recommendations favoring less restrictive forms of punishment (May et al., 1975). Still, few of the studies in which this class of punishment was used noted that less restrictive methods were first attempted or that the target behavior was dangerous. This latter finding illustrates a conflict that has been evident for some time yet remains unresolved. It is clear that punishment involving direct or intense stimulation (e.g., chemical, electrical, or mechanical) is judged as the most intrusive by members of the professional community (e.g., May et al., 1975), and perhaps by the public in general as well (Kazdin, 1980). Thus, from the standpoint of treatment ethics (Martin, 1975), punishing stimuli, such as electric shock, currently would seem appropriate only following unsuccessful application of milder forms of punishment (e.g., timeout, response cost, overcorrection). On the other hand, very little empirical knowledge has been accumulated regarding the relative efficacy of various punishment techniques. The issue of treatment efficacy is important in discussing treatment ethics because it is possible that the more ethical treatment would involve exposure to an intense punishing stimulus for a brief period of time, rather than repeated and lengthy exposure to milder but less effective punishing stimuli; this is especially true if the eventual outcome is to use the intense stimulus after the milder ones have failed.

    Data from nonhuman studies suggest that in order to maximize the effects of punishment, the punishing stimulus should be delivered at a high intensity and introduced at maximum strength rather than increased gradually (Azrin & Holz, 1966). Similarly, Burchard and Barrera (1972) found that reductions in disruptive/aggressive behavior were directly related to the magnitude of response cost and the duration of timeout. Finally, White, Nielson, and Johnson (1972) investigated the effects of differing lengths of timeout and found not only that relative response suppression varied as a function of timeout duration, but also that the effectiveness of a given duration may depend on its sequence relative to other timeout durations. These and other studies have, as a group, yielded rather mixed findings regarding the question of treatment efficacy; thus, it is apparent that much additional research needs to be done before it will be possible to assess the ethics of a treatment within the context of its likelihood for success when compared to alternative forms of treatment.

3. Overall, less than half of the punishment studies provided follow-up data, information on side effects (i.e., data on nontarget behaviors), or qualifications regarding the procedure or its implementation. Although this general finding seems undesirable, the data are encouraging for the following reasons.

First, although it is difficult to compare the present data to those reported in the Keeley *et al.* (1976) survey (our definition of follow-up was more liberal than the 6-month criterion used by Keeley *et al.*), the inclusion of follow-up data in 50% of the punishment studies published in JABA, BT, and BRT for the past 3 years is much higher than one would have estimated from the 6.2% figure cited by Keeley *et al.* for all studies published in the same journals during 1972 and 1973. Thus, it appears that the evaluation of follow-up effects has become a relatively common practice in research on punishment.

Second, attempts to assess side effects, which averaged 20.7% of all punishment studies in the present survey, also compared quite favorably with the average of 8.9% found by Keeley *et al.* It is also important to note that large between-journal differences were found in the present study: over 40% of the JABA punishment articles assessed side effects, whereas the results for BRT (6.3%) were more consistent with the figure obtained by Keeley *et al.*

Third, the data regarding procedural qualifications indicate that, in many cases, authors and/or editors realize the importance of describing potential problems associated with punishment techniques. About half of the punishment studies published in JABA and BT over the past 4 years have done so. And, although no studies published in BRT during the past 2 years have included qualifying information, these years do not appear representative, because over 60% of punishment studies published in BRT during the previous 4 years did include such information.

Finally, one would not expect that all research on punishment should require the gathering of data on follow-up or side effects (e.g., if the focus of the research was very circumscribed), or would benefit from additional qualifying information (e.g., if the researchers used a well-known technique in a standard manner). In light of these considerations, results of the present survey suggest that the assessment of sustained, indirect, and untoward effects has taken on greater importance in applied punishment research.

4. Of all punishment studies reviewed, 21.8% contained information related to the procurement of consent. This figure is much higher than the 1% average cited by McNamara and Woods (1977), who surveyed all articles published in JABA, BT, JEP (*Journal of Educational Psychology*), and JPSP (*Journal of Personality and Social Psychology*) from 1971 to 1974. Still, the present finding is troublesome in several respects.

First, there were several differences between the McNamara and Woods survey and the present one. The years covered by the McNamara and Woods survey generally predated the publication of ethical standards for research with human subjects by APA, whereas a majority of studies reviewed in the present survey followed publication of the APA standards. McNamara and Woods also reviewed all types of articles, whereas the present survey (with regard to consent) only reviewed articles pertaining to the use of punishment. One might expect that greater care would be taken to obtain consent following publication of official guidelines, especially in cases where the treatment contained aversive components.

Second, the one factor most likely to take ethical precedence over all those examined in the present survey is that of consent. Regardless of the type of treatment used and the nature of the data collected, the provision of informed consent by subjects and/or their guardians would seem to mitigate a number of ethical problems, assuming that the research was carried out in a competent manner.

Finally, any conclusions regarding the adequacy of current efforts to obtain informed consent are limited due to inconsistencies in reporting. Articles reviewed in the present survey that did mention consent were generally vague with respect to the actual methods employed. Furthermore, in the absence of editorial policies concerning the public disclosure of information pertaining to consent, it is virtually impossible to determine the true percentage of studies in which consent was actually obtained, but merely not reported. The latter problem poses a particularly important question: Should our journals adopt a formal policy for the publication of studies involving human subjects? Arguments against such a policy include the fact that guidelines in the profession, federal granting agency requirements, and institutional review boards have clearly spelled out appropriate measures to be taken in the conduct of research, and that the actual reporting of such measures is therefore unnecessary. There is also concern that in some cases data obtained through unethical means may have immense heuristic value, and that the automatic exclusion of such data from the literature may obstruct the course of science and be particularly wasteful, in that subjects' participation—perhaps at great risk—would have yielded no benefit whatsoever. On the other hand, an analysis of at least some of the variables that control researchers' behavior would suggest that unethical experimentation is less likely when the resulting data are not published. In this respect, it is interesting to note that a growing number of medical journals now require, as one condition of publication, the inclusion of specific statements regarding the protection of human subjects.

The issues of consent practices and editorial policies governing them in behavioral research are complex ones that will require careful consideration of a number of factors and perhaps even some unusual exceptions. At the present time, however, further evaluation of experimental ethics in the behavioral literature will be extremely difficult without improvements in the area of public disclosure. In light of the frequent criticism that has been voiced against the use of behavioral procedures in general and punishment in particular, such improvements will only benefit the continued development of the field and the public that it serves, and will provide a noteworthy model for the objectification of effective and humane treatment.

REFERENCES

American Psychological Association. (1973). *Ethical principles in the conduct of research with human participants.* Washington, DC: American Psychological Association.

Azrin, N. H., & Holz, W. C. (1966). Punishment. In W. K. Honig (Ed.), *Operant behavior: Areas of resarch and application* (pp. 380–447). New York: Appleton-Century-Crofts.

Bailey, J. S., & Bostow, D. E. (1979). *A handbook of research methods in applied behavior analysis.* Tallahassee, FL: Copy Grafix.

Berecz, J. M. (1973). Aversion by fiat: The problem of "face validity" in behavior therapy. *Behavior Therapy, 4,* 110–116.

Berkun, M. M., Bialek, H. M., Kern, R. P., & Yagi, K. (1962). Experimental studies of psychological stress in man. *Psychological Monographs, 15,* 1–8.

Berscheid, E., Baron, R. S., Dermer, M., & Libman, M. (1973). Anticipating informed consent: An empirical approach. *American Psychologist, 28,* 913–925.

Bitgood, S. (1975). Response. In W. S. Wood (Ed.), *Issues in evaluating behavior modification.* Champaign, IL: Research Press.

Bloom, B. S. (Ed.). (1956). *Taxonomy of educational objectives. Handbook 1: Cognitive domain.* New York: David McKay.

Bostow, D. E., & Bailey, J. S. (1969). Modification of severe disruptive and aggressive behavior using brief time out and reinforcement procedures. *Journal of Applied Behavior Analysis, 2,* 31–37.

Bradshaw, C. M., Szabadi, E., & Bevan, P. (1976). Behavior of humans in variable-interval schedules of reinforcement. *Journal of the Experimental Analysis of Behavior, 26*, 135–141.

Brady, J. (1973). Behavior therapy: Fad or psychotherapy of the future? In R. Rubin, J. Brady & J. Henderson (Eds.), *Advances in behavior therapy*. New York: Academic Press.

Brady v. United States, 397 U.S. 742 (1970).

Burchard, J. D., & Barrera, F. (1972). An analysis of timeout and response cost in a programmed environment. *Journal of Applied Behavior Analysis, 5*, 271–282.

Croxton, T. A., & Tropman, J. E. (1977). The new puritans. In J. E. Krapfl & E. A. Vargas (Eds.), *Behaviorism and ethics* (pp. 331–354). Kalamazoo, MI: Behaviordelia.

Darrah v. Kite, 301 N.Y.S. 2d 286 (1969).

Davison, G. C., & Stuart, R. B. (1975). Behavior therapy and civil liberties. *American Psychologist, 30*, 755–763.

Department of Health, Education, and Welfare. (1971). *The institutional guide to DHEW policy on protection of human subjects* (NIH Publication No. 72–102). Washington, DC: U.S. Government Printing Office.

Epstein, J. C., & Lasagna, L. (1969). Obtaining informed consent. *Archives of Internal Medicine, 123*, 682–688.

Favell, J. E., McGimsey, J. F., & Jones, M. L. (1978). The use of physical restraint in the treatment of self-injury and as positive reinforcement. *Journal of Applied Behavior Analysis, 11*, 225–241.

Friedman, P. (1975). Legal regulations of behavior modification. *Arizona Law Review, 17*, 39–100.

Getchell v. Mansfield, 489 P. 2d 953 (1971).

Goldiamond, I. (1977). Protection of human subjects and patients. In J. E. Krapfl & E. A. Vargas (Eds.), *Behaviorism and ethics* (pp. 129–187). Kalamazoo, MI: Behaviordelia.

Gray, B. H. (1975). An assessment of institutional review committees in human experimentation. *Medical Care, 13*, 318–328.

Griswold v. Connecticut, 381 U.S. 479 (1965).

Horner, R. D. (1979). Accountability in habilitation of the severely retarded: The issue of informed consent. *AAESPH Review, 4*, 24–35.

Kaimowitz v. Michigan Department of Mental Health, 42 U.S.L.W. 2063 (1973).

Katz v. United States, 389 U.S. 347 (1967).

Katz, J. (1972). *Experimentation with human beings*. New York: Russell Sage Foundation.

Kazdin, A. E. (1980). Acceptability of alternative treatments for deviant child behavior. *Journal of Applied Behavior Analysis, 13*, 259–273.

Kazdin, A. E., & Bootzin, R. B. (1972). The token economy: An evaluative review. *Journal of Applied Behavior Analysis, 5*, 343–372.

Keeley, S. M., Shemberg, K. M., & Carbonell, J. (1976). Operant clinical intervention: Behavior management or beyond? Where are the data? *Behavior Therapy, 7*, 292–305.

Kelman, H. C. (1970). Deception in social research. In N. K. Denzin (Ed.), *The values of social science*. Chicago, IL: Aldine.

Knecht v. Gillman, 488 F 2d 1136 (8th Cir. 1973).

Krapfl, J. E., & Vargas, E. A. (1977). *Behaviorism and ethics*. Kalamazoo, MI: Behaviordelia.

Kryspin, W. J., & Feldhusen, J. F. (1974). *Writing behavioral objectves*. Minneapolis, MN: Burgess.

Lasagna, L. (1969). Special subjects in human experimentation. *Daedalus, 449*, 456–457.

Mackey v. Procunier, 477F 2d 877 (1973).

Maley, R., & Hayes, S. C. (1977). Coercion and control: Ethical and legal issues. In J. E. Krapfl & E. A. Vargas (Eds.), *Behaviorism and ethics* (pp. 265–284). Kalamazoo, MI: Behaviordelia.

Mann, R. A. (1972). The behavior-therapeutic use of contingency contracting to control an adult behavior problem: Weight control. *Journal of Applied Behavior Analysis, 5,* 99–109.

Martin, R. (1975). *Legal challenges to behavior modification.* Champaign, IL: Research Press.

May, J. G., Risley, T. R., Twardosz, S., *et al.* (1975). Guidelines for the use of behavioral procedures in state programs for retarded persons. *MR Research, 1.*

McNamara, J. R., & Woods, K. M. (1977). Ethical considerations in psychological research: A comparative review. *Behavior Therapy, 8,* 703–708.

Menges, R. (1973). Openness and honesty vs. coercion and deception in psychological research. *American Psychologist, 28,* 1030–1034.

Merriken v. Cressman, 364 F Supp 913 (1973).

Milgram, S. (1963). Behavioral study of obedience. *Journal of Abnormal Psychology, 67,* 371–383.

Milgram, S. (1969). Some conditions of obedience and disobedience to authority. *Human Relations,* 57–75.

Miller, R., & Willner, H. A. (1974). The two-part consent form: A suggestion for promoting free and informed consent. *The New England Journal of Medicine, 290,* 964–966.

O'Dell, S. (1974). Training parents in behavior modification. *Psychological Bulletin, 81,* 418–433.

O'Leary, K. D., & Drabman, R. (1971). Token reinforcement programs in the classroom: A review. *Psychological Bulletin, 75,* 379–398.

O'Leary, D. K., O'Leary, S., & Becker, W. C. (1967). Modification of a deviant sibling interaction pattern in the home. *Behavioral Research and Therapy, 5,* 113–120.

Pappworth, M. H. (1967). *Human guinea pigs: Experimentation on man.* Boston, MA: Beacon Press.

Porterfield, J. K., Herbert-Jackson, E., & Risley, T. R. (1976). Contingent observation: An effective and acceptable procedure for reducing disruptive behavior of young children in a group setting. *Journal of Applied Behavior Analysis, 9,* 55–64.

Relf v. Weinberger, 372 F Supp 1196 (1974).

Risley, T. R. (1968). The effects and side effects of punishing the autistic behavior of a deviant child. *Journal of Applied Behavior Analysis, 1,* 21–34.

Roe v. Wade, 410 U.S. 113 (1973).

Rosoff, A. J. (1981). *Informed consent: A guide for health care providers.* Rockville, MD: Aspen Systems.

Schloendorff v. Society of N.Y. Hospitals, 105 N.E. 92 (1914).

Shetter v. Rochelle, 409 P. 2d 74 (1965).

Skinner, B. F. (1957). *Verbal behavior.* New York: Appleton-Century-Crofts.

Skinner, B. F. (1968). *The technology of teaching.* New York: Appleton-Century-Crofts.

Skinner, B. F. (1971). *Beyond freedom and dignity.* New York: Vintage.

Skinner, B. F. (1974). *About behaviorism.* New York: Knopf.

Stolz, S. B. (1975). Ethical issues in research on behavior therapy. In W. S. Wood (Ed.), *Issues in evaluating behavior modification.* Champaign, IL: Research Press.

Stolz, S. B. (1977). Why no guidelines for behavior modification? *Journal of Applied Behavior Analysis, 10,* 541–547.

Stuart, R. B. (1978). Protection of the right to informed consent to participate in research. *Behavior Therapy, 9,* 73–82.

Stuart, R. B. (1973). Notes on the ethics of behavior research and intervention. In L. A. Hamerlynck, L. D. Handy, & E. J. Mash (Eds.), *Behavior change: Methodology, concepts, and practice* (pp. 221–233). Champaign, IL: Research Press.

Sullivan, D. A., & Deiker, T. E. (1973). Subject-experimenter perceptions of ethical issues in human research. *American Psychologist, 28,* 587–591.

Tramontana, J. A. (1971). A review of research on behavior modification in the home and school. *Educational Technology, 11,* 61–64.

Tuskeegee Syphilis Study Ad Hoc Advisory Panel. (1973). *Final Report.* Washington, DC: U.S. Public Health Service.

Ulrich, R. (1967). Behavior control and public concern. *Psychological Record, 17,* 229–234.

Vargas, E. (1977). Rights: A behavioristic analysis. In J. E. Krapfl & E. A. Vargas (Eds.), *Behaviorism and ethics.* Kalamazoo, MI: Behavioredia.

Wahler, R. G., Winkel, G. H., Peterson, R. F., & Morrison, D. C. (1965). Mothers as behavior therapists for their own children. *Behavior Research and Therapy, 3,* 113–124.

Walker, M. (1963). *The nature of scientific thought.* Englewood Cliffs, NJ: Prentice-Hall.

Waltz, J. R., & Scheuneman, T. W. (1970). Informed consent to therapy. *Northwestern University Law Review, 628,* 637–645.

Warwick, D. P. (1975). Social scientists ought to stop lying. *Psychology Today,* pp. 105–106.

White, G. D., Nielsen, G., & Johnson, S. M. (1972). Timeout duration and the suppression of deviant behavior in children. *Journal of Applied Behavior Analysis, 5,* 111–120.

Willems, E. P. (1974). Behavioral technology and behavioral ecology. *Journal of Applied Behavior Analysis, 7,* 151–165.

Winters v. Miller, 446 F 2d 65, 68 (2d cir.), cert. denied, 404 U.S. 985, 1971.

Wolf, M. M. (1978). Social validity: The case for subjective measurement or how applied behavior analysis is finding its heart. *Journal of Applied Behavior Analysis, 11,* 203–214.

Wolf, M., Risley, T., & Mees, H. (1964). Application of operant conditioning procedures to the behavior problems of an autistic child. *Behavior Research and Therapy, 1,* 305–312.

12

Social Validation of Applied Behavioral Research

A Selective Review and Critique

R. WAYNE FUQUA AND JOHN SCHWADE

INTRODUCTION

Among the defining features of applied behavioral research is the emphasis on socially important behaviors and the insistence that treatment-produced changes in those behaviors be of practical value (Baer, Wolf, & Risley, 1968). These criteria have been broadly embraced by applied researchers and practitioners. Despite the concern for social importance and clinical significance in applied research, a methodology to evaluate how much of these valued characteristics a behavioral intervention possesses has been slow in developing.

Kazdin (1977) and Wolf (1978) have described a strategy for evaluating the goals, methods, and outcomes of applied behavioral research. This strategy, referred to as social validation, features the inclusion of people other than the researchers or therapists in the evaluation process. These evaluators may include the recipient of the services, individuals paying for the service, public policymakers, significant others whose reaction to the subject defines the problem (e.g., those who label the subject as deviant), experts in some aspect of the behavior targeted for change, and persons presumed to represent community standards. These evaluators are often directly or indirectly affected by the provision of services or are financially responsible for the charges incurred. They may thus be considered to be consumers of behavior change services

R. WAYNE FUQUA • Department of Psychology, Western Michigan University, Kalamazoo, MI 49008. JOHN SCHWADE • Murdoch Center, Butner, NC 27509.

and recent writings on consumer satisfaction with behavior therapy (e.g., Bornstein & Rychtarik, 1983; McMahon & Forehand, 1983) are relevant to the ensuing discussion.

After arguing for the development of better measures of social importance, Wolf (1978) suggested that society would need to validate applied behavioral research on at least three levels:

> 1. The social significance of the *goals*. Are the specific behavioral goals really what society wants?
> 2. The social appropriateness of the *procedures*. Do the ends justify the means? That is, do the participants, caregivers, and other consumers consider the treatment procedures acceptable?
> 3. The social importance of the *effects*. Are consumers satisfied with the results? *All* the results, including any unpredicted ones? (p. 207)

Wolf further suggests that reliance on these judgments of "social validity" might "bring the consumer, that is society, into our science, soften our image, and make more sure our pursuit of social relevance" (p. 207). Surely, the rise of consumerism in our society has been an important impetus in the development and widespread adoption of social validation procedures for applied behavioral research. Additional factors that may have contributed to the concern with social validation and consumer satisfaction deserve brief mention as they will provide some perspective on the uses and limitations of social validity and consumer satisfaction procedures.

Behavioral research has been subjected to criticisms regarding the selection of target behaviors (e.g., Nordyke, Baer, Etzel, & LeBlanc, 1977; Winett & Winkler, 1972; Winkler, 1977). Much of the discussion centers on the potential for authority figures (e.g., parents, teachers) to select target behaviors for their wards (children and students respectively) that may be more for the convenience of the authority figure than for the ultimate benefit of the individual whose behavior is being changed. Procedures for selecting treatment goals have not been clearly delineated and social validation may provide some guidance in the selection of target behaviors and treatment goals.

As the judiciary has become more active in regulating behavior change procedures so as not to infringe on client rights (Martin, 1975), institutional review boards have been charged with overseeing behavioral programs. Kazdin (1980b, 1981) has argued that review boards, in evaluating the appropriateness of a treatment procedure for a specific client and problem behavior, are essentially making subjective judgments of the treatment acceptability. He has conducted research to isolate the variables influencing judgments of treatment acceptability. This concern with the regulation of behavioral treatment procedures on ethical and legal grounds has also contributed to the development of social validation procedures to assess treatment acceptability.

As clinical psychology has expanded its emphasis from a scientific, empirical focus to include a practice-oriented professional focus, and as government funding of clinical research has been curtailed, interest in third-party payments for services rendered has increased. To the extent that competing for these third-party payments involves some evaluation of the adequacy of the services being purchased, interest in consumer satisfaction with behavior therapy has increased (Bornstein & Rychtarik, 1983).

Several other factors may have spurred interest in social validation. Behavioral psychology has been the subject of controversy and misunderstanding since its inception and the current emphasis on social validation and consumer satisfaction may be one means of improving the public image of applied behavioral psychology and making it more responsive to the consumers of its services. Finally, there is an assumption that satisfaction with treatment may be related to client dropout rates and other more direct measures of treatment efficacy and that improving consumer satisfaction might also improve therapeutic outcome.

In this chapter, we will review the methods of social validation recommended by Wolf (1978), Kazdin (1977), and Van Houten (1979). Articles that exemplify the application of these procedures will be selectively reviewed. Social validation procedures have become standard in applied behavioral research and an exhaustive review of this literature would be beyond the scope of this chapter and tangential to its primary function. Finally, a critique of social validation procedures will be offered.

VALIDATION OF TREATMENT GOALS

In many situations the treatment goals of an applied research project or clinical application seem obvious and noncontroversial. For example, if a child is emitting unprovoked aggressive behavior directed toward the child's classmates, then an obvious treatment goal might be to reduce the frequency of hitting, kicking, and verbally abusive behavior emitted by this child. Careful examination of even this simple hypothetical example reveals at least three problems that contribute to the interest in social validation of treatment goals. Even when there is agreement on the topography of the behavior that constitutes the problem, there may be disagreement on the level of behavior that should be achieved before terminating therapy. Some might argue that a low level of unprovoked aggression is typical of children of a certain age and that suppression to zero is an unnecessary and unrealistic goal. Others might challenge the therapy goal for failing to consider the stimulus conditions under which the target behaviors occurred, noting that aggression in self-defense should not be eliminated because of its adaptability in the child's current or future environment. Finally, others, adopting a constructional approach (Goldiamond, 1974), might question the appropriateness of the therapy goals based on the failure to specify appropriate behaviors that might be increased to supplant the aggressive behavior. Thus, controversy regarding treatment goals may exist even with seemingly simple treatment goals. Social validation involves community members in assessing the social significance of the treatment goals and thus provides some guidance in the specification of target behaviors and acceptable levels of those target behaviors.

Questionnaires and Interviews

Wolf (1978) described two methods for selecting treatment objectives that, if achieved, should produce favorable reactions from community members. The first method, questionnaires and informal interviews with experts or significant others who interact with the subject, presumes that these individuals can specify the behaviors that determine their reactions to the subject. For example, Werner et al. (1975) conducted informal interviews with, and then administered questionnaires to, police officers in an attempt to ascertain which behaviors influence whether an officer arrests a youth in situations where the officer has the option of exercising discretion. The police officers indicated that a youth is less likely to be arrested if the youth expresses cooperation, faces the officer, and acts politely. Werner et al. (1975) taught these behaviors to their subjects in an effort to help youthful offenders avoid further arrests. This study illustrates the use of interviews and questionnaires with relevant professionals as a means of identifying target behaviors that meet a socially mediated criterion, judgments regarding arrest of the suspect.

Other uses of interviews and questionnaires to identify target behaviors have differed with respect to the qualifications of the judges filling out the questionnaires and whether the appropriateness of the target behaviors is based primarily on socially defined criteria (e.g., social skills) or on something other than social criteria (e.g., fire safety skills).

For example, Dow (1985) divided college students into "socially inadequate" and "socially adequate" groups based on their score on the Social Avoidance and Distress scale (Watson & Friend, 1969). Each socially inadequate subject then participated in three separate 10-minute introductory meetings with a different socially adequate peer in each meeting. Each of the socially adequate peers then rated the subject on various dimensions of social desirability using 1 to 9 Likert scales. Additionally, each socially adequate peer rated the degree of change that they would recommend on 13 specific behaviors, 9 of which had received prior research support as a relevant social skill. The socially adequate peer then suggested changes in the socially inadequate conversant's behavior and physical appearance. The results generally validated the relevance of the nine previously identified social skills, indicated individualized patterns of skill deficits, and suggested specific behavior and physical appearance changes for the socially inadequate subjects. Although no subsequent attempts to modify the social behavior of the subjects were reported, this study illustrates the use of questionnaires completed by judges with no unique qualifications other than their scores in the "socially adequate" range of a survey as a method of identifying socially defined target behaviors.

On occasion, opinions are solicited from others who by virtue of their professional expertise are uniquely qualified to guide the selection of target behaviors. Prior to teaching fire safety skills to elementary school children, Jones, Kazdin, and Haney (1981) consulted published sources and local and national organizations for information on fire safety skills. From this information they constructed 42 hypothetical fire emergency situations and suggested responses for each situation. These scenarios were then presented to 14 city firefighters to evaluate whether each response was correct or incorrect for the emergency situation described. Items judged as correct by 64% or more of the firefighters were retained. The remaining items were revised and presented to 11 firefighters with items receiving a correct rating from 73% or more of this group of firefighters being retained. Three items were once again revised and rated by 10 firefighters before a final list of situations and appropriate responses was adopted. The degree to which each successive sample of firefighters overlapped was not specified. Although the level of disagreement between firefighters and between authoritative publications and firefighters is somewhat disturbing, this study exemplifies the use of experts to identify target behaviors whose appropriateness is based on something other than socially defined criteria, that is, the probability of surviving a fire. Additionally, this study is laudable in its systematic approach to the validation of therapy goals.

A similar use of experts is reported by Iwata, Wong, Riordan, Dorsey, and Lau (1982), who had "Ph.D. psychologists who taught graduate courses, supervised interns, and/or conducted research in areas related to child behavior therapy" (p. 199) complete a survey in which specific therapist responses were rated for their "usefulness" in conducting a clinical interview. Although the survey was conducted after completion of the experiment, the experts showed a high degree of agreement regarding the relevance of the therapist responses to the interviewing process.

Social Comparison Method

The essential feature of the social comparision or known groups method (McFall, 1976) of identifying treatment objectives is the collection of normative data on a group of prospective clients and a group of peers that differ on a global dimension relevant to the target behavior. Those behaviors that are unique to the normal or more successful group suggest the target behaviors for the clients. This method was used by Minkin *et al.* (1976) to select treatment objectives for predelinquent girls who had been judged as poor conversationalists. Based on an informal review of videotaped conversations between high school and university female students and a previously unknown adult, the investigators noted that the college students tended to ask more questions and provide more positive feedback than their high school counterparts. They developed objective definitions of conversational questions and positive conversational feedback and scored the tapes for the occurrence of these behaviors and for the amount of time the girls talked. They then had adult residents of the local community rate the conversational ability of each girl. Judges were cautioned to "try not to be influenced by the conversant's age or appearance" (p. 131). The mean rating by the judges of the conversational ability of the university girls exceeded that of the high school girls in this and a subsequent replication using different girls and judges. The researchers concluded that the component behaviors distinguishing the university girls from the high school girls were probably responsible for the differences in ratings of conversational ability. Predelinquent girls were then trained so as to attain such conversational skills. The results of training were then socially validated by comparing judge's ratings of the conversational skills of the predelinquent girls on tapes recorded prior to training with ratings of tapes recorded after training. Thus community representatives were used initially to verify that university students were better conversationalists than high school students. The conversational behaviors that distinguished these two groups were objectively defined and recorded, assumed to be the source of these discrepant ratings, and thus adopted as target behaviors for the predelinquent girls.

A similar approach to the selection of treatment objectives was reported by Holmes, Hansen, and St. Lawrence (1984), who compared the conversational skills of normal community members with those of formerly hospitalized psychiatric patients. This study is noteworthy in that observed discrepancies between the two groups were used not only to identify target behaviors but also to specify criterion levels of the conversational skills that approximated community norms. A similar approach but with a different target behavior was described by Nutter and Reid (1978), who observed over 600 women in community settings to determine popular clothing color combinations. They then trained institutionalized mentally retarded women to select clothing combinations that approximated local fashion.

One of the problems with the social comparison method is the adoption of treatment objectives based on "normal" peer groups. As Kazdin (1977) notes

> For many behaviors, normative or standard levels may be an inappropriate criterion against which to evaluate change. Indeed, for many programs, the goal might be to *change* the normative level. (p. 439)

Noting similar concerns about the adequacy of treatment goals based on norms from untreated peers, Van Houten (1979) has suggested a variation of the social comparison procedure that requires first the identification of individuals who are widely acknowledged for their competence at a given behavior. Treatment objectives and standards of competence would then be based on the behavior of competent individuals rather than the performance of untreated individuals who may or may not display exemplary performance. Unfortunately, selection of performance standards and treatment objectives based on competent individuals is not yet widespread.

Experimentally Based Procedures

Van Houten (1979) has also suggested two experimentally based procedures for determining the optimal level of a behavior. In one of the procedures, the level of the target behavior is systematically varied to determine the level at which the relevant treatment effect is most closely approximated. For example, Jones and Azrin (1969) systematically varied the time between successive metronome beats to determine what temporal interval allowed stuttering clients to sound most "natural" when they paced their speech to the metronome. The "naturalness" of the resulting speech cadence was subjectively evaluated by judges listening to audio tapes of speech paced at different metronome settings.

Using a different standard of evaluation—the impact on the subsequent acquisition of different or more complex skills—allows for the experimental evaluation of a target behavior that is a prerequisite for other important behaviors. Such an approach might provide some experimentally based standards for sight word reading rate if mastery of a more complex skill, such as comprehension of textual material, was shown to be optimal only when a minimum rate of sight word decoding was exceeded. Examples of experimentally validated treatment objectives are relatively scarce and those that exist focus primarily on the optimal level of an identified target behavior rather than the identification of the target behavior itself.

Critique

Social validation of treatment objectives is a relatively new area and consequently a number of conceptual and methodological problems have yet to be resolved. First, the psychometric characteristics of the procedures used to assess the social validity of treatment objectives have yet to be established. Few of the issues typically addressed in the construction of paper-and-pencil tests (Nunnally, 1967; Salvia & Ysseldyke, 1981) have been applied to questionnaires regarding treatment objectives. With the exception of the Treatment Evaluation Inventory (Kazdin, 1980), a questionnaire designed to assess the appropriateness of treatment procedures, most of the questionnaires have relied solely on face validity. Little is known about the stability (i.e., test–retest reliability) of questionnaire data or of judge's ratings in social comparison procedures. This is in marked contrast to the care with which dependent variables are typically defined and measured in most behavioral studies.

The predictive validity of questionnaire data is at least as important as the stability of the judge's responses to questionnaires. If, for example, the police officers' identification of behaviors emitted by a youth that increase or decrease the probability of arrest had predictive validity then changes in those behaviors would indeed alter the probability of being arrested. If the identified behaviors fail to correlate with the criterion measure, for example, the probability of being arrested, then predictive validity is low and the value of the officer's response to the questionnaire is questionable. In the absence of data to attest to the predictive validity of the questionnaire data, we must assume that the officers can accurately select specific stimuli from a complex social situation that are functionally related to the probability of arresting the youth. This seems to be a tenuous assumption in the absence of supporting data.

Concerns with predictive validity are not circumvented with the social comparison methods of selecting treatment objectives. For example, the judges in the Minkin et al. (1976) study rated the conversational abilities of college-aged females above that of high school aged females. The degree to which the conversational behaviors that differentiated these two groups actually controlled the judges' ratings cannot be determined from the first two studies reported in this experiment. It is possible that some other factor, such as the conversant's physical appearance or the topic the conversant chose to discuss, may have controlled the ratings more than the conversational behaviors that were actually targeted. To their credit, the experimenters instructed the judges "not to be influenced by the conversant's age or appearance" (p. 131). Whether instructions of this sort are sufficient to offset the effects of physical appearance or other variables (some of which may be unrecognized by the experimenters) on the judges' ratings is not known. The most convincing way to remove the confound between conversational skills, conversational topic, and physical appearance is to hold all of the variables constant except one. Had the judges rated two tapes that differed only in the frequency of specific conversational behaviors (e.g., question asking), firm conclusions regarding the role of that specific behavior in controlling ratings of conversational ability could be drawn. Fortunately, Minken et al. approximated this ideal when they had judges rate the conversational skills of the predelinquent girls both during baseline and after receiving training to increase the identified conversational skills. They reported an increase in the judges' ratings that could not be attributed to differences in age or physical appearance. Although one might quibble about the failure to control the content of the pre- and posttraining conversations or the failure to isolate the impact of each separate conversational skill on the ratings, this study provides convincing evidence that increasing conversational questions and positive feedback improved perceptions of conversational skills. Ideally, the definitive analysis that isolates the impact of a prospective target behavior on social judgments should occur prior to the clinical intervention.

Disagreements between judges is perplexing, especially when they are disagreeing about target behaviors whose appropriateness is based on something other than social judgment. For example, Jones et al. (1981) consulted published sources on fire safety to devise their descriptions of fire emergency situations and appropriate responses to each situation.

They then consulted local authorities and revised their treatment objectives accordingly; this process was repeated three times before adequate agreement between experts regarding the appropriateness of each targeted emergency skill was attained. One would assume that there is a right or a best response in each emergency situation. That items would have to be adopted based on seemingly low percent agreement (64% for the first evaluation) raises serious concerns about the accuracy of the published sources, the ability of the experimenters to translate the advice of published material into response descriptions, the expertise of the firefighters, or all three. Although relying on the opinion of the majority of the firefighters seems a straightforward solution to this conflict of opinions, majorities have been wrong on many occasions. It is entirely possible that the firefighters, even those with extensive experience, knew less about fire safety skills for children than the experimenters did after studying authoritative publications. Conducting additional research to determine which fire emergency skill yielded optimal results would be an ideal although impractical strategy for resolution of such conflicts. A more practical solution requires a careful analysis of the credentials of judges selected for their expertise and, on occasion, the willingness to override the opinion of the majority when compelling evidence suggests that alternative treatment objectives might be more appropriate.

Not only is it important to analyze the credentials of experts, but it is also important to determine whose opinion is represented by your judges. If we wish to identify the treatment objectives that society wants, it is necessary that the judges be randomly selected from the population they are purported to represent (e.g., society, local community), hardly a simple task given the diversity in society or less global community groups. The degree to which the judges are a representative sample of a larger population has yet to be addressed in social validation methodologies. Furthermore, it is not always clear that the manner in which questionnaires are phrased and target behaviors adopted directly addresses the client's problem or the needs of society. For example, the officers queried in the Werner et al. (1975) study indicated the behaviors that if altered might reduce the probability of arrest for a youth. It is unclear that these behaviors represent "what society wants." If asked, "Do you think it is in the best interest of society to teach suspected juvenile offenders to avoid arrest?" we suspect that many people, including the officers queried in this study, would say no. We suspect that a treatment objective with broader support would be for juveniles to cease committing crimes. Simply teaching them to avoid arrest may solve few problems for either the juvenile or the society.

Another serious flaw in the methods by which treatment objectives are socially validated is the focus on the topography of the target response, often to the exclusion of discriminative stimuli and response consequences. Complete specification of a treatment objective should include the antecedent stimuli and response consequences that will control the target behavior after the conclusion of formal treatment. Failure to specify the controlling variables that together with the response define an operant-response class has been called the formalistic fallacy (Skinner, 1969). The failure to describe a complete operant-response class when specifying treatment objectives may result in the premature termination of treatment before the target behaviors are controlled by the contrived or naturally occurring stimuli that must ultimately maintain the responses after termination of treatment. For example, many of the therapist responses suggested by Iwata *et al.* (1982) are appropriate only under certain circumstances. To give an obvious example, "schedules next appointment" should not precede "gives name" during the course of an assessment interview. The appropriateness of a therapist response during an interview is probably based on a number of factors, including the occurrence of prior therapist questions, the client's response to those questions, and whether the client is currently talking. We have no reason to suspect that any of the subjects in this study did so, but it would have been entirely possible to attain a high percent correct score while continuing to emit therapist responses at inappropriate times during the interview. Similar arguments can be made for the importance of specifying a complete three-term contingency for conversational skills.

Finally, there are some situations where the selection of treatment goals may be justifiably based on legal and ethical grounds rendering social validation of treatment goals, regardless of the procedure used, largely superfluous. For example, attempting to increase community survival skills of the developmentally disabled, such as independent walking skills (e.g., Gruber, Reeser, & Reid, 1979), may be justified solely on the basis of ethical and legal principles regarding the rights of handicapped individuals to an education (e.g., Irvin, 1976), to live in the least restrictive environment possible (Council for Exceptional Children, 1976), and federal accreditation standards regarding freedom of movement within institutional grounds (Joint Commission on Accreditation of Hospitals, 1971). Although social validation procedures may prove useful in targeting specific components of a community survival skill, whether or not such a skill should be a training objective is more appropriately a matter of client rights than social validation. One would hope that treatment goals based on ethical and legal principles would be supported by social-validation procedures, although frequent reports of local opposition to certain treatment goals, such as the integration of developmentally disabled people into the community through placement in community facilities, suggest that what the community wants for a treatment goal may vary from legal mandates for treatment goals. In situations where public opinion is at odds with legally mandated treatment goals, public opinion should not simply be dismissed but efforts should be directed to isolating the factors controlling adverse public opinion and steps taken to improve public relations, especially when public support may expedite the achievement of treatment goals.

SOCIAL VALIDATION OF TREATMENT PROCEDURES

The acceptability of behavioral treatment procedures has also been subjected to social-validation research. To the extent that those involved in the social validation of treatment procedures are often direct (i.e., clients) or indirect (e.g., parents, teachers, administrators) consumers of those services, the literature on consumer satisfaction with treatment procedures is relevant to this aspect of social validation. Recent reviews of this literature (e.g., Bornstein & Rychtarik, 1983; Lebow, 1982; McMahon & Forehand, 1983) suggest great variation in the measures of consumer satisfaction, when those measures are taken, the sources from whom data are solicited, and the dimension along which consumer satisfaction with treatment procedures are assessed.

A variety of direct and indirect measures of consumer satisfaction have been reported. For example, unobtrusive measures such as premature withdrawal from treatment (e.g., McLean & Hakstian, 1979; Tracy, 1977) are occasionally reported as indicators of consumer satisfaction. Such unobtrusive measures of satisfaction are thought to be less reactive than other, more direct measures of satisfaction (Webb, Campbell, Schwartz, Sechrest, & Grove, 1981) and may thus prove to be useful adjuncts to other measures of satisfaction. Among other unobtrusive measures of consumer satisfaction that might be reported are unsolicited comments, referrals of friends for treatment, and institutional adoption of treatment procedures.

By far the most commonly reported measure of consumer satisfaction with treatment procedures is self-report, either to informal questions regarding treatment procedures or to formal questionnaires (e.g., Kazdin, 1980a; Larsen, Attkisson, Hargreaves, & Nguyen, 1979). These measures are often taken from service recipients upon completion of treatment or at some extended interval after completion of treatment, although they may be taken prior to treatment implementation from people who may or may not be prospective service recipients. The use of questionnaires to assess the acceptability of a treatment prior to its implementation is best exemplified by a series of studies by Kazdin (Kazdin, 1980a,b, 1981; Kazdin, French, & Sherick, 1981). He first developed and validated a 15-item rating scale, the Treatment Evaluation Inventory (TEI), to assess the degree to which treatment procedures for child behavior problems were viewed as "appropriate, fair and reasonable for the problem or client" (Kazdin, 1981, p. 493). Using a 7-point Likert-type scale, subjects are asked to rate 15 items whose content reflects

> how acceptable treatment was, how willing they would be to carry out the procedure, how suitable the procedure would be for children with problems other than those described in the study, how cruel or unfair treatment was, and how much the student liked the procedure. (Kazdin, 1980a, p. 261)

With the exception of Kazdin *et al.* (1981), who used children on a psychiatry inpatient ward and their parents and staff as raters, college jstudents have been used as the source of treatment ratings. In an effort to standardize the presentation of treatment details, treatments were described on cassette tapes to which raters listened. Whether raters had other exposure to the treatment procedures, either as a recipient, provider, or student, was not reported.

With the use of this format, the relative acceptability of various treatment procedures has been identified and factors determining treatment acceptability ratings isolated. For example, reinforcement of incompatible behavior was rated as more acceptable than time out, drug therapy, and electric shock for the treatment of deviant child behavior (Kazdin, 1980a). Among the factors that appear to influence the acceptability ratings are severity of the behavior problem (Kazdin, 1980a), the manner in which treatments are presented and implemented (Kazdin, 1980b), and the presence of undesirable side effects (Kazdin, 1981). Surprisingly, the effectiveness of treatments in altering behavior did not influence acceptability ratings (Kazdin, 1981). Although children rated treatment acceptability lower than either parents or staff, all three groups yielded the same relative ranking of four treatments for a hypothetical "seriously disturbed child" (p. 902); the order was, from most acceptable to least acceptable, reinforcement of incompatible behavior, positive practice, medication, and time out (Kazdin *et al.* 1981). This series of studies is noteworthy for the use of a validated assessment instrument and rigorous experimental methodology, and for its systematic approach to isolating the determinants of treatment acceptability.

Others have based their evaluation of the acceptability of treatment on the ratings of consumers who have had direct exposure to the procedure. Most researchers who have assessed consumer satisfaction with treatment procedures have relied on the subjective evaluations of service recipients as their primary measure. Although some have used informal interviews with unspecified content (e.g., Horne & Matson, 1977), most researchers have relied on questionnaires to solicit client evaluations of their satisfaction with treatment procedures. Standardized questionnaires with known psychometric properties are not yet widely used to assess consumer satisfaction. Most questionnaires require the participant to give a global rating of the usefulness of a technique or their overall satisfaction with the treatment procedures. On occasion, participants are asked to rate treatment procedures along another dimension that is relevant to social validation of treatment procedures. For example, Baum and Forehand (1981) had parents rate the difficulty of various parenting skills for the management of noncompliant children. Only on rare occasions have consumers been asked to rate specific aspects of a multicomponent treatment program (e.g., Ashby & Wilson, 1977) rather than rating the entire treatment program as an undifferentiated whole.

Generally speaking, participants report very positive mean ratings of satisfaction and helpfulness with respect to behavioral approaches to such diverse problems as public-speaking skill deficits (Fawcett & Miller, 1975), muscle tics (Miltenberger, Fuqua, & McKinley, 1985) and lack of senior citizen participation in a community-based meals program (Bunck & Iwata, 1978). Several investigators have compared the treatment efficacy and consumer satisfaction with behavioral treatments to that attained with nonbehavioral approaches. In a number of studies, no differences in consumer satisfaction with the two approaches was documented despite the superiority of behavioral approaches on objective measures of the problem (e.g., Hall, Bass, Hargreaves, & Loeb, 1979; Kingsley & Wilson, 1977). Others have reported greater satisfaction with behaviorally based treatments than comparison treatments (Coyne, 1978; Hall, Loeb, Coyne, & Cooper, 1981). Interpretation of these data is somewhat complicated by the global nature of the subjective evaluation (e.g., "Were you satisfied with this treatment?") making it difficult to determine whether clients were evaluating the acceptability of the treatment alternatives, the likability of the therapist, or the satisfaction with the results. Summarizing their review of studies comparing behavioral and nonbehavioral approaches, Bornstein and Rychtarik (1983) noted "no study was found in which the behavioral approach was less satisfactory or less favored" (pp. 194–195). Whereas this bodes well for behavioral interventions, it must be interpreted cautiously in light of generally high ratings for all interventions, behavioral or otherwise, and the imperfect correlation between treatment efficacy and treatment acceptability. All of the previously mentioned studies have relied on some form of verbal report (e.g., questionnaire responses) to assess consumer satisfaction. An alternative approach is described by Martin, Pallotta-Cornick, Johnstone, and Goyos (1980), who used a variation of a two-choice selection procedure (Mithaug & Hanawalt, 1978) to assess the preferences of mentally retarded clients for working under typical vocational workshop conditions versus a workshop condition featuring a number of behavioral programming components. Client preference for the contrasting workshop arrangements was assessed twice after baseline and twice after exposure to the multicomponent behavioral workshop by having the clients choose between two tables, each associated with a different set of workshop contingencies. Preference for the behavioral contingencies was evinced by selection of the behavioral table on 75% of the choices. Lockhart (1979) describes additional procedures for the behavioral assessment of human preference.

Critique

On a methodological level, efforts to socially validate treatment procedures have been characterized by a number of weaknesses that render interpretation of the results problematic. With the exception of the Treatment Evaluation Inventory (Kazdin, 1980a), consumer satisfaction has been assessed with questionnaires for which validity or reliability data are lacking. Because many of the assessment questions are developed by the experimenters for their own study, rating scales and question phrasing may differ widely between studies, making comparisons of the results across studies difficult.

A sizable minority of the studies of treatment acceptability have solicited ratings from subjects who have not directly experienced the interventions. For example, most of Kazdin's research on treatment acceptability was conducted with college students. In the one study in this series that was conducted with children, their parents, and staff on a psychiatric ward (i.e., Kazdin et al. 1981) prior exposure to all four of the treatments rated seems unlikely, although it is not specified. With few exceptions (e.g., Ashby & Wilson, 1977; Hagen, Foreyt, & Durham, 1976), attempts to compare consumer satisfaction between behavioral and nonbehavioral interventions or between different components of a behavioral intervention have suffered from the same problem, lack of direct exposure to all of the treatments being compared. Most of this group of studies rely on group designs in which consumer satisfaction of a group exposed only to a behavioral treatment procedure is compared with the ratings of a different group that was exposed to a different treatment procedure. Whether the lack of direct exposure to more than one treatment procedure accounts for the generally positive but undifferentiated ratings that clients give all treatment procedures is not known at this time.

There are a number of other methodological problems that may relate to the generally high, undifferentiated positive evaluations that consumers bestow on most interventions, behavioral or otherwise. First, only a very small number of studies (e.g., Keane, Black, Collins, & Vinson, 1982; Kingsley & Wilson, 1977; Kirigin, Braukmann, Atwater, & Wolf, 1982) actually specified that questionnaires were collected anonymously, thus limiting the possibility of bias and reactivity effects on their consumer satisfaction measures. Furthermore, as Kiesler (1983) points out, those who present themselves for therapy may not be randomly drawn from the general population but may be coming to therapy with positive expectations about therapy and the resolution of their problems. In the absence of a pretest of consumer acceptability of an impending treatment, it may be impossible to determine if a positive evaluation after completion of treatment represents a preformed opinion that was not altered by exposure to the treatment or a favorable change in opinion engendered by the treatment.

Interpretation of consumer satisfaction ratings is by no means straightforward. Most consumer satisfaction surveys request a global rating of the treatment without asking about specific aspects of what may be a complex, multicomponent therapy program. Thus, it is difficult to determine if some components engendered more satisfaction than other components. Furthermore, many of the statements on consumer satisfaction scales are sufficiently vague ("were you satisfied . . ."; "was . . . acceptable") as to render interpretation of these statements and their corresponding answers questionable. We have simply no way to know that "satisfied" means the same thing to any two people completing a consumer survey. Fortunately, some researchers have asked consumers about more specific aspects of the treatment procedure, such as the difficulty of implementation.

Finally, there are a number of variables, in addition to details of the treatment procedures, that could positively influence subjective evaluations. Among these confounding variables are the therapist's social skills, the therapist's physical appearance, and the amount of time and money the client has invested in psychological services. Comparison of pretreatment measures (i.e., prior to baseline, after completion of baseline but prior to treatment) of client attitudes about therapy procedures with posttreatment measures might allow changes in client satisfaction measures to be attributed to relevant treatment procedures with more confidence.

In addition to the methodological issues raised above, conceptual issues regarding the appropriate use of treatment acceptability data merit brief discussion. Consumer satisfaction with treatment procedures should not be used in lieu of objective data on treatment efficacy to guide decisions regarding adoption of treatment procedures. The primary criteria for adding an intervention to the behavioral armamentarium should continue to be the experimentally documented effects of that intervention, effects that include not only changes in the target behavior but information on treatment side effects and generalization and maintenance of behavior change. For those problems where the efficacy of more than one behavioral technique has been documented, data on treatment acceptability should be considered in recommending treatments for specific problems. As important as treatment acceptability may be in choosing between equally effective interventions, it is but one source of adjunct data on which such treatment decisions might be based. In addition to measures of consumer acceptability of treatments, data on cost effectiveness and ease of implementation should be considered in selecting between a number of effective treatments.

On yet another level, one might ask why treatment acceptability should be used to guide the selection of treatment alternatives, even when those alternatives are equally effective. Kazdin (1981) suggested that

> treatments that are viewed as more acceptable may be more readily sought, initiated, and adhered to than those viewed as less acceptable. Hence, acceptability may have direct implications for dissemination and utilization of treatments. (p. 494)

Although the purported relationship between treatment acceptability and both treatment initiation and adherence to therapeutic regimen seems conceptually sound, convincing experimental data to support these claims are not yet available. As noted by Bornstein and Rychtarik (1983), the relationship between consumer satisfaction and therapy outcome is inconsistent, with some studies reporting differences in treatment efficacy without corresponding differences in consumer satisfaction (e.g., Goldfried, Linehan & Smith, 1978; Loro, Fisher, & Levenkron, 1979), whereas other studies have reported differences in treatment acceptability without attaining differences in treatment efficacy (e.g., Kantorwitz, Walter, & Pezdek, 1978). The inconsistencies in this body of literature suggest a complex relationship between consumer satisfaction and treatment efficacy. Research that directly addresses the relationship between treatment acceptability and the probability of initiating treatment and, once initiated, the probability of adhering to therapy regimens, would be useful in justifying the efforts devoted to assessing treatment acceptability. Should such research be undertaken, the points in time at which treatment acceptability is assessed (e.g., prior to the initial assessment session, after the initiation of treatment, immediately upon completion of treatment, and well after completion of therapy) may prove to be an important consideration.

Finally, concern with treatment acceptability and consumer satsifaction seems merited for its potential public relations benefits. Misconceptions about behavioral psychology are all too prevalent (O'Leary, 1984; Todd & Morris, 1983; Turkat & Feuerstein, 1978) and may have contributed to the negative opinion that some people, who often lack direct experience or extensive knowledge about behavioral psychology, seem to have about behavior modification and behavior therapy. Thus, concern with consumer satisfaction with treatment procedures is merited, if for no other reason than to improve the public image of behavioral psychology. Although the public relations function of social-validation research is important, it should be recognized that improving treatment acceptability is but one element of what should be a coordinated public relations effort that might also include public school education, legislative lobbying, promoting media coverage, and correcting misconceptions in media and textbooks.

SOCIAL VALIDATION OF TREATMENT EFFECTS

The most extensive body of social-validation research, and the one which most closely approximates the focus of consumer-satisfaction research, concerns the social importance of treatment outcome. Wolf (1978) described the purpose of social validation of effects in the following manner:

> Are consumers satisfied with the results, all of the results, including those that were unplanned? Behavioral treatment programs are designed to help someone with a problem. Whether or not the program is helpful can be evaluated only by the consumer. Behavior analysts may give their opinions, and these opinions may even be supported with empirical objective behavioral data, but it is the participants and other consumers who want to make the final decision about whether a program helped solve their problems. (p. 210)

Thus, social validation of treatment effects is proposed as a method of assessing the clinical significance of a treatment effect. It is distinct from assessments of the reliability or statistical significance of behavior changes produced by an intervention; that is, determination of whether or not a treatment effect occurred. It is also distinct from the question of whether the treatment objectives have been achieved; if improper treatment objectives were adopted, achieving those objectives would not solve the client's problem.

Social validation of treatment effects has relied on two basic procedures, social comparison and subjective evaluation (Kazdin, 1977). Because the procedures closely parallel those used in the social validation of treatment goals and treatment procedures, they will be described only briefly.

Social Comparison

Like the social comparison method of socially validating treatment objectives, this method requires the identification of peers who differ from the client only with respect to the presence of the target behavior. Assuming that the behavior of the peer group is considered adequate and in no need of intervention (usually a subjective judgment), one should then judge as clinically important behavior changes that bring the client's behavior within the range of behaviors exemplified by the peers.

For example, van den Pol *et al.* (1981) taught mentally retarded subjects to eat independently at a fast food restaurant. They socially validated the treatment effects by comparing their subject's posttraining performance with that of 10 customers who ate alone at the same restaurant. They reported that the performance of their subjects generally exceeded that of the normative sample with respect to the percent of target behaviors performed. Others have used the social comparison method to determine clinically acceptable levels of behaviors as diverse as appropriate behavior in the classroom (e.g., Walker & Hops, 1976), laundry skills with the developmentally delayed (Thompson, Braam, & Fuqua, 1982), and the social behaviors of withdrawn or aggressive children (e.g., Matson, Kazdin, & Esveldt-Dawson, 1980).

Subjective Evaluation

The social importance of treatment effects can be assessed by having clients, experts or other consumers of services subjectively evaluate the treatment effects. Typically, participants provide a global rating for questions concerning the resolution of the presenting problem or their satisfaction with either the therapist or with the treatment outcome. In general, satisfaction with the treatment outcome for behavioral research appears to be quite high.

Social evaluation of treatment effects has been extensively used in studies from Achievement Place, a behaviorally based living facility for predelinquent youths. The application of this approach is perhaps best illustrated by a recent comparative evaluation of group homes based on the Achievement Place model (referred to as teaching-family group homes) with a group of comparison programs (Kirigin, Braukmann, Atwater, & Wolf, 1982). The authors collected a range of objective measures on program effectiveness from court and police files including information on the number of alleged offenses and percentage of youths institutionalized. They also collected subjective measures of consumer satisfaction from the youths who participated in the program and from other relevant consumer groups, such as the board of directors for a program, juvenile court personnel, parents, and teachers. Participants from these various consumer groups anonymously completed questionnaires on which the programs were rated on a Likert scale along a variety of dimensions, including staff effectiveness and quality of the treatment environment. Some of the rating dimensions, such as staff cooperation and pleasantness, may more accurately reflect consumer satisfaction with treatment procedures than with treatment outcome. Whether consumers were directly asked for their evaluation of the clinical significance of the treatment effects was not stated. Composite scores of consumer satisfaction suggested that with one exception, social welfare personnel, each consumer group was more satisfied with the teaching-family programs than with the comparison programs. Furthermore, they reported a positive correlation between consumer satisfaction ratings, especially those provided by the youths in the program, and official records of criminal offenses, which suggests the validity of both subjective and official measures of program effectiveness.

Critique

Many of the concerns with the methods by which treatment effects are socially validated have been discussed earlier and will only be briefly mentioned in this section. The concerns with psychometric characteristics of questionnaires (i.e., test–retest reliability, predictive validity) that were raised with respect to validating treatment objectives are also relevant to their use in validating treatment outcome.

For example, the validity of a subjective opinion regarding the clinical significance of a treatment effect might be established by its correlation with objective indexes that the problem was indeed solved.

As noted previously, Kirigen *et al.* (1982) report statistically significant correlations between composite scores of consumer satisfaction with teaching-family group homes and official records reflecting treatment effectiveness. Note, however, that the consumer satisfaction measures were composite scores that probably reflected more than just consumer satisfaction with treatment outcome. Thus the degree to which consumer ratings of treatment efficacy, unconfounded by other influences, related to the objective outcome measures was not reported. Despite this weakness, this study is exemplary in that it is one of the few that validates its consumer-satisfaction measures by reporting their relationship to other outcome measures. Unfortunately, validation of subjective judgments of clinical significance through correlations with other outcome measures is rare. If consumer-satisfaction instruments with established validity are not used, then validation efforts will be necessary with each application, a truly formidable task requiring the measurement of multiple-treatment outcomes. Kaplan (1984) recently raised similar concerns about the impact of behavior medicine interventions on health status; readers interested in validating treatment effects are referred to this article.

Closely related to concerns about the validity of subjective ratings are concerns about the ability of clients and other consumers to detect clinically significant changes in behavior. Bornstein and Rychtarik (1983) noted that the "assessment of consumer satisfaction and the assessment of treatment outcome can yield different conclusions" (p. 196). Moreover, the correlations between client ratings of therapy outcome and therapist ratings are not especially high (Garfield, 1983). A number of explanations might be offered for these discrepancies. The possibility that clients and consumers cannot accurately discriminate or describe clinically significant changes in problem behaviors has not yet been ruled out as an explanation for these discrepancies. In fact, the widespread concern with the reliability and validity of self-recording would suggest that clients and consumers, lacking training in behavioral observation and assessment, might have difficulty detecting changes in problem behaviors and thus labeling the social importance of the qualitative and quantitative changes produced by a behavioral treatment. At issue is not only the accuracy with which judges label behaviors (or people) as presenting a problem but also their sensitivity to changes in those problem behaviors. This is not to suggest the abandonment of such subjective evaluations but to suggest, as do Kazdin and Wolf, that such measures are never to be used to determine whether a treatment effect has occurred; objective measures are more appropriate for this task. Subjective judgments are most appropriately applied to evaluating the clinical or social impact of a behavior change and, even for this limited application, their sensitivity and validity is problematic. Perhaps a more direct way to assess the clinical and social significance of a treatment effect is to determine whether treatment produced behavior changes are contacting and being maintained by appropriate sources of reinforcement, be they contrived or naturally occurring, after termination of therapy.

Additional methodological concerns pertinent to the social validation of treatment effects that have been previously discussed with respect to the validation of objectives or procedures involve (a) isolating specific behavior changes that are responsible for subjective evaluations of clinical significance; (b) between-judge disagreements with respect to treatment efficacy; (c) focus on the topography of the response or the criterion level of the response to the exclusion of the controlling variables; and, (d) concerns about locating an appropriate comparison group to set therapy outcome standards. With respect to the last issue, Kazdin (1977) and Van Houten (1979) have cautioned against the uncritical acceptance of normative standards, as they may be lower than the ideal or attainable level of performance. It is noteworthy, however, that there is at least one situation where the use of normative standards is not only permissable but even desirable. This is when the problem is defined by the unfavorable reactions of others to the client and the achievement of normalcy contributes to the resolution of this problem. This standard would seem most relevant to matters of etiquette or fashion where variations from the norm often subject a person to social censure.

CONCLUSIONS

Social validation is a recent and potentially influential development in applied behavioral research. In this chapter we have attempted to describe the range of social-validation procedures and to analyze critically their methodological characteristics and conceptual foundations. As seen in our commentary throughout this chapter, social-validation efforts to date are characterized by a number of methodological weaknesses that limit conclusions that can be drawn from the data. This lack of methodological sophistication should not be especially surprising given the relatively recent emergence of concern with social validation. However, many of our methodological concerns involve the reliability and validity of measures and the necessity of experimentally isolating variables controlling the evaluative behavior of judges. These concerns involve basic principles of behavioral assessment and experimental methodology and we look forward to behavioral researchers applying the same methodological rigor to the collection of social-validation data as they currently do to the collection of their primary experimental data.

In the introduction, we mentioned several factors that may have promoted the current interest in social validation. In closing we will briefly review the relevance of social validation to those factors, as this should give some perspective on the conceptual strengths and limitations of social validation.

Can we rely on social-validation procedures to select meaningful treatment objectives? No, other factors should be considered. Social validation can provide guidance in selecting treatment goals if an appropriate peer group or exemplary performer is used in the social-comparison method or if questionnaire and interview data are collected from qualified experts. In either case, care must be taken to isolate the prospective target behaviors that are functionally related to either the subjective judgments of experts or the differences between the client and the client normal peer group.

In addition to social-validation concerns, a number of other issues merit consideration when selecting target behaviors. Among the questions that might be asked in selecting target behaviors are the following: Are the prospective target behaviors mandated as legal rights of the client? Do the prospective target behaviors interfere with the legal rights of the client? What is the problem for which services are being sought and would modification of the target behavior really solve this problem? Is a complete three-term contingency required to adequately define the target behavior? What parties are interested in changing the target behavior and why? If the target behavior was not changed, what consequences would occur for the client and for others? How might changes in the proposed target behavior benefit or harm the client, both now and in the foreseeable future? Are the proposed target behaviors likely to contact and be maintained by natural and contrived reinforcers in the posttreatment environment? Is the identification of the target behavior and a therapeutically acceptable level of that behavior most appropriately based on social-validation data or are other factors more relevant? This list of questions could be extended but the important point is that the selection of a meaningful treatment goal is a complex process requiring consideration of a number of issues, some of which require expertise in behavior analysis. Social-validation data, although valuable, are but one source of information that should be considered in selecting target behaviors.

Will social validation of treatment acceptability insure that interventions meet ethical and legal guidelines? No. Social validation was never proposed for this purpose. These issues are more appropriately determined by the judiciary and by institutional review boards familiar with legal and ethical principles regarding client rights.

Will social-validation research on treatment acceptability promote the development of procedures that are sought by more clients, retain a larger percentage of those clients partaking of the service, and promote better compliance to the therapy regimen? Maybe. The factors determining treatment acceptability have yet to be isolated but to the degree that ratings of acceptability can be traced to the reinforcing aspects of the treatment procedure, one might expect an impact on drop out rates and subsequent requests for services from those having experienced the reinforcing aspects of therapy. We suspect that an alternative set of variables are involved in compliance to treatment regimens. Unfortunately, experimental support for this application of social validation is lacking.

Will social validation improve the prospects for attaining third-party reimbursements for behavioral procedures? Probably not. We agree with Parloff (1983), who argued that treatment efficacy and cost effectiveness should be the relevant criteria for decisions regarding the expenditure of taxpayer and insurance carrier funds on a treatment procedure.

Will social validation meet the emerging demands of consumers for input into the development of science and technology? Maybe. Surely consumers who directly or indirectly finance scientific and technological activities should have some input into the manner in which those funds are spent. On one level, that of the therapist–client relationship, we suspect that consumer input is regularly solicited and incorporated into outpatient therapy plans. On other levels, involving programatic issues and client advocacy, the issues rapidly become complicated and beyond the purview of this chapter. Suffice it to say that the interpretation of social-validation data as an index of consumer input should be largely predicated on the sophistication of the consumer with respect to behavioral psychology. Efforts should be made to educate consumers with respect to scientific research and behavioral applications, for such knowledge may influence consumer satisfaction with treatment procedures and treatment outcomes.

Will social validation improve the public image of behavioral psychology? Maybe, but not on a large scale and not by itself. As mentioned previously, social validation should be but one component of a coordinated public relations effort that includes efforts to correct misconceptions about behavioral psychology and its applications, efforts to promote favorable media coverage of the numerous contributions that behavioral psychology has already made to our society, and efforts to educate increasingly larger portions of the populace with respect to behavioral philosophy and applications. Although the tone of this review has been critical, it was not meant to be negative. Given appropriate methodological considerations, social-validation procedures have much to contribute to behavioral research. However, the limitations of social-validation procedures should be acknowledged. Social-validation research has yet to develop the methodological sophistication that characterizes applied behavioral research. This perhaps is understandable given the relatively recent emergence of this topic but, if social-validation data are important, they should be collected with the same methodological rigor and subject to the same level of scrutiny as other behavioral research data. Furthermore, social-validation data should be acknowledged as adjuncts to, not replacements for, other sources of information regarding important research and clinical decisions. In closing we would like to caution behavioral practitioners and researchers neither to abbrogate their professional responsibility nor underestimate the value of behavioral training by relying exclusively on social-validation methods for the selection of treatment objectives, evaluation of treatment acceptability, or assessment of clinical outcome.

REFERENCES

Ashby, W. A., & Wilson, G. T. (1977). Behavior therapy for obesity: Booster sessions and long term maintenance of weight loss. *Behaviour Research and Therapy, 15,* 451–463.

Baer, D. M., Wolf, M. M., & Risley, T. R. (1968). Some current dimensions of applied behavior analysis. *Journal of Applied Behavior Analysis, 1,* 91–97.

Baum, C. G., & Forehand, R. (1981). Long term follow-up assessment of parent training by use of multiple outcome measures. *Behavior Therapy, 12,* 643–652.

Bornstein, P. H., & Rychtarik, R. G. (1983). Consumer satisfaction in adult behavior therapy: Procedures, problems and future perspectives. *Behavior Therapy, 14,* 191–208.

Bunck, T. M., & Iwata, B. A. (1978). Increasing senior citizen participation in a community based nutritious meal program. *Journal of Applied Behavior Analysis, 11,* 75–86.

Council for Exceptional Children. (1976). *P. L. 94–142 Works for Children.* Reston, VA: Author.

Coyne, P. D. (1978). The effects of peer tutoring with group contingencies on the academic performance of college students. *Journal of Applied Behavior Analysis, 11,* 305–307.

Dow, M. G. (1985). Peer validation and idiographic analysis of social skill deficits. *Behavior Therapy, 16,* 76–86.

Fawcett, S. B., & Miller, L. K. (1975). Training public-speaking behavior: An experimental analysis and social validation. *Journal of Applied Behavior Analysis, 8,* 125–135.

Garfield, S. G. (1983). Some comments on consumer satisfaction in behavior therapy. *Behavior Therapy, 14,* 237–241.

Goldfried, M. R., Linehan, M. M., & Smith, J. L. (1978). Reduction of test anxiety through cognitive restructuring. *Journal of Consulting and Clinical Psychology, 46,* 32–39.

Goldiamond, I. (1974). Toward a constructional approach to social problems: Ethical and constitutional issues raised by applied behavior analysis. *Behaviorism, 2,* 1–84.

Gruber, B., Reeser, R., & Reid, D. H. (1979). Providing a less restrictive environment for profoundly retarded persons by teaching independent walking skills. *Journal of Applied Behavior Analysis, 12,* 285–297.

Hagen, R. L., Foreyt, J. P., & Durham, T. W. (1976). The dropout problem: Reducing attrition in obesity research. *Behavior Therapy, 7,* 463–471.

Hall, S. M., Bass, A., Hargreaves, W. A., & Loeb, P. (1979). Contingency management and information feedback in outpatient heroin detoxification. *Behavior Therapy, 10,* 443–451.

Hall, S. M., Loeb, P., Coyne, K., & Cooper, J. (1981). Increasing employment in ex-heroin addicts I: Criminal justice sample. *Behavior Therapy, 12,* 443–452.

Holmes, M. R., Hansen, D. J., & St. Lawrence, J. S. (1984). Conversational skill training with aftercare patients in the community: Social validation and generalization. *Behavior Therapy, 15,* 84–100.

Horne, A. M., & Matson, J. L. (1977). A comparison of modeling, desensitization, flooding, study skills, and control groups for reducing test anxiety. *Behavior Therapy, 8,* 1–8.

Irvin, T. (1976). Implementation of public law 94–142. *Exceptional Children, 43,* 135–137.

Iwata, B.A., Wong, S. E., Riordan, M. M., Dorsey, M. F., & Lau, M. M. (1982). Assessment and training of clinical interviewing skills: Analogue analysis and field replication. *Journal of Applied Behavior Analysis, 15,* 191–203.

Joint Commission on Accreditation of Hospitals. (1971). *Standards for residential facilities for the mentally retarded.* Chicago: Author.

Jones, R. J., & Azrin, N. H. (1969). Behavioral engineering: Stuttering as a function of stimulus duration during speech synchronization. *Journal of Applied Behavior Analysis, 2,* 223–229.

Jones, R. T., Kazdin, A. E., & Haney, J. I. (1981). Social validation and training of emergency fire safety skills for potential injury prevention and life saving. *Journal of Applied Behavior Analysis, 14,* 249–260.

Kantorwitz, D. A., Walters, J., & Pezdek, K. (1978). Positive versus negative self-monitoring in the self-control of smoking. *Journal of Consulting and Clinical Psychology, 46,* 1148–1150.

Kaplan, R. M. (1984). The connection between clinical health promotion and health status. *American Psychologist, 39,* 755–765.

Kazdin, A. E. (1977). Assessing the clinical and applied importance of behavior change through social validation. *Behavior Modification, 1,* 427–452.

Kazdin, A. E. (1980a). Acceptability of alternate treatments for deviant child behavior. *Journal of Applied Behavior Analysis, 13,* 259–273.

Kazdin, A. E. (1980b). Acceptability of time out from reinforcement procedures for disruptive child behavior. *Behavior Therapy, 11,* 329–344.

Kazdin, A. E. (1981). Acceptability of child treatment techniques: The influence of treatment efficacy and adverse side effects. *Behavior Therapy, 12,* 493–506.

Kazdin, A. E., French, N. H., & Cherick, R. B. (1981). Acceptability of alternative treatments for children: Evaluations by inpatient children, parents and staff. *Journal of Consulting and Clinical Psychology, 49,* 900–907.

Keane, T. M., Black, J. L., Collins, F. L., Jr., & Vinson, M. C. (1982). A skills training program for teaching the behavioral interview. *Behavioral Assessment, 4,* 53–62.

Kiesler, C. A. (1983). Social psychological issues in studying consumer satisfaction with behavior therapy. *Behavior Therapy, 14,* 226–236.

Kingsley, R. G., & Wilson, G. T. (1977). Behavior therapy for obesity: A comparative investigation of long-term efficacy. *Journal of Consulting and Clinical Psychology, 45,* 288–298.

Kirigin, K. A., Braukmann, C. J., Atwater, J. D., & Wolf, M. M. (1982). An evaluation of teaching-family (Achievement Place) group homes for juvenile offenders. *Journal of Applied Behavior Analysis, 15,* 1–16.

Larsen, D., Attkisson, C., Hargreaves, W., & Nguyen, T. (1979). Assessment of client patient satisfaction: Development of a general scale. *Evaluation and Program Planning, 2,* 197–207.

Lebow, J. (1982). Consumer satisfaction with mental health treatment. *Psychological Bulletin, 91,* 244–259.

Lockhart, K. A. (1979). Behavioral assessment of human preference. *The Behavior Analyst, 2,* 20–28.

Loro, A. D., Jr., Fisher, E. B., Jr., & Levenkron, J. C. (1979). Comparison of established and innovative weight-reduction treatment procedures. *Journal of Applied Behavior Analysis, 12,* 141–155.

Martin, G., Pallotta-Cornick, A., Johnstone, G., & Goyos, A. C. (1980). A supervisory strategy to improve work performance for lower functioning retarded clients in a sheltered workshop. *Journal of Applied Behavior Analysis, 13,* 183–190.

Martin, R. (1975). *Legal challenges to behavior modification: Trends in schools, corrections and mental health.* Champaign, IL: Research Press.

Matson, J. L., Kazdin, A. E., & Esveldt-Dawson, K. (1980). Training interpersonal skills among mentally retarded and socially dysfunctional children. *Behaviour Research and Therapy, 18,* 419–427.

McFall, R. M. (1976). Behavioral training: A skill acquisition approach to clinical problems. In J. T. Spence, R. C. Carson, J. W. Thibaut (Eds.), *Behavioral approaches to therapy* (pp. 227–259). Morristown, NJ: General Learning Press.

McLean, P. D., & Hakstian, A. R. (1979). Clinical depression: Comparative efficacy of outpatient treatments. *Journal of Consulting and Clinical Psychology, 47,* 818–836.

McMahon, R. J., & Forehand, R. L. (1983). Consumer satisfaction in behavioral treatment of children: Types, issues and recommendations. *Behavior Therapy, 14,* 209–225.

Miltenberger, R. G., Fuqua, R. W., & McKinley, T. (1985). Habit reversal with muscle tics: Replication and component analysis. *Behavior Therapy, 16,* 39–50.

Minkin, N., Braukmann, C. J., Minkin, B. L., Timbers, G. D., Timbers, B. J., Fixsen, D. L., Phillips, E. L., & Wolf, M. M. (1976). The social validation and training of conversational skills. *Journal of Applied Behavior Analysis, 9,* 127–139.

Mithaug, D. E., & Hanawalt, B. A. (1978). The validation of procedures to assess vocational task preferences in retarded adults. *Journal of Applied Behavior Analysis, 11,* 153–162.

Nordyke, N. S., Baer, D. M., Etzel, B. C., & LeBlanc, J. M. (1977). Implications of the stereotyping and modification of sex role. *Journal of Applied Behavior Analysis, 10,* 553–557.

Nunnally, J. C. (1967). *Psychometric theory.* New York: McGraw-Hill.

Nutter, D., & Reid, D. H. (1978). Teaching retarded women a clothing selection skill using community norms. *Journal of Applied Behavior Analysis, 11,* 475–487.

O'Leary, K. D. (1984). The image of behavior therapy: It is time to take a stand. *Behavior Therapy, 15,* 219–233.

Parloff, M. B. (1983). Who will be satisfied by "consumer satisfaction" evidence? *Behavior Therapy, 14,* 242–246.

Salvia, J., & Ysseldyke, J. E. (1981). *Assessment in special education and remedial education* (2nd ed.). Boston, MA: Houghton, Mifflin.

Skinner, B. F. (1969). *Contingencies of reinforcement.* New York: Appleton-Century-Crofts.

Thompson, T. J., Braam, S. J., & Fuqua, R. W. (1982). Training and generalization of laundry skills: A multiple probe evaluation with handicapped persons. *Journal of Applied Behavior Analysis, 15,* 177–182.

Todd, J. T., & Morris, E. K. (1983). Misconception and miseducation: Presentations of radical behaviorism in psychology textbooks. *The Behavior Analyst, 6,* 153–160.

Tracy, J. J. (1977). Impact of intake procedures upon client attrition in a community mental health center. *Journal of Consulting and Clinical Psychology, 45,* 192–195.

Turkat, I. D., & Feuerstein, M. (1978). Behavior modification and the public misconception. *American Psychologist, 33,* 194.

van den Pol, R. A., Iwata, B. A., Ivancic, M. T., Page, T. J., Neef, N. A., & Whitley, F. P. (1981). Teaching the handicapped to eat in public places: Acquisition, generalization and maintenance of restaurant skills. *Journal of Applied Behavior Analysis, 14,* 61–69.

Van Houten, R. (1979). Social validation: The evolution of standards of competency for target behaviors. *Journal of Applied Behavior Analysis, 12,* 581–591.

Walker, H. M., & Hops, H. (1976). Use of normative peer data as a standard for evaluating classroom treatment effects. *Journal of Applied Behavior Analysis, 9,* 491–497.

Watson, D., & Friend, R. (1969). Measurement of social-evaluative anxiety. *Journal of Consulting and Clinical Psychology, 33,* 448–457.

Webb, E. J., Campbell, D. T., Schwartz, R. D., Sechrest, L., & Grove, J. B. (1981). *Nonreactive Measures in the Social Sciences* (2nd ed.). Boston, MA: Houghton Mifflin.

Werner, J. S., Minkin, N., Minkin, B. L., Fixsen, D. L., Phillips, E. L., & Wolf, M. M. (1975). "Intervention package": An analysis to prepare juvenile delinquents for encounters with police officers. *Criminal Justice and Behavior, 2,* 55–83.

Winett, R. A., & Winkler, R. C. (1972). Current behavior modification in the classroom: Be still, be quiet, be docile. *Journal of Applied Behavior Analysis, 5,* 499–504.

Winkler, R. C. (1977). What types of sex-role behavior should behavior modifiers promote? *Journal of Applied Behavior Analysis, 10,* 549–552.

Wolf, M. M. (1978). Social validity: The case for subjective measurement or how applied behavior analysis is finding its heart. *Journal of Applied Behavior Analysis, 11,* 203–214.

13

The Science of Behavior in the Design of Cultures

ROBERT G. BROWN, JR.

Skinner (1953, 1969, 1972, 1979) has suggested that the solutions to many problems that confront our society rest in implementing a science of cultural design based on the principles and technology of the analysis of behavior. Skinner's novel *Walden Two* (1948) presented his vision of how the application of the science of behavior to the design of cultural institutions and practices might be accomplished. *Walden Two* presents the picture of a community in which most of the evils of society, such as poverty, hunger, crime, violence, and exhausting labor, have been eliminated, and in which all members lead a good life free from material want and debilitating social conditions. It is a community with an egalitarian social structure in which jealousy, hate, envy, bigotry, and oppression have been all but eliminated. It is a community in which the arts and sciences flourish and in which creativity and accomplishment are maximized. In short, it is a utopia. But it is a special type of utopia that has been brought about by the judicious use of the natural sciences in general and the science of behavior in particular; it is a behavioral utopia.

For Skinner and many other behaviorists, the science of behavior provides the key to the fulfillment of the utopian dream. In *Contingencies of Reinforcement* (1969), Skinner wrote,

> Life in Walden Two is not only good, it seems feasible. It is within reach of intelligent men of goodwill who will apply the principles which are now emerging from the study of human behavior to the design of culture. (p. 29)

ROBERT G. BROWN, JR. • Department of Psychology, Western Michigan University, Kalamazoo, MI 49008.

But to date, in spite of some noteworthy attempts (Kinkade, 1973; Ulrich, 1973), no behavioral utopias have developed from the existing culture. Indeed it could be argued that even with the tools of an emerging science of behavior at our disposal many local, national, and worldwide cultural conditions have worsened. In this country crime rates continue to increase, racism and bigotry are still widespread, and millions still live in abject poverty. The economies of large and small nations alike continue to worsen, producing local and worldwide shortages and suffering. Regional wars continue unabated; civil wars and internal conflicts claim the lives of thousands of people each year. The spread of thermonuclear weapons among nations and the accelerated buildup of weapons within nations increase the likelihood of the virtual annihilation of humans and other species in even a "limited" nuclear war (Schell, 1982).

If Walden Two was within reach in 1969, what has prevented its establishment? Undoubtably, some of the reasons have to do with the size and the complexity of the task of overhauling major cultural institutions. It is also possible that the relatively young science and technology of behavior have developed only to the point where it can be applied to the solution of specific intracultural problems, such as littering (Fawcett, Mathews, & Fletcher, 1980), or in restricted settings, such as group homes or college dormitories (Miller, 1976). Fawcett et al. concluded their survey of the application of behavioral technology to community problems with the observation that

> Long standing community problems, such as poverty, alienation, and a lack of a sense of belonging, place rigorous demands on any single method of inquiry. Despite the power of behavioral methods and the promise of even more appropriate technologies for solving community problems, these means may not be sufficient. Other knowledge, including that gained from the special experience on which scientific inquiry is based and from the common experience on which philosophical inquiry is founded, may be required (Adler, 1965). Further work may clarify whether the apparent limitations of behavioral community technology reflect temporary or permanent gaps in our understanding. (pp. 515–516)

One limitation of behavioral community technology as it is currently formulated is the experimental model upon which it is based. In the typical laboratory operant-conditioning experiment that serves as the basic model for most behavioral technologies there exists an asymmetrical controlling relationship between the experimenter and the subject. During the experiment the subject is usually confined to the experimental chamber and home cage that are designed to minimize extraneous stimuli outside the control of the experimenter. In addition, the subject is usually an experimentally naive animal that has been raised in a tightly controlled environment to minimize accidental conditioning of idiosyncratic behavior. Furthermore, although the experiment may be designed to allow the subject to escape from various stimuli, the subject is never free to escape from the experiment itself. Consequently, experimenters can shape behavior using almost any type of stimulus or contingency they choose. They can administer extremely punishing consequences; they can stretch schedules of reinforcement; they can deprive the subject of food and drink. Achieving this same degree of control in a large scale behavioral community experiment is unlikely not only because of the difficulty of manipulating major variables in the cultural environment, but also because of extensive countercontrols in the functional relationships existing between the subject(s) and the experimenter(s).

Although it is almost a cliche to cite the reciprocal control existing between the experimenter and the subject in the typical nonhuman operant conditioning experimenter (e.g., the experimenter must design the experiment to conform to the biological and behavioral parameters of the subject; the subsequent behavior of the experimenter will be shaped by the results of the experiment, etc.), experimenters usually do not include a discussion of this reciprocal control in their reports. The various experimental manipulations that the experimenter arranges are treated as independent variables requiring no functional analysis.

The controlling relationships in behavioral community experimentation differ from those in nonhuman conditioning experiments in the laboratory in several important ways. Unless the behavioral community experiment is a clandestine one carried out on a group of unwitting subjects, the experimenter is directly or indirectly accountable to his subjects, that is, the members of the community. As Fawcett *et al.* point out, the first objective of the behavioral community engineers is to ascertain from the community members the specific goals towards which the behavioral technology should be applied. Next, behavioral community engineers must rely on members of the community to provide them with whatever stimuli they are to manipulate to achieve these goals. In addition to controlling the objectives and techniques of the experiment, the community members control other important stimuli affecting a wide range of the behavioral engineers' behavior (like whether or not they get paid or rehired for some other project). In the behavioral community experiment these types of countercontrols are likely to have such a confounding effect on the results as to cast considerable doubt on the suitability of the nonhuman conditioning experiment as the model for behavioral community engineering.

In a large scale behavioral community experiment of the sort necessary to establish a behavioral utopia, the issue of countercontrol becomes even more important in the analysis of controlling relationships. In the limited behavioral community experiment, it is possible to conceive of a behavioral engineer who, by virtue of the fact of being hired from outside a given community to engineer behavioral contingencies from a presumably objective vantage point, functions as a controller in an asymmetrical controlling experimenter–subject dichotomy. However, in a behavioral utopian experiment, the experimenters who thoroughly integrate themselves into the designed culture must ultimately come under the explicit experimental control of their own experiment. In other words, the behavior of the experimenters becomes both the independent and the dependent variables of the experiment, at which point the behavioral utopian experiment becomes an experiment in self-management and self-control at the personal and cultural levels.

If the typical laboratory operant conditioning experiment no longer suffices as the model upon which a behavioral science of cultural design can be constructed, we must either abandon the science of behavior as a useful tool in redesigning cultural practices on a large scale or carry on with more basic research into the principles of behavior, with particular emphasis on the dynamics of reciprocal control and self-control.

A first step in such research must involve a functional investigation and operational definition of the term *self* as it applies to the researcher and participant in the behavioral community experiment. The very notion of self-control implies the existence of two entities: a controlling self and a controlled self. But behavioral science has gone far in refuting the conception of the self as a controlling entity. An independent ego, prime mover, or functional I is not supportable from a deterministic perspective. Skinner (1979) noted that, "There's a kind of intellectual suicide in the sense that an analysis of behavior moves towards the conception in which there is no functional I . . . no capital I" (p. 47). Any research that is to be useful in the establishment of a behavioral utopia must be devoid of the notion of the functional I and must account for the behavior of the experimenter as a completely determined system, just as it accounts for the behavior of the subject. This is a very large undertaking, but it is one we must attempt if we are to continue to hold on to the behavioral utopian dream.

There is, however, an existing body of knowledge that may provide useful information on this subject. Mikulas (1981) suggested that the body of literature and set of behavioral practices known as Buddhism might be in actuality a highly evolved and empirically tested applied science composed of the objective and systematic observations of those overt and covert behaviors that make up what is commonly referred to as the self or sense of self. Mikulas asserts that the Buddhist technique of meditation is a method by which the individual can learn to be an "objective observer of the behavior of his or her mind," after which one can learn "to observe such behaviors as coverants, self statements, images, expectancies, and attributions, all within a particular cognitive style, as well as related antecedents and consequences" (p. 336). In his article, Mikulas noted several similarities between the basic principles of Behaviorism and Buddhism. For example, both are basically ahistorical, preferring to deal primarily with stimuli that are currently impinging on the individual as the major determinants of behavior; both stress objectivity and avoid theoretical and metaphysical constructs; both stress the importance of distinguishing between the behavior of the person and the person herself or himself. Mikulas proposed that a synthesis of Behaviorism and Buddhism could yield more general principles of behavior than are currently contained in either discipline by itself.

If, as Mikulas contends, both disciplines have similar sets of axioms, then the primary differences between them are a function of different domains of investigation and different levels of instrumentation. Behaviorism has traditionally taken as its field of study those overt behaviors that lend themselves most easily to instrumental forms of measurement and manipulation. Buddhism, on the other hand, has taken as one of its major fields of investigation covert behaviors that are accessible only to the individual and are not easily measured by instruments.

To the extent that Buddhism can shed light on those areas of behavior that have been ignored by behavior analysis it could prove useful to the behavioral scientist interested in the design of culture. Given the current impasse in behavioral community technology, it would be foolish for the behavioral community scientist to forego a serious study of Buddhism, or for that matter, any discipline that shows promise for expanding our understanding of the processes of behavior, no matter how divergent from the current behavioral literature that discipline may at first appear to be. It may well be the case that the road to a Behavioral Utopia will include a stop in a Buddhist Nirvana.

REFERENCES

Adler, M. J. (1965). *The condition of philosophy.* New York: Atheneum.
Fawcett, S. B., Mathews, R. M., & Fletcher, R. K. (1980). Some promising dimensions for behavior community technology. *Journal of Applied Behavior Analysis, 13,* 505–518.
Kinkade, K. (1973). *A Walden Two Experiment.* New York: Morrow.
Mikulas, W. L. (1981). Buddhism and behavior modification. *Psychological Record, 31,* 331–342.
Miller, L. K. (1976). Behavioral principles and experimental communities. In W. E. Craighead, A. E. Kazdin, & M. J. Mahoney (Eds.), *Behavior modification: Principles, issues,*

and applications (pp. 479–502). Boston, MA: Houghton Mifflin.

Schell, J. (1982). *The Fate of the earth.* New York: Knopf.

Skinner, B. F. (1948). *Walden Two.* New York: Macmillan.

Skinner, B. F. (1953). *Science and human behavior.* New York: Macmillan.

Skinner, B. F. (1969). *Contingencies of reinforcement: A theoretical analysis.* Englewood Cliffs, NJ: Prentice Hall.

Skinner, B. F. (1972). *Cumulative record: A selection of papers.* New York: Appleton-Century-Crofts.

Skinner, B. F. (1979). Interview with B. F. Skinner. *Behaviorists for Social Action Journal, 2,* 47–52.

Ulrich, R. E. (1973). Toward experimental living. *Behavior Modification Monographs, 2,* 1–74.

14

The Role of Applied Behavior Analysis in Evaluating Medication Effects

ALAN POLING AND JAMES CLEARY

INTRODUCTION

One need look no further than the *Journal of Applied Behavior Analysis* (JABA) to see that applied behavior analysts have largely ignored drugs as independent variables. Since the inception of the journal in 1968, less than a dozen studies primarily concerned with drug effects have graced its pages. This perhaps is understandable, for applied behavior analysis traditionally has involved the use of operant (or, less commonly, respondent) conditioning procedures to improve socially significant human behavior. Given this orientation, the majority of independent variables evaluated have consisted of response–consequence (reinforcement or punishment) operations. Pharamacotherapies are not easily conceptualized in terms of operant or respondent conditioning, and seem to imply faith in a medical model of behavioral problems that few behavior analysts share. We are nevertheless of the opinion that the research philosophy and analytical strategies characteristic of applied behavior analysis could serve as the basis for a fruitful science of clinical psychopharmacology. To demonstrate this, we will discuss seven dimensions of applied behavior analysis research as they relate to clinical drug evaluations. These characteristics were initially set forth by Baer, Wolf, and Risley (1968) in the inaugural issue of JABA, and serve as a set of goals

ALAN POLING • Department of Psychology, Western Michigan University, Kalamazoo MI 49008.   JAMES CLEARY • Department of Psychology, University of Minnesota, Minneapolis, MN 55455. Manuscript preparation was partially supported by Grant 1 RO1 NS202-01 from the National Institutes of Health and a Faculty Research Grant from Western Michigan University.

for research in applied behavior analysis.[1] We will argue that worthwhile research in clinical psychopharmacology must possess these same characteristics, regardless of the theoretical persuasion of the researcher.

Obviously, acceptable research must employ sound experimental design—in Baer et al.'s terms, this is the analytical dimension of research. Unfortunately, it is abundantly clear that many, in fact most, clinical drug evaluations lack methodological rigor. This is exampled by the results of an exhaustive review of studies of chlorpromazine's (Thorazine's) clinical effects conducted by Klein and Davis (1969). They found only 11 methodologically sound studies among over 12,000 published reports. Even those 11 studies were subsequently criticized by Marholin and Phillips (1976) as containing sufficient methodological errors to render their findings inconclusive. As a number of authors have recently indicated (e.g., Aman & Singh, 1983; Breuning & Poling, 1982b; Poling, Picker, & Wallace,1983; Wysocki & Fuqua, 1982), methodological errors are not confined to studies of any particular drug or subject population. Further, despite publication of several articles describing common design errors and offering guidelines for improvement (e.g., Sprague & Werry, 1971, Sulzbacher, 1973), there is little evidence to suggest that the methodological quality of drug evaluations has consistently improved over time, a contention supported by recent writings offering further suggestions for improving research quality (e.g., Aman & Singh, 1983).

One recommendation concerning clinical drug evaluations that has been made with increased frequency over time is to increase the use of within-subject research designs (e.g., Poling & Clearly, in press; Wysocki & Fuqua, 1982). Two such designs, the withdrawal and multiple baseline, were advocated by Baer et al.

The withdrawal design evolved in basic research laboratories (Sidman, 1960) and involves a sequence of manipulations in which the independent variable (treatment) is alternately presented and withdrawn,

---

[1]The seven dimensions of applied behavior analysis discussed by Baer et al. seemingly were at least in part intended as characteristics that ought to be present in articles published in JABA. Hayes, Rincover, and Solnick (1980) evaluated articles published in the first 10 volumes of that journal with respect to four of these dimensions (applied, analytical, generality, conceptual principles). They found that, across time, (a) interest in conceptual issues declined, (b) concern for maintenance (of treatment effects) increased, but interest in other forms of generality decreased, (c) analytical studies decreased in popularity, and (d) relatively simple research designs grew in popularity. These findings indicate that applied behavior analysis is not static, and that the dimensions outlined by Baer et al. are by no means homogeneous across studies. This notwithstanding, these dimensions provide a reasonable means of characterizing applied behavior analysis as a whole, and for considering its relationship to clinical psychopharmacology.

with the behavior(s) of interest repeatedly assessed under both conditions. If behavior systematically differs during the presence and absence of treatment, this difference is assumed to result from the independent variable.

A study by Marholin, Touchette, and Stewart (1979) demonstrates how a withdrawal design (sometimes misleadingly termed a reversal design, as Hersen and Barlow, 1976, explain) can be used to evaluate medication effects. In that study, four subjects were first observed during 19 days in which chlorpromazine was given. Several workshop and ward behaviors were systematically monitored. These same behaviors were then recorded across a 23-day drug-free period, followed by 25-day period in which chlorpromazine was given again. Although results differed across subjects (an outcome likely to have been obscured had a between-subjects analysis been used), there was no consistent evidence of improvement when chlorpromazine was given, although in some instances disruptive behaviors emerged when the drug was discontinued.

The multiple-baseline design requires that two or more (usually three or four) dependent variables be monitored, and involves the temporally staggered introduction of treatment, so that each dependent variable is in turn measured in the presence of treatment. In drug research, each dependent measure is usually the behavior of an individual person. Here, the target behaviors of all subjects are first assessed for a time in the absence of the drug. Then one subject receives medication, whereas the remaining subjects continue to be monitored in the absence of drug. When the performance of the first subject stabilizes, the drug is given to the second subject. This temporally staggered introduction of treatment continues until all subjects are exposed to the medication. The effectiveness of treatment is demonstrated by showing that behavior changes only when an individual subject receives the drug.

A variant of this design can be used to assess the effects of withdrawing medication. Here, all subjects receive medication that is withdrawn from each in turn in the temporally staggered sequence just described. Medication efforts are inferred when behavior changes as a function of termination of the drug regimen.

The use of a multiple-baseline across subjects designs in drug evaluation is demonstrated in a study by Davis, Poling, Wysocki, and Breuning (1981). Those authors evaluated the effects of withdrawing the antiepilepsy drug phenytoin (Dilantin) on the workshop and matching-to-sample performance of mentally retarded subjects. In all instances, workshop performance improved only after the drug was totally withdrawn. Similar results were obtained with respect to matching-to-sample performance. Other recent studies also have successfully used this design (e.g., Wysocki, Fuqua, Davis, & Breuning, 1981).

Hersen and Barlow (1976) provided a good general discussion of withdrawal and multiple-baseline designs, whereas Poling and Cleary (in press) and Wysocki and Fuqua (1982) specifically examined their usefulness in drug evaluations. For our purposes, it is enough to note that both designs are adequate for demonstrating that a drug reliably produces a particular effect, and that neither poses intrinsic problems for the researcher. The withdrawal design does, however, require countertherapeutic behavior change (when treatment is withdrawn) to show the value of treatment, and for this reason may be less acceptable than the multiple-baseline design.

The withdrawal and multiple-baseline designs historically have stood first and second, respectively, in popularity among applied behavior analysts (Kelly, 1977), and there is every reason to believe that they offer an excellent alternative to the between-subjects analyses commonly and often badly (see Sprague & Werry, 1971) employed in clinical psychopharmacology.

Regardless of research design, Baer et al. argue that a treatment is of interest to applied behavior analysts only if its effects are socially significant. This means that the problem being studied is of interest to society. That is, treatment must be applied in that, if successful, it solves some real and pressing problem.[2] In most instances, clinical drug evaluations are clearly applied in that drugs are prescribed to treat behavioral problems that are obviously troublesome to the patient and to society at large. Nonetheless, it cannot be taken for granted that the behavior actually measured in a given study has any relation to the alleged problem for which drugs are given. Baer et al. note that an actual problem-solving orientation is an important dimension of applied behavior analysis; the same is true for clinical psychopharmacology.

Beyond being applied, useful research shows that a treatment is effective, which is the term Baer et al. use to designate clinical, as opposed

[2]Applied research almost always implies the study of naturally occurring behaviors in their usual social setting. However, controlled laboratory studies of drug effects on the learning and performance of behaviors not socially significant in their own right (e.g., lever pressing, memorization of nonsense syllables) can be of great value in understanding clinically significant drug effects, as can investigations involving laboratory analogues of socially significant behaviors (e.g., driving simulations). Behavioral pharmacologists have utilized laboratory procedures to determine the effects of many drugs in nonhumans and, occasionally, humans. These findings can provide clues to the probable behavioral effects of drugs in applied settings, and should not be ignored by individuals conducting clinical drug evaluations (cf. Poling, Picker, & Hall-Johnson, 1983).

to experimental or statistical, significance, and consider as the third dimension of applied behavior analysis research.

Certainly, the evaluation of any pharmacotherapy requires the researcher to consider the magnitude and consequent utility of any demonstrated drug effect. Put simply, is the patient really better off when the drug is given? As Marholin and Phillips (1976) indicated, negative side effects, as well as beneficial actions of treatment, must be considered in answering this question. Applied behavior analysts have begun to recognize this (e.g., O'Leary, 1980; Willems, 1974), and have taken steps to develop procedures for socially validating their treatments (Van Houten, 1979; Wolf, 1978).

Social validation presupposes that the effects of treatment can be adequately indexed. Unfortunately, drug evaluations often fail to pay due attention to the dependent variable—whatever it is that the drug is supposed to improve. The importance of this dimension of research was documented by Sulzbacher (1973), who found that the probability of a beneficial drug effect being reported in pediatric psychopharmacology was greatest when global clinical evaluation formed the basis of treatment evaluation, and considerably lower when more direct measures of behavior were used.

Since 1968, when Baer et al. wrote that one dimension of applied behavior analysis was an insistence that treatment effects can be shown only through direct measures of behavior, applied behavior analysts have developed a powerful technology for quantifying a wide range of human behaviors. Yet, with some noteworthy exceptions, the data collection procedures of applied behavior analysis have had little influence on either preclinical or clinical psychopharmacology (Poling, Cleary, & Monaghan, 1980; Poling, Picker, & Wallace, 1983). This is distressing, for pharmacotherapies are used with the avowed intent of changing a patient's behavior. They are successful only to the extent that behavior changes in the desired direction, and to the desired extent, and this can be determined only if reliable, valid, and sensitive samples of the behavior of interest are actually taken. Clinical psychopharmacology, quite as much as applied behavior analysis, should take overt behavior as its primary datum, and in so doing, must eventually share data collection strategies with applied behavior analysis. These strategies have been analyzed at length elsewhere (e.g., Hersen & Barlow, 1976; Johnston & Pennypacker, 1981; Kazdin, 1982).

We have discussed four dimensions of applied behavior analysis and their possible application to clinical psychopharmacology. Beyond these dimensions, Baer et al. emphasized that research in applied behavior analysis ought to be presented with sufficient clarity to allow others to fully replicate treatments. They called this the technological dimension of research, and its relevance to clinical psychopharmacology is readily apparent. At minimum, treatments must be fully described with respect to subject characteristics, dose and schedule of drug administration, the environmental conditions under which behavior is measured, the manner in which behavior is assayed, and the precautions taken to ensure that double-blind and placebo control conditions are not violated. As Sprague and Werry (1971) and Poling, Picker, and Hall-Johnson (1983) pointed out, a sizable number of published articles in clinical psychopharmacology fail to provide such basic information as the dose of drug given and the procedures used to quantify behavior. These studies are at best of little value, and serve primarily as reminders of the importance of the technological dimension of research.

Related to the technological adequacy of research is the analysis of procedures in relation to accepted principles and conceptual systems. This sixth dimension of research is difficult to evaluate, for there can be legitimate disagreement as to what principles, and hence what literature, is relevant to a particular treatment. With regard to the present discussion, it is interesting to consider the existence of a large literature in basic behavioral pharmacology that seems to have had relatively little influence on the conduct or interpretation of clinical psychopharmacology research. In some respects, this resembles the alleged separation of the experimental analysis of behavior and applied behavior analysis that has been bemoaned in a number of articles (e.g., Deitz, 1978; Pierce & Epling, 1980; Poling, Picker, Grossett, Hall-Johnson, & Holbrook, 1981). It is beyond our purposes to consider the extent to which basic research findings in either behavioral pharmacology or behavioral psychology influence applied investigations, or whether current practices are profitable. We would, however, like to suggest that although few individuals know the collective literatures of applied behavior analysis, the experimental analysis of behavior, behavioral pharamacology, and clinical psychopharmacology, each of these literatures contains information valuable to scientists interested in therapeutic drug effects in humans.

A seventh and final dimension of research discussed by Baer et al. is the generality of treatment effects.

> A behavior change may be said to have generality if it proves durable over time, if it appears in a wide variety of possible environments, or if it spreads to a wide range of problem behaviors. (Baer et al., 1968, p. 96)

As discussed elsewhere (Breuning & Poling, 1982b), pharmacotherapy with the mentally retarded seems to rest in part on the belief that drugs that have been shown to affect beneficially the mentally ill will likewise affect the mentally retarded, who may emit superficially similar behaviors. This generalization is not strongly supported by data (see Breuning & Poling, 1982a). In this regard, within-subject research designs are likely to be more valuable that between-subjects designs, for the former are especially well suited for disclosing the variables that determine whether subjects do or do not benefit from treatment.

The foregoing indicates that Baer *et al.*'s analysis of the important aspects of applied behavior analysis research can be related meaningfully to clinical psychopharmacology. The behavioristic position requires all treatments to be evaluated similarly and, to a behaviorist, any drug evaluation that possesses the seven characteristics discussed by Baer *et al.* would provide useful information. In the next section, we encourage applied behavior analysts to focus greater attention on drugs as independent variables.

DRUGS AS INDEPENDENT VARIABLES

Over 1500 compounds have been classified primarily as psychotropic agents (Usdin & Efron, 1972), which essentially means that they are prescribed to treat behavioral problems. These drugs, commonly classified as neuroleptics, anxiolytics, stimulants, antidepressants, and antimaniacs (or mood-stabilizers), are prescribed by the millions each year. Baldessarini (1980), for example, writes: "Today, 20% of the prescriptions written in the United States are for medications intended . . . to sedate, stimulate, or otherwise change mood, thinking, or behavior" (p. 391). It is estimated that over 50 million patients received chlorpromazine between 1953 and 1963 (Ray, 1978), whereas in 1975 Americans spent nearly half a billion dollars on anxiolytics, mainly chlordiazepoxide (Librium) and diazepam (Valium) (Cant, 1976). In addition, approximately 600,000 to 700,000 children receive stimulants for hyperactivity during the school year (O'Leary, 1980). These figures underscore the popularity of pharmacotherapies. And, despite recent judicial pronouncements limiting carte blanche drug use with institutionalized populations, especially the mentally retarded (see Sprague, 1982), there is no good reason to believe that the use of drugs to treat behavioral problems will diminish in the foreseeable future.

Unfortunately, far too little is known concerning (a) the variables (e.g., kinds of subjects, specific behavior problems) that determine whether a given compound produces a therapeutic effect, (b) the behavioral side effects of psychotropic agents, and (c) the comparative value of the specific pharmacotherapies relative to non-drug treatments, such as behavior modification. This is not to say that drugs have not been studied in detail. Some surely have. For example, studies of neuroleptics' effects in psychotic patients are legion, although as mentioned earlier many are methodologically flawed. Enough sound evaluations have nonetheless appeared to convince most scientists that neuroleptics can often be of value in this population (see Berger, 1978).

Often is a critical qualifier here, for it is certain that not all patients, psychotic or otherwise, benefit from neuroleptics. Within-subject research performed in the applied behavior analysis tradition and exemplified by the studies mentioned earlier should prove particularly useful in clarifying who does and does not benefit from these drugs. In this regard, it is worth noting the conclusions of a recent review of neuroleptic drug effects in the mentally retarded by Ferguson and Breuning (1982).

> A fairly impressive number of studies have been conducted in an attempt to examine the efficacy of antipsychotic drug use with the mentally retarded. However, the overwhelming majority of these studies are methodologically inadequate and the results are largely uninterpretable. The results of the methodologically stronger studies suggest that compared to a placebo, a few antipsychotic drugs may be effective in reducing some inappropriate behaviors. The most impressive evidence (while not overwhelming) for efficacy is from studies showing that thioridazine can reduce self-stimulatory behaviors. However, these same studies have also shown that merely engaging the mentally retarded in another activity is at least as effective as the drug. (p. 199)

Beyond emphasizing how little actually is known about the actions of neuroleptics in a population that often receives them, Ferguson and Breuning's summary indicates the need for, and potential value of, comparative research.

It is noteworthy that several studies of drugs as independent variables that have appeared in JABA compared medication to behavioral treatments. In four such studies (Ayllon, Layman, & Kandel, 1975; Pelham, Schnedler, Bologna, & Contreras, 1980; Shafto & Sulzbacher, 1977; Wulbert & Dries, 1977), methylphenidate (Ritalin) was compared to contingency management in controlling the behavior of hyperactive children. Whereas medication alone produced some beneficial effects in each study, contingency management also facilitated desired behavior. In addition, in three studies (Ayllon *et al.*, 1975; Shafto & Sulzbacher, 1977; Wulbert & Dries, 1977), medication was at least occasionally associated with adverse behavioral changes, whereas contingency management was never observed to produce such effects. However, Pelham *et al.* (1980) did not observe deleterious side effects with methylphenidate alone, nor with combined drug and behavioral treatment, which they found to be more effective than either component alone.

Although these studies do not resolve the complex issue of how hyperactivity ought to be managed (for a discussion of this issue see O'Leary, 1980), they do demonstrate conclusively that the research philosophy and methodology characteristic of applied behavior analysis can be used to compare medications to alternative treatments and to assess the behavioral side effects of pharmacological interventions.

Given this, it is our opinion that much would be gained if scientists interested in pharmacotherapies adopted the approach to research described in its rudiments by Baer *et al.* (1968). This could occur in two ways. First, researchers now working in clinical psychopharmacology, most of whom are not trained in behavioral psychology, could come to generally accept the value of within-subject research intensively analyzing how drugs affect carefully defined and measured target behaviors. Second, applied behavior analysts could begin to examine drug effects with greater frequency.

Recent writings by us and others (e.g., Breuning & Poling, 1982b; Poling & Cleary, in press; Wysocki & Fuqua, 1982) were intended at least in part to convince clinical psychopharmacologists of the merits of the behaviorists' approach to treatment evaluation. Although the success of these efforts remains to be determined, it seems unlikely that many established researchers will be easily convinced to accept what is to them a novel paradigm. Thus, if one believes as we do that careful empirical examination of drug effects in individual patients is the only adequate way to evaluate pharmacotherapies (both in the context of research and everyday clinical evaluation), it is crucial that researchers who now understand and accept the methodology of applied behavior analysis begin to examine drug effects.

Some steps in this direction have already been taken and enough studies have been published to demonstrate that the research methodology characteristic of applied behavior analysis can be profitably adopted to drug evaluations. However, although drugs are in principle independent variables that can be studied in the same manner as other treatments commonly evaluated by behaviorists, they do have certain unique characteristics that must be considered in designing and interpreting studies.

One peculiarity of pharmacotherapies involves the question of who can manipulate the treatment. In contrast to most independent variables examined by applied behavior analysts, psychotropic drug treatments can be legally administered, withdrawn, or otherwise manipulated only by licensed medical doctors. Because few people trained in applied behavior analysis hold the M.D. degree, to perform drug evaluations they must enlist the aid of a sympathetic physician.

Securing such support can be difficult, although we have found that the majority of physicians condone objective drug evaluations if they are contacted in a professional manner, the well-being of their patients is ensured, and their role in the project is consistent with accepted medical practice. It is perhaps easier to convince physicians to be involved in within-subject drug evaluations than to take part in a traditional between-subjects analysis for, in contrast to many between-subjects evaluations, within-subject designs do not require withholding medication from anyone and often require no actions by the physician beyond those that would normally be performed in the course of treatment.

For example, in the Davis et al. (1981) study of the effects of withdrawing phenytoin described earlier, the patients were by virtue of being free of seizures for an extended period of time due to receive a drug-free period (drug holiday). This was not affected by our study; we simply conferred with the responsible physician concerning the exact schedule of phenytoin withdrawal, and systematically monitored behavior across conditions. Wysocki et al. (1981) employed a similar strategy to investigate the effects of thioridazine (Mellaril) withdrawal on titrating-delayed-matching-to-sample performance in mentally retarded adults. These studies show that empirical drug evaluations are by no means incompatible with good clinical practice. In fact, such evaluations provide the only compelling means of determining the effects of pharmacotherapy, a point that will escape surprisingly few physicians.

Beyond securing a physician's assistance, studying drugs as independent variables requires basic knowledge of pharmacology. This may prove troublesome for applied behavior analysts not formally trained in the area. For example, drugs regularly produce effects that endure, or emerge, long after the medication regimen is terminated. To become aware of the problems potentially involved in unequivocally showing that drugs produce particular effects, one need only consider that metabolites of chlorpromazine can be detected in urine weeks after treatment is terminated (Ferguson & Breuning, 1982), whereas tricyclic antidepressants produce therapeutic effects only with extended (perhaps 2 weeks) exposure (Berger, 1978). Although multiple-baseline and withdrawal designs are perfectly capable of detecting treatment effects that are delayed in time, most of the interventions studied by applied behavior analysts produce dramatic and rapid effects. Hence the extended time periods required to analyze drug effects completely may not be fully appreciated.

However, O'Leary (1980), writing in JABA, has convincingly argued that long-term research assessing a range of dependent measures at a number of dosages is unavoidable if the efficacy of pharmacotherapy is ever to be known with certainty, which indicates that at least some applied behavior analysts are aware of the potential methodological issues associated with drug evaluation. In view of these problems, O'Leary (1980) contended that, with regard to evaluating treatments for hyperactive children: "Single researchers or single research teams cannot well address long- and short-term treatment efficacy problems. A large multiclinic research effort is now needed" (p. 201).

Few such multiclinic studies have been attempted. Yet even if such collaborative efforts remain rare, more modest studies conducted in the applied behavior analysis tradition, and published in such archtypically behavioral journals as JABA, provide good evidence that practically feasible and scientifically sound drug evaluations are possible.

Perhaps these studies will help to convince applied behavior analysts that pharmacotherapies deserve detailed examination as independent variables. Society, especially those individuals whose lives are personally affected by drugs, need and demand information concerning their behavioral actions. Applied behavior analysts, perhaps to a greater degree than any other group of scientists, are capable of providing this information and of developing and evaluating alternatives to pharmacotherapies as well. The promise of applied behavior analysis will not be fulfilled if they fail to do so.

ACKNOWLEDGMENTS

We wish to thank the members of the Behavioral Pharmacology Laboratory, Western Michigan University, for their comments on an earlier draft of this paper.

REFERENCES

Aman, M. G., & Singh, N. N. (1983). Pharmacological intervention. In J. L. Matson & J. A. Mulick (Eds.), *Handbook of Mental Retardation* (pp. 317–337). New York: Pergamon Press.

Ayllon, T., Layman, D., & Kandel, H. J. (1975). A behavioral-educational alternative to drug control of hyperactive behavior. *Journal of Applied Behavior Analysis, 8*, 137–146.

Baer, D. M., Wolf, M. M., & Risley, T. (1968). Some current dimensions of applied behavior analysis. *Journal of Applied Behavior Analysis, 1*, 91–97.

Baldessarini, R. J. (1980). Drugs and the treatment of psychiatric disorders. In A. Goodman Gilman, L. S. Goodman, & A. Gilman (Eds.), *The pharmacological basis of therapeutics* (pp. 391–447). New York: Macmillan.

Berger, P. A. (1978). Medical treatment of mental illness. *Science, 200,* 974–981.

Breuning, S. E., & Poling, A. (1982a). *Drugs and mental retardation.* Springfield, IL: Charles C Thomas.

Breuning, S. E., & Poling, A. (1982b). Pharmacotherapy with the mentally retarded. In J. L. Matson & R. P. Barrett (Eds.), *Psychopathology in the mentally retarded* (pp. 195–252). New York: Grune & Stratton.

Cant, G. (1976, February 1). Valiumania. *New York Times Magazine,* pp. 34–44.

Davis, V. J., Poling, A., Wysocki, T., & Breuning, S. E. (1981). Effects of phenytoin withdrawal on matching to sample and workshop performance of mentally retarded persons. *The Journal of Nervous and Mental Disease, 169,* 718–725.

Deitz, S. M. (1978). Current status of applied behavior analysis: Science versus technology. *American Psychologist, 33,* 805–814.

Ferguson, D. G., & Breuning, S. E. (1982). Antipsychotic and antianxiety drugs. In S. E. Breuning & A. Poling (Eds.), *Drugs and mental retardation* (pp. 168–214). Springfield, IL: Charles C Thomas.

Hayes, S. C., Rincover, A., & Solnick, J. V. (1980). The technical drift in applied behavior analysis. *Journal of Applied Behavior Analysis, 13,* 275–286.

Hersen, M., & Barlow, D. (1976). *Single case experimental designs: Strategies for studying behavior change.* New York: Pergamon Press.

Johnston, J. M, & Pennypacker, H. S. (1981). *Strategies and tactics of human behavioral research.* New York: Erlbaum.

Kazdin, A. E. (1982). *Single-case research designs.* New York: Oxford University Press.

Kelly, M. B. (1977). A review of the observational data collection and reliability procedures reported in the Journal of Applied Behavior Analysis. *Journal of Applied Behavior Analysis, 10,* 97–102.

Klein, D., & Davis, J. (1969). *Diagnosis and treatment of psychiatric disorders.* Baltimore, MD: Williams & Wilkins.

Marholin, D., & Phillips, D. (1976). Methodological issues in psychopharmacological research. *American Journal of Orthopsychiatry, 46,* 477–495.

Marholin, D., Touchette, P. E., & Stewart, R. M. (1979). Withdrawal of chronic chlorpromazine medication: An experimental analysis. *Journal of Applied Behavior Analysis, 12,* 159–171.

O'Leary, K. (1980). Pills or skills for hyperactive children? *Journal of Applied Behavior Analysis, 13,* 191–204.

Pelham, W. E., Schnedler, R. W., Bologna, N. C., & Contreras, J. A. (1980). Behavioral and stimulant treatment of hyperactive children: A therapy study with methylphenidate probes in a within-subjects design. *Journal of Applied Behavior Analysis, 13,* 221–236.

Pierce, W. D., & Epling, W. F. (1980). What happened to analysis in applied behavior analysis? *The Behavior Analyst, 3,* 1–9.

Poling, A., & Cleary, J. (in press). Within-subject designs. In K. D. Gadow & A. Poling (Eds.), *Advances in learning and behavioral disabilities (Supp. 1): Methodological issues in human psychopharmacology.* Greenwich, CT: JAI Press.

Poling, A., Cleary, J., & Monaghan, M. (1980). The use of human observers in psychopharmacological research. *Pharmacology Biochemistry and Behavior, 13,* 243–246.

Poling, A., Picker, M., & Hall-Johnson, E. (1983). Human behavioral pharmacology. *Psychological Record, 33,* 473–493.

Poling, A., Picker, M., & Wallace, S. (1983). Some methodological characteristics of psychopharmacological studies with the mentally retarded. *Mental Retardation and Learning Disability Bulletin, 11,* 110–121.

Poling, A., Picker, M., Grossett, D., Hall-Johnson, E., & Holbrook, M. (1981). The schism between experimental and applied behavior analysis: Is it real and who cares? *The Behavior Analyst, 4,* 143–152.

Ray, O. (1978). *Drugs, society, and human behavior.* St. Louis, MO: Mosby.

Shafto, F., & Sulzbacher, S. (1977). Comparing treatment tactics with a hyperactive preschool child: Stimulant medication and programmed teacher intervention. *Journal of Applied Behavior Analysis, 10,* 13–20.

Sidman, M. (1960). *Tactics of scientific research.* New York: Basic Books.

Sprague, R. L. (1982). Litigation, legislation, and regulations. In S. E. Breuning & A. Poling (Eds.), *Drugs and mental retardation* (pp. 377–415). Springfield, IL: Charles C Thomas.

Sprague, R. L., & Werry, J. S. (1971). Methodology of psychopharmacological studies with the retarded. In N. R. Ellis (Ed.), *International review of research in mental retardation,* (Vol. 5, pp. 147–219). New York: Academic Press.

Sulzbacher, S. I. (1973). Psychotropic medication with children: An evaluation of procedural biases in results of reported studies. *Pediatrics, 51,* 513–517.

Usdin, E., & Efron, D. H. (1972). *Psychotropic drugs and related compounds.* Washington, DC: Government Printing Office.

Van Houten, R. (1979). Social validation: The evaluation of standards of competency for target behaviors. *Journal of Applied Behavior Analysis, 12,* 581–591.

Willems, E. P. (1974). Behavioral technology and behavioral ecology. *Journal of Applied Behavior Analysis, 7,* 151–166.

Wolf, M. M. (1978). Social validity: The case for subjective measurement or how applied behavior analysis is finding its heart. *Journal of Applied Behavior Analysis, 11,* 203–214.

Wulbert, M., & Dries, R. (1977). The relative efficacy of methylphenidate (Ritalin) and behavior-modification techniques in the treatment of a hyperactive child. *Journal of Applied Behavior Analysis, 10,* 21–32.

Wysocki, T., & Fuqua, R. W. (1982). Methodological issues in the evaluation of drug effects. In S. E. Breuning & A. Poling (Eds.), *Drugs and mental retardation* (pp. 138–167). Springfield, IL: Charles C Thomas.

Wysocki, T., Fuqua, R. W., Davis, V. J., & Breuning, S. E. (1981). Effects of thioridazine on titrating delayed matching to sample performance in the mentally retarded. *American Journal of Mental Deficiency, 85,* 539–547.

15

Fraud, Fakery, and Fudging

Behavior Analysis and Bad Science

ELBERT BLAKELY, ALAN POLING, AND
JEFFREY CROSS

INTRODUCTION

The business of scientists is collecting, interpreting, and disseminating data. A difficult business it is, but honorable. Or is it? A look at the historical record might suggest otherwise, for it appears that unethical conduct in the name of science, including the falsification of data, is by no means rare. In fact, myriad cases of apparent fraud are evident in the history of science (Broad & Wade, 1982).

For example, Claudius Ptolemy, an Egyptian who lived in the second century A.D., promoted a geocentric model of planetary movement, wherein other planets revolved around the earth in circular orbits. This model, widely accepted until Copernicus proposed a heliocentric planetary system, was supported by astronomical data allegedly collected by Ptolemy, and by an anthropocentric worldview. A careful examination of Ptolemy's data reveals, however, that many of his reported observations are grossly inaccurate. Evidence exists that Ptolemy presented as his own data actually collected by Hipparchus of Rhodes. These observations were made from a location well north of that supposedly used by Ptolemy, and hence differed from those that would have resulted had Ptolemy actually scanned the heavens (Newton, 1977).

ELBERT BLAKELY and ALAN POLING • Department of Psychology, Western Michigan University, Kalamazoo, MI 49008. JEFFREY CROSS • Department of Psychology, Allegheny College, Meadville, PA 16335. Preparation of this manuscript was partially supported by National Institutes of Health Grant 1 RO1 NS20216–01.

Galileo, a proponent of Copernicus' theory, published many works on the laws of motion. An avowed empiricist, Galileo reported a plethora of experiments. Historians have speculated, however, that he often arrived at preexperimental conclusions that were not precisely supported by experimental results, but were nonetheless reported. In fact, the results of some of Galileo's experiments have not been replicated, leaving doubt as to whether the initial investigations were even conducted (Cohen, 1957). It should be noted in passing that a translator's error, as well as his own apparent willingness to play fast and loose with data, appears to have contributed to Galileo's reputation as a researcher. In one English translation of Galileo's writings concerning the properties of motion, the translator apparently added the words "by experiment" to suggest that Galileo's discoveries were a result of empirical research. These key words do not appear in the original Italian version (Broad & Wade, 1982).

The blind devotion to personal theories that afflicted Ptolemy and Galileo also is evident in the work by Isaac Newton. Newton argued that scientific truth was realized only when there was a perfect correlation between observations and theory. Thus, in an inexorable search for this perfect correlation, he apparently made certain "adjustments" in his calculations so that they would agree with his theoretical propositions. For instance, Newton used different air density constants until the final computation of sound velocity fell within the appropriate range. Newton also engaged in questionable conduct of another sort when he used his position of authority in the Royal Society of London for Improving Natural Knowledge (a powerful English scientific organization generally known as the Royal Society) to discredit the work of Leibniz, with whom he was vying for the honor of discovering calculus, although his success in so doing had more to do with politics than science (Broad & Wade, 1982).

Gregor Mendel was an Austrian monk who in the 19th century described many basic genetic relations, supported by data that corresponded with theoretical predictions to an amazing degree. Fisher (1936) and van der Waerden (1968) have argued that Mendel probably selected data that supported his preexperimental notions, although Fisher raised the possibility that Mendel was an unwitting victim of data selection by an assistant who was aware of expected (and desired) experimental outcomes.

Robert Millikan, winner of a 1923 Nobel Prize for discovering the electrical charge of the electron, is another successful researcher who appears to have been guilty of presenting only results consistent with theory. Millikan performed numerous experiments that, he concluded, categorically demonstrated that electrons carried a single negative charge.

This contention was opposed by Felix Ehrenhaft, who proposed the existence of subatomic particles with fractional charges (Broad & Wade, 1982). A post hoc analysis of Millikan's raw data revealed that he discarded many outlier observations that did not conform to his theory, and actually noted in his records whether a particular trial observation should be published (Holton, 1978). Millikan's publications, based at least in part on carefully selected data, were instrumental in procuring the Nobel Prize and discrediting the work of Ehrenhaft, although it now appears that the latter's observations and conclusions were correct (Broad & Wade, 1982).

Psychology gives us an excellent example of unethical scientific conduct, and the potential gains associated therewith, in the bizarre case of Cyril Burt. Sir Cyril was at various times responsible for the mental testing of all London school children, chair of the most prestigious psychology department in England (University College, London), and editor of an important journal (*British Journal of Statistical Psychology*). During his lifetime, Burt was renowned for his work in factor analysis, and for steadfastly arguing for the inherited basis of intelligence. Burt's claim that intelligence was largely inherited rested primarily on data from his own studies. These data indicated that there was a strong positive correlation in the intelligence quotients (IQs) of identical twins reared apart. In fact this correlation, reported as .771, did not change substantially across the course of several studies, in which the number of pairs of twins studied grew from less than 20 to more than 50.

Such an outcome is so unlikely as to be practically impossible. Leon Kamin noted this (see Kamin, 1974), and the scientific community began to rumble with concerns abut the apparent "carelessness" of Burt, who died in 1971. Five years after Burt passed on, the medical correspondent of the London *Sunday Times*, Oliver Gillie, revealed that two women who allegedly collected and analyzed Burt's data (Margaret Howard and J. Conway) either did not exist, or could not have been in contact with Burt when he wrote the papers bearing their names, and accused the deceased of outright fakery. It soon became apparent that the charge was valid, and it is now generally accepted that in his later career (i.e., after 1940) Burt fabricated data on identical twins, kinship correlations in intelligence, and declining levels of intelligence in Great Britain (Dorfman, 1978; Hearnshaw, 1979; Gould, 1981). Burt also misrepresented factor analysis in an attempt to support the hereditarian nature of intelligence in which he so strongly believed (Gould, 1981), and in whose defense he would eventually prostitute himself.

Burt's fabricated data were used by Arthur Jensen (1969) to support his contention that: (a) intelligence is largely genetically determined; (b) blacks are by virtue of heredity intellectually inferior to whites; and (c) since (a) and (b) hold, educational programs designed to produce equal performance in blacks and whites are doomed to failure. That Burt's egregiously flawed data were once used for such a purpose—and are occasionally so used today—clearly emphasizes that the consequences of unethical scientific conduct extend beyond the hallowed halls of academia.

Burt's misdeeds took place over two decades ago, although the hereditarian conception of intelligence is with us still (see Gould, 1981). A more contemporary but equally audacious case of skulduggery involves Elias Alsabti. Alsabti was an Iraqui who claimed to be related to the royal family of Jordan. He emigrated to this country in 1977 professing to bear a Ph.D. and an M.D., and was initially funded by the Jordanian government to study medicine and conduct cancer research. Within a period of 3 years, Absabti published over 60 articles. Well done, perhaps, unless one considers that the authenticity of Alsabti's degrees could not be verified; it was unclear where (or if) he had obtained the Ph.D., and the medical school he supposedly attended had no record of his matriculation. In addition, examination of the papers he published reveals outright pirating (Broad, 1980c). For example, while working in a lab at Jefferson Medical School, Alsabti absconded with a copy of a research grant application, which he summarily turned into three review papers—all his own.

In another noteworthy sleight of hand, Alsabti, while working as an M.D. at Anderson Hospital in Houston, happened upon an article sent to a professor of medicine for editorial review. Unbeknownst to the journal's editor, the professor had died and the article was languishing in his mailbox from whence Alsabti retrieved it. He then prepared a new title page bearing his name and the names of two fictitious coauthors, and sent it to another journal for review. The article was accepted and published before the original version!

A veneer of deceit so thin as Alsabti's is easily penetrated; Elias Alsabti, M.D., Ph.D., research scientist, is no more. Unfortunately, Alsabti's actions cannot be dismissed as the laughable lies of a medical dilettante, for he managed to secure a rotation as a medical student in a Houston hospital. There, by virtue of a lack of training, he had ample opportunity to compromise the treatment delivered to patients.

Alsabti perpetrated an unlikely hoax; Helena Rodbard was the victim of another (see Broad, 1980a, b). The story begins in 1978, when Rodbard submitted to the *New England Journal of Medicine* a manuscript describing insulin binding in patients afflicted with anorexia nervosa. The research described therein was a logical outgrowth of other studies where defective insulin binding was detected in obese patients. Despite this, the manuscript was not accepted for publication, largely because one of the referees reviewed it unfavorably.

This referee, Philip Felig, passed the manuscript along to an associate, Vijay Soman, then an assistant professor of medicine at Yale University. Shortly after perusing the Rodbard paper, Soman submitted a paper to the *American Journal of Medicine* detailing insulin binding in anorectic patients. Incredibly, this manuscript was sent to Rodbard's supervisor at the National Institutes of Health, who then asked her to review it. To her incredulity, she discovered the paper to be much like her rejected submission, with some portions being identical reproductions. A brouhaha ensued, complete with charges of plagiarism, fabrication, and conflict of interest. Felig eventually confronted Soman and extricated an admission that he, Soman, had used the Rodbard paper in writing his own. A subsequent audit of Soman's work revealed that his insulin binding data either were not available or did not support reported conclusions. In addition, there was evidence that four of the subjects who supposedly participated in the study did not do so. These findings resulted in the withdrawal of Soman's submission, and eventually culminated in the retraction of 11 papers published in other journals. The scandal also tainted Felig, who was forced to resign a newly acquired chair at the Columbia College of Physicians. When questioned, Soman related that his nefarious actions were a result of great pressure to publish his data in order to establish "priority."

No field has provided more evidence of fraudulent activity than parapsychology nor, perhaps, has any been more closely scrutinized. Many scientists view claims of extrasensory perception and other psychic powers with obvious disdain, believing the claims to be based on less than compelling data (Barber, 1976); even magicians have called into question the methods, findings, and ethics of parapsychologists (e.g., Randi, 1982). Certainly some of this criticism is merited, for there are documented instances of parapsychologists engaging in obvious deceit in the interest of substantiating seemingly untenable claims of psychic phenomena. J. B. Rhine (1973, 1974a,b), a leading parapsychologist, has detailed several cases of fraud in his field, including the case of Walter J. Levy, Jr.

Just over a decade ago, Dr. Levy was a young but respected researcher employed by the Institute of Parapsychology at Duke University, which Rhine directed. Among other activities, Levy published an abstract reporting the interesting but unlikely finding that chicken embryos had powers of psychokinesis. These powers were demonstrated by placing fertilized chicken eggs in an incubator where heat was turned on and off by a randomizing device supposedly designed so that the incubator would be on (i.e., heated) about half of the time unless somehow perturbed. Despite this, Levy's data indicated that the incubator was on significantly more than it was off, which lead him to conclude that the chicken embryos had influenced the randomizing device through psychokinesis, presumably exercised because of the reinforcing effects of heat. Hard boiled eggs, however, provided no evidence of psychic powers.

Levy employed a similar experimental strategy to demonstrate that rats were able to influence a mechanical device so as to increase the probability of receiving pleasurable brain stimulation (see Gardner, 1981). However, his claims for the psychokinetic powers of rats and embryos were shattered when suspicious coworkers observed him tinkering with recording equipment so as to produce data consistent with his expectations. Clandestinely installed equipment provided data that disagreed with those reported by Levy, refuting his claims and revealing his chicanery.

Dozens of other examples of questionable conduct under the guise of science are explored by Barber (1976), Broad and Wade (1982), and Gardner (1981). Although the examples described in these texts rarely involve behavior analysts, Broad and Wade have questioned the veracity of Watson and Rayner's (1920) famous "Little Albert" study:

> In 1980 Franz Samelson of Kansas State University raised grave doubts about the experiment. Little Albert existed, but a study of Watson's letters and records strongly suggests that the conditioning could not have occurred as Watson described. (Broad & Wade, 1982, p. 80)

Quite recently, two individual scientists and one pair of researchers who have published studies in applied behavior analysis have been accused of unethical scientific practices, including the presentation of falsified data. The final resolution of each case is pending as this is written, thus the extent of wrongdoing, if any, is unknown. It is clear that the alleged misconduct is serious enough to have initiated in all cases formal investigations by employing and/or granting institutions and, in one case, a spot on *Sixty Minutes.*

The balance of this chapter considers why some scientists engage in fradulent activities, how such activities harm science, and what can be done to prevent their occurrence.

HOW AND WHY SCIENTISTS CHEAT

What behaviors constitute fraud in science, and why do such behaviors occur? Neither question affords easy answer. Documented cheating in science has involved outright fabrication of data, selection and manipulation (including inappropriate statistical analysis) of results to increase apparent orderliness or confirm a theoretical prediction, misleading descriptions of experimental procedures, and plagiarism.

In law, *actual* and *constructive* fraud are distinguished; the former involves "actual wrongful intent to deceive," the latter "though not originating in any actual evil or fradulent design, has a tendency to deceive or mislead other persons, to violate public or private confidence, or to impair or injure the public interests" (*Webster's New Twentieth Century Dictionary,* 1979, p. 729). Determining whether a particular example of fraud in science is "actual" or "constructive" is difficult, but it appears that scientists whose activities might constitute constructive fraud have been criticized only as bad scientists, not as unethical charlatans. Barber (1976), for example, describes several general pitfalls in research, one of which he terms "fudging," a common euphemism for the bald and bold "fraud." According to Barber, fudging occurs "when an investigator intentionally reports results that are not the results he actually obtained" (p. 36).

This definition is reasonable, but conscious intent to misrepresent results is difficult to prove. As Broad and Wade (1982) note,

> There may appear to be a clear distinction between conscious and unconscious manipulation of data, but the two phenomena probably lie at opposite ends of a spectrum, with a murky region of semiaware legerdemain in between, rather than being totally separate behaviors. (p. 85)

Two factors make it difficult to discern whether a scientist's behavior involves premeditated intent to deceive. First, intent to deceive cannot be assessed directly, but must be inferred, either on the basis of observed precursors to fraud (e.g., arranging conditions such that data are not publicly accessible), or on the basis of self-reports. An investigator who intends to cheat is likely to be as careful in camouflaging preparations for so doing as in hiding the actual fradulent activity. Moreover, the accuracy of verbal reports concerning intent to defraud is questionable, especially when they come from an individual accused of substantial misconduct, hence unlikely to admit premeditation. Second, it is possible that fradulent behavior sometimes may go unobserved by the perpetrator. That is, the behaver may not realize what has been done in the sense of being unable to report the unethical behavior. In such cases, stimulus control of self-descriptive behavior is defective, and the unethical behavior continues unnoticed and unchanged. Skinner (1953) described general contingencies that could shape and maintain the defective self-description and resultant perpetuation of illicit behavior commonly termed repression. When applied to fraudulent activity by scientists, these contingencies might operate as follows.

Ethical training, in the form of punishment of deceptive behavior, is a substantial component of most scientists' operant history. Stimuli (including behaviors) correlated with the punished behavior come to function as aversive stimuli in that their termination or avoidance is reinforcing. One class of behavior most likely so correlated, and thus aversive, is self-observation of the fradulent activity. The aversive consequences of realizing that one is engaging in previously punished (i.e., deceptive) behavior can be terminated by turning one's self-observation elsewhere, which is thereby automatically reinforced.

This analysis certainly does not imply that all perpetrators of fraud are unaware of their misdeeds. On the contrary, the activities of Cyril Burt and his ilk are too flagrant to be explained readily as actions of the incognizant. One might argue nonetheless that awareness may be lacking in the incipient stages of fraudulent practice and, once the behavior is performed and reinforced, emergent self-knowledge fails to weaken the tendency to behave illicitly, for such behavior is then strongly (though unintentionally) maintained by the reinforcement contingencies of the scientific community.

For example, French scientists in the early 1900s strongly believed in the existence of N-rays; in 1904 alone, over 100 papers reporting their characteristics appeared in a single French journal (de Solla Price, 1961). N-rays have no physical status. As Barber (1976) explains, "all of the effects attributed to N-rays were due to wishful thinking and to the immense difficulties involved in estimating by eye the brightness of faint objects" (p. 7). Nye (1980) has suggested that French scientists continued to argue for the existence of N-rays even in the face of seemingly unassailable evidence to the contrary in part because of fierce national pride. Apparently, the reputation of French scientists in the early 1900s had suffered much at the hands of the Germans. N-rays became almost a national cause celebre (Broad & Wade, 1982), and French researchers whose work affirmed their status were reinforced accordingly. Nonetheless, like the baker in Lewis Carroll's poem *The Hunting of the Snark*, by 1910 N-rays had "softly and suddenly vanished away."

Nye (1980) reports that N-rays were observed by at least 40 people and analyzed by over 100. Jean Bacquerel, Gilbert Ballet, and Andre Broca, all of whom made substantial contributions to science, were among those beguiled by N-rays (Rostand, 1960). These men were not, and probably should not have been, accused of fraud for their role in the defense of N-rays. The way of science is a circuitous and poorly mapped course, marked by false starts and uncertain progress. All scientists pursue their work with preconceived notions concerning the nature of reality and how the subject matter of their field can best be studied and understood. These preconceptions guide scientists in conducting experiments, and determine the manner in which data are collected, portrayed, and interpreted. Scientists are not, and cannot be, perfectly objective. In light of this, departures from objectivity are generally recognized as constituting fraud only when a researcher behaves so as to intentionally misrepresent findings.

There is, however, little consensus as to who should attempt to detect fraudulent activities within various disciplines, or how they should be dealt with if suspected. The obvious exception occurs when it appears to a plaintiff (a) that a contractual arrangement has been abrogated through fraudulent practices, as when a researcher supported by federal grant monies publishes falsified data, or (b) that copyright laws have been violated through plagiarism. Formal judicial procedures and rules of evidence exist for evaluating these forms of fraud, which are surprisingly rare.

Ethically suspect but not clearly criminal activities by their peers appear to be ignored by many scientists (Broad & Wade, 1982). This probably occurs in part because there is no consensus as to precisely what behaviors constitute fraud in a particular field. For instance, the Ethical Principles of Psychologists published by the American Psychological Association (1983) advances 10 general ethical principles (dealing with responsibility, competence, moral and legal standards, public statements, confidentiality, welfare of the consumer, professional relationships, assessment techniques, research with human participants, and care and use of animals), but fails to describe the standards of honesty incumbent upon a researcher. In the absence of detailed and formal standards, admittedly hard to contrive, scientists can judge the ethicality of their peers' behavior only in light of standards established on the basis of rules given and behaviors modelled by instructors and other professional intimates. Contrary to lay belief, these standards are not fixed; some researchers are sloppy, others punctilious. Certain behavior analysts, for instance, may find it perfectly acceptable to expose a client to three successive treatments in an A/B/A/C/A/D/A design, then describe in print only the last three phases, data from which indicate that the final (D) intervention was effective. Others would label such behavior poor science if not pure perfidy, and would certainly be willing to argue against it in the abstract.

The likelihood that they would formally accuse a peer of unethical conduct if that peer were suspected of selecting data as described above is nevertheless small. The reasons for this are three.

First, unless one works closely with another scientist, one can never know precisely what that person has done. In most cases, suspicion of fudging is just that, and the majority of scientists are unwilling to accuse a peer of unethical conduct in the absence of incontrovertible evidence.

Second, unless criminal activity is involved, there is no obvious forum for judging the ethicality of scientific conduct. Dr. A. may believe that Dr. B. has perpetrated a hoax, but who will impartially evaluate the charge? Perhaps the institution that employs B; nearly all universities and research facilities make provision, cumbersome though they may be, for dealing with an employee's alleged moral turpitude.

Assume, then, that B's employer takes A's accusation seriously, and assesses whether the selection of data was unethical. Given the controversial nature of the alleged offense, full or partial exoneration is the probable outcome. A recent example of this involves the case of Mark and Linda Sobell, who reported success in training chronic alcoholics to drink moderately (1973a,b). This was a radical departure from the normal treatment approaches of the day, which involved total abstinence. Pendery, Maltzman, and West (1982) essentially accused the Sobells of falsely reporting follow-up interview data and challenged their claim that most subjects succeeded in moderating their drinking. This challenge resulted in intensive inquiries by the Sobells' employers (The Addiction Research Foundation in Toronto), by the National Institute of Alcohol Abuse and Alcoholism (NIAAA), which partially funded the Sobells' research, and, ultimately, by a Special Steering Committee to the Administrator of the Alcohol, Drug Abuse and Mental Health Administration (ADAMHA).

The end result of these investigations was that the Sobells were criticized for "being careless" in estimating the frequency of post-treatment interviews with controlled-drinking subjects. The Sobells reported that they contacted subjects every 3 to 4 weeks throughout the entire follow-up period, whereas the review committee found evidence that in some cases 3 to 6 months elapsed between interviews. In view of this, the ADAMHA Steering Committee somewhat evasively concluded that Mark and Linda Sobell were "ambiguous but not fradulent" in their 1973 article on controlled drinking by chronic alcoholics. The response of the scientific community to Pendery and co-workers' criticisms of the Sobells has been less than favorable. Peele (1984), for example, has questioned the validity of the Pendery *et al.* (1982) report because of methodological flaws cited by an independent investigative committee funded by the Addiction Research Foundation of Toronto (Dickens, Doob, Warwick, & Wingard, 1982).

Third, the case of Mark and Linda Sobell indicates that researchers accused of fraud are likely to be cleared of charges and, moreover, that when researchers are fully or partially acquitted their initial accusers are likely to be chastised. Apparently inept witch hunters are accessories most scientists can do without. Accusing a peer of fraud is serious business; the reinforcement contingencies arranged by scientific communities support it only when the wrongdoing is obvious and malicious.

In fact, many scientists downplay the significance of fraud in science, a sentiment clearly echoed by Sir Peter Medawar (1984):

> Enough examples of fraud in science have been uncovered in recent years to have given rise to scary talk about "tips of icebergs" and to the ludicrous supposition that science is more often fraudulent than not—ludicrous because it would border upon the miraculous if such an enormously successful enterprise as science were in reality founded upon fictions. (p. 32)

Surely, science has been successful. Nonetheless, the reinforcement contingencies to which scientists are exposed are such that it would be amazing if serious fraud did not occur occasionally. Although to our knowledge there is no published behavioral analysis of the variables responsible for unethical scientific practices, several authors (e.g., Barber, 1976; Beck, 1961; Glaser, 1964; Reif, 1961) have duly noted that fudging can increase a scientist's ability to produce what appear to be "good" data, that is, data that are orderly and interesting, ergo publishable. By producing good data, a researcher increases access to a variety of reinforcers—good positions, grant monies, professional and personal recognition, to name a few. For some individuals, such reinforcers maintain fraudulent activities.

If, however, fraudulent practices can gain a scientist ready access to potent reinforcers, why are they not characteristic of all, or even most, scientists? Perhaps they are. If one is willing to define fraud with sufficient breadth, no scientist living or dead is beyond reproach. Despite this, it appears that a jury of their peers would judge few scientists as guilty of fraud; at least, few have been so judged.

Honesty in science appears to be supported in most scientists by a learning history in which accurate reporting of data is reinforced, and in which strong rules describing the aversive consequences of fraud are provided. These consequences are real enough, for the scientific community deals harshly with known cheaters. Barber (1976) made this point clearly:

> The motivation to report results correctly is strong since the investigator knows that if he is caught fudging his data, he will immediately be expelled from the fraternity of scientists and, if he is even suspected of fudging, he will be treated as a pariah by his colleagues. (p. 44)

Graduate school provides a mileau in which ethical research practices can be established as rule-governed or contingency-shaped behaviors. In addition, the long and (often) closely supervised research training characteristic of scientific education provides ample opportunity for the detection of incipient fraud; students found guilty of cheating on research projects typically do not become scientists.

Graduate training is intended to produce ethical researchers. When this goal is not achieved, there are a number of safeguards that may protect against fraud. These safeguards, and the consequences of fraudulent research practices, are discussed in the following.

CONSEQUENCES OF FRAUD

The harm that follows from a particular scientist's fraudulent activities is practically impossible to assess. In general, however, four kinds of damage can result when researchers misrepresent the results of their studies. One involves the erosion of public confidence in, and consequent willingness to support, science. A second entails harm done to patients who receive clinical treatments that are not in actuality beneficial, but are thought to be so on the basis of fabricated data. Related but more pernicious damage occurs when fabricated data are used to support abominable social biases; Jensen's citation of Burt's data is the apotheosis of this practice, and of the third kind of harm wrought by fraud. A fourth consequence is what economists term "opportunity cost." What one investigator reports frequently affects the kinds of studies her or his peers conduct. If a scientist publishes interesting but falsified data, other investigators may attempt to replicate or, more probably, extend, the findings. These follow-up studies may consume considerable time, effort, and other resources, which perhaps could have been put to better use in the conduct of different kinds of studies.

Although fraudulent research practices can lead scientists momentarily astray, and in that sense extract a considerable opportunity cost, replication often is touted as a major protection against fraud in science. Other protections include the referee system that governs the publication of scientific articles, and peer review of grant applications (Broad & Wade, 1982).

Much research is funded by the federal government, which grants support only after the proposed studies are favorably reviewed by established scientists. Presumably, grant reviewers have an opportunity to inspect proposed research strategies and to identify any potential for nefarious activity. However, this affords little real protection against fraud, for it is unlikely that a grant proposal will reveal illicit machinations. In addition, government funding is not needed to conduct research or publish scientific papers; many legitimate scientists receive little or no grant money. An individual who intends to fudge data need not apply for a grant, although grant money is one of the reinforcers that assumedly maintains illicit (as well as licit) scientific practices.

Peer reviewers of grant applications are, however, unlikely to award support to a scientist known or suspected of unethical research practices. Knowledge of this contingency, and that the contractual arrangement between a researcher and a funding agency may render fraudulent research illegal and hence subject to penalty of law, may reduce the probability that a researcher will fudge.

The manner in which federal grant monies are awarded provides a means, albeit imperfect, for punishing fraud and reinforcing appropriate scientific behavior. Nonetheless, governments can become involved in actually perpetuating questionable scientific practices, as shown by the support the Soviet Union provided for the work of Trofim Lysenko. Lysenko, the son of a peasant, argued that vernalization, the soaking and chilling of wheat seedlings, would improve what in the early 20th century had for the Soviets been dismal harvests (Joravsky, 1970). Vernalization was consistent with a Lamarckian conception of evolution, one in which characteristics acquired by parents could be transmitted genetically to offspring.

Though data support neither, officials in the Soviet Union accepted vernalization as well as Lamarckism. Lysenko and his followers dominated Soviet biology for three decades and, at least in the area of plant sciences, effectively denied it the fruitful and overarching conceptual organization afforded by Darwin's theory of evolution and Mendelian genetics. Lysenko's rise to power illustrates that governmental involvement in science provides no prophylaxis against fools and frauds, and that those who support and utilize the results of research are no more likely to judge it objectively than are scientists themselves.

Before a scientific article is accepted for publication in a respected journal, it must be evaluated favorably by a set of peer reviewers. Articles published in the *Journal of the Experimental Analysis of Behavior* (JEAB), for instance, typically are reviewed by an associate editor and two other editors. Publication depends on these individuals' favorable evaluation, and reviewers are free to ask authors for clarification of data, procedures, and theoretical analyses.

Referees of journal articles are in principle capable of detecting plagiarism, inappropriate data analysis (e.g., the wrongful use of a particular inferential statistic), and the drawing of conclusions not supported by the data at hand. They usually cannot know whether any or all of the data presented in an article were fabricated or otherwise fudged, or if procedures were actually imposed as described.

In science, findings are accepted to the extent that they (a) make sense in light of existing conceptual systems, and (b) are replicable (cf., Kuhn, 1970). Replication provides a mean whereby erroneous findings, that is, those that demonstrate a functional relation that cannot be reproduced generally, are recognized as such: science is not infallible, but it is eventually self-correcting.

Despite this, attempts to replicate findings do not provide a compelling protection against fraud. The reasons for this are three. First, a researcher can present data that, though fabricated, portray a relationship legitimate researchers can reproduce. Second, direct (i.e., exact) replication is relatively rare in science, including behavior analysis, unless the original findings are either of remarkable clinical or theoretical significance, or are highly anomalous in light of current theories. Replication of specific studies that report relatively unimportant and easily believable results have little payoff. One has merely to consider the venerable status of a Jonas Salk, Christian Barnard, or Thomas Edison to realize that fame and fortune come not to investigators who merely duplicate others' work, but to pioneers and risktakers.

Third, the difficulty of determining what is responsible for failure to replicate reported results is a reason why replications of studies rarely reveal fraud in the original. As Barber (1976) noted,

> If an investigator in the behavioral sciences is unable to cross-validate an earlier study, the author of the earlier study will very likely argue that there were some important differences in the procedure which led to the failure to replicate. (p. 45)

In point of fact, the author of the original study will rarely be called on to make such an argument, for the author of its sequel is likely to point out procedural or parametric variations that seem to account for the disparate results. Unless there is reason to believe otherwise, scientists must assume that their peers are honest; in most cases, cheating is the last variable suspected to be responsible for unreplicable results.

On occasion, researchers report results that are too good to be true in the sense of being miraculously orderly, easily generated, and conceptually important. Whether this reflects the touch of a Midas or a Merlin is rarely obvious. The latter typically is suspected, or at least publically voiced as a suspicion, only when insiders who have access to raw data or original experimental materials that question the prodigy's ethicality. This happened to Mark Spector, an apparently brilliant cancer researcher who formulated a data-based theory that explained how a wide range of cancers develop.

Spector's research in support of his "kinase cascade" theory of cancer generation was not challenged by researchers outside Spector's lab; colleagues who had access to his materials suspected, however, that his work was flawed. Although the extent of Spector's wrongdoing is uncertain, it appears doubtless that he willingly modified a substance used in the research such that results were generated in accordance with his seemingly brilliant theory (see McKean, 1981; Wade, 1981).

The case of Mark Spector indicates that those who directly interact with a scientist are in the best position to detect wrongdoing. Researchers have on several occasions brought the unethical practices of close associates to public attention, although reinforcement contingencies operating within research facilities may render it unlikely that a junior scientist will openly criticize a senior (Broad & Wade, 1982). Moreover, many researchers uncritically accept the reports of professional associates; it is not unusual for researchers to appear as authors of articles for which they have never seen raw data and so cannot verify its validity. Though it would serve no good end if scientists were to constantly demand assurance of their colleagues' ethicality, it does appear that anyone willing to take credit for data collected by another must be equally willing to share the blame should those data prove fabricated. Despite this, a common defense of established scientists accused of fraud is to acknowledge "irregularities" in the data, but to assert that those irregularities are the result of the misconduct of an underling, a journeyman not committed to the higher goals of science.

There is no assurance that colleagues will openly challenge or even recognize an individual's questionable research practices, or that these practices will be revealed through peer review of grant applications, referees' evaluations of articles submitted for publication, or attempts to replicate fabricated results. Gross misconduct in the name of science can go undetected for years, even for the lifetime of the perpetrator as in the case of Cyril Burt, especially in situations where those in a position to detect the hoax are inclined to believe the fraudulent conclusions. Minor fudging is rarely made an issue by scientists, but may well be widespread. If one is to believe journalists who have branded science as widely marred by fraud and fakery (e.g., Broad & Wade, 1982), by current standards even Ptolemy, Galileo, Newton, and Mendel engaged in questionable if not downright fraudulent practices. Whether anything is to be gained by denigrating the work of long departed scientists, and whether it is fair to apply the evaluative standards of 20th century science to their work, is moot.

Nonetheless, science is conducted by men and women, not by angels, often in relative privacy and under conditions where the temptation to cheat must be great. The fact that scientists do engage in fraudulent practices—though how often no one knows—should be widely recognized. If it is recognized by behavior analysts, it evokes passingly little concern. Major texts dealing with strategies for behavioral research (e.g., Johnston & Pennypacker, 1981; Kazdin, 1982; Sidman, 1960) do not address what practices are fraudulent, or how such practices can be averted. In addition, behavior analysts have done little to analyze experimentally or theoretically the variables responsible for unethical scientific behavior. Although Azrin, Holz, Ulrich, and Goldiamond (1961) fortuitously found that many undergraduate and graduate students asked to conduct an impossible study would report success in so doing, further research in this or related areas has not been forthcoming.

Like the poor, the unethical are with us always, and some are involved in research. Fraud can be a serious problem in science, hence it appears judicious for behavior analysts to begin addressing the thorny issues of what behaviors actually constitute fraud, and how can such behaviors be prevented, or detected and punished if they occur.

Though fraudulent practices are detestable, they have neither doomed nor damned science. The possibility of their occurrence, as well as the countless other errors even the most ethical scientist can make, suggest that the slogan of the Royal Society of London, *Nullius in verba*, is perhaps the best possible for a scientific society. That motto, as sagacious as straightforward, roughly translates as "don't take anybody's word for it" (Medawar, 1984). Well put.

ACKNOWLEDGMENTS

The helpful comments of Cathy Karas and Rod Clark on an earlier version are gratefully acknowledged.

REFERENCES

American Psychological Association. (1983). *Ethical standards of psychologists.* Washington, DC: Author.
Azrin, N. H., Holz, W., Ulrich, R., & Goldiamond, I. (1961). The control of the content of conversation through reinforcement. *Journal of the Experimental Analysis of Behavior, 4,* 25–30.
Barber, T. X. (1976). *Pitfalls in human research.* New York: Pergamon Press.
Beck, W. S. (1961). *Modern science and the nature of life.* Garden City, NJ: Doubleday.

Broad, W. J. (1980a). Imbroglio at Yale (I): Emergence of a fraud. *Science, 210,* 38–41.
Broad, W. J. (1980b). Imbroglio at Yale (II): A top job lost. *Science, 210,* 171–173.
Broad, W. J. (1980c). Would-be academician pirates papers. *Science, 208,* 1438–1440.
Broad, W. J., & Wade, N. (1982). *Betrayers of the truth.* New York: Simon & Schuster.
Cohen, I. B. (1957). *Lives in science.* New York: Simon & Schuster.
de Solla Price, J. (1961). *Science since Babylon.* New Haven: Yale University Press.
Dickens, B. M., Doob, A. N., Warwick, O. H., & Wingard, W. C. (1982). *Report of the committee of inquiry into allegations concerning Drs. Linda and Mark Sobell.* Toronto: Addiction Research Foundation.
Dorfman, D. D. (1978). The Cyril Burt question: New findings. *Science, 201,* 1177–1186.
Fisher, R. A. (1936). Has Mendel's work been rediscovered? *Annals of Science, 1,* 115–137.
Gardner, M. L. (1981). *Science: Good, bad, and bogus.* New York: Avon Press.
Glaser, B. G. (1964). *Organizational scientists: Their professional careers.* Indianapolis: Bobbs-Merrill.
Gould, S. J. (1981). *The mismeasure of man.* New York: W. W. Norton.
Hearnshaw, L. S. (1979). *Cyril Burt psychologist.* London: Hodder & Stoughton.
Holton, G. (1978). Subelectrons, presuppositions, and the Millikan-Ehrenhaft dispute. *Historical Studies in the Physical Sciences, 9,* 166–224.
Jensen, A. R. (1969). How much can we boost IQ and scholastic achievement? *Harvard Educational Review, 33,* 1–123.
Johnston, J. M., & Pennypacker, H. S. (1981). *Strategies and tactics of human behavioral research.* New York: Erlbaum.
Joravsky, D. (1970). *The Lysenko affair.* Cambridge, MA: Harvard University Press.
Kamin, L. J. (1974). *The science and politics of IQ.* Potomac, MD: Erlbaum.
Kazdin, A. E. (1982). *Single-case research designs.* New York: Oxford University Press.
Kuhn, T. (1970). *The structure of scientific revolutions.* Chicago, IL: University of Chicago Press.
McKean, K. (1981). A scandel in the laboratory. *Discover, 11,* 18–23.
Medawar, P. B. (1984). *The limits of science.* New York: Harper & Row.
Newton, R. R. (1977). *The crime of Claudius Ptolemy.* Baltimore, MD: Johns Hopkins University Press.
Nye, M. J. (1980). N-rays: An episode in the history and psychology of science. *Historical Studies in the Physical Sciences, 11,* 125–156.
Peele, S. (1984). The cultural context of psychological approaches to alcoholism: Can we control the effects of alcohol. *American Psychologist, 39,* 1337–1351.
Pendery, M. L., Maltzman, I. R., & West, L. J. (1982). Controlled drinking by alcoholics: New findings and a reevaluation of a major affirmative study. *Science, 218,* 169–175.
Randi, J. (1982). *Flim-flam!* Buffalo, NY: Prometheus Books.
Reif, F. (1961). The competitive world of the pure scientist. *Science, 134,* 1957–1962.
Rostand, J. (1960). *Error and deception in science.* New York: Basic Books.
Rhine, J. B. (1973). Some avoidable heartaches in parapsychology. *Journal of Parapsychology, 37,* 355–366.
Rhine, J. B. (1974a). A new case of experimenter unreliability. *Journal of Parapsychology, 38,* 215–255.
Rhine, J. B. (1974b). Security versus deception in parapsychology. *Journal of Parapsychology, 38,* 99–121.
Sidman, M. (1960). *Tactics of scientific research.* New York: Basic Books.
Skinner, B. F. (1953). *Science and human behavior.* New York: Macmillan.

Sobell, M. C., & Sobell, L. C. (1973a). Individualized behavior therapy for alcoholics. *Behavior Therapy, 4,* 49–72.

Sobell, M. C., & Sobell, L. C. (1973b). Alcoholics treated by individualized behavior therapy: One year treatment outcome. *Behaviour Research and Therapy, 11,* 599–618.

van der Waerden, B. L. (1968). Mendel's experiments. *Centaurus, 12,* 275–288.

Wade, N. (1981). The rise and fall of a scientific superstar. *New Scientist, 9,* 781–782.

Watson, J. B., & Rayner, R. (1920). Conditioned emotional reactions. *Journal of Experimental Psychology, 3,* 1–14.

Webster's New Twentieth Century Dictionary. (1979). New York: Simon & Schuster.

Index

Peer review
  ethics and, 245–246
  fraud and, 325, 327
  journal articles, 325–326
Pennypacker, H. S., 29–54, 55–83
Pharmacology. *See* Medication effects
Physicians, 307–308, 316–317
Poling, Alan, 7–27, 299–311, 313–330
Prediction, 190–192
Predictive validity, 272–273
Procedural descriptions, 86, 88, 93
Psychopharmacology. *See* Medication
    effects
Punishment
  journal reports and, 249
  reinforcement and, 249–250
  surveys of, 252–255
  types of, 257
  See also Aversive control
Pure behavioral research, 32–38
  behavior and, 29–32
  defined, 32
  dimension/measurement in, 33
  experimental design in, 34–35
  experimental inference in, 35–36
  inferential statistics and, 43–49
  methodological contingencies, 52–54
  observation/recording in, 34
  quantification and display, 35
  unit of analysis in, 32–33
  uses and limitations of, 36–38
  See also Quasi-behavioral research

Quantification
  pure behavioral research, 35
  quasi-behavioral research and, 42
Quasi-behavioral research, 38–43
  behavior and, 29–32
  defined, 38
  dimension/measurement in, 40
  experimental inference, 42–43
  inferential statistics and, 43–49
  limitations and uses of, 49–52
  methodological contingencies and, 52-
    54
  observing/recording, 40–41
  quantification/display, 42
  research designs in, 41–42
  unit of analysis in, 39–40
  See also Pure behavioral research

Questionnaires
  consumer satisfaction, 276–277, 278,
    279–280
  critique of, 272–273
  social validation and, 268–270
Questions. *See* Experimental questions
Quetelet, Adolphe, 43–44

Recording
  pure behavioral research, 34
  quasi-behavioral research, 40–41
Reinforcement
  consent and, 236–237
  consumer satisfaction and, 277
  ethics and, 247–248
  fraud and, 323
  punishment and, 249–250
Reliability
  application limitations and, 85–86
  autocorrelation and, 204
  graphic analysis and, 163
  interobserver agreement, 100
  types of, 101–102
Replication
  application limitations and, 86
  fraud and, 326
  medication effects and, 303–304
  statistical significance and, 216–218
  See also Direct replication; Systematic
    replication
Research designs, 7–27
  A/B designs, 9–11
  alternating-treatment design, 20–
    23
  analytic consistency and, 218–219
  between-subjects design, 7–8
  case study designs, 9
  changing-criterion designs, 19–20
  external validity and, 23–25
  fine-grained graphic analysis and,
    174–181
  fraud and, 321
  graphic analysis and, 161, 162–163
  inferential statistics and, 44, 46
  medication effects and, 300–302
  multiple-baseline designs, 15–17
  multiple-probe designs, 17–19
  pure behavioral research, 34–35
  quasi-behavioral research, 41–42
  selection of, 25–26